THE BEST
and Worst
of Thoroughbred Racing

By Steve Davidowitz

DRF Press

NEW YORK

Published by
Daily Racing Form Press
100 Broadway, 7th Floor
New York, NY 10005

ISBN: 1-932910-88-3
ISBN13: 978-1-932910-88-9
Library of Congress Control Number: 2006936646

Cover and jacket designed by Chris Donofry
Text design by Neuwirth and Associates

Printed in the United States of America

*To my late mother, Sarah Shapiro Davidowitz
(1915-2006), who wanted me to write this book
and left her four adult children with inspirational
poetry and paintings that too few have seen.*

CONTENTS

ACKNOWLEDGMENTS

As INDICATED IN the dedication, this book was born from a discussion with my dying mother, who came to appreciate horse racing as she followed her son's career as a horseplayer and racing writer. I am similarly grateful for the support of my sisters Maxine and Rita; my brother, Sid; my son, Brad, and his family; my good friend Bill Stevenson; and my ex-partner in life, June Davila. All made various important contributions.

My grateful thanks also go to a long list of professional associates who provided invaluable editorial guidance and specific historical content. These include Steven Crist, publisher of *Daily Racing Form*, who agreed from the first mention that this was a project DRF Press should do and followed up with substantial editorial guidance along the way; Robin Foster, an expert editor of copy who added meaningful suggestions and diligently checked obscure facts; and Dean Keppler of DRF Press, who coordinated the project. Also, many thanks to several members of racing institutions who graciously provided hard-to-find news articles and exact dates, including Alan Carter, historian at the National Museum of Racing; Sandy Baze, assistant publicity director at Hollywood Park; Ray Paulick, editor in chief of *The Blood-Horse* magazine; Dan Smith, semi-retired vice president of media relations at Del Mar racetrack; Eric Donovan of the New York Racing Association public-relations department; the staff at the Keeneland Library; Cindy Pierson Dulay, editor of Horse-Races.net; handicapper-writer John Pricci of MSNBC; Bill Heller, author of *Saratoga Tales;* Paula Welch-Prather, editor of *The American Racing Manual;* Joe Hirsch, retired *Daily Racing Form* executive columnist; and Lauren Stich, breeding historian and DRF columnist. In addition, many jockeys, jockey agents, trainers, horseplayers, and racing officials contributed their recollections, and invaluable source material was provided by DRF's historical books *Champions: The Lives, Times, and Past Performances of the 20th Century's Greatest Thoroughbreds* and *The American Racing Manual.*

My thanks also for access to the archives of several publications and Internet resources, most notably *The New York Times, The Baltimore Sun, Los Angeles Times, The Courier-Journal* of Louisville, Kentucky, the *Lexington Herald-Leader,* the Minneapolis *Star Tribune,* Equibase.com, TrackMaster.com, Brisnet.com, and the NBC, CBS, and ABC television networks.

Most of all, after watching, wagering on, and writing about horse racing for more than four decades, I am most appreciative of the gallant racehorses who provided so many stunning moments to remember, the very reason for sharing the *Best* they have given us and the *Worst* of a game that must fight to be better—on their behalf, as much as for those who love it.

—Steve Davidowitz

INTRODUCTION

THE FIRST TIME I went to a racetrack, in April 1960, I saw a jockey get thrown from his mount at the starting gate, dust himself off, put his goggles back on straight, and ride the horse to win the race.

I also saw a speed duel set up a thrilling three-way photo finish that had fans in the stands arguing for several minutes about who was first, second, or third. And, before all of that occurred, I already had won a $221 daily double to propel me on a trip with my college buddies to Fort Lauderdale, Florida, where *all* the best-looking college girls were partying. Although that sequence of events should explain my connection to Thoroughbred horse racing, it does not.

Actually, I became a devoted horseplayer and racing writer because a New Brunswick, New Jersey, bookie (and railroad-station taxi dispatcher) gave me a copy of the 1959 *American Racing Manual*. This was after he had taken me for about $1,200 in the three months that followed my Florida adventure.

"Here, kid, you seem to like this game," he said, "but you don't know nuttin' and I hate to see somebody be so damn stupid."

The *American Racing Manual*, which was published by *Daily Racing Form*, proved to be much more interesting than *War and Peace*, or whatever book

I was supposed to be reading for American Lit 101. I was fascinated with the history of the sport, the statistics, and the tales and exploits of Man o' War, Seabiscuit, and Gallant Fox. I loved the race-by-race details imbedded in the past-performance profiles of top horses in training, and was blown away by the amount of information contained in result charts of the best races of the previous year.

I spent hours reading about Triple Crown races and other historical tidbits, just as I had studied Mickey Mantle's and Warren Spahn's baseball stats on the backs of bubble-gum cards throughout my youth.

I loved the track diagrams of Churchill Downs, Pimlico, and Belmont Park, just as I had been fascinated by the unique dimensions of Yankee Stadium, Fenway Park, and Wrigley Field. The parallels were important to me because until my sojourn to Florida, I had been on a swift path toward a career as a professional baseball player. An arm injury ended that dream virtually at the same time I discovered horse racing.

Less than two years after my bookie gave me the book that would bring me closer to the game, he began to lay off my bets on horses I liked. I may have been near the bottom of my Rutgers graduating class, but I was magna cum laude in horse-race betting at nearby Garden State Park. My bookie took pride in my progress. So did a music teacher at Rutgers, who helped me graduate by giving me a higher grade than I deserved after I tipped him on the winning daily double while bumping into him one lucky Saturday at Garden State.

Some four decades later, I am happy to have overcome my share of losing streaks to be ahead of the game while also working as a reporter, columnist, handicapper, and racing editor for various newspapers, magazines, and Internet outlets in every region of the country. I have seen virtually all the top jockeys, trainers, horses, Triple Crown, and Breeders' Cup races and have logged more than 500,000 miles betting and writing about the sport at more than 60 different tracks in North America. I have covered the birth of several new tracks and the death of several that I wish were still in existence.

I have shared long hours of debate and conversation about horses and courses with many of the most knowledgeable racing writers and horseplayers in America. Some of the best trainers and jockeys have revealed intimate details of their working operations, on and off the record; I can name others who usually run the other way when they see me coming. In other words, I've been around a few racetracks through the years and still find it fascinating to connect the past to the present, the same way that I annually invest countless hours pursuing a good Derby horse and a good key to a million-dollar pick six.

All this background is provided to suggest that the compelling idea behind this book is grounded in a deep catalogue of experiences that helped formulate the various lists of the bests and worsts of the modern era in a great game.

Objectivity is the intended backbone of all these lists, but there is a lot to be said for a good eye and a good opinion forged from a professional handicapping approach.

I confess, I did not see Upset defeat Man o' War in 1919, just as I did not see Babe Ruth hit any of his 714 regular-season home runs. Yet there are reliable accounts in dated issues of *Daily Racing Form* and other sources to support Man o' War's standing among the great Thoroughbreds of all time, just as baseball historians can say with conviction that Ruth, not Hank Aaron, was the most prolific slugger in baseball history. For one thing, Ruth's home-run output dwarfed his contemporaries. For another, Aaron's 755 lifetime home runs came with several thousand more at-bats in a much longer career.

Barry Bonds? Mark McGwire? Sammy Sosa? You have to be kidding. What we have seen with our own eyes during the steroid era in baseball is sufficient to know that their records should not be measured on the same playing field.

Man o' War? I make him the Babe Ruth of the horse kingdom during the early years of the 20th century, even though I saw Secretariat, Seattle Slew, Affirmed, Kelso, Spectacular Bid, Cigar, Ruffian, Damascus, and many other great horses who deserve to be compared—one against the other.

Some of the lists in this book admittedly are perched on the fringes of any previously published in any sport. A few are designed to focus attention on important but overlooked aspects of the game. I've even included some lists that reflect the opinions of people who know far more than I about breeding and bygone eras.

You probably will disagree with some of my rankings. Perhaps often enough to send me a note or pull me aside when we pass each other at Del Mar or Saratoga. By all means, please do wake me up to the horse, jockey, trainer, or historical event you think I overrated or missed. All of us who love horse racing are 100 percent sure of only one thing: This is a game built on heartfelt opinions and on our ability to change our views in a few fifths of a second.

My hope is that you will not only think about or learn something new about some of the people, horses, tracks, and events chronicled in this book, but that you may also be moved to remember *your* best moments, *your* most satisfying victories, and seek to relive such experiences with a new cast of contemporary characters and past-performance profiles for races yet to be run.

1

STUNNERS:

The Greatest Upsets and

Worst DQs of Modern Times

10. *Dark Star Narrowly Defeats an Unlucky Native Dancer in the 1953 Kentucky Derby.*

The very first horse race I ever saw was on a seven-inch black-and-white television used as a curiosity item in my father's camera store in Bayonne, New Jersey. I was 11 years old, proudly wearing my Little League uniform for the Leon's Fotoshop Athletics. The TV was tuned to the broadcast of the 1953 Kentucky Derby, one of the earliest racing events to be nationally televised.

Little did I know I was peeking into my future as a racing writer and horseplayer, bearing vague witness to one of the biggest upsets in racing history, the only race the great horse Native Dancer ever would lose.

Called the Grey Ghost by his admirers in the press, Native Dancer was a star of the highest magnitude, a sleekly built, long-striding winner of 11 straight prior to the Kentucky Derby. He already was a household name in an era when more people attended racetracks than baseball or football games. All the horses lined up in the Churchill Downs starting gate, including Dark Star, were presumed to be four-legged foils destined to become Native Dancer's latest victims.

Although Dark Star was nearly 25–1 that day, he was a good horse, having won three of six starts as a 2-year-old, plus the Derby Trial stakes just four days before the Kentucky Derby. Still, no one really believed that any horse other than Native Dancer would win the world's most famous race.

Dark Star did not follow the script. Neither did Native Dancer.

While Dark Star sprinted to the lead with the determination of a horse with a chance, Native Dancer was bumped on the first turn by Money Broker, a 45–1 shot, forcing jockey Eric Guerin to make a wide rally on the final turn that was destined to fall a head short.

The announced crowd of 100,000 at Churchill Downs was stunned; so was an 11-year-old boy in Bayonne, New Jersey, who had been told by the television announcers that the improbable had just happened, that the horse-racing equivalent of "Casey at the Bat" had been acted out. Mighty Casey had struck out.

The invincible Native Dancer was no longer so. But the defeat did have an unexpected impact on the estimated 300,000 people who tuned in, as well as on many who read about it in newspapers from coast to coast. Native Dancer became a sympathetic as well as charismatic story. Having been so unlucky and so gallant in defeat, he would become the sport's first true media star, the most popular horse since the 1930s, when Seabiscuit drew record crowds to train stations to see him pass by.

Native Dancer did not let down his growing legion of fans, winning the other two Triple Crown races and never once tasting defeat in his remaining 11 races into 1954. While the crushing Derby upset would haunt trainer W. C. Winfrey and owner-breeder Alfred Gwynne Vanderbilt, who never came that close again to a redeeming Kentucky Derby victory, they took solace in the fact that Native Dancer attracted more interest and more television coverage for the sport. I, for one, regularly stopped on the racing page on my way to the daily baseball scores looking for details of the Grey Ghost's next race, a habit acquired by thousands of people who might not have ever seen a horse race.

Dark Star? He never would win again, fading badly in the Preakness two weeks later, suffering a career-ending tendon injury shortly after Native Dancer ranged up alongside to launch his winning bid. He did, however, go on to be a moderately successful sire of 26 stakes winners, including My Dad George, second in the 1970 Kentucky Derby and Preakness. Moreover, Dark Star had the kind of bright, shining moment that will be remembered for a thousand years.

9. *Sherluck Wins the 1961 Belmont Stakes; Carry Back Finishes Seventh.*

The extremely popular and very exciting stretch-runner Carry Back won the 1961 Kentucky Derby and Preakness with devastating rallies. He came to the Belmont Stakes as the shoo-in favorite to complete a rare sweep of the American Triple Crown races, a feat not accomplished since Citation in 1948.

Unfortunately, Carry Back could only manage a weak and tired seventh-place finish in the grueling 1½-mile "Test of the Champion" that has foiled so many potential Triple Crown winners through the years.

Former president Dwight D. Eisenhower was one of many thousands of fans at Belmont Park seen ripping up parimutuel tickets on Carry Back that day. I was there too, doing the same. Ironically, someone who wasn't there probably should have been: the great Hall of Fame jockey Eddie Arcaro.

Arcaro, a winner of five Kentucky Derbies in his legendary career, had watched Sherluck win the Blue Grass Stakes at Keeneland and got the mount in the Derby nine days later when Sherluck's original rider, Braulio Baeza, opted to ride the talented Crozier for owner Fred W. Hooper. Hooper, an owner, breeder, and great judge of jockey talent, was responsible for bringing Baeza to America from his native Panama.

Arcaro did not like what he experienced in the Derby, finishing a tired and dirty fifth, as Carry Back rallied from far back in the 15-horse field to outfinish Crozier for the blanket of roses. When Arcaro told Sherluck's trainer, Harold Young, to find another rider for the Preakness, Young gave the mount to Sammy Boulmetis, who would experience a virtual replay of Arcaro's ride in the Derby: Carry Back winning from last to first; the Derby pacesetter, Globemaster, second; Crozier a respectable third; and Sherluck fifth again, with no apparent excuse.

About a week before the Belmont, Young told Arcaro that Sherluck was training very well and seemed to be handling the Belmont racing surface as well as he did Keeneland's. This was consistent with a fact that was known to very few people at the time: The old Belmont racing strip was built out of the same compatible mixture of sand and clay that was in use at Keeneland.

"I'd like you to ride him for me," Young told Arcaro. But the great jockey reportedly had a straightforward reply. "No thanks, Harry . . . I've got a golf game in mind for Belmont Day."

Arcaro confided to friends that "Sherluck can't win that race, he's seen his best days; he's just another hopeless longshot."

While I have no idea how many strokes Arcaro needed to complete his round of golf, he was lucky he didn't have a stroke watching the telecast of Sherluck winning the Belmont by a comfortable 2 ½ lengths under Baeza. Yes, Braulio Baeza. The young and highly skilled jockey became available when Crozier was forced out of the Belmont with a minor physical problem incurred during his third-place finish in the Jersey Derby on Memorial Day. Sherluck paid $132.10 for every $2 bet.

Despite Arcaro's embarrassment, it should be reported that he graciously called Young the next day to offer his congratulations on a miracle job of training. Baeza, by the way, quickly emerged as one of the best jockeys in the world, a Hall of Famer with steel nerves who would ride 1963 Kentucky Derby-Belmont Stakes winner Chateaugay and 1969 Belmont Stakes winner and Horse of the Year Arts and Letters, among many champions.

8. *Desert Stormer Wins the 1995 Breeders' Cup Sprint.*

Desert Stormer, a 5-year-old mare, paid $31 (hardly earth-shattering) while winning the 1995 Breeders' Cup Sprint at Belmont Park. But for the vast majority playing the Breeders' Cup card around the world, this was an incredibly difficult outcome to predict or accept, even after the race was run.

Desert Stormer probably would have paid at least twice as much had she not been part of the "mutuel field." Since most racetracks' tote boards can only accommodate 12 betting interests, horses that are considered longshots by the track's linemaker are lumped together in the mutuel field when there are 13, 14, or more horses in the starting gate. In such a situation, anyone buying a parimutuel ticket on number 12 also gets the other horses in the field at no extra cost—in this case, Ovington and Lit de Justice.

Although Ovington was a complete throwout, Lit de Justice was a dangerous stretch-runner whose only shortcoming was that he was presumed to be more effective at seven furlongs than the six-furlong distance of the Breeders' Cup Sprint. Lit de Justice hardly was an impossible winner in a race that had several fast-breaking horses ready to get involved in a taxing, perhaps suicidal, pace duel, and I actually thought the pace scenario set up so well that he just might overpower the field at a decent payoff. While Desert Stormer had good early speed, she would have been 30–1 or higher if she had not been linked with Lit de Justice in the betting pools.

The pace was indeed hot, just what Lit de Justice needed, and he did run well to finish a good third, a year before he actually would win the 1996 Sprint. But Desert Stormer, trained by the little-known Irishman Frank Lyons and ridden by Future Hall of Famer Kent Desormeaux, kept right on going at a breakneck pace, pressed by the ultraquick Mr. Greeley. Somehow, the two speedballs continued to fight for the lead all the way to the finish line, with Desert Stormer winning by a desperate neck.

Lyons, an affable, knowledgeable racing lifer, might not have been confused with a Breeders' Cup-winning trainer such as D. Wayne Lukas, but he had great faith in his mare's ability to compete on the highest level and was not only rewarded in the Sprint, but also parlayed her surprise victory into a successful career as a horse buyer and later as a primary commentator for Television Games Network's extensive racing coverage.

I benefited too, having used number 12 (the field) on my Breeders' Cup pick-seven ticket, which eventually paid $22,000 for $1. All things considered, Desert Stormer remains the most obscure one-hit wonder in Breeders' Cup history—a lucky afterthought that only her connections and a small number of horseplayers still have cause to remember.

7. *Bee Bee Bee Wins the 1972 Preakness.*

It rained so much for the 1972 Preakness that many in the crowd probably expected to go home in canoes. It rained so much that Lucien Laurin, the trainer of Riva Ridge, confided to jockey Ron Turcotte and owner Penny Tweedy that they might be better off scratching the horse, an impossibility from a public-relations standpoint. You can't scratch the fit winner of the Kentucky Derby from the middle jewel of the Triple Crown.

I did not have any such problem eliminating Riva Ridge as a contender in the Preakness despite having won a sizable bet on him in the Derby. I had reason to bet against Riva Ridge on that rain-soaked Preakness Day, as my friend and colleague Andy Beyer can attest. I was at Saratoga the previous summer when Laurin scratched Riva Ridge from the Hopeful Stakes simply because it rained the day before the race. Of equal import, Riva Ridge's worst race of the season was his poor fourth-place finish in the Everglades Stakes at Hialeah, his only defeat in his last nine races, stretching back to a pair of sprint wins on somewhat wet tracks that convinced Laurin that the colt won those races simply because he was tons the best.

"He was slippin' and slidin' all over the place," Laurin explained. "If he ever has to run against a good horse on a wet track, I would be very worried."

Laurin knew what he was talking about. Beginning with the Everglades and continuing through the end of his career, Riva Ridge would finish fourth, fourth, fourth, and seventh in the four races he would run on wet tracks.

Searching through the rest of the Preakness field for a likely upset winner, my thinking went like this:

Key to the Mint was a very promising horse, but was not yet in top condition, having been rushed to make the Kentucky Derby after a minor winter injury. (Later in the year, Key to the Mint would win four major stakes and even outpoll Riva Ridge for the Eclipse Award given to the best 3-year-old of 1972.)

No Le Hace, second in the Kentucky Derby, was a stretch-runner—and that was not a good thing to be at Pimlico on May 20, 1972. All day long, the sloppy but "sealed" (packed-down) racing surface was strongly favoring front-runners. Race after race was decided in the first few yards out of the starting gate. Nothing was winning from off the pace. So the big handicapping question of that soggy day in Maryland was: Which horse in this field would take the early lead and go on from there to a historic Preakness victory?

My answer was, unfortunately, an obscure 47–1 shot named Eager Exchange who was trained by the late Johnny Campo, a roly-poly New

York-born trainer who was winning lots of races there after learning his craft under Hall of Famer Eddie Neloy. Ten years later, Campo would become a household name while winning the Kentucky Derby and Preakness with Pleasant Colony, but on this afternoon, Eager Exchange jumped out to challenge for the lead for about 20 yards and packed it in.

Even if I had known in advance that Eager Exchange was going to do that, my final Preakness pick would not have been Bee Bee Bee, who wrested control of the pace 10 strides out of the gate and somehow turned out to be the right answer on the wrong day for me—and for most others who had deciphered the prevailing conditions. Consider these facts:

Bee Bee Bee was a promising 2-year-old, but had been a major disappointment in a pair of Florida stakes during the early months of his 3-year-old season. He was a bigger bust losing to an exceedingly weak field of Maryland-breds when shipped back to Bowie racecourse in March.

The horse that defeated Bee Bee Bee in that March race at Bowie was named Right Judex, who previously had failed to defeat $5,000 claiming horses! Now, I ask you, can a horse be expected to win a classic stakes race after losing to a horse that was unable to beat slow-footed $5,000 claimers?

The answer is no, he can't. Or he shouldn't. But Bee Bee Bee did. I know, I saw it with my own two eyes and that's all the reason I need to rank Bee Bee Bee's front-running upset of Riva Ridge seventh on this list. Oh, yes, Riva Ridge did go on to win the Belmont Stakes three weeks later over Key to the Mint, while Bee Bee Bee skipped the Belmont in favor of an obscure $25,000 stakes race at Liberty Bell Park. I guess his trainer, Del Carroll, knew that Bee Bee Bee really wasn't capable of beating top-notch horses on a fast track. Case closed.

6. *Undefeated Seattle Slew Finishes Fourth in His First Race Since Sweeping the 1977 Triple Crown.*

It was one of the pleasures of my life to have spent the five weeks of both the 1977 and 1978 Triple Crown races in private daily consultations with Billy Turner Jr., trainer of Seattle Slew, and Lazaro S. Barrera, trainer of Affirmed.

Having such access and trust with these two outstanding horsemen became the most significant learning experience of my life.

Almost every day, I was up at 5:00 a.m. and at their respective barns before anyone else. I clocked their horses' workouts and gallops along with all the workouts and gallops of every other Derby horse each morning from a small booth near the horse gap on the backstretch, the cramped and chilly Churchill Downs clockers' stand (subsequently expanded to include an attached porch). After all horses left the track and the media horde dissipated following their daily pack interviews, I would share what I saw on the track with Turner in 1977 and Barrera in '78.

The passing of information was not one-sided. What I got in return was a college-level education in what a good horse should look like and how to detect various states of physical condition and/or physical flaws.

Turner, a rangy, down-to-earth young man with wild eyes and a quick mind that might have matched wits with a world-class chess champion, was the first to take me under his wing in this manner. Having learned his horsemanship from patient Burley Cocks and other renowned steeplechase trainers in Maryland, Turner seemed happy to bounce ideas off me, as if I knew what he was talking about, which I didn't.

I can recall one specific lesson he passed on when I asked him—as most of the press was asking him—"When are you going to work Seattle Slew fast, like a Derby horse usually works?"

Turner stared at me for a split second as if he wanted to send me to a corner with a dunce cap or hit me over the head with a hammer.

"Are you paying attention at all?" he said. "Haven't you figured out anything?" Turner was laughing, but the tone in his voice conveyed annoyance.

"Why would I want to work Seattle Slew fast when he's got all the speed in the world already? . . . Here I am trying my best to get him to relax, telling the owners to lay back and stop asking me to do this or do that and you're asking me what they're asking me. . . . Doesn't anybody get it? It's taken me months to get him ready to go a mile and a quarter and you and everybody else wants me to burn him up on the training track!"

I felt like crawling into a hole as Turner walked away, shaking his head. A few hours later, while crossing paths near the Churchill Downs paddock, Turner was calm as a summer breeze, smiling from ear to ear when he pulled me aside and repeated his thoughts. This time the words helped me understand how and why this oft-criticized, extremely unorthodox young horseman was gingerly handling the high-strung Thoroughbred that was going to be the first undefeated horse to sweep the American Triple Crown.

"The key," he explained, "is to keep him from sensing a race is coming up, to keep him as comfortable and as relaxed as possible up to the last minute. . . . He's a big goofball most of the time, but if you were going to put him in a boxing ring with nine other horses, he'd be the only one to come out. He's so strong; so competitive; very willful, a very proud son of a gun."

The Derby was a tour de force, with Seattle Slew overcoming a bad start and knifing through the field in a blur to reach front-running For The Moment entering the first turn and taking over from that rival turning into the long Churchill Downs homestretch. One by one, the stretch-runners loomed menacingly into contention. But it was too late; Seattle Slew had the Derby won, and Turner admitted after the race that he purposely had undertrained him so that there would be room for improvement in the Preakness and Belmont.

Indeed there was, as "Slew" won a swiftly run Preakness and scored a wire-to-wire romp in the Belmont to complete the elusive Triple Crown sweep. Almost immediately, Turner cautioned owners Karen and Mickey Taylor and Jim and Sally Hill not to be swayed by offers of big money to race Seattle Slew for at least a few months.

"He needs some rest," Turner said. But instead of heeding Turner's advice, the owners prevailed on him to train Slew for a trip to California to run in the Swaps Stakes against what most believed to be a moderate field. Turner never forgave himself for caving in.

"Everybody thinks because Slew won the Triple Crown so convincingly that he had easy races. Everybody is wrong," Turner said. "There is no such thing as winning the Triple Crown easily. Each of these races takes an awful lot out of a young horse, never mind one who won all three under the kind of pressure we put on him."

When Hollywood Park increased the purse for the Swaps Stakes to $300,000 to attract Seattle Slew, it became too tantalizing to resist. But trainer Laz Barrera, who would sweep the 1978 Triple Crown with Affirmed, had a sneaky-good horse in the field, the English import J.O. Tobin, who had not run a true race when well beaten by Seattle Slew in the Preakness.

Barrera was salivating for the rematch at Hollywood Park. He worked J.O. Tobin extra furlongs to peak on Swaps Day as if it would be the race of the century.

"I made mistakes with this horse for the Preakness," Barrera said. "He's a really good horse. . . . I'm so glad they're going to run here on my home track. They're in for a big surprise."

As Barrera expected, the Swaps was run at a dizzying pace, with J.O. Tobin in front every step of the way through a half-mile in 45 $^2/_5$ and six furlongs in a blistering 1:09 $^1/_5$ en route to 1 $^1/_4$ miles in a smashing 1:58 $^3/_5$, just two-fifths of a second off the existing world record.

J.O. Tobin was eight lengths in front of Barrera's second-place finisher, Affiliate, and neither of Barrera's horses was challenged while Seattle Slew struggled to keep up, finishing a bad fourth. The result was a national shock to millions who had become convinced during the Triple Crown that unbeaten Seattle Slew could not possibly lose to horses that were seemingly so inferior. The upset made headlines around the world. But it really was no mystery to Billy Turner. Seattle Slew was a tired race-horse who performed as if he wished his connections had left him alone in his stall at Belmont to recover from the grueling Triple Crown.

"I should have stuck to my guns," Turner admitted. "But after a while you can convince yourself into believing a horse like that can do anything. . . . We let him down. He never should have been in the race."

Seattle Slew's first loss was also the first real tear in the relationship between Seattle Slew's owners and the trainer who developed him. In fact, the rift eventually would lead to Turner's shocking dismissal during the winter. But Seattle Slew—despite suffering a nearly fatal illness and being handled by relatively inexperienced trainer Doug Peterson—came back in the fall of his 4-year-old season to run some of the most astonishing races in history. There will be more about that in a later chapter, but for now, it is important to point out that this is one of the few horses in racing history that probably never should have lost a race.

5. *Birdstone Stops Smarty Jones's 2004 Triple Crown Bid.*

Smarty Jones was not quite Seattle Slew, but he was the undefeated winner of the Kentucky Derby and Preakness when he came to Belmont Park with a record of 8 for 8 in early June 2004. Fact is, no American horse in more than two decades had achieved such widespread popularity and there was not a horse in the Belmont field that seemed to belong in the same race.

Maybe Rock Hard Ten, who had finished second to Smarty Jones in the Preakness, could provide some competition; maybe Purge, who had won the local Peter Pan Stakes, could make a bid. Certainly not Eddington, a soundly defeated third in the Preakness, or Royal Assault, a Nick Zito-trained winner of a moderate stakes at Pimlico on the Preakness undercard. By any handicapping analysis, none of those horses seemed to pose a serious threat.

And they didn't. At least not a win threat. But Purge set a brisk pace through the first mile (clocked in 1:35 $^2/_5$), and Rock Hard Ten was right there with him. Unfortunately, so was Smarty Jones, who was expending valuable energy tracking the leaders under jockey Stewart Elliott.

Still, Smarty Jones was able to open up a seemingly decisive lead on the final turn as he moved through a very fast 1¼ miles in 2:00 $^2/_5$. The crowd roared in anticipation of a long-awaited Triple Crown winner, the same way they roared when Secretariat seemed ready to break a 25-year drought taking an insurmountable lead in the 1973 Belmont.

It had been 26 years since Affirmed won the 1978 Triple Crown. In the interim, nine horses had come to Belmont with the Kentucky Derby and Preakness victories in hand, only to fall short of the ultimate reward. There was Smarty Jones moving in front of the pack with less than a quarter of a mile to racing immortality.

Some in the huge crowd of 120,139 who were not intoxicated by the moment, and those who vividly recalled Real Quiet's nose defeat to the late-closing Victory Gallop in the 1998 Belmont, could not have liked what they saw through their binoculars on the final turn.

Nick Zito's other horse in the race, the erratic Birdstone, was less than five lengths behind, a set of fresh legs aimed at the favorite, gaining ground steadily, heading for a confrontation inside the twelfth and final furlong. Dismissed at 36–1 despite having won the Grade 1 Champagne Stakes at Belmont as a 2-year-old, Birdstone now was running as if *he* were the horse poised to sweep the Triple Crown.

For a few strides in midstretch, it still appeared that Smarty Jones might hold off Birdstone's late surge. For a few more strides after the pair raced together approaching the final sixteenth, it still seemed possible.

But, in the final few strides, the Triple Crown bid was over, Smarty Jones was weakening, and Birdstone pulled clear, the $74 upset winner.

Except for the few who were rejoicing with their winning parimutuel tickets and except for Nick Zito, owner Marylou Whitney, and a few dozen friends, the crowd gasped in unison, falling instantly silent at the realization that such a promising Triple Crown bid had been dashed.

Later that summer, Birdstone showed that his victory hardly was a fluke as he won the Travers Stakes at Saratoga, but Smarty Jones was not in the field. A couple of months after the Belmont, Smarty Jones became one more high-flying 3-year-old who was prematurely whisked off to stud with a relatively minor problem rather than risk any further damage to his reputation or breeding value. No upset there.

4. *Onion Beats Triple Crown Winner Secretariat.*

Secretariat was the horse that finally broke the 25-year drought in Triple Crown winners. He was an extremely handsome chestnut with three white feet and a white blaze down the center of his regal face.

Secretariat seemed to know he was special from the first day his handlers put him under tack at the Meadow, the Virginia farm where he was foaled. As a 2-year-old, he ran faster than 4-year-olds while making electrifying moves in several stakes at Saratoga, Garden State Park, and Laurel racecourse. Before his first start as a 3-year-old, he was syndicated for a record $6 million to help owner Penny Tweedy save Meadow Stable and pay the crushing inheritance taxes that followed the death of her father, Christopher Chenery.

Ironically, Tweedy might not have owned Secretariat were it not for a losing a coin flip on a complicated foal-sharing arrangement between her father and Ogden Phipps, whose family owned champion sire Bold Ruler. Under their agreement, Chenery would send the same pair of mares to Bold Ruler for two consecutive years of matings, and the owners would meet every other year for a coin flip to determine the order of selection. The winner would get first choice from the current pair of foals, and second choice of next year's offspring. In the summer of 1969, the Phippses won the coin flip and selected a filly by Bold Ruler out of Chenery's mare Somethingroyal. The filly, named The Bride, proved to be slower than most stable ponies. Penny Tweedy, standing in for her ailing father, got the second choice of that year's foals, but also got a consolation prize. Somethingroyal was already back in foal to Bold Ruler, but the other mare in the arrangement had failed to become pregnant, so there would only be one foal to choose from the next year. That meant that Meadow Stable, the "loser" of the coin toss, automatically got the next year's Somethingroyal colt—Secretariat.

While sweeping the 1973 Triple Crown, Secretariat more than lived up to the hype that was building around him, turning in successively more impressive performances.

In the Derby, he made two breathtaking moves sweeping past the good horse Sham, who could not match Secretariat's long, effortless stride while finishing second, 2 ½ lengths behind "Big Red." The winner's time was 1:59 ²/₅ for 1 ¼ miles, the first sub-2:00 minute clocking in Kentucky Derby and Churchill Downs history.

In the Preakness two weeks later, Secretariat made a move for the ages, sweeping widest of all on the first turn to go from last to first and take his familiar 2 ½-length lead over Sham before hitting the stretch. Veteran Pimlico observers said they had never seen any horse make a wide move on the first turn at Pimlico as a prelude to victory.

Sham was a helpless foe as jockey Laffit Pincay Jr. was all over the colt, trying to get him to close the gap, but to no avail as Ron Turcotte barely moved a muscle aboard Secretariat.

This time Secretariat set another track record, but you would never know it from the official record book, because the Pimlico teletimer did not run nearly as well as Secretariat. Moreover, even after a hearing with the Maryland Racing Commission to challenge the erroneous clocking —a hearing I help convene through contacts with the CBS television network and Mrs. Tweedy—the commission decided only to accept a compromise clocking, faster than originally posted, but slower than the track record he deserved. This decision, which went against a mountain of evidence, still stands as a disgraceful chapter in the way horse racing treated one of its most significant records by one of its most important horses.

In the final leg of the Triple Crown, Secretariat won the 1 ½-mile Belmont Stakes by an incredible 31 lengths, smashing the world record for the distance and beating Gallant Man's stakes and track record by an otherworldly 2 ³/₅ seconds. This great horse not only swept the 1973 Triple

Crown, he broke three track records doing it with the flair and charisma of an immortal.

That was why Secretariat was on the cover of *Newsweek* and *Time* magazine during that Triple Crown season. That was why he turned so many people on to racing and knocked the Watergate scandal off the front pages of the nation's newspapers for a while. He was a phenomenon, a legend in his own time, a racehorse who later would be voted one of the top athletes of the 20th century by *Sports Illustrated,* which also put him on the cover the same week that *Time* and *Newsweek* did.

So here came the conquering champion to historic Saratoga, after having ventured to Arlington Park in Chicago during July for a gift $100,000 exhibition race. Now, in early August, without any significant rest, he was entered in the Whitney Handicap as the biggest cinch in decades. Except for one thing. Or one man, trainer Allen Jerkens.

Jerkens, a master horseman, had already earned the nickname "the Giant Killer" after upsetting five-time Horse of the Year Kelso twice in 1962 and once more in 1963 with his first good horse, Beau Purple. Now Jerkens was taking on the mighty Secretariat with a sprinter named Onion, who had run one of the fastest 6 ½-furlong races in Saratoga history only five days earlier.

A huge crowd bet on the great horse as if he were a bank certificate, sending Secretariat to the post at 10 cents on the dollar.

Onion raced to the lead in the middle of the track and never looked back. Secretariat, apparently weakened from his rigorous campaign, was further hampered by trying to rally along a very deep rail path, something that was contributing to Saratoga's notorious reputation as "the Graveyard of Favorites." It was not to be. The great horse lost this Whitney just as Man o' War had lost to Upset over the same track in 1919 and just as champion Gallant Fox lost to the improbable 100–1 shot Jim Dandy in the Travers stakes two months after Gallant Fox swept the 1930 Triple Crown.

It happens. But as a postscript to this historic upset, Allen Jerkens proved later in the same year that he was not a one-trick pony, upsetting both Riva Ridge and Secretariat in separate races with the vastly underrated Prove Out. Still, Secretariat hardly went downhill in the latter part of his 3-year-old season, in spite of losing twice to Jerkens-trained horses.

In three other starts before he was retired, Secretariat merely set a course record while winning the Man o' War Stakes in his turf-racing debut against the top grass horses in America and defeated the best horses in training in the Marlboro Cup while setting another world record for 1⅛ miles at Belmont Park. In his final career race, while still a maturing 3-year-old, Secretariat easily defeated a solid field of grass horses in the Canadian International at Woodbine Racecourse.

3. *Arcangues Wins the 1993 Breeders' Cup Classic at 133-1.*

The Breeders' Cup was in its 10th year when it provided a forum for one of the most astounding results in racing history. The nerve of his European-based owner and trainer to think they could win the richest race in America with Arcangues, a moderately accomplished grass specialist. Were they crazy? Did they really believe that such a horse could win the Breeders' Cup Classic on a fast dirt track?

They had at least four good reasons to believe.

1. America's top jockey, Jerry Bailey, readily accepted the mount.
2. Owner Daniel Wildenstein was one of the most astute horse owners in Europe and his trainer, Andre Fabre, was the most successful horseman on that side of the pond, a man who had won four stakes and more than $1.2 million in America during the previous season, including a solid third-place finish with Jolypha in the 1992 Breeders' Cup Classic.
3. Bertrando, the American-based favorite for the 1993 Classic, was a fast horse relatively light in stamina.
4. On October 2 at Longchamp, Arcangues had run a creditable fourth in the 1½-mile Prix de l'Arc de Triomphe, Europe's toughest and most prestigious race.

Yet despite those hints, no public handicapper in any major newspaper mentioned Arcangues among the possible longshots for a prospective in-the-money finish.

Arcangues was brilliantly ridden through a crowded pack to catch front-running Bertrando in midstretch to score an upset that reverberated around the world. While many more shocking upsets have been posted in top international contests, this victory at such an outrageously large parimutuel payoff validated the suspicion that a top European grass horse could compete in the richest of the Breeders' Cup races on dirt. Indeed, it inspired several other notable attempts in the Classic, including those by Giant's Causeway and Sakhee, who were narrowly defeated by Tiznow in the 2000 and 2001 Classic, respectively. But Arcangues's success also played an interesting role in changing the boundaries of international racing as they had been understood for several decades.

According to Simon Crisford, manager for the Godolphin stable of Sheikh Mohammed bin Rashid Al Maktoum, the victory also "helped build support in Europe for a Breeders' Cup-style racing day in Dubai," an idea that would take form (as the Dubai World Cup) when Nad Al Sheba racecourse was ready to host the event in 1996.

2. *Volponi Wins the 2002 Breeders' Cup Classic.*

Before getting to the greatest upset of modern times, it seems only fair to share the following upset, which was not only highly unexpected but also probably ranks as the most infamous, given its surrounding details.

The 2002 Breeders' Cup card was at Arlington Park for the first time, having been at Hollywood, Aqueduct, Churchill Downs, Belmont, Santa Anita, Gulfstream, and Woodbine in various years.

Arlington is a spectacularly beautiful racing facility, rebuilt from the ashes of a devastating 1985 fire. This Breeders' Cup Day was similarly spectacular on many levels, none more so than the shocking victory scored by Volponi at 43–1 odds in the Classic, far and away the longest price in the 2002 Breeders' Cup. But the significance of this upset cannot really be told through a description of the race or the horses Volponi defeated. It comes from what occurred through microfiberoptic wires.

The magic word is Autotote, the parimutuel totalizator company that was handling all Breeders' Cup bets through computerized links to dozens of racetracks, offtrack betting centers, and simulcast facilities. Magic is what seemed to be involved when those of us who were paying attention found out that someone actually had included Volponi on their winning Breeders' Cup Ultra Pick Six tickets along with several other major upsets that dominated the Breeders' Cup card.

I was sitting with friends at Mohegan Sun casino in eastern Connecticut when the Ultra Pick Six results—posted later than usual—flashed a confounding fact that six tickets were sold on the obscure winning combination, paying $428,392 apiece.

"Impossible," several of us said almost simultaneously. The same word was being repeated incredulously at betting venues throughout the land.

"Impossible," said Bill Nader, a New York Racing Association vice president who was monitoring the handle at the Belmont Park betting hub. Almost instantly, Nader called Breeders' Cup officials at Arlington, who responded by halting payments on the winning tickets. This in turn led to an internal investigation, which took less than 24 hours to discover that all the winning tickets had been purchased through an upstate New York offtrack phone-wagering system via calls from a single Delaware customer whose pattern of bets was unusual, to say the least.

Despite Autotote and Catskill OTB officials saying there was nothing fishy about the winning tickets, the in-depth investigation launched by the National Thoroughbred Racing Association and the Breeders' Cup quickly discovered a conspiracy taking advantage of glitches in the security system that was supposedly designed to prohibit such things.

The investigation zeroed in on three former Drexel University fraternity brothers: Glen DaSilva, Derrick Davis, and the ringleader, Chris Harn.

Harn was a computer-savvy employee of Autotote who used his security clearance to finagle his way into the Ultra Pick Six parimutuel pool to alter the numbers on tickets bought by Derrick Davis via Davis's Catskill OTB phone account. DaSilva helped concoct the scam and participated in an earlier fleecing of a smaller pick-six payoff in New York that served as a practice run.

By design, Harn waited until four Breeders' Cup Ultra Pick Six races were run before changing Davis's tickets to the winning numbers, while selecting all of the horses in the fifth race yet to be run and all in the sixth and final race, the race that would be won by Volponi, the biggest longshot in the 12-horse Classic field.

The mistake that Harn made was typical of a criminal who thinks he has stolen a map to King Solomon's mines. He was not satisfied to buy one winning ticket. By converting all six of Davis's tickets to the eventual winning combinations, he gave his conspiracy five more winning tickets than any rational bettor would have bought in the expensive-to-play pick six.

The winning tickets stood out from any previously observed betting pattern. They looked like this:

Race 5: Horse #5, wins, pays $54

Race 6: Horse #10, wins, pays $7.40

Race 7: Horse #11, wins, pays $28.40

Race 8: Horse #6, wins, pays $10.20

Race 9: All 8 horses, winner pays $3.80

Race 10: All 12 horses, winner pays $89

The irony was clear. The upset here was not so much that Volponi won, but that his victory caused such a cinch conclusion that something was rotten with the system. The stench led to an astute investigation and the swift arrest and conviction of the three fraternity brothers who thought they had orchestrated the biggest betting coup in racing history.

When all was said and done, Harn and his friends went to jail and the Breeders' Cup Ultra Pick Six pool was redistributed to all players who had five winners, which amounted to $43,937.60 per winning ticket. There also was at least one other extremely positive fact that got lost a bit in this scandal.

Volponi was a moderately accomplished racehorse trained by 77-year-old Phil Johnson, an extremely popular figure on the New York backstretch, where he built a Hall of Fame career without ever having a victory quite like this in 60 years on the racetrack. Johnson also bred and co-owned Volponi, and remains the only person to have bred, owned, and trained a Breeders' Cup winner. For their faith in Volponi, the Johnson family earned $2.2 million the hard way that day. They earned it.

1. *THE GREATEST UPSET OF MODERN TIMES:*
The least-appreciated, most astounding upset of them all

In late 1970, I took a 15-month left-hand turn with my life to become a travel agent. St. Maarten, Puerto Rico, and Jamaica were my specialties, even though I never had been to any of those islands until one of those perks that keep people in the travel-agency business came along.

I was sent to Puerto Rico to canvass a dozen hotels and sample their fare, accommodations, side trips, and the like. Essentially it was a paid vacation. I could do what I wanted when I wanted, so long as I came back with useful information.

The date of departure was Friday, April 30, 1971, and the significance escaped me until a fellow travel agent asked a very strange question on Thursday night: "Who do you think is going to win the Kentucky Derby on Saturday?"

I hadn't opened a *Daily Racing Form* in more than a year, I had regularly skipped past the entries and result pages in the New York *Daily News* en route to the ball scores. The Kentucky Derby? I barely knew the names of three or four horses in the race.

"Here's the entries," said a friendly fellow agent. "An OTB shop just opened a few doors down and we're gonna make a bet for the office."

I looked at the names and the newspaper descriptions of the horses in the race for about five minutes and said, "This horse from South America, Canonero? The newspaper says he's already won a race at 1 1/4 miles in Venezuela. I don't remember any horse having run a race at the Derby distance before the Derby itself. He might be worth a play."

"Are you nuts?" my fellow agent said. "Canonero II? He's just a bum."

Arriving in Puerto Rico the next day, I was astounded to find that most of the country had a bad case of Kentucky Derby fever. Even the El San Juan Hotel limo driver wanted to know "Que caballo su gusto?" (*Which horse do you like?*)

While I knew the Derby was the most famous horse race in the world, I had no idea anyone in Puerto Rico cared much about it.

They didn't. But this year was different. The South American horse I had picked out of the *Daily News* the day before was a *big* Puerto Rican story. Not only had Canonero raced in Venezuela, he was owned by Latin American Edgar Caibett and was going to be ridden by a native of Puerto Rico, Gustavo Avila, a jockey well known to the local population.

I wasn't sure why they had adopted Avila as a personal hero. Angel Cordero Jr., the best jockey in America, was from Puerto Rico and nobody was going bananas over him riding his third Derby. But when it came time for the running of the race, I was sitting by the hotel pool when a television was wheeled over, connected by a long extension cord. The nearby bar was packed with newly born racing fans. Dozens of mint juleps—the official Derby drink that needs an overload of sugar to suit my taste—were being handed out to everyone.

Canonero II was not the longest shot on the board, but with the way he was being bad-mouthed by the television announcers and the way he had been written about in the press, he could have been, should have been, 100–1. He was in fact only 8.70–1 because Churchill Downs lumped him together with five other horses as part of the Derby's large mutuel field. The oddsmaker at Churchill Downs who put together this mutuel field was right about every horse except Canonero.

The other five finished 16th, 17th, 18th, 19th, and dead last in the field of 20.

Canonero? He was 18th for the first half-mile, 15th approaching the end of a mile, and first by more than three lengths at the wire to score one of the most spectacular, mind-numbing upsets in Thoroughbred-racing history.

According to many who were at Churchill Downs, the vast majority of astute observers didn't have a clue what was happening during the race.

"Who's THAT HORSE making a run in those black jockey silks?"

Many had to look at their track programs while the horse was moving strongly to the lead to realize that it was the South American invader.

Where I was watching the race—poolside at the El San Juan Hotel—everybody everybody knew "THAT HORSE."

"*Viva Canonero!*"

"*Viva Avila!*"

The busboys, the waiters, the bartenders, and the pool attendants all knew. Within a few moments after the blanket of roses was draped on Canonero in the winner's circle, someone on the hotel staff disconnected the TV and promptly threw it into the deep end of the pool. Everybody in the place roared with laughter and immediately took it as a signal to begin a rip-roaring party that would last well past dawn and be talked about for decades.

"*Viva Canonero!*"

"*Viva Avila!*"

I was amazed at the passion I had seen and experienced. So when I returned home to Brooklyn, I could not help but read everything I possibly could about what had happened in Louisville on the first Saturday in May.

What I found out bothered me a great deal and ignited my curiosity to the point where I called a few friends in Maryland who were tuned in to the goings-on leading up to the Preakness, the second jewel in the American Triple Crown scheduled for the third Saturday in May, two weeks after the Kentucky Derby.

It seems that most did not believe what their eyes had seen. They called Canonero a fluke, a skinny horse who looked undernourished who somehow had managed to win the Kentucky Derby through a lot of blind luck. The Kentucky-based racing industry also was unwilling to give the horse, his owner, his trainer, and his jockey any credit. It was embarrassing that Canonero had just beaten the best-bred, most expensive horses in the land, most of them born and raised in Kentucky.

In 1969, Caibett bought Canonero at a Kentucky yearling sale for a paltry $1,200, because the colt had modest breeding and a crooked foreleg that scared away all but a few bidders on the low end of the buying market. A few months later, Canonero made a successful debut over modest rivals, winning his first career start in Venezuela, but a September journey to Del Mar racetrack in Southern California resulted only in a fair third and a disappointing return trip to Caracas after a poor try in the Del Mar Futurity.

As a young 3-year-old during the winter and spring of 1971, the same horse blossomed into a major stakes-winner for trainer Juan Arias, even scoring an important victory at the 1 ¼-mile Derby distance in the high altitudes of Venezuela and another at 6 ½ furlongs over older horses in April. Caibett and his trainer, especially his trainer, had seen enough to warrant paying the nominating fee to make the horse eligible for America's greatest racing prize, the Kentucky Derby.

Nobody believed Caibett would have the chutzpah to actually ship the runty South American reject to Kentucky. Nobody in the blue-blooded world of Kentucky breeding believed the horse belonged in the race. That is only part of the story.

What I found out about Canonero and what his people went through to get to the Derby and the Preakness was the stuff that movies are made of, movies that cannot be made until the world lets the great Seabiscuit story fade away just long enough to accept a more improbable adventure.

Nevertheless, I will tell you the story of Canonero here as I learned it from racing writers and reporters Clem Florio, Andrew Beyer, Gerry Strine, Jim Bolus, Charles Hatton, and Joe Hirsch, because it needs to be told. I will also tell you that if it were not for the amazing Canonero II and a simple twist of fate, I probably would still be a travel agent.

On May 15, 1971, my wife was out shopping when I quietly tuned in to see the national telecast of the Preakness. The Kentucky Derby winner was not the betting favorite even after he had beaten all his major rivals, including Eastern Fleet, in the Kentucky Derby. Juan Arias was belittled and snickered at while his methods were criticized openly by prominent horse trainers and members of the press.

Perhaps they were jealous, perhaps they did not understand what he was doing or saying. Arias spoke not a single word of English. But if anyone was really paying attention, they would have witnessed a master horseman at work. Let me take you back to the week before the Kentucky Derby.

To get Canonero II to Louisville, Caibett booked the colt on a small cargo plane to Miami, where he was scheduled to be held in quarantine for 48 hours before U.S. Customs would permit him to be vanned to Kentucky, 1,000 miles away.

Unfortunately, a terrible tropical storm broke out in midflight, forcing the pilot to return to Venezuela, where Canonero remained on the plane for about 12 hours before a revised flight plan was approved for a restart. Once in the air, engine trouble forced still another return to Venezuela. About six hours later, the third attempted flight took off and detoured an extra four hours to avoid more turbulence en route to Miami. Everybody aboard, including Canonero, had suffered some form of illness during the arduous flights.

Upon arrival in Florida, Canonero was kept onboard the aircraft, sitting on the Tarmac for the duration of the 48 hours of quarantine. The van to Louisville turned out to be a single-horse trailer hooked up behind a 1965 Oldsmobile. Arias, the leading trainer in Venezuela, and his groom, Pedro Quintero, shared the driving chores straight through the 26-hour trip.

When Canonero II was checked into his barn at Churchill Downs, bones were showing through his girth area and he was unimpressive to the naked eye as he walked the shed row and jogged under the historic Twin Spires at Churchill Downs.

Newspaper columnists and radio commentators in Louisville were quick to take shots at the South American contingent.

"They're making a mockery out of America's most famous race."

"They should be barred from running this horse in the Derby."

Some writers even went so far as to suggest new rules of eligibility that would prevent any future horse from South America be permitted entry. Others of a more temperate nature publicly urged the owner and the trainer to reconsider their folly.

"The best thing to do would be to scratch the horse from the race."

After the Derby shocker, the people who wrote and spoke such things did not change their tune very much. In fact, their comments turned vitriolic and suggested that the Derby result was a pure fluke that surely would be reversed in the Preakness, now that the scrawny horse from South America would be taking no one by surprise.

The newspaper reporters who covered the Preakness knew a good story when they had one, but with few exceptions, the majority also believed that the South American wonder horse would be exposed to certain defeat in the slightly shorter Preakness, a race that usually required more overall speed than the longer Kentucky Derby.

Every horseman and racing writer anxiously awaited the morning during Preakness Week when Canonero would have his customary workout over the Pimlico surface. Everyone wanted to see if the horse had gotten stronger or lost more weight after his incredible journey and his come-from-behind finish in the grueling Kentucky Derby. Most expected to see Arias put the colt though a relatively fast clocking of 48 seconds for a half-mile or 1:00 or so for five-eighths. That was a typical Preakness Week workout for a fit horse.

Shortly after dawn on Wednesday of Preakness Week, Arias led his colt out to the track and spoke instructions to Gustavo Avila that no one within earshot could hear or understand. At least 60 reporters shadowed the six-foot-three-inch, dark-skinned Arias as he moved to his vantage point in front of the finish line to watch his horse train.

Canonero jogged slowly past them all and went into a light gallop heading around the clubhouse turn toward the backstretch. Picking up the pace just a bit, the bay son of French bred Pretendre broke off into a half-mile workout that could have been timed with an hourglass.

Talk about sl-o-o-o-w.

Several clockers looked at their watches and shook their heads.

"Fifty-three seconds for a half-mile? A donkey could do that," one of them said.

Muffled laughter could be heard rattling though the empty grandstand as trainers of other Preakness starters stood in the shadows, trying to measure the competition.

"That's the Derby winner?" asked one trainer in disbelief.

"That horse has no chance whatsoever!"

The reporters turned slowly toward Arias, who was already moving down onto the track to get to his horse. Only Clem Florio of the *Baltimore News American* followed him quickly enough. Florio was the only one there who spoke any Spanish and he was elected by default to ask the trainer what he thought of the way his horse had trained.

Florio had seen dozens of Preakness winners before 1971. A former professional boxer and a stablehand in Chicago for the legendary Sunny Jim Fitzsimmons (whose worst mistake as a horseman was to okay the sale of Seabiscuit), Florio had a keen eye for horse talent, but even he was confused by what he had just witnessed.

"*Porque?*" he asked Arias, meaning, "What in the world was that?" In response, the tall man from Venezuela leaned over and, while staring straight into Florio's eyes, quickly cupped his right hand in a way that curled his thumb and forefinger into a clear O, with the other three fingers upright—giving Florio the universal sign that says "Okay"—and proudly answered with a huge smile, "*PERFECTO. Canonero es perfecto!*"

All of which can be translated as follows: "The horse trained absolutely perfect, he went just the way I wanted him to go, he's ready to run the race of his life."

Florio was stunned, but he saw the convincing look of happiness in Arias's eyes and instantly believed him. In fact, Florio was the only one in the crowd of reporters who took Arias at his word, picking the horse to win the Preakness in his newspaper column and emptying his wallet with one of the biggest bets he would ever make on a horse race.

This time Canonero II did not come from out of left field to win the race, this time he broke sharply from the gate, raced head-to-head with Calumet Farm's impeccably bred speedster Eastern Fleet, and proceeded to leave that one in his wake in the upper stretch while en route to a new track-record clocking!

It was an astonishing performance, one that confirmed the sheer greatness of this improbable South American horse, a performance that would lead to a prestigious breeding farm offering an irresistible $1 million to buy the horse before the Belmont Stakes. It was an electrifying Preakness performance that would attract a record crowd to Belmont Park, including thousands of Spanish-speaking Americans, all there to be witness to Canonero's improbable bid for a sweep.

It also affected me personally as I watched on my home TV, 200 miles away. I was so thrilled, so moved by what had occurred, I knew I had to get back into this wonderful game that revolved around such noble creatures.

Canonero did not win that Belmont Stakes. In fact, he should not have run in it, because as race day approached, he developed a case of hives and was not in peak condition for the longest and toughest of the Triple Crown events. The decision to run him was blamed first on Caibett, then on Arias, and finally on King Ranch, which paid big bucks for his racing ability, not as a breeding prospect. But the new and old owners felt almost forced into the contest with so many people hanging on to Canonero, the newly crowned folk hero of two continents.

Canonero was not going to die from the experience, but he was not going to run anywhere near his best, and his people secretly knew it, even though they were hoping against hope that the South American wonder horse would overcome this adversity as he had overcome the harrowing flights from Venezuela.

More important was the behavior of the racing industry after the Belmont toward the people who had brought Canonero to America for his amazing Triple Crown run. Caibett was treated well enough as a member of the wealthy class, but Arias never was accepted as a bona fide training talent despite his success, mostly because he used highly unorthodox training methods that did not accent speed.

Ignored and dismissed as lucky, Arias was not even invited to attend the Kentucky Derby trainers' dinner that always includes every trainer of a Kentucky Derby horse, nor was he given any token recognition at the end of the year for developing Canonero from a two-time loser in California into a dual-classic winner and the unanimous 3-year-old champion racehorse of 1971.

Arias was not even given a real opportunity to practice his craft in America, though he was so talented that he made it back to the Derby in 1972 with a cheap horse he bought and developed for a small-time owner, Hassi Shina. The horse was a weakly bred, relatively slow-footed colt named Hassi's Image and there is serious doubt that any other trainer could have developed him into a legitimate Derby starter.

Even that encore performance did not attract any American sponsors or horses to train, and Arias returned to his native Venezuela to spend the rest of his working life breaking yearlings and training horses on various farms throughout South America. He earned a good living working with the animals he loved best, but never again ventured into the active world of racehorse training, living in relative obscurity to this day, one of the great horse trainers of the 20th century.

I have always felt that the American racing industry owes Juan Arias something it was unwilling to give while he was proving his skill in the toughest arena the sport has to offer with a horse that did not have a gilt-edged path to glory. Years later, Cuban-born Hall of Fame trainer Laz Barrera told me he thought that Arias's training ability was a personal inspiration that should be studied more closely by modern trainers who wear horses down with too many fast workouts. He also said that a Juan Arias Training Award should be instituted annually for the most outstanding achievement by a foreign-based horse trainer in the United States.

In my own case, I had no trouble realizing that I should give up the travel-agency business and get involved more seriously in the game. That summer, my wife and I took a cottage in Lake Luzerne, New York, and went to the races at Saratoga every day.

THE WORST DISQUALIFICATIONS OF THE MODERN ERA
Sometimes three judges and all the technology in the world does not help.

Back in the day when stewards did not have videotape replays and there were no photo-finish cameras, mistakes happened more often than historical accounts will confess.

In the modern era, in which there are technological aids to help stewards and placing judges make accurate calls, some will argue that the mistakes are just as frequent. Whether that is true or not, it seems hard to believe that the following disqualifications—the three worst of the modern era—actually occurred.

3. *Thistledown, November 20, 2005, Sixth Race, a $16,000 Allowance Sprint.*

Favored at 2–5, Slewrenity finished first by 3 ½ lengths with jockey Julio Felix aboard. Lac Grape was second at 7–1 with jockey Lyndon Hannigan.

The official Equibase result chart states: "SLEWRENITY battled for the lead along the rail into the stretch, drifted a bit then drew clear late under strong handling. LAC GRAPE battled for the lead off the rail, threw his head sharply near the sixteenth pole and finished clear for second. . . ."

After a stewards' inquiry and a claim of foul by Hannigan, the order of finish was reversed and Lac Grape was declared the official winner, making thousands of dollars of tickets worthless to those players who had keyed the 2–5 shot in the win pool, the exacta, trifecta, superfecta, and multirace pools.

Lac Grape paid $17.40 to win. In $2 units, the exacta with Lac Grape first and Slewrenity second paid $33.20; the trifecta, $417; the superfecta, $1,509.40; and the pick three, $618. The win pool for this race was $24,716; the exacta pool; $22,346; the trifecta pool, $23,139; the superfecta pool, $9,739; and the pick-three pool, $2,791.

The stewards, Allen Fairbanks, Kim Sawyer, and Joel McCullar, said that they felt compelled to disqualify Slewrenity after watching the videotape replay, thinking that Felix had hit Lac Grape's head with his whip, which ordinarily does call for a DQ.

Unfortunately, no such thing occurred, as a closer examination of the video evidence clearly demonstrated. Felix was so upset with the DQ that he canceled his remaining mounts.

Five days later, after trainer Jerry Hollendorfer's assistant, Butch Marshall, protested the decision on behalf of Slewrenity and other interested parties—most notably, several bettors—the three stewards were forced to admit their mistake.

The official statement by the Thistledown stewards read in part: "A review of the videotape of the race fails to confirm that Felix's whip struck Lac Grape, even though Lac Grape throw [sic] its head up in the air."

Given that the stewards had access to the same videotape evidence before they disqualified Slewrenity, they were fined $2,000 apiece by the

Ohio State Racing Commission. The commission also reversed the incorrect order of finish and redistributed the purse.

Of course, there was no relief for horseplayers who lost their wagers on Slewrenity. The lucky bettors who had been given a 7–1 return on Lac Grape probably felt no remorse, having occasionally been victimized themselves by close calls and disqualifications that went against them.

2. *The 1967 Jersey Derby at Garden State Park.*

This race will be discussed in greater detail in the next chapter, in Hall of Famer Manny Ycaza's profile as one of the best jockeys of modern times. This was the race that was awarded to In Reality by the stewards after Dr. Fager crossed over in front of the field heading into the first turn. While Dr. Fager did tighten up a few rivals with Ycaza's typically aggressive handling, Dr. Fager was so much the best of that group entering the turn, and at every stage of the race, that the infraction was dwarfed by the injustice it rendered.

The move to the inside in front of the field was so mild compared to what occurs several times a week in races throughout the country— with no penalty—that to this day, the decision ranks as one of the worst calls ever made in a stewards' booth. One of the worst, but not *the* worst. That (dis)honor has to go to the most bizarre disqualification anyone has ever seen.

1. *The Second Race at Saratoga, August 2, 1986.*

On this day at precisely the moment the stewards posted the official order of finish, I was on the phone from Minneapolis seeking conversation with handicapper John Pricci, of *Newsday,* a friend since the mid-1960s. His phone line was picked up by Mark Berner, another friend and handicapper from *Newsday.*

"John's not here, Steve," Mark said. "He's in the stewards' booth telling the three blind mice they just disqualified the wrong horse!"

So it was that the three Saratoga stewards—Dick McLaughlin, Sal Ferrara, and Robert F. Kelley Jr.—were informed that they had made the worst disqualification possible.

Pricci, whose best bet of the day was the unofficial and disqualified winner, number 8, Allumeuse (at 7–1 odds), later explained that he controlled his emotions as best he could while politely asking the stewards to cue up the videotape.

Pricci patiently pointed out that number 8 had rallied down the center of the track, far away from an incident that had caused the inquiry to be held. When he saw the suddenly concerned looks on the stewards' faces, Pricci simply left the room, having made his point.

Left aghast and severely embarrassed by their error, the stewards refused to show the videotape replay of the race for the rest of the day and finally came into the press box with a statement after the final race. The details, as refreshed in a 2006 interview with Bill Heller, who did considerable reporting on this incident in his book *Saratoga Tales* (Whitston Publishing Company, 2004), went something like this:

Jerry Bailey was aboard Fasta Dancer when the horse to his immediate outside, number 11, Syntronic, ridden by apprentice Wigberto Paneto, took a sharp left-hand turn, knocking Fasta Dancer down and vaulting Bailey over the inner hedge, lucky not to be seriously injured.

With Fasta Dancer lying on the turf, Robbie Davis was unable to avoid a spill while riding Utah Pine. Fortunately, Davis was only shaken up as horse and rider also recovered without serious injury.

The unofficial order of finish was:

8 ALLUMEUSE
2 FESTIVITY
11 SYNTRONIC
1 DAWN'S FANCY

The stewards erroneously blamed number 8, Allumeuse, for the infraction, and disqualified her to 10th. They then moved number 2, Festivity, into the winner's circle, followed by the actual offender, number 11, Syntronic, in second, with number 1, Dawn's Fancy, placed third.

All this despite the fact that Jose Santos, who rode Allumeuse, told them they were making a big mistake.

"Not the eight," Santos said. *"No ocho, no ocho,"* he repeated.

Even worse, when they interviewed Bailey, he categorically told them that it was number 11, Syntronic, that had caused the foul.

After consulting with the New York State Racing and Wagering Board, the stewards composed the following mea culpa and walked into the press box.

> "The stewards erred in disqualifying the No. 8 horse, Allumeuse, in today's second race. Following the finish of the race on the main turf course in which two horses unseated their riders near the eighth pole, we reviewed a video replay and inadvertently disqualified Allumeuse instead of the No. 11 horse, Syntonic, who did interfere with No. 3, Fasta Dancer. We have corrected the purse distribution accordingly.
>
> "We regret that, because of our concern for the condition of jockey Robbie Davis, who was injured in the incident, we did not discover our error until after the race was declared official and betting payoffs began. Under State Racing and Wagering Board Rule 4008.1, the betting payoff cannot be changed after the 'Official' sign has been posted."

Naturally, a firestorm of protests was set off by this decision. Players in the Saratoga grandstand wanted their $16.40 to win and/or the $97.20 for a winning $2 daily-double ticket with Passing Thunder, winner of the first race. Instead, they got nothing, even after former heavyweight boxer David Zyglewicz, a resident of Watervliet, New York, filed a lawsuit against the New York Racing Association on behalf of his $24 daily double tickets and nine other Allumeuse bettors.

Years later, Bailey told Heller that he was completely shocked that the stewards could have made such a mistake in the face of the videotape evidence and his own testimony.

The fate of these three stewards was predictable. Ferrara was demoted to Finger Lakes and retired. McLaughlin was fined and given a desk job, but left New York to take a steward's job at Rockingham Park in New Hampshire, where he had once worked as a stable boy. Kelley, a substitute steward that season for regular NYRA steward Jerry Burke, who was attending to his wife's illness, was fined and demoted to assistant steward.

In my own review of these cases, especially the Thistledown and Saratoga disqualifications, two things stand out that deserve a closer look by racing commissions everywhere.

1. Stewards are likely to make mistakes, but when those mistakes are quickly addressed, why isn't there a provision in the parimutuel law that commands payment to the correct winning bettors?

Surely a portion of the $1 million or more that usually winds up in the "uncashed ticket fund" can be reserved to pay bettors who are penalized by such injustices through no fault of their own. Wouldn't this alleviate a problem that historically has given racing so much bad publicity?

2. Had the Thistledown or Saratoga DQ occurred in California, there would have been no option at all to reverse the stewards' bad decision. According to California's current racing rules, no appeal of a stewards' decision based on a riding infraction can be filed with the California Horse Racing Board. CHRB Rule 1761a states: "From every decision of the stewards, *except a decision concerning the disqualification of a horse due to a foul or riding or driving infraction,* an appeal may be made to the Board."

Thus, no appeal of Slewrenity's disqualification in Ohio, or Allumeuse's disqualification in New York, could have been entertained if these bad disqualifications had occurred in California. That seems to be a rule that closes the door on correcting a terrible decision.

2 THE GREATEST JOCKEYS

DURING THE SECOND half of the 20th century, there were about two dozen jockeys who easily could be placed on anyone's Top 10 list. Among those who qualified, but did not make my list, were Hall of Famers Johnny Rotz, Bobby Ussery, Johnny Longden, Jorge Velasquez, Sandy Hawley, Jacinto Vasquez, Walter Blum, Kent Desormeaux, Julie Krone, Russell Baze, Mike Smith, and several contemporary riders who are building Hall of Fame careers, including John R. Velazquez, Edgar Prado, Patrick Valenzuela, Victor Espinoza, and Garrett Gomez.

Longden was the toughest to cut, and several others on the list were extremely hard to separate. Longden was the winningest jockey in history when he retired in 1966, but most of his best work was in the 1940s and early 1950s. He also had a near Hall of Fame career as a trainer well into the 1970s and rightfully will deserve prominent mention in a later chapter—"Before My Time," which is devoted to the best in the sport who were prolific prior to the mid-1950s.

I also do not have a "Worst Jockey" in the strictest sense, because it seems unfair to skewer men and women who risk their lives every time they jump aboard a racehorse. I do, however, have some candidates for the worst *rides* I have ever seen—including a few by jockeys who made this list, as you will see in the recaps below and in commentaries about specific races and horses scattered throughout the book.

That said, I have expanded this category to a baker's dozen: The Top 12, plus one special jockey who, for a very brief time, was absolutely the best jockey I have ever seen, bar none. There also is a lot more to Steve Cauthen's story than his meteoric rise to stardom, including a glimpse at the harsh realities faced by every jockey in racing history.

The most unusual interview of my reporting career took place in April 1977, while taking an early-morning shower in the basement of Aqueduct racetrack. I was cleaning up after having worked all night in the press box researching a story for the short-lived *Philadelphia Journal* newspaper. When the soap cleared my eyes, I just happened to notice that 17-year-old jockey sensation Steve Cauthen was using the next shower in the open stall.

After dominating Ohio, Kentucky, and Chicago racing for several months, Cauthen, still an apprentice jockey, moved his tack to New York when ace jockey agent Lenny Goodman agreed to line up his mounts. Goodman had helped Hall of Fame jockey Braulio Baeza, as well as other top riders, break in with good New York outfits. He liked what he saw of Cauthen on film.

Goodman saw the brilliant talent that stunned astute horsemen and professional horseplayers in race after race during the 1977 season. Cauthen was far more polished than any apprentice to come down the pike in decades. He broke horses alertly, settled them into an easy stride, saved ground when needed, moved outside or inside as the situation commanded, and always seemed to get his horses to finish well, even when he barely used the whip. Most amazingly, Steve Cauthen projected the common sense of a fully grown adult—a young man of such natural intelligence that he could have pursued any number of elite professions in settings of higher learning.

From the day he arrived at Aqueduct in December 1976 and virtually every day through the ensuing winter and spring, Cauthen's name appeared in three-inch headlines on the back pages of the New York tabloids. Three wins per day was commonplace. Four happened as often as other jockeys got two, and during one astonishing 10-day stretch in January, Cauthen rode five winners three times and six winners once. Let me spell that out: Steve Cauthen rode five winners on January 12, five more on January 14, five on January 15, and topped off this scorching streak with six winners on January 22!

In all, Cauthen had three different days in which he won six races during that single meet, while no other jockey in history has ever won six races on a single New York racing card three different times during a career of any length.

Surprisingly, Cauthen's horses sometimes paid fancy prices. Form reversals were commonplace as this young riding savant turned proven losers into sudden winners as if the whip he twirled in his oversized hand were a magic wand.

So there he was, after a morning of galloping and working horses, and here I was, with an outrageous opportunity to get some good inside stuff.

Cauthen and I exchanged a few basic hellos. I identified myself as a reporter, and to my surprise that didn't put a lid on anything, so I queried him on several reasonable issues—from his life away from the comfort of his Kentucky-based family to his impressions of New York City, to the size of his hands and his approach to a race. All the while I knew I was going to ask him something that had been planted in my head for more than a decade when I witnessed jockey Sidney Cole fatally thrown from his mount into a furlong pole at this same racetrack in the mid-1960s, and soon afterward heard about the crippling injuries suffered by a high-school mate, James Moriarty, who became a jockey in New England.

While Cauthen and I talked, I also knew that this great young athlete had been lucky to escape a fall just a week earlier. So I popped the question: "Steve, what kind of precautions do you take to protect yourself from something like that happening?" I asked, knowing that if we were anywhere else, I never would have gotten an answer.

I was surprised when he looked me straight in the eye through the cascading water and said, "One of the first things I learned about falling or being thrown is that you can't be thinking about that . . . you're just increasing the chance of it happening. To answer your question, though—to really answer your question—I prepare by keeping sharp, staying in shape . . . I practice concentration. Zen breathing, it relaxes me. Been doin' that since I was 13."

Cauthen also said he studied the *Daily Racing Form* and watched replays every day, taking mental notes on the way certain horses handle the turns and the way other jockeys do things. "All good riders do that," he said. I asked for an example.

"A few days ago there was a horse in front of me that has been hard to keep from bearing out on the turn, so I took a hold and angled to the inside, waiting 'till he started floating out. When a race is jammed up, if there's no place to go, I try to feel my way to a position where I might make a quick move out of there; your head has to be in the game to take advantage or you might as well be watching in the grandstand."

Cauthen realized he would be asking for trouble if he took anything about race riding lightly. He also seemed unusually focused and intensely aware that he was performing at a higher level than anyone around him—the way Tiger Woods would be focused and perform two decades later as the young king of golf.

As many readers may know, Cauthen was going to finish 1977 on top of the jockey world, the winner of unprecedented double Eclipse Awards as both outstanding apprentice and outstanding jockey over all other riders in North America. He also was destined to raise his game to stratospheric levels during the next 14 months while becoming the darling of the national media, expertly riding Affirmed to the 1978 Triple Crown over the stubborn Alydar, ridden to the hilt by eventual Hall of Famer Jorge Velasquez. Yet, it did not take long after this triumphant Triple Crown for the Steve Cauthen story to take a rather diabolical, negative turn.

Riding in the third race at Saratoga on August 9, 1978, he broke his knee in a fall. Despite all his preparation, there had been no way for Cauthen to escape what every jockey eventually has to deal with—a spill, broken bones, or sometimes so much more. Fans in the grandstand or watching on television may have an inkling of the dangers involved, but few fans, even experienced veterans, know that many jockeys spend significant portions of their lives in hospitals and rehab centers. Every year, several jockeys are maimed for life or pay the ultimate price for their work.

George Woolf, the star of the 1930s who rode Seabiscuit to his match-race win over War Admiral, died in a racing accident in 1946; Red Pollard, Seabiscuit's regular rider, suffered his share of major injuries in races and in morning workouts; Alvaro Pineda died in a starting-gate accident at Santa Anita in 1975 that was witnessed by his close friend Laffit Pincay Jr., the all-time winning jockey who would retire 28 years later due to neck and head injuries he suffered in a fall. Julie Krone was seriously injured twice in the last six years of her Hall of Fame riding career. Ditto for Hall of Famer Chris McCarron.

Gary Stevens still suffers from badly damaged knees that forced him to prematurely give up the game. Bill Shoemaker, who spent the last few years in a wheelchair after an automobile accident, also spent more than two years in hospitals and rehab centers dealing with assorted racing injuries, the worst of which occurred in 1968 when a horse tossed him off and rolled on top of him. Ron Turcotte, who rode Secretariat to his immortal 1973 Triple Crown sweep, has been paralyzed from the waist down since a Belmont spill in 1978.

On February 10, 2004, as part of a story on the death of jockey Michael Rowland from a racing accident, *The Courier-Journal* newspaper in Louisville, Kentucky, reported that the University of North Carolina at Chapel Hill had found that nearly 20 percent of all jockey injuries are to the head or neck. From 1993 through 1996, the UNC study found that U.S. jockeys suffered 6,545 injuries serious enough for treatment. Furthermore, according to information supplied to the Kentucky newspaper by the Jockeys' Guild, there have been 144 documented racing-related cases of death and/or paralysis to jockeys and exercise riders in North America since 1940.

The list of life-threatening injuries on horseback I personally know about could run through several pages in this book and would reflect much more than the sport's occupational hazards. It is a profound tragedy for families, for the racing industry, for insurance companies, and for the public at large, all of whom have to deal with drastically changed lives and ultra-expensive medical care.

In Steve Cauthen's case, the injury was not life-threatening, but there was considerable pain and a noticeable loss of flexibility in his left knee that cost him the mount on Affirmed in the 1978 Travers Stakes. Apparently, the time on the sidelines made him nervous about his place in the game for the first time in his meteoric career.

Cauthen denied it in public, but having watched him perform so closely for months at his peak, there was no doubt in my mind that Cauthen rushed his way back to riding before he was healed completely. Instead of riding with supreme confidence, communicating so intuitively with his mounts, Cauthen seemed slightly out of balance and certainly less effective.

Steve Cauthen never would ride at the same level of brilliance he displayed as a 17- and 18-year-old phenom, when for 18 months he won more than 650 races and was the best jockey in America. It wasn't even close. Through that remarkable run, Cauthen was the best jockey I have ever seen, bar none.

But that was then and this was now. During the winter of 1979, he would go winless for nearly six straight weeks after heading out west against his agent's advice, a move that eventually led to his frustrated agent's premature return to New York in the middle of the losing streak.

The unthinkable was unfolding. Steve Cauthen, winner of the Triple Crown just nine months earlier, was going to permanently lose the mount on Affirmed to Laffit Pincay. After all, Affirmed had lost four straight races with Cauthen aboard.

As I mentioned in the previous chapter, trainer Laz Barrera was a personal friend and professional confidant. We shared many consultations during Affirmed's career. One such conversation occurred by phone in early February 1978, days before Barrera was going to tell Cauthen the bad news.

"I love him like one of my sons," Laz said. "But I have to do this for his sake as much as for Affirmed. . . . He has too much pressure on him; he feels so bad about the way he lost the last two races. He's riding like a good [baseball] player in a bad slump. He's trying too hard and it has to be done."

Losing Affirmed was a major blow to Cauthen's confidence. To ease the pain just a bit, Barrera vowed that he would do everything he could to put him on a winner, and a few days later Barrera put Cauthen aboard a cheap maiden-claiming horse named Father Duffy, who was clearly better than his opposition. Thus came Cauthen's first winner of the year, stopping the incredible losing streak at 110, one of the longest droughts by a nationally ranked jockey in modern times.

Even though the losing streak was over, Cauthen seemed precariously placed for a very hard fall from grace. Suddenly and seemingly out of the blue, a great gift came his way, a gift that helped him escape the heavy criticism that had been gaining momentum the same way unbridled adoration had accompanied his rock-star popularity,

Through the intercession of many well-connected friends, 18-year-old Steve Cauthen was tendered a $1 million contract to ride for high-powered Robert Sangster in Great Britain. Across the Atlantic, he would encounter less scrutiny and be able to ride in the longer stirrups utilized by European jockeys while his legs would take less pounding on relatively soft grass courses.

Cauthen accepted the offer with minimal hesitation and, after a few months of cultural adjustments, proved to be a quick study, recovering his form well enough to become a three-time champion jockey in England during the 1980s, a reign that was going to be stopped only by another nasty fall in 1988—at Goodwood racecourse. This fall would lead to fewer mounts over the next five years and to Cauthen's eventual retirement. In 1993, he returned to his native Kentucky with wife and family, beginning a second career in public relations at the ripe age of 33.

In recounting the career of this extraordinary athlete, a man I respect greatly, there is one more detail that has to be included. Even while he was successful in his second career as a British-based jockey, Steve Cauthen returned to America on more than a dozen occasions to ride good horses in the Breeders' Cup, the Arlington Million, and other international racing events. Cauthen never won a single stakes in any of those trips.

While he deserved huge credit for making all the needed adjustments to be successful in Europe, Cauthen had not regained the smooth form that turned American racing upside down in 1977 and 1978. Obviously, the fall he took in 1978 was to blame. Yet, the best thing to remember about that fall is that it did not cost Cauthen his life, or limbs, or an opportunity for a second career in England doing what he loved the most.

"Some things you just can't prevent, no matter how hard you might try," he had admitted philosophically and somewhat prophetically at the end of our impromptu interview in 1977. "I think positive about things I'm doing all the time, but we all know the risks."

In the early 21st century, Steve Cauthen remains one of the most admired jockeys ever to ride the American turf, a quiet icon and gentle ambassador for the best elements of the game. Even as he ages toward his social-security years, there is little doubt that Cauthen will be remembered forever as the wunderkind of American racing. He was elected to Racing's Hall of Fame in 1994.

THE BEST JOCKEYS OF MODERN TIMES: SUPERIOR PERFORMERS WHO WERE NOT PERFECT BY ANY MEANS

---

12. *Manuel Ycaza*

Manuel Ycaza was one of the great riding stars of the 1960s, the first of many exceptional jockeys to come to America from Panama. Ycaza also was the most aggressive rider of the modern era, a man alternately applauded and penalized for his daring style.

Ycaza was the one who would ride an aging $5,000 claimer through the narrowest opening on the rail, picking up shards of white paint on his black leather boots. He was the jockey you wanted to be aboard the horse you were betting on because you had no doubt he would ride for all he was worth. Once the race was on, you held your breath, knowing he was even money to be involved in a foul claim, or to be victimized by officials who had their binoculars trained on him to catch him when he sneezed.

The New York stewards had a special eye out for Ycaza, setting him down for days at a clip for infractions that would get other riders polite warnings. But if truth be told, there were justifications for the stewards to be ready to cut the hard-bodied, sharply conditioned Ycaza down to size.

To Manny Ycaza, race riding may not have been a contact sport, but he played the game the way Sugar Ray Robinson boxed. Ycaza regularly angled his horse deftly in front of rivals, or nudged them wide going into the first turn, or subtly put key contenders into tight quarters just enough to take his edge. Sometimes it was more than a deft move, or a nudge; sometimes Manny Ycaza seemed hell-bent on impersonating a kamikaze pilot.

But Ycaza was a superb athlete with all the moves, extremely tough to pass in stretch battles, absolutely fearless in any riding situation. In many ways, Manny Ycaza was Angel Cordero Jr. before the racing world would discover Cordero.

Unlike Cordero, who would refine and tone his own aggressiveness into an art form in the 1970s and '80s, Ycaza rode with such abandon that he went over the line several times a season, costing himself quality mounts and important stakes victories.

The most famous and most important horse Ycaza ever rode too aggressively was Dr. Fager, regarded by many to be among the fastest horses of all time. After Ycaza piloted Dr. Fager to victory over Damascus in the 1967 Gotham Mile at Aqueduct, trainer John Nerud gave the mount back to him for the Jersey Derby at Garden State Park while Braulio Baeza was busy riding the 4-year-old Buckpasser in the Metropolitan Mile at Belmont the same day.

Dr. Fager was tons the best on paper of his three Jersey Derby rivals. Only Francis Genter's In Reality seemed to present a remote challenge. A few strides out of the starting gate, Dr. Fager was clearly in front as expected. From there to the wire, he would improve his position, scoring by 6 ½ widening lengths over In Reality. The other two overmatched horses were far back.

The stewards instantly lit the Inquiry sign, as they did so often at other tracks when Ycaza was involved. In this case, it was hard to see why. Dr. Fager was guilty of running too fast. All Ycaza did was angle Dr. Fager sharply over to the rail entering the clubhouse turn while about two lengths clear of the three horses who were left in his dust.

Sure, the film-patrol cameras caught Ycaza being his aggressive self, taking command of the inside racing lanes. Sure, the stewards saw the other jockeys flinch a bit in response. But this disqualification was based on a mirage, or more likely on Ycaza's exaggerated reputation, which preceded his trip to Garden State.

Later, Nerud, one of the great horseman of the 20th century, said that the decision was patently unfair to Ycaza. But nevertheless, the disqualification cost the rider a return engagement on Dr. Fager when the mount came open later in the year. Nerud, in fact, chose jockey Bill Boland to ride Dr. Fager in the 1967 Woodward, one of the most important races of modern times.

"I couldn't ride him back," Nerud said. "They had a bulls'-eye on his back."

All that notwithstanding, Ycaza rode first string for future Hall of Fame trainer Woody Stephens for more than a decade and was aboard many of the best horses of the 1960s for other great horsemen who recognized his superb riding skills. These included Ack Ack for Frank Bonsal; Bald Eagle and Never Bend for Stephens; Sword Dancer for Elliott Burch; Lamb Chop for J. W. Maloney; Dark Mirage for E. W. King;

Damascus for Frank Whiteley Jr; Ridan for LeRoy Jolley; and of course Dr. Fager, who never should have had his number taken down.

In all, and somewhat lost in the infamous highlights of his controversial career, Manny Ycaza won more than 22.4 percent of 10,561 races, the second-highest win percentage of more than 300 American jockeys who have won at least 1,900 races. The only other riders with higher win percentages in racing history are Avelino Gomez (24 percent), who rode almost exclusively in Canada, and the still active Russell Baze. At the bottom line, Manuel Ycaza was one of the very best jockeys anyone will ever see.

11. *Eddie Delahoussaye*

After he completed his career of 39,214 races with 6,384 wins, I had the pleasure of sharing a Las Vegas handicapping seminar on Kentucky Derby Day with Eddie Delahoussaye, a rider who raced mostly in the shadow of other jockeys on this list, but was nearly flawless in every respect.

"I preferred to ride horses coming from off the pace," Delahoussaye told the crowd at the Orleans Hotel. "Not only was it more enjoyable to reach back and catch the leaders in full stride, or win a stretch battle, but I had a knack for it. I felt at my best on a horse reaching out for his best, trying to win. It suited my personality."

Delahoussaye's personality was straightforward. He rarely spoke deceptively; rarely resorted to tricks on horseback. He was larger than most jockeys, but thin at the waist, with powerful arms and wrists. He had begun to learn his craft as a preteen on the bush tracks of Louisiana and was the best jockey at the Fair Grounds in New Orleans for a dozen years before he moved to Southern California to become one of the most reliable "money riders" on a tough, competitive circuit.

"Eddie D." was soft-spoken, extremely intelligent, and highly articulate. An easy interview under any circumstance, Delahoussaye usually illustrated what he was thinking with rare precision and economy of language.

"Look for horses moving up with minimal urging," Delahoussaye told the Orleans crowd while showing them how to spot live contenders in classic-distance races. "If a rider has to use his horse to move up before he gets to the three-eighths pole, he won't be in the money."

Delahoussaye should know. He rode back-to-back winners of the Kentucky Derby—Gato del Sol in 1982 and Sunny's Halo in 1983, as well as Preakness-Belmont winner Risen Star in 1988 and Belmont and Breeders' Cup Classic winner A.P. Indy in 1992. Beyond his deft handling of classic horses over a distance of ground, Delahoussaye also was a master sprint rider, and won back-to-back runnings of the Breeders' Cup Sprint with Thirty Slews and Cardmania in 1992 and '93, respectively.

The leading jockey in America in 1978, Delahoussaye won everywhere he ventured and was especially effective with stretch-running stakes contenders at Belmont Park.

"I loved the long, soft turns at Belmont," Delahoussaye said. "I always felt I could get a horse to relax better on a larger track. When they relax they finish; when they're too aggressive they usually stop."

Delahoussaye's mounts won more than $193 million. Always at his best in the clutch, he was far from finished when forced to retire in 2002. He had not lost any of his skills and had little difficulty maintaining his racing weight at 117 pounds, thanks to a sensible diet, good metabolism, and rigorous conditioning. But, as pointed out previously, jockeys usually do not escape falls. They survive them if they are lucky. They mend and pick themselves up again for more danger, more thrills, more high-stakes poker on horseback.

At the handicapping seminar in the Las Vegas casino on Kentucky Derby Day, 2003, Eddie Delahoussaye seemed sadly out of place. He knew he deserved to be riding in the world's most famous race that afternoon. Instead, Eddie D. was doing his best to satisfy an audience of horseplayers who, while expressing their appreciation for his life's work, wanted most of all to know who was going to win the race. Nothing more, nothing less.

Delahoussaye was enduring what many jockeys before him had endured; having suffered one too many broken bones and injuries to his knees and hip. The spirit was willing, but the body could no longer take the punishment. If he persisted, one more fall might leave him in a wheelchair.

Speaking for many dozens of thousands of fans who cashed a few bets on Eddie D.'s mounts through three decades of excellence on horseback, I told him that I was glad he was sitting in the next chair, in relatively good health, with good bucks in the bank, his Hall of Fame reputation secured, never again to be put in such a precarious position.

"I guess it really is about that time for me to enjoy the pleasures of my family and friends," he responded. "There are a few new things I'd like to try, too; like maybe cash a few good bets on these races from the sidelines. I think I know what it takes to win."

10. *Pat Day*

According to Pat Day's own testimony, and *testimony* is precisely the right word, his life changed dramatically one sleepless night in 1984 when he was startled by a "presence" in his Miami hotel room. The presence seemed to tell Day to turn on his TV set. What he saw was an Evangelical minister encouraging his flock to be "born again" into the Christian faith.

"In that instant, I realized that I was ruining a good life with drugs and alcohol. I was getting a personal call to change everything."

So said the four-foot-eleven-inch, 100-pound former Colorado high-school wrestling star and rodeo rider who reformed on the spot and would retire 21 years later at age 51, with more money won than any other rider in history.

"In my case, the pot at the end of the rainbow was empty without more meaning to my life."

Thus Pat Day became an evangelical presence on the national racing scene, a presence who sometimes seemed at odds with the world of horse-race gambling and occasionally made those who were interviewing him feel uncomfortable with his religious zeal. But on horseback, Pat Day was all business, and a complex, amazing jockey to analyze.

In Illinois and Kentucky, where Day was the dominant rider at numerous meets, he was affectionately nicknamed God, the same way the celestially talented guitarist Eric Clapton was flattered in the 1960s by "Clapton Is God" graffiti in London.

Day owned Churchill Downs and Arlington Park to such an extent that any horse he was scheduled to ride would attract inordinate play in the mutuels, lowering legit 5–1 shots to 5–2, and 5–2 shots to 6–5. He may have frustrated value bettors, but not his loyal fans, as Day delivered win after win at an uncanny 25 to 30 percent rate in meet after meet.

In New York, however, Pat Day was not so well regarded. Far from being labeled God, Pat Day became Pat "Wait All" Day to hard-core bettors who were hypercritical of his extremely patient riding style. In particular, large numbers of New York fans never forgave Day for two important defeats he suffered aboard one of New York's favorite horses, Easy Goer.

After Sunday Silence won the 1989 Kentucky Derby over heavily favored Easy Goer, the latter's legion of New York fans (and many others in Kentucky) expected a reversal of that result in the Preakness, if only Day would abandon his laid-back style and ride the stretch-running Easy Goer more aggressively.

In the Preakness, that is exactly what Pat Day did, moving Easy Goer early on the backstretch after an awkward start to put the strongly built son of Alydar in a good striking position right outside front-running Houston before the far turn. Day had gotten a big jump on Sunday Silence, who had lost position after being bumped and forced offstride at virtually the same time Easy Goer was moving forward.

It didn't matter, as Sunday Silence recovered his balance in a split second, lengthened his stride instantly, and turned on the burners to engage Easy Goer en route to a great stretch battle and a narrow victory. Once more Day took the heat for a narrow defeat as Easy Goer's supporters believed that jockey Pat Valenzuela, aboard Sunday Silence, had outfinished Day—even intimidated him while keeping Easy Goer pinned on the inside rail.

"I tried everything, the horse tried everything, and there was no difference between them at the wire, except the half-inch the camera showed," Day said. "Give credit to both horses; they ran super."

After Easy Goer spoiled Sunday Silence's bid for a Triple Crown sweep with a dominating eight-length victory in the Belmont Stakes, the pair met one last time five months later in the 1 1/4-mile Breeders' Cup Classic at Gulfstream Park. In this all-important showdown, Easy Goer was bet down to 50 cents on the dollar, having comfortably won his last four races. Sunday Silence was the 2–1 second choice. Unfortunately, Day did not get Easy Goer off to an alert start and fell a diminishing neck short of catching Sunday Silence (with Chris McCarron aboard) to incur more blame from the fans of the New York-based star.

While this last meeting may have added fuel to the criticism, I believe that Day's aggressive ride in the Preakness and the extraordinary recovery by Sunday Silence proved beyond any argument that Sunday Silence was a more agile, more athletic racehorse with a quicker burst of speed, which helped him win the Breeders' Cup. Yet, there were many other races in which Pat "Wait All" Day earned his unflattering moniker by overplaying his hand, getting his mounts trapped behind horses, where they inevitably moved too late. This was particularly true late in Day's career and especially in turf races.

But, in dozens and dozens of races I saw, with what I hope was an objective eye, Pat Day was a crucial difference-maker who contributed to many improbable victories. Frequently, he timed his stretch-running moves to a split-second cadence. Moreover, no rider I have ever seen has been able to get more response from his horse while on the lead, or near the pace.

Day's sensitive hands and powerful wrists helped him "put horses to sleep" on the lead, giving them the breather they would need to resist a challenger emerging from the pack. When Pat Day came into the stretch in front, you knew he had horse left. When he had a horse close to the lead, he invariably would mount a stiff challenge. These skills were especially deadly in seven-furlong races around one turn, a distance that tends to place extra emphasis on pace-pressing tactics. Day usually was the last rider in the race to resort to the whip. Frequently, "Wait All" Day would put the whip away in the final sixteenth of a mile without any loss of speed or rhythm.

All in all, few riders have ever been so successful and so underrated by so many seemingly astute fans of the sport. Consider these phenomenal career stats:

Pat Day retired at age 51 in 2005 after hip-replacement surgery with 8,803 career victories and a record $297,941,912 in purse earnings. He had 12 Breeders' Cup wins and nine victories in Triple Crown races, including the 1992 Kentucky Derby on Lil E. Tee, five victories in the Preakness, and three in the Belmont Stakes.

Day also won the 1991 Canadian Triple Crown against male horses aboard the filly Dance Smartly, who added the Breeders' Cup Distaff later the same year. He is the all-time leading rider at Churchill Downs with 2,481 wins, including 155 Churchill stakes races, and had five winners on a single Churchill racing card an amazing 21 times, a record unmatched by any jockey at any other track. Day also set a North American record in 1989 when he won eight races from nine mounts in one day at Arlington Park. He led the nation in victories six different years, including three in succession, 1982–84, and was the Eclipse Award winner as the nation's top jockey four times (1984, 1986, 1987, and 1991). To top it off, he was so respected by his peers that he won the George Woolf Memorial Jockey Award in 1985 and the Mike Venezia Award in 1995, a pair of citizenship awards named for riders who died on the track.

Pat Day also served as president of the Jockeys' Guild and in his retirement has continued his evangelical work with the Racetrack Chaplaincy of America.

"I don't want to leave the racing industry," Day explained at the 2005 retirement ceremony held in his honor at Churchill Downs. "I'm merely giving up my tack, no longer participating as a jockey; I just want to be a positive contributing member of the racing community."

9. *Bill Hartack*

Bill Hartack was master of the Kentucky Derby with five victories—including the Johnny Longden-trained Majestic Prince in 1969—but he also won the Preakness three times and the Belmont Stakes once. He was a four-time national leader in races won and a two-time leader in purses won, and later became a respected racing official, which apparently was a shock to those who covered his career in the 1960s.

Hartack was not the friendliest interview in the jockeys' room, turning his back on reporters who approached, or limiting his responses to postrace questions to a single-syllable word—"Yes," or "No," or a devastating silent stare. Hartack marched to his own drummer and he had no sense of public relations, nor did he give a damn. The root cause of this defiance, which bordered on disrespect, was in itself a form of disrespect, as he hated to be called Willie, or William Hartack. "Call me Bill," he insisted, almost the same way heavyweight boxing champ Cassius Clay hated to be called Cassius or Clay after he officially changed his name to Muhammad Ali in 1964.

Yet, despite his surly manner with the press, it was Bill Hartack who provided some of the most insightful racing commentary when he served briefly as an analyst for a handful of television broadcasts in the late 1970s, and it was Hartack who held one of the most memorable, most informative press conferences as an adviser to the Hollywood Park stewards after the roughly run 1984 Breeders' Cup Classic.

In contrast to the usual cryptic explanation for a controversial stewards' decision that passes for information conveyed to the racegoing public, Hartack painstakingly demonstrated what the stewards had seen and why they had disqualified Gate Dancer from second to third for interfering with Slew o' Gold. It was a memorable, eloquent performance by a tough-minded, extremely competitive athlete who had been in many similar tight spots on horseback. The unfortunate irony of that rare moment had nothing to do with Hartack. It is a simple fact that nothing quite as thorough has been attempted by any other racing official regarding any disqualification since.

A native of Blacklick Township in rural Pennsylvania, Hartack began riding at 16 and was indisputably one of the great jockeys of the 20th century. Beyond his raw statistical totals, Bill Hartack was one of the few jockeys to get the better of Bill Shoemaker and Eddie Arcaro and even Braulio Baeza on more than one occasion in the highest-class races in America.

In the 1960 Belmont Stakes, Hartack timed his move perfectly aboard Celtic Ash to sweep past Kentucky Derby winner Venetian Way, ridden by Arcaro. For the 1964 Kentucky Derby, Shoemaker had his choice between Hill Rise and Northern Dancer and chose Hill Rise, only to see Hartack outride him aboard Northern Dancer en route to a new track record in the Derby and another win in the Preakness.

In the 1969 Triple Crown, Hartack was aboard unbeaten Majestic Prince and used every trick in the book to narrowly outride Baeza aboard Arts and Letters to win both the Kentucky Derby and Preakness. Baeza did win the Belmont Stakes in their third meeting, but it was clear to everyone but Majestic Prince's owner that Majestic Prince was not 100 percent healthy for the race.

The record books say that Hartack was the nation's leading jockey four times and that he and Arcaro are the only five-time winners of the Kentucky Derby. But just two weeks before the 1958 Kentucky Derby, Hartack fell and broke a leg and had to give up his ride on Tim Tam, who won the race.

A man of his own choices, Bill Hartack was one of the first American jockeys to explore the burgeoning world of Asian racing, riding in Hong Kong from 1978 to 1980 before coming back to America to ride out the final year of his outstanding 21-year career.

Excluding his Hong Kong totals, Hartack rode 4,272 winners from 21,535 mounts, for career earnings of $26,466,754, and retired in good health at age 49 in 1981.

8. *Chris McCarron*

Chris McCarron, a native of Massachusetts, was a precocious jockey pro-tégé of trainer Odie Clelland, a Maryland-based Irish horseman who also raced in New England and had a penchant for developing young Irish riders whose last name was McCarron.

Chris McCarron was following the lead of his brother, Gregg, schooled by Clelland in the early 1970s. Gregg was the leading rider at Rocking-ham Park as an apprentice in 1971 and had a good career in his own right. But *good* is an inadequate word to describe Chris McCarron's 28-year Hall of Fame career.

In 1974, his first full year, Chris earned his first of two Eclipse Awards while breaking Bill Shoemaker's single-season record for most wins (485) with two months to spare. McCarron finished with 546, a record for apprentice jockeys that still stands.

McCarron won another Eclipse Award in 1980, and was the world's leading money-winning rider four times, retiring in 2002 at age 47 in good health after enduring his share of serious falls and broken bones. He had 7,141 victories and was the all-time money leader with more than $264 million in purse earnings.

McCarron won six Triple Crown races—the Kentucky Derby, Preak-ness, and Belmont, twice each—and nine Breeders' Cup races, includ-ing five Classics. Two of those were aboard Tiznow, the only repeat winner in America's richest race.

It was Chris McCarron, his wife, Judy, and their friend Tim Conway, the well-known actor-comedian, who formed the Don MacBeth Memo-rial Jockey Fund in 1987. The organization is dedicated to raising money to assist injured or disabled riders and their families.

McCarron's sense of personal responsibility surfaced often on the race-track. For instance, during that same year, he squarely took the blame for Alysheba's surprising fade to fourth in the 1987 Belmont Stakes, despite the fact that trainer Jack Van Berg seemed to make a crucial tactical mis-take in the colt's workout regimen for the grueling climax to the difficult Triple Crown series. I clocked all of Alysheba's workouts for Van Berg throughout the 1987 Triple Crown and sat with him during an impor-tant workout a week before the race, one that was never properly recorded by the official Belmont clockers. The workout was a full 1 ½ miles at a moderate pace (2:34), but probably was four furlongs farther than needed, given the tough races Alysheba had endured. The next time I saw the horse on the track for a gallop, he looked lighter in body weight and not as playful or as energetic as he had appeared prior to the unusually long workout.

McCarron's career was loaded with high points—riding John Henry through his 1984 Horse of the Year campaign when the great gelding was 9; stealing the 1994 Kentucky Derby wire to wire in the slop aboard Nick Zito's inconsistent Go for Gin, a colt that won only one other race in 11 starts that year and lost all three of his starts the following season; riding Tiznow to consecutive nail-biting victories in the 2000 and 2001 Breeders' Cup Classics over a pair of hard-hitting Europeans, Giant's Causeway and Sakhee, respectively; and winning several meet titles in Maryland and Southern California, including an extraordinary Del Mar title that he won in the final race on the final day of racing there in 1998, after overcoming the effects of a bad spill earlier in the year.

McCarron was an exceptional tactician, a marvel on the grass course, a finesse rider who fearlessly rode between horses or would take the inside route whenever possible and was an equal match in any stretch duel against the game's strongest finishers, including Laffit Pincay Jr., Eddie Delahoussaye, and Angel Cordero Jr.

McCarron was a lot like Manny Ycaza, without any excesses. He was a full-time trier, a jockey who rode as much for the players in the grandstand as for the owners and trainers who hired him. He was a winner of both the George Woolf Memorial Jockey Award (1980) and the Mike Venezia Award (1991) and was elected to the Hall of Fame in 1989.

When Chris McCarron retired in 2003, he became president of Santa Anita Park, but was a fish out of water. Eighteen months later he moved to Lexington, Kentucky, to establish the North American Racing Academy, a school for budding jockeys.

7 . *Gary Stevens*

Gary Stevens may have become more famous for his excellent portrayal of George Woolf in the 2003 movie *Seabiscuit* than for his excellence as one of the best jockeys in racing history. Such is the age we live in.

Frankly, it takes some doing to fully recap Stevens's impressive riding career, which includes more than $200 million in purses won and a batch of Kentucky Derby and Breeders' Cup victories. Yet it is sometimes better to integrate statistical details with specific events that provide more insight.

Born March 5, 1963, Stevens began his riding career at age 18 in 1979, at Les Bois Park in his home state of Idaho. After routing the Idaho competition, he first drew national attention while setting records atop the jockey standings at Portland Meadows in Oregon and Longacres Park in Washington State from 1981 through '84. This success led him to Southern California, where the horses were faster, the purses much bigger, and the jockey colony loaded with Hall of Fame competition.

Struggling to get rolling, Stevens was hesitant to remain in Southern California until encouraged to give it a more patient trial by a close friend, Mark Kaufman, the media-relations director at Longacres. Kaufman's belief in Stevens was just the boost the young rider needed, but to really appreciate how much it meant, we should move ahead quickly to May 5, 1995, when Stevens arrived at Churchill Downs the day after Kaufman suffered a fatal heart attack in his car exiting the Kentucky Derby media party at a Louisville hotel.

Stevens was in Louisville to ride Thunder Gulch, a colt that had shown considerable promise winning the Remsen Stakes as a 2-year-old in 1994 with Stevens aboard. Thunder Gulch continued to act like a serious Derby contender in the winter of 1995, winning the Fountain of Youth Stakes and the Florida Derby at Gulfstream Park under Mike Smith. But in his final Kentucky Derby prep, Thunder Gulch finished a weak fourth in the Blue Grass Stakes under Pat Day while Stevens was engaged to handle Santa Anita Derby winner Larry the Legend, who was going to miss the Kentucky Derby due to a training injury. With the Blue Grass defeat at 6–5 odds, Thunder Gulch suddenly seemed past his peak and dropped like a rock in most handicappers' Kentucky Derby rankings.

As usual, I was clocking the training moves of all the Derby contenders and there was nothing encouraging to report about Thunder Gulch, at least not until Stevens arrived. A trainer friend of mine, Phil Thomas, who mostly breaks yearlings in Kentucky and evaluates horses for sale purposes, saw Stevens with Thunder Gulch on the day before the Kentucky Derby when trainer D. Wayne Lukas brought the colt into the paddock to familiarize him with the unique Churchill Downs surroundings.

"I had watched Thunder Gulch all week," Thomas said, "and he had his head down, he was lethargic, he looked like crap. But I noticed when Stevens went up to the colt in the paddock, he caressed his head and was speaking to him as if he was a human being and it caught my attention. That's all it took. Thunder Gulch picked his head up and shook it vigorously. He was much more alert. I watched him walk around the paddock, walk out the tunnel, and out to the track for a light gallop toward the gap to the barn. He wasn't dead on his feet anymore, he was alive, kicking and playing, he looked *brand new!*"

The Kentucky Derby itself was a revelation, with Stevens guiding Thunder Gulch to an easy striking position a few lengths off the leader from post 16 and moving smoothly on the final turn to engage the tiring front-runner, the Lukas-trained filly Serena's Song, with the emerging Talkin Man moving through along the rail at the top of the stretch. At $24.50–1, a huge overlay, Thunder Gulch was in complete command through the final quarter-mile. When Stevens crossed the finish line, he did what was in his heart ever since he met Thunder Gulch in the Churchill Downs paddock.

"This one's for you, Mark," Stevens said, pointing to the sky. "This one's for you!" Later, Stevens explained that he sent a message to Kaufman's wife before the race: "I told her that I was going to have a copilot with me today. I told her that I expected to give [Thunder Gulch] the most thrilling ride of his short life."

In my view, this Kentucky Derby performance not only illustrates the special connection between a top-notch jockey and a fast racehorse when all the positive vibes are pointing in the same direction, it also specifically shows just what kind of a positive force Gary Stevens could be on horseback.

Despite several interruptions and aborted comebacks due to multiple fractures and four different surgeries and repeated battles with Legg-Calve-Perthes syndrome, a degenerative disease that forced Stevens to wear a metal brace on his right leg as a child, he rode successfully for more than two decades. Somehow, Stevens shook off his pain to become a silky-smooth performer with the rare skill of being able to get good position from any starting post at any distance, on grass or dirt. Never flashy in any way, Stevens was a complete rider, a good horse-man whose postrace suggestions to trainers usually helped improve the horses he rode.

Even after he suffered a horrendous fall aboard Storming Home in the 2003 Arlington Million when that robust turf runner took a nasty left-hand turn nearing the wire to be disqualified from an apparent victory, Stevens readily accepted the mount to ride him again—to victory—five weeks later in the Clement Hirsch at Del Mar. Stevens may have been cleared to resume riding, but he was not fully recovered from a punctured lung and other injuries.

Among the top horses this fearless jockey rode were Kentucky Derby winners Winning Colors (1988), Thunder Gulch (1995), and Silver Charm (1997); Preakness winners Silver Charm and Point Given (2001); Belmont winners Thunder Gulch, Victory Gallop (1998), and Point Given; plus eight Breeders Cup winners, including 1998 Juvenile Fillies winner Silverbulletday; Distaff winners One Dreamer in 1994 and Escena in 1998; Mile winners Da Hoss in 1996 and War Chant in 2000; Turf winner In the Wings in 1990; and Juvenile winners Brocco in 1993 and Anees in 1999.

Stevens also won 15 different meet titles at Santa Anita, Hollywood Park, and Del Mar; was the youngest jockey in history to reach $100 million in earnings at age 30 in 1993; won nine Santa Anita Derbies to pass Bill Shoemaker's record in that race; and was inducted to Racing's Hall of Fame in 1997—a year before he would win the Eclipse Award as the nation's top jockey.

Stevens also had great success riding abroad, winning the 1991 Japan Cup with Golden Pheasant and the 1998 Dubai World Cup with Silver Charm. One year later, while trying to save wear and tear on his painful knees, Stevens spent the summer in England and won the riding title at the York meeting for trainer Michael Stoute. In 2004, Stevens rode five months in France, winning 55 races, before returning to the United States in late August. As a tribute to his overall approach to his craft and classy demeanor in the spotlight, Stevens won the George Woolf Memorial Jockey Award in 1996, seven years before he would play that great jockey of the 1930s in *Seabiscuit*. He formally retired at the end of 2005 with 4,888 victories and career purse earnings in excess of $221 million, and became a television horse-racing analyst in 2006.

6. *Laffit Pincay Jr.*

The world's leading jockey with 9,530 victories, Laffit Pincay Jr. could have ridden many more winners had he not been forced to retire in 2003 with a neck brace still in place from a severe fall at Santa Anita.

Pincay was a prolific performer who uniquely demonstrated one of the most difficult facets of jockey life. Keeping his weight at a manageable 114 to 117 pounds was a 24-hour, 365-day-a-year chore that few of us in the grandstand or press box would ever accept. On a flight from New York back to his California base in the mid-1990s, Pincay was seen eating the following meal: five green peas, a glass of water, and two flatbread crackers.

With the help of a nutritionist, Pincay expanded his dietary regimen to include vitamins and protein supplements, but it took extraordinary dedication for him to keep his weight under control while still maintaining the health and strength of a top-class professional athlete. He was not alone in having to do this to ride racehorses for a living.

Pincay had amazing strength and athletic prowess. At Saratoga in the mid-1970s we played a jockeys-writers softball game and the two most impressive jockey players on the field were Laffit Pincay and Robyn Smith, a pioneer woman rider who rode several winners for Allen Jerkens and horses owned by Alfred Vanderbilt, before she married dancer-actor Fred Astaire. She pitched and Pincay played shortstop.

She pitched well enough to make fools out of many of us and Pincay scooped up grounders like he had professional talent. To top it off, he hit a rocket over my head in center field to win the game.

But at that particular time, I was not overly impressed with Pincay on the racetrack. I saw Angel Cordero Jr. and Jacinto Vasquez and Howard Grant and Bill Shoemaker ride rings around him more than once, as if he was not quite as sharp as his California reputation suggested. Frankly, Pincay did not fit in with the tough New York jockey colony at the time.

Not until 1984 and 1985 would I see how blind I had been to the real Laffit Pincay Jr. In 1984, Pincay won the Kentucky Derby and Belmont Stakes aboard Swale in two excellent performances. I was at Santa Anita the following winter when he rode Skywalker to an amazing victory in the 1985 Santa Anita Derby that finally made me wonder how anyone could ride a better race. Skywalker was in front and seemingly in trouble turning for home. Fast Account was ready to pass him and Nostalgia's Star was looming up boldly with plenty of energy. But Pincay had not yet asked his colt to run—not even when both horses passed him in the upper stretch. Approaching the final furlong, Laffit finally wound up and uncorked a series of powerful finishing strokes that put Skywalker back into top gear, winning narrowly. His ride was dead-solid perfect in every respect and was responsible for Skywalker's victory, just as it would be 18 months later when Skywalker would upset the Breeders' Cup Classic field over the same racetrack.

From that point forward, it was impossible not to fall in line with the Western-based observers who had labeled Pincay as one of the best of modern times.

5. *Angel Cordero Jr.*

Through much of his excellent career, Angel Cordero Jr. was the most popular rider in America. He won numerous meet titles in New York, including 11 in a row at Saratoga, probably the toughest one-month race meet in the world. He also was the most daring rider to come along since Manny Ycaza.

Cordero was the great intimidator on horseback, a frequent winner of major stakes races who sometimes seemed as if he were riding two or more horses in the same race. In the 1980 Preakness, for example, while Jacinto Vasquez was riding the Kentucky Derby-winning filly Genuine Risk, Cordero angled wide on the final turn, forcing Vasquez to move the filly farther out in the track to avoid interference. While the replays for the race show that Cordero's mount, Codex, might have brushed against the filly, the contact was not significant enough to reverse the order of finish. As he saw it, Cordero merely was doing his best to take whatever edge he could within the boundary lines of aggressive race-riding.

Just as Ycaza paid a price for his aggressive riding style in the 1960s, Cordero took a daring approach to race-riding that bordered on arrogance, and it did not always pay off the way he wanted. Riding Slew o' Gold in the 1983 Marlboro Cup, he was so intent on keeping the California horse Bates Motel wide on the final turn that he lost sight of eventual winner Highland Blade moving up along the inside.

For several years, Angel Cordero was no angel at all, getting into scrapes with other riders and drawing unflattering attention to himself and other members of the New York jockey colony for a number of questionable rides and other borderline violations of racing ethics. Still, just as Ycaza had previously won over so many fans for his commitment to win, so too did Cordero become the $2 bettor's best friend on horseback. His appetite for victory was insatiable.

"He's got all the tools to handle any horse at any distance on any track surface at any level of competition," said Hall of Fame trainer D. Wayne Lukas. "I love using him when I can, just as much as the players love to bet on him."

Of equal import, perhaps, Cordero curbed his excesses noticeably as he matured and took it upon himself to become a father figure and teacher to young riders whom he competed against.

Born in 1942 in Santurce, Puerto Rico, Cordero learned his craft under the tutelage of his father and uncles, all prominent trainers at El Comandante Racetrack in San Juan. Cordero was 20 when he arrived in New York in 1962, ready to take on the world, and three decades later he had won more than $164 million in purses and many of the most important stakes in the game, including six Triple Crown races—the Kentucky Derby three times, the Preakness twice, and the 1976 Belmont Stakes, a storied victory in which he seemed to carry the exhausted Laz Barrera-trained speedball Bold Forbes across the finish line.

Cordero also rode four Breeders' Cup winners and dozens of Grade 1 stakes winners and divisional champions for Hall of Famers Barrera, Lukas, LeRoy Jolley, Angel Penna, and Shug McGaughey. There could have been many more, but he was unable to fully recover from a serious fall in 1992 that left him on the fence of retirement for his last three years in competition.

But even in retirement, Cordero's competitive zeal did not abate, nor his devotion to the game. He helped the young riding star John R. Velazquez get started in New York and became his full-time agent while also exercising horses regularly for Eclipse Award-winning trainer Todd Pletcher.

"I never want to retire from the game," Cordero said. "I love the horses, I love the people; I love the racetrack life too much to disappear . . . I love to win too much, too."

In addition to 7,057 victories and his extraordinary success at Saratoga, Cordero was national leading money-winning jockey three times (1976, 1982, and 1983) and twice the national leader in races won, in 1982 and 1983, when he was voted Eclipse Awards as champion jockey. Cordero also won the George Woolf Memorial Jockey Award in 1972 and the Mike Venezia Award in 1992. He was inducted into Racing's Hall of Fame in 1988.

4. *Braulio Baeza*

Braulio Baeza was the first of several great Panamanian jockeys brought to America by owner-breeder Fred W. Hooper in the 1960s. Three others—Laffit Pincay Jr., Jorge Velasquez, and Jacinto Vasquez—are also members of the Hall of Fame.

Baeza was, in my opinion, the best of them all, even though he rode only 3,140 winners—less than one-third as many as Pincay's 9,530; less than one-half of Velasquez's 6,795; and 2,088 fewer than Vasquez's 5,228.

Born in 1940, the son and grandson of Panamanian jockeys, Baeza reportedly won 37 percent of about 1,000 races as 19-year-old apprentice in Panama the year before Hooper brought him to America. At 20, Baeza was a stranger in a strange land, breaking ground for other Panamanian riders. It was astonishing to see him jump instantly from obscurity to ride with great success against the legendary Eddie Arcaro, as well as the other Hall of Famers—Eric Guerin, Bobby Ussery, and Johnny Rotz—who were dominating New York racing at the time.

Baeza was a distinctive sight in the saddle, an immovable statue on horseback with a profile that looked as if he had been cast in a bronze mold. Perfectly balanced, tall and erect, Baeza was Mr. Cool, completely undisturbed by rain, wind, or the noises that came from the Aqueduct grandstand or the low-flying airplanes heading into nearby Idlewild airport (now JFK). At least that is what he seemed in the post parade. Once the gates opened, Baeza's crouch on horseback looked as if he had been taught how to minimize drag in a wind tunnel—low to the mane, back straight as a board, knees and legs pinned to his mount at perfect angles, feet using the stirrups as they were meant to be used, as guides for the horse and as natural cushions to absorb the shocks to the base of the spine felt by every rider with every stride.

You barely noticed Baeza holding a whip, so smoothly did he cock it in his right hand, flipping it over to his left and back again more efficiently than anyone else in the race. A few good cracks to the hindquarters were followed by equally powerful, rhythmic pushes with his hands and arms. More than a passenger, Baeza always seemed to blend in with his mount as he urged it to keep going forward, keep up the tempo.

Nearing the wire, Baeza would often employ a trick he probably copied from Eddie Arcaro or Bill Hartack. With a head-bobbing finish in sight, Baeza would turn his whip forward, placing the tip under his mount's head, pushing lightly to assist the forward thrust—helping him gain a few millimeters in a close photo finish. It's something I've seen many riders do through the years, but no one ever did it more effectively than Braulio Baeza. Rarely, it seemed, did he lose a photo.

He was the most technically correct rider in the game. Baeza won races, especially the biggest races. He was cool all right, but he must have carried a burning fire to win in his heart. The very best trainers sought out Baeza to ride their top horses. In fact, he rode 24 different champions during his relatively brief 17-year riding career, including nine Hall of Famers.

In 1962 he was the regular rider for the champion mare Primonetta for J. P. Conway, and he also rode Conway's Chateaugay to upset victories in the 1963 Kentucky Derby and Belmont Stakes. Baeza rode 2-year-old champions Bold Lad, Queen Empress, Queen of the Stage, Successor, Vitriolic, and Buckpasser for Eddie Neloy and was aboard Buckpasser for 15 straight victories as a 3- and 4-year-old in 1966 and 1967.

He rode Dr. Fager for John Nerud 13 times, winning 12, including a world-record mile clocking in the 1968 Washington Park Handicap to erase the world record he set aboard Buckpasser at the same track two years earlier. Baeza rode Arts and Letters for Elliott Burch, finishing second in the 1969 Kentucky Derby and Preakness before stopping Majestic Prince's Triple Crown bid in the Belmont Stakes. By year's end he had ridden Arts and Letters to consecutive victories in the Jim Dandy, Travers, Woodward, and Jockey Club Gold Cup to complete a Horse of the Year campaign.

Baeza also was the regular rider for 1965 Horse of the Year Roman Brother for Burley Parke; 1972 sophomore champ Key to the Mint for Burch; 1975 champion 3-year-old Wajima for Steve DiMauro; and he was aboard Foolish Pleasure for LeRoy Jolley in the infamous 1975 match race that cost the life of the great filly Ruffian.

In all, this master craftsman, who had trouble keeping his weight down in his mid-30s, led the nation in money won five times, won two Eclipse Awards (1972 and 1975), was a George Woolf Memorial Jockey Award winner, and was elected to the Hall of Fame in 1976.

In probably his most remarkable ride, one that I only saw on film and one that has not received the attention it deserves, Baeza was sent to England to ride 3-year-old Roberto for John Galbreath in the 1972 Benson and Hedges Gold Cup at York. Roberto, who had won the Epsom Derby earlier in the British racing season, had most recently run poorly despite no apparent physical issues. Baeza was chosen for this unusual assignment in the somewhat desperate hope that his quiet demeanor might settle the high-strung, classy colt.

Taking early control of the race, Baeza rode the undulations of the unfamiliar York course as if he had been a 10-year regular, keeping the previously undefeated Brigadier Gerard at bay to the finish, giving "Brigadier" his only career defeat. In some circles, Brigadier Gerard is regarded as one of the top half dozen horses ever to race in Europe, and Baeza's flawless ride is regarded as one of the best of all time.

3. *Eddie Arcaro*

I could have copped out and listed Eddie Arcaro among the jockeys who were the best in the game before my time. He was by far the best in the game during the 1940s, when he rode two Triple Crown winners—Whirlaway and Citation—and had 11 other victories in the Kentucky Derby, Preakness, and Belmont Stakes. But I saw enough of Eddie Arcaro in his final two years, 1960 and 1961, when he was well past his prime, dealing with nagging injuries. He was at least equal to the best jockeys of that era, too. One can only imagine how good Arcaro must have been when he had all his reflexes, all the strength and guile that led the great writers of the 1940s and '50s to call him the Master.

Joe Hirsch, the revered racing writer whose *Daily Racing Form* columns spanned the second half of the 20th century, said that Arcaro "had no peer," and that he was "years ahead of his time" in the way he balanced himself on horseback and the way he strategically won so many races on horses that were not quite the best in the race.

Arcaro was born in Cincinnati in 1916 and rode his first race at 15 at Bainbridge Park in May 1931 near Cleveland, but did not win a race for more than 2 ½ years. He rode more than 100 consecutive losers before getting his first win aboard Eagle Bird on January 14, 1932, at Agua Caliente in Mexico. The next year, he was the leading apprentice jockey in Louisiana but suffered a fractured skull and punctured lung in a spill in Chicago that summer. When Arcaro returned in 1934, he had modest success, while incurring the wrath of stewards sufficiently to earn several suspensions and warnings that threatened his status as a professional jockey. But the young Eddie Arcaro made a strong positive impression on trainer Ben A. Jones, who, along with his son, H. A. "Jimmy" Jones, would turn Calumet Farm into the dominant stable in America.

Ben Jones put Arcaro on his first Kentucky Derby winner, Lawrin, in 1938 when "the Jones Boys" were working for Woolford Farm. Arcaro was aboard Calumet's Whirlaway when he set a track record winning the 1941 Kentucky Derby en route to the first of Calumet's and Arcaro's two Triple Crown sweeps.

In 1945, Arcaro won two Triple Crown races with two different horses for different outfits, including his third Kentucky Derby in seven years aboard Hoop Jr., the first horse Fred W. Hooper ever owned. He won his third Belmont Stakes with Walter Jeffords's Pavot, who had been 2-year-old champion in 1944, but had not won a race in '45 until Arcaro climbed aboard. In 1948, Arcaro and Calumet teamed up for their second Triple Crown sweep aboard Citation. In a year when none of the richly endowed Triple Crown races had a purse of $100,000, Arcaro's mounts earned $1,686,230, a record in winnings that he would break with $1,859,591 in 1952.

Beyond his Triple Crown exploits and so many other career highlights, Arcaro probably is best remembered for his exceptionally crafty ride aboard Preakness-Belmont winner Nashua in the 1 ¼-mile match race against Kentucky Derby winner Swaps at Washington Park in Chicago on August 31, 1955.

Swaps had skipped the Preakness and Belmont after winning the 1955 Kentucky Derby under Bill Shoemaker's wily front-running ride. The public clamored for and got a rematch that was anticipated as much as the match race between Seabiscuit and War Admiral in 1938. Arcaro, studying the tactics employed by Seabiscuit's rider, George

Woolf, knew his best chance to win the race was to take the lead away from the speedy Swaps right at the start.

With Arcaro nursing Nashua along while narrowly in front for the first six furlongs in a rapid 1:10 $^4/_5$ on a drying-out track, Shoemaker thought he might have Arcaro at his mercy until he looked over and saw the Master sitting absolutely still, with a ton of horse left.

"I practically waved bye-bye to him," Arcaro later said. At the wire, Nashua won by a decisive 6 $^1/_2$ lengths to clinch the 1955 Horse of the Year title, while Swaps would need time off for a nagging foot injury before he became one of the best 4-year-olds in history the following year.

I never saw Eddie Arcaro while he was winning Triple Crown races and setting earnings records, but I did see him win with a high percentage of his mounts at Aqueduct and Belmont Park in 1960 and 1961 and cashed my very first $100 wager on a horse he rode one rainy afternoon toward the end of his career. I made the bet because Arcaro was so impressive riding the great horse Kelso through 11 wins in 11 tries at those two tracks from September 1960 through October 1961—in particular, the 1961 Metropolitan Handicap at Belmont Park. I saw Eddie Arcaro guide, exhort, and will Kelso to a victory over longshot All Hands that seemed beyond the normal limits of human or equine capability. Think of Forego catching Honest Pleasure in the 1976 Marlboro Cup or Victory Gallop catching Real Quiet in the 1998 Belmont Stakes. This one was better.

Kelso, then a 4-year-old making his second start of the year, was losing ground on the final turn after showing no inclination to compete through a half-mile in 46 seconds, a good pace, but not insane for a one-turn mile at Belmont. Arcaro was nudging Kelso, but not using the whip. Entering the stretch, after six furlongs in 1:10 $^3/_5$, they were moving slightly better, between tiring rivals, picking up the tempo when a horse blocked their path and Arcaro had to switch Kelso out to the middle of the track.

Approaching the furlong pole, All Hands still was going strong at least four lengths in front. But now Arcaro was all over Kelso, prodding him with the whip, showing that he had not lost his strength or his rhythm, as horse and rider moved closer and closer with the wire coming up too fast for them to make it, or so it seemed. Kelso won by a neck to begin a campaign that would lead to his second of five consecutive Horse of the Year titles. Arcaro would ride him all the way through that season and quit the game immediately afterward.

"I rode Citation and Whirlaway, but Kelso was the best horse I ever rode," Arcaro said. "He hooked everybody, every place, on every kind of racetrack. He could sprint, go a distance, run all day. He could do it all."

If Kelso could talk, I am sure he would have heaped praise on Ismael Valenzuel, who rode him to 22 victories after Arcaro retired, but I'd bet everything I own that he would return the compliment and label Arcaro as the best jockey who ever sat on his back, or rode against him.

Arcaro was inducted into racing's Hall of Fame in 1958 and ended his career with 4,779 wins, including 554 stakes victories, 3,807 seconds, and 3,302 thirds from 24,092 mounts. He earned $30,039,543, and might have eclipsed 10 times that sum had he had ridden in the era of the Breeders' Cup and $1 million purses. He died at the age of 81 on November 14, 1997.

2. *Bill Shoemaker*

Legendary jockey Bill Shoemaker was finished by 1986, or so most of the West Coast racing writers believed. "The Shoe" had been atop the race-riding world for nearly four decades, but he was 54, and not many athletes in any sport can sustain their verve and nerve at that age.

As I watched him perform in major stakes at Santa Anita and on the Triple Crown trail, I had to agree. Shoemaker definitely was finished. A race that comes to mind immediately was the 1984 Preakness Stakes, when he picked up the mount on Taylor's Special from Sam Maple, who had had a rough trip en route to a sixth-place finish in Swale's Kentucky Derby.

Trainer Billy Mott was someone I had marveled at while he trained a small string at Churchill Downs after working for Jack Van Berg, the future Hall of Famer who would develop Alysheba. Apart from his horsemanship, Van Berg was famous for giving promising assistant trainers a world-class education.

In 1984, it was hard not to miss Mott's natural talent while he turned Taylor's Special from a pure sprinter into the winner of the Louisiana Derby and Blue Grass Stakes prior to his disappointing Kentucky Derby. Mott was not sure he should send the colt to Baltimore for the Preakness until after I called him the day before entries were taken with a report that piqued his interest.

"There's not going to be a lot of early speed in the race," I said. "If you ship here you could get the lead and control the pace and the rail. Everything is winning on the rail. It's playing like an interstate highway."

So Mott shipped to Baltimore and gave the mount to Bill Shoemaker, thinking he had acquired a world-class jockey who would ride the Pimlico rail for all he was worth. But inexplicably, after breaking alertly as if he could easily have taken the lead heading to the first turn, Shoemaker grabbed the reins and snuggled Taylor's Special back to third, where he essentially remained until reaching the backstretch. Shoe moved his mount off the golden rail to lose any chance of victory. It was that precise moment when Shoemaker demonstrated that he was through.

Bill Shoemaker was not a coward; he had ridden thousands of tough races for nearly 40 years, and no one could accuse him of that. He had even overcome one of the worst mistakes in racing history, standing up in the saddle aboard Gallant Man 30 yards from the finish of the 1957 Kentucky Derby, losing that all-important race by a nose to Iron Liege. Shoe showed his grit and determination at his next opportunity, when trainer Johnny Nerud put him back aboard Gallant Man to win the Belmont Stakes and the Jockey Club Gold Cup among six subsequent victories that year. Shoe may have been humiliated by a mistake that never would be forgotten, but he proved his winning acumen many times over, leading the nation in money won for the next seven consecutive seasons.

I had seen him in terrific form in his visits to New York and New Jersey tracks and was impressed by how skillful, how relaxed he was, and how hard it was to outsmart him or beat him when the chips were down. His winning Belmont Stakes rides aboard Jaipur in 1962 and Avatar in 1975 were among the best in that storied race's history; his handling of three-time horse of the Year Forego in a desperate stretch drive to win the 1976 Marlboro Cup by a nose under 137 pounds over Honest Pleasure still is regarded as an impossible outcome, even by those who witnessed it. At his best, and for a very long time, with a resume that includes dozens of meet titles, a good case can be made that Bill Shoemaker was the greatest jockey this country has ever produced.

But now, in 1984, the Shoe seemed to ride mostly to preserve his horse's energy and to minimize the danger of getting jammed up in a crowd. In other words, the great Bill Shoemaker was tentative, riding out in the clear, refusing to go inside, riding without the aggressiveness it takes to win world-class races.

By the spring of 1986, Shoemaker was going through the motions, yet still getting his share of live mounts for his longtime friend Charlie Whittingham, the peerless Southern California trainer known as the Bald Eagle. Whittingham had won more major stakes at Santa Anita and Hollywood Park than any other horseman; many of them had been with the Shoe.

Whittingham, an extremely patient trainer who specialized in developing older distance horses, had no interest in the Kentucky Derby after saddling Gone Fishin to an eighth-place finish in 1958 and Divine Comedy to a disappointing ninth in 1960. He hated the hoopla and vowed never to go back to Churchill Downs "without a horse that could really win it."

That all changed during the winter and spring of 1986, when Whittingham told Shoemaker that he finally had a young horse that seemed ideally suited to the world's most famous race. Whittingham also confessed to a handful of close friends that he would like to cap his career with a Kentucky Derby victory.

The two veteran champions—Shoemaker and Whittingham—were on the same wavelength, getting the large-bodied, slow-to-develop Ferdinand to improve his concentration and strength steadily through the winter. To complete the colt's preparation, Whittingham shipped Ferdinand to Louisville three weeks before the Derby after a modest third-place finish behind the highly regarded Snow Chief in the Santa Anita Derby.

Whittingham knew that something dramatic was needed to bring Ferdinand to peak form, so he brought the top-notch filly Hidden Light to Churchill Downs, ostensibly to train for the Kentucky Oaks, but more realistically to serve as a high-class training partner.

Shoemaker quietly was living the same dream and the two old pros used all their combined experience to work on Ferdinand through every important training move, including a sensational mile drill in company nine days before the Derby. Along with one of Whittingham's private clockers, I caught the work in a very fast 1:36, with a last quarter in a super-sharp 23 flat, galloping out nine furlongs a shade under 1:50, one of the best workouts I have ever seen.

The most telling thing was the way Hidden Light had to be put to a hard drive to keep up while the Derby-bound colt breezed on by. She may not have been a sacrificial lamb, but it was clear that Whittingham and Shoemaker had successfully pushed Ferdinand to another level of performance.

By the time post positions were drawn two days prior to the Derby, I was ready to clean out my bank account to bet on this colt, who was likely to be 12–1 at minimum and perhaps 20–1 or higher.

Then Ferdinand drew post number 1 in a very large field, the kiss of death for the Kentucky Derby, especially with 16 horses ready to run at 36 to 40 miles per hour on a one-mile track that invariably tightens up the bulky field in the frenzied run to secure a ground-saving position around the sharp clubhouse turn. With Shoemaker aboard, the very rider who had shown no inclination to ride inside anymore, I canceled any thought of making a win bet, convinced that Shoemaker would not be able to handle the predicament. What an expensive mistake!

What transpired in the 1986 Kentucky Derby was simply the most astounding, daredevil ride in Derby history, certainly the best ride I've ever seen, a ride that remains a historic monument to Bill Shoemaker's greatness.

Right out of the gate, Ferdinand was bumped solidly toward the inside rail. Through the run past the grandstand for the first time, while many horses were angled to the inside for better position, Shoe was forced to stand up in the saddle, extending the reins to keep from falling off, to keep Ferdinand from running off, while the pint-sized rider on the over-sized horse scraped against the rail. Entering the first turn, while horses were bouncing off each other like bowling pins, Shoemaker was squeezed back to last, still held in tight with nowhere to go. But this was a different Shoemaker than anyone had seen in several years. There was no panic, no effort to safely swing Ferdinand out of trouble.

Instead, Shoemaker used his soft, experienced hands and a steel nerve to settle Ferdinand into a more relaxed stride. Without hesitation, the two of them began to pick their way forward, passing a horse here and a horse there, threading their way into the top 10, then the top six as the massive field fanned out against the roar of 123,000 fans for the tense stretch run.

Ferdinand was on the outside now, moving fluidly, his head pointing toward the leaders as several other contenders also made their bids along the inside and from between horses. Then, for a brief instant, a very brief instant, a gap between two horses opened up toward the inside and

Shoemaker, as he must have done many times in his youth, quickly angled Ferdinand sharply to the left, toward the rapidly disappearing hole just in front of hard-charging Rampage, who had to take up abruptly when Ferdinand beat him to the slim passage through the wall of horses.

Moments earlier, Bold Arrangement and Broad Brush made their respective moves and seemed on their way to a 1–2 finish, but here came Bill Shoemaker aboard the long-striding Ferdinand with his bright bronze coat gleaming in the sun.

"Here comes Ferdinand along the rail!" called track announcer Mike Battaglia, but Battaglia was a few beats behind what had already occurred. Ferdinand was in the lead, inside of both horses, approaching midstretch with the finish line his to claim.

I had missed out on one of the best bets in Kentucky Derby history because I did not believe in the champion rider who later would admit that this was the most satisfying moment of his amazing career. Ferdinand could not win that Kentucky Derby, no, not with the ancient Bill Shoemaker riding him; no, not from the rail! But he did, and it happened because the venerable horse trainer Charlie Whittingham still believed in Bill Shoemaker and because Bill Shoemaker still believed in himself.

After this amazing victory, Shoemaker continued to ride aggressively for most of the next two years and would even win the 1987 Breeders' Cup Classic aboard Ferdinand in a thriller over Kentucky Derby-Preakness winner Alysheba. In the early 1990s he became a successful trainer who persisted with that career for more than a year after he was tragically paralyzed from the waist down in an automobile accident. In 1995, Shoemaker told friends that he had found personal inspiration for the rebirth of his flailing career from golf champion Jack Nicklaus, who at 46, was supposed to be well past his prime when he won the Masters a month before the 1986 Kentucky Derby.

"I told myself after watching him do that," Shoemaker said, "that if Nicklaus could rise to the occasion at his age like that, I could too."

Here are some of the amazing highlights from his lifetime record, which includes four Kentucky Derby victories, two in the Preakness, and five in the Belmont Stakes. Among his more remarkable achievements, Shoemaker won 1,009 stakes, including 250 worth $100,000 or more, mostly during an era when there were many fewer races with similar purses. He won 18 meet titles at Hollywood Park, including 15 in succession (1953–67) and was the Eclipse Award winner in 1976 and 1981 and surely would have won many more if that honor had existed during the 1950s and 60s.

After winning his first race in 1949, Shoemaker led the nation in wins five different years, including one tie with Joe Culmone in 1950, as well as 1953,1954, 1958, and1959. He also was leading money winner a record 10 times, as well as the regular jockey for numerous champions, including Round Table, Gallant Man, Swaps, Cicada, Damascus, Jaipur, Ack Ack, Cougar II, Exceller, Forego, Spectacular Bid (during his unbeaten season at 4 in 1980), Turkish Trousers, Typecast, Ferdinand, and John Henry in 1981–82.

1. *Jerry Bailey*

Although Jerry Bailey was closing in on 5,900 wins and had more than $296 million in purse earnings when he retired early in 2006, he knew it was time to go, the same way that Chris McCarron left plenty of winners on the track when he retired in 2002.

"I've been as lucky as any rider I know, escaping serious injuries through most of my career," he said. "But I have plenty of aches and pains and I've reached all of my goals, so this is the right time for me to begin the rest of my life."

The winner of an astonishing seven Eclipse Awards during a spectacular nine-year run from 1995 through 2003, Bailey was the late-20th-century version of Bill Shoemaker and Eddie Arcaro rolled into one. Almost every trainer with a good horse pointing for a rich stakes race called Bailey first, or wanted to call him. Bailey was a prolific winner at the highest level the game has to offer.

But it wasn't always like that, as he admitted to himself as much as to anyone when he turned his life around in the late 1980s while heading nowhere fast, a journeyman rider with an alcohol problem. His addiction got so bad that he even continued to drink through a straw while his jaw was wired shut from a racing accident, one of the few accidents he suffered in his 31-year riding career.

"Something had to change," he said. "That something was me."

Bailey did not make the conversion to a mature outlook on life on his own, but he did take the first essential steps with his wife, Suzee, and the

12-step program of Alcoholics Anonymous that has helped so many before him.

"The world at large cannot imagine how a man widely declared to be the leading rider of his era, one of the greatest jockeys ever to break from the starting gate, could have handled a 1,200-pound thoroughbred with so much ease but have no control of himself," wrote Bailey in his revealing 2005 autobiography *Against the Odds: Riding for My Life,* which he cowrote with *USA Today* sports reporter Tom Pedulla.

Success on the racetrack followed his personal change to the highest degree imaginable. Bailey suddenly became the most relaxed, best jockey in the East and was quickly joined at the hip with future Hall of Fame trainer Bill Mott, who realized—as Ben Jones had realized 50 years earlier, when he hooked up with Eddie Arcaro—that Jerry Bailey was someone who would help Mott achieve what both men wanted to accomplish on the national stage.

"I watched him get better and better," Mott explained at Saratoga during the summer of 1995. "He was flawless and at the time, he was not in high demand by too many other trainers. . . . We just struck up a perfect working relationship that helped us both."

Bailey's modus operandi was simple to describe, but so rarely executed by most other riders: break well, get a good position—preferably along the rail, or just outside and behind the logical speed horses—and be in the right spot to launch a winning bid coming off the final turn into the stretch.

A Bailey ride was a blueprint to the winner's circle. A Bailey ride was a road map that minimized traffic problems and maximized his mount's natural ability. Front-runners were not strangled to hold them in reserve; they were allowed to get the lead on their own power, without using them up with excessive restraint. Stretch-runners were not taken back, they were allowed to settle into a comfortable stride and never forced to move up before they began to show interest in making a run.

Stalkers, the horses that tended to have just enough speed to race within a length or two of the lead, always seemed to have a serious bid to offer when Bailey was aboard. Jerry Bailey was the equal to California-based grass specialist Fernando Toro in turf races; equal to Angel Cordero Jr. in sprints; equal to Cajun-born Randy Romero on muddy tracks; equal to Bill Shoemaker in distance races; and equal to Eddie Arcaro when the biggest money was on the line.

Jerry Bailey was strong, but not overpowering; he was a wonderful tactician, but rarely tried to make a race into a jigsaw puzzle. He rode to get position, and once he got it, he knew precisely how to use it to best advantage.

Bailey was not a robot who lacked creativity, as his stretch-running ride from 13th to first aboard Sea Hero in the 1993 Kentucky Derby clearly demonstrated. Bailey and his horse zigzagged through the field like a New York taxi driver cutting through Midtown traffic. Not once did Bailey act as if he feared running into a red light. Not once did Sea Hero have to break stride.

That was Bailey's first of two Kentucky Derby winners and a grand present for 71-year-old trainer Mack Miller, who had supported Bailey since their first meeting in the early 1980s and would retire two years later. But it was just a hint of what this jockey ultimately would accomplish. Try some of these facts on for size.

Fifteen career wins in Breeders' Cup races, including five in the Breeders' Cup Classic; two wins each in the Kentucky Derby, Preakness, and Belmont Stakes; four in the Dubai World Cup; seven Saratoga riding titles; nine Belmont riding titles; set a national earnings record three consecutive years (2001–03); won a national record of 70 stakes in 1993 and was the regular rider for a gateload of champions, including Skip Away for Sonny Hine; Hansel for Frank Brothers; Orientate for D. Wayne Lukas; Soaring Softly for Jimmy Toner; Squirtle Squirt and Aldebaran for Bobby Frankel; Perfect Sting for Joe Orseno, and the Bill Mott-trained Cigar, whom he rode to an undefeated Horse of the Year season in 1995 and to 16 consecutive victories, including an amazing performance by horse and rider in the inaugural $4 million Dubai World Cup on March 27, 1996.

As with so many of the top jockeys and horses of the past half-century and beyond, there is no substitute for seeing the performance to truly appreciate how deep runs the winning spirit in the best of the two-legged and four-legged athletes who grace this sport. In the case of Cigar and Jerry Bailey, their records speak well to that point, but when the gallant horse and the well-matched rider were in midstretch at Nad Al Sheba racecourse, with hard-charging Soul of the Matter breathing fire on their flank, poised to go on by, it is difficult to imagine how much talent it takes to resist, to push on, and to reach down for a final response and take the win anyway. But when it happens, we know we have seen the unusual, the freakishly wonderful thing that separates the good from the great and the best of the great from all the rest.

There was no way to deny Cigar victory in that Dubai World Cup, no way that Cigar would have won that race and many others without Jerry Bailey on his back.

He was the best jockey I have ever seen.

As a footnote to the profiles on the top jockeys of the modern era, it should be pointed out that jockeys do not line up mounts themselves. That responsibility falls on the jockey agent, who is a horse-talent scout, an insightful handicapper, a personal confidant, and an expert reader of the condition book that lists races to be run at the local track.

It may seem axiomatic that the majority of great jockeys have had great agents, but they do not get nearly the credit they deserve. Here are several jockey agents who most often get positive mention by racing insiders: First, Harry Silbert, who represented Bill Shoemaker with considerable grace and intelligence through most of Shoe's lengthy career. "He was the one everybody looked up to," said Dan Smith, Del Mar's former media-relations director, who co-wrote a Shoemaker autobiography. "Loyalty was his thing, and it was the same way with Shoe. They were a perfect match." Also, there were Ron Anderson, who represented Gary Stevens for more than a decade and Jerry Bailey for the final five years of his amazing career; George O'Bryan, agent for Hall of Famer Manny Ycaza in the 1960s and Laffit Pincay Jr. in the 1980s; Lenny Goodman, who represented Braulio Baeza during that Hall of Famer's spectacular run atop the nation's jockeys in the 1960s and also represented Steve Cauthen when the boy wonder of racing turned the game on its ear in 1977–78; Chick McLelland, who represented Sandy Hawley, Fernando Toro, and Alvaro Pineda, among other high-class California-based jockeys; and Vince DeGregory, who represented Hall of Famers Angel Cordero Jr. and Jorge Velazquez, as well as Darrel McHargue.

Also: Fred Aimie, who was Pat Day's longtime agent in Illinois and Kentucky; Harry Hacek, who recruited Hawley, McCarron, McHargue, and Eddie Delahoussaye for the West Coast jockey colony; George Hollander, a legendary agent in Southern California who briefly represented Ycaza and was the longtime agent for the unsung Don Pierce and for Ismael Valenzuela, who rode Kelso after Eddie Arcaro retired; and Tony Matos, who represented Angel Cordero for several years in New York and later handled Pincay and Victor Espinoza when Matos moved to California.

Since his retirement as a jockey, Hall of Famer Cordero has become a great jockey agent, handling the bookings and the other aspects of this work for two-time Eclipse Award winner John R. Velazquez.

All of the jockey agents listed above probably would be good candidates for a plaque on some racetrack wall honoring their own "hall of fame" careers in a thankless profession. Jockey agents deserve far more recognition than they get.

3 THE BEST TRAINERS

WHEN I WAS a young editor of *Turf and Sport Digest* magazine (R.I.P) in the mid 1970s, a reader asked the following question, which led to series of articles and a new section in the magazine.

Question: In handicapping, which is more important, the jockey or the horse?

After thinking about this at length, I realized that the question missed a vital point. The answer really is neither. From a handicapping perspective, it's a triangle—horse, jockey, and trainer. More often than not, it's the trainer that is most important.

The trainer recognizes the horse's talent, develops and harnesses its speed, zeros in on its distance and surface preferences, sets the schedule of races in harmony with the horse's natural maturation, and makes the necessary adjustments to stay on top of its day-to-day physical condition. Just as a great football coach usually wins a high percentage of games no matter where he is employed, great horse trainers win a high percentage of races at various tracks and invariably have success, year after year.

Some trainers have unique specialties. Others apply their skills to a variety of racing situations. Some are great working with aged horses that have been limited by a variety of foot ailments; some have the winning eye for young, untested racehorses with the potential to become high-class performers. Many are most comfortable working with small or modest-sized stables, while a select few effectively train 150 or more horses at three or four different tracks without missing a beat.

The best-known horse trainers tend to make their mark with Kentucky Derby prospects, or with beautifully bred 2-year-olds that dominate summer and fall stakes. But many good trainers stay far away from high-profile races for young horses, preferring a patient approach, hoping to develop their best prospects for long-distance races on dirt and turf when they are more mature. Yet, from what I have observed through the years, the best trainers—regardless of their preferred style—share at least two common traits.

*They regularly outperform most of their contemporaries in a variety of settings.

*They display their absolute best skill with unusually gifted, if not difficult, horses.

Few trainers—even the biggest winners in the sport—manage to escape painful slumps or bizarre changes in fortune that come with owners leaving the game or with harsh turns of fate. All of the good ones recover from such setbacks to reclaim their high standing, and a select few in each generation—including the greats who came before my time—set standards for others to emulate.

Many that I considered for this list were Hall of Famers and were spectacular with turf horses, or 2-year-olds, or one particular group of horses. Preference was given to trainers involved with more than one type of horse, or more than one top horse and more than one outstanding achievement. As with the top jockeys of modern times, it was painful to pare down a long list from more than three dozen highly qualified horsemen to a baker's dozen.

Among those who did not make the cut were Lucien Laurin, who trained dual champion Riva Ridge and the great Secretariat during the early 1970s; Nick Zito, a two-time Kentucky Derby winner; Buddy Delp, a terrific claiming-horse trainer who won the 1979 Kentucky Derby and Preakness with Spectacular Bid and went on to record an unbeaten Horse of the Year campaign with that colt in 1980; Billy

Turner Jr., who did Hall of Fame work with Seattle Slew; Dale Baird, a prolific, high-percentage winner of more than 9,000 races who never gets a tumble for the Hall of Fame because he deals exclusively with cheap stock in West Virginia; King Leatherbury, a winner of more than 6,000 on the Maryland racing circuit; Jack Van Berg, a national leader in races won nine times, who also trained 1984 Preakness winner Gate Dancer and 1987 Kentucky Derby-Preakness winner/1988 Horse of the Year Alysheba; Frank "Pancho" Martin, who trained several dozen stakes winners, including Secretariat's chief Triple Crown rival, Sham, and also won 12 training titles in New York during the 1970s; LeRoy Jolley, who seemed to win everything during the late 1970s into the early 80s; Jerry Hollendorfer, another overlooked candidate for the Hall of Fame who has done well with limited top-quality horses on the national stage and won every meet training title in Northern California for two decades.

The two hardest cuts were Todd Pletcher and Ron McAnally. Pletcher, a tall, elegantly attired disciple of Hall of Famer D. Wayne Lukas, has been training only since 1996, yet won 20 meet titles in New York in his first $10\frac{1}{2}$ years, with the meter still running. He also set new standards for races won at Saratoga and led the nation in purses won in 2004 and 2005. He had broken his own seasonal earnings record by early October 2006, with more than $21 million in purse winnings, and was challenging D. Wayne Lukas's record for the most stakes wins in a year as well. Although Pletcher has not won a Triple Crown race despite many attempts, he is on the fast track to the Hall of Fame.

McAnally, an easygoing, affable fixture on the Southern California racing scene, certainly is one of the best horsemen in America. Among many accomplishments, McAnally trained the great gelding John Henry to four national turf championships and two Horse of the Year Awards, including a remarkable title in 1984 when John Henry was 9.

Beyond John Henry, McAnally trained two other turf champions, Tight Spot and Northern Spur, and two female champions, Bayakoa and Paseana, each of whom won back-to-back Eclipse Awards as the nation's top filly or mare. McAnally himself was a three time Eclipse Award winner as America's top trainer in 1981, 1991, and 1992 and still is producing winners in his sixth decade of training on the Southern California circuit.

13. *Neil Drysdale*

The British-born Neil Drysdale had a great deal to celebrate in the year 2000. Not only did he win the Kentucky Derby with Fusaichi Pegasus and the Breeders' Cup Mile with War Chant, he was also elected to the Hall of Fame for all his accomplishments prior to those two stellar victories.

Drysdale already had trained numerous Grade 1 winners, including the high-class filly Bold 'n Determined, a multiple Grade 1 winner in 1980, and 1989 Breeders' Cup Turf winner Prized (in his first start on grass), plus five national champions: Princess Rooney, the 1984 Breeders' Cup Distaff winner and champion mare of 1984; Tasso, the 1985 Breeders' Cup Juvenile winner; A.P. Indy, the 1992 Horse of the Year, who won the Belmont Stakes and the Breeders' Cup Classic; Hollywood Wildcat, winner of the 1993 Breeders' Cup Distaff and champion 3-year-old filly; plus Fiji, the top female turf horse of 1998.

A former assistant to Charlie Whittingham during the early 1970s, Drysdale learned quite a bit from that great horseman, accenting the long-term development of his stock for distance races, especially on the turf. The vast majority of Drysdale's 1,000-plus winners in his 30-year career have been at one mile or longer.

Always a sly fox and sometimes difficult to get close to, Drysdale is meticulous with his preparation for each horse and sometimes takes great pleasure putting over a few on the clockers and his competition.

Fusaichi Pegasus was trained in the dark at Churchill Downs for the Kentucky Derby, partly to avoid the horde of media who might spook the high-strung colt, but partly because that is just Drysdale's way. Nothing was left to chance in any of Drysdale's preparations, not for Fusaichi Pegasus, not for any horse in his barn. Perhaps this might be best illustrated by something I saw while clocking horses during the 1997 Triple Crown run. Although Drysdale did not have a single horse good enough to compete in that year's Derby, he was at Churchill with a half dozen horses, training them for future stakes engagements.

I was packing my watch away when I saw a trio of Drysdale trainees enter the gap for the turf course 10 minutes after the course was supposed to be closed. Standing in the nearly vacant grandstand, I could hear Drysdale barking instructions from his pony to one of the riders as the trio tracked back to the start of a lengthy work that was going to start and end at the finish line. The work began with two of these three horses opening up a few lengths on the third horse. It continued with the trio keeping their relative positions all the way around the track until the lead pair reached the eighth pole in good stride together, about two horse widths separating them from each other.

Suddenly, the third horse, the one who was tracking the top pair about three lengths behind, was asked for a serious run. Almost instantly, he caught up and split them, reaching the finish line in front by about a length. Beyond the wire, this fast-working colt galloped out well in front of the other two as Drysdale beamed from ear to ear.

Later that same morning, I checked the work tab and found three Drysdale-trained workers listed on the turf, all credited with seven furlongs in 1:29, breezing, although it was obvious that the middle horse had worked the best. So, I made my way over to Drysdale's barn and complimented him on the good-looking workers, asking him what his plan was for the middle horse, not daring to ask him for his name.

Drysdale looked at me as if I had just stolen his wallet. But he did mumble something that sounded like this: "Oh, he's just a young horse who's going to take a while to get ready. Nothing special." Yeah, right.

Almost two weeks to the day after that workout, I was at Pimlico in the press box when the field for a one-mile allowance race at Belmont Park was on display via the television monitors. The same horse, with the same physical markings, was on the track and he was 5–1 with 10 minutes to post. His name was Storm Trooper, and despite getting off to a bad start, he split horses in midstretch to win the race going away after getting crushed in the betting, down to even-money odds. In my mind's eye I could see Drysdale's grin. There he was in the winner's circle at Belmont, feeling as if he were Sylvester the cat, catching more than Tweety's feathers.

Storm Trooper, by the way, had been a moderately effective horse in Europe, and this race at Belmont was his first start in North America. Drysdale was right—he did take a long time to develop into a top horse, but as a 5-year-old in 1998, he won the Grade 1 Charles Whittingham Handicap, among other races.

As for statistics and the like, Drysdale's resume does not contain the usual array of meet titles. Neil Drysdale has only won one meet title in his career—a tie with Paul Aguirre for the 1998 fall meet at Hollywood

Park—but his horses have persistently won at a solid 22 percent rate, earning more than $75 million from fewer than 5,700 starters.

Anyone who has watched him through the years, anyone who has seen his horses come out sharp as a tack after extended layoffs, anyone who saw his handling of his six Breeders' Cup winners—including Prized, who defeated a world-class field in his turf debut in the Breeders' Cup Turf at Gulfstream Park in 1989—or his patient, expert development of the freakishly talented but injury-prone Fusaichi Pegasus into a convincing winner of the Kentucky Derby, or his extremely patient handling of 1992 Horse of the Year A.P. Indy, knows that Neil Drysdale is a master horseman.

Prior to the 1992 Kentucky Derby, A.P. Indy was considered to be a very strong favorite, but a minor hoof injury forced him out of the race a few days before it took place.

"He might've run in the Derby, but it never pays to run them in any race when they're dealing with something," he explained.

A completely healed A.P. Indy won the Peter Pan Stakes at Belmont Park and used that race to defeat the British import My Memoirs in the Belmont Stakes, with Preakness winner Pine Bluff third. The colt's nagging injuries forced Drysdale to skip the Travers in midsummer, but he slowly brought A.P. Indy back to form with a fifth in the Molson Million at Woodbine in September and a fair third in the Jockey Club Gold Cup in October after a bad stumble at the starting gate.

Drysdale's brilliant assessment of that race provides a rarely seen view of his exceptional talent.

"The race we want is the Breeders' Cup Classic," Drysdale pointed out. "His stumble didn't help him win the Jockey Club, but it did give him a boost in confidence that he could run on those legs that had been a problem for him. It was tough to watch, but I was very pleased."

In his next and final career outing, A.P. Indy rallied smoothly to win the 1992 Classic by two lengths, driving clear. Not a bad way to complete a Horse of the Year campaign and just one of many examples of Neil Drysdale's enormous talent.

12. *Dick Mandella*

Richard Mandella's two biggest days in racing occurred at Del Mar racetrack in August 1996 and at Santa Anita in late October 2003.

At Del Mar, in the 1996 Pacific Classic, he orchestrated the upset of Cigar, the Billy Mott-trained superstar who had won 16 races in succession, only to fall victim to a relay-team battle that Mandella perfectly executed. It can be argued that Mandella began to formulate his game plan the day he found out that Cigar was coming to the West Coast to compete in the $1 million race.

Cigar had been through a stern series of tests, beginning with the inaugural running of the $4 million Dubai World Cup, which he won by a hard-fought half-length over the Mandella-trained Soul of the Matter. The latter seemed on his way to a sure victory in midstretch until the stubborn Cigar reached down for one last surge to repulse Soul of the Matter's strong bid and score his 14th straight win. While the world saluted Cigar's performance, Mandella left Dubai with the feeling that he had been denied a sure victory in the world's richest race.

When Cigar returned to the United States, he did what few horses have managed since—he won his first race back after the 12,000-mile round trip, taking the Massachusetts Handicap on June 1, 1996. He then tied Citation's 16-race winning streak in the specially convened Citation Handicap at Arlington on July 13 and was pointed for the $1 million Pacific Classic at Del Mar on August 10, close to owner Allen Paulson's home base. Paulson's intent, of course, was to give California racing fans the chance to see the great Cigar in action.

Mandella, an ardent admirer of Cigar's talent, still harbored feelings that he should have won the Dubai World Cup. But Soul of the Matter was recuperating from his Dubai adventure and could not be part of the Pacific Classic equation. No sweat—Mandella had two more high-class horses in the barn worthy of a double-edged challenge.

Siphon had won the Hollywood Gold Cup wire to wire and loomed a front-running threat if left alone on the lead in the Pacific Classic. Dare and Go was the lesser regarded of the Mandella pair, but was trained specifically to give his best rally after some of the starch had been taken out of Cigar.

The plan was a throwback to the work of veteran trainers who regularly employed pacesetting "rabbits" to sap the strength of highly ranked rivals.

It worked to perfection.

Cigar was forced to chase Siphon through six furlongs in 1:10 $\frac{1}{5}$ before taking the lead under pressure at the mile mark in 1:35$\frac{3}{5}$. This left Cigar vulnerable to Dare and Go's late surge, ending the historic streak and giving Mandella his private revenge for losing the richest race in the world five months earlier.

"People asked me if I was sad to see Cigar lose," Mandella said the next morning. "Hell no . . . the object in this game is to win, and if you beat great horses, that's all the better."

On October 25, 2003, Dick Mandella had the most successful day of any trainer in racing history. He won four Breeders' Cup races, each with a purse of $1 million or more, including the $4 million Breeders' Cup Classic.

The Breeders' Cup had been in existence since 1984 and had been the forum for some amazing performances by Hall of Fame trainers, jockeys, and horses, including the aforementioned Cigar in the 1995 Classic. But no trainer or jockey had ever won four Breeders' Cup races on the same racing program, a program that began with seven Cup races and expanded to eight in 1999.

The 2003 Breeders' Cup was at Santa Anita, rotating back to that Southern California track for the first time since 1993, and Mandella used the home-field advantage to great effectiveness, winning the Juvenile with Action This Day, who never would win another race, and the Juvenile Fillies with the very impressive Halfbridled, who never would win another race. Mandella also scored a dead-heat victory with Johar in the $2 million Breeders' Cup Turf for that horse's final career victory.

Pleasantly Perfect's win at 14–1 odds in the 2003 Classic, however, only foreshadowed a great string of successful efforts, which was more typical of Mandella's handiwork. As most Southern California horseplayers will attest, once Mandella-trained horses reach top form, they usually stay in form.

"He was always a very talented horse who was hard to keep on the track," Mandella said, explaining why Pleasantly Perfect had to miss several engagements early in his career, including the 2002 Breeders' Cup, due to nagging injuries. "But I always believed in him and knew he was worth the time and effort we spent on him. When he was healthy, he was outstanding."

During his stellar career, which began in 1974 and continues into the 21st century, Mandella has not won a Triple Crown race and has never been the national leader in races won, or money earned; but he annually has won close to 20 percent of all attempts and has been leading trainer at several Southern California race meets, repeatedly finishing among the top half dozen in purses won nationally. He also has trained several Eclipse Award champions, including a trio of 2-year-olds— Phone Chatter, Halfbridled, and Action This Day—plus the 1993 turf champion and Horse of the Year, Kotashaan. Mandella was inducted into the Hall of Fame in 2001 and remains one of the most respected horsemen in America.

11. *Elliott Burch*

J. Elliott Burch was born to be a top trainer, and he was schooled in the art of horsemanship as well. His grandfather, William P. Burch, was a Hall of Fame trainer; his father, Preston Burch, was a Hall of Fame trainer who also wrote a classic instructional book, *Training the Thorough-bred Racehorse.*

Apparently Elliott inherited the talent to perform admirably in the family's chosen craft, and he must have studied the lessons and watched his father's daily routines with considerable dedication, because he too was elected to the Hall of Fame, giving the Burch family the distinction of having three plaques on the Hall of Fame wall.

Elliott Burch earned his way in. He trained many outstanding horses to victories that other trainers might not have managed. For instance, after Quadrangle lost the 1964 Kentucky Derby and Preakness Stakes to Northern Dancer, he entered the 3-year-old colt in the Metropolitan Mile, not so much to win that race against older horses, but to tighten him up for a stronger try in the grueling 1 1/2-mile Belmont Stakes. Quadrangle finished second in that Met Mile and did win the Belmont.

Five years later, Burch repeated this pattern with the hard-hitting Arts and Letters, who had finished a close second in the Derby and Preakness before he went to the Met Mile, won that race, and then defeated the previously unbeaten Majestic Prince in the Belmont. Under Burch's handling, Arts and Letters went on to win four more races in succession— the Jim Dandy, Travers, Woodward, and Jockey Club Gold Cup—to complete a six-race winning streak that earned him Horse of the Year over the retired Majestic Prince.

Winning streaks were, in fact, part of the Elliott Burch modus operandi. When his horses reached peak form they stayed in form for longer periods than those of most trainers I have seen in my handicapping career. For example, the Burch-trained Bowl of Flowers raced 16 times at 3 and 4 years old in 1960 and 1961, never finishing out of the money and reeling off six wins in succession from October 1960 through May 1961.

Burch was a firm believer in using prep races to get his horses where he wanted them. The Met Mile approach extended to races of lesser value, including simple allowance races that either set a horse up for a longer, tougher contest or prepared him for something new, such as learning how to ration his speed and rally from behind horses. Burch horses did tend to finish well, rather than break out of the gate in hot pursuit of the lead. Quadrangle was a stretch-runner; so were Arts and Letters and Bowl of Flowers and all of his other top runners.

Fort Marcy, one of the top turf horses ever developed in America, was another perfect example of the Burch training method. After Fort Marcy compiled a mediocre record of two wins and two seconds from his first 12 races—all on dirt—Burch decided to move him to the grass. First time out on the turf was a ninth-place finish. Second time was a vastly improved second. The next time Fort Marcy was in a grass race, he won by three lengths after rallying from far back in the pack. From that day forward, Fort Marcy was a steadily improving grass horse who would win two titles as the best turf horse in America (1967 and 1970) and culminate his career as the 1970 Horse of the Year.

Key to the Mint was another top-class horse Burch developed slowly but surely, until he was able to nudge Kentucky Derby-Belmont winner Riva Ridge out of the 3-year-old championship in 1972. With his training interrupted due to minor physical setbacks, Key to the Mint did not make it to the 1972 Derby and was an immature fourth in the Belmont. But Burch had him moving forward during the summer, and in typical fashion, Key to the Mint reeled off eight straight races in which he was first or second from July through the following June. The streak included wins over older horses in the Brooklyn, Whitney, and Woodward, sandwiched around a win in the historic Travers Stakes.

Among other top horses Burch trained were Run the Gantlet, champion turf horse of 1971, who had a five-race winning streak during his championship campaign, and Summer Guest, winner of the 1972 Monmouth Oaks, Coaching Club American Oaks, and the Alabama Stakes in another patented Elliott Burch winning streak.

The private trainer for Rokeby Stable throughout the 1960s and early 1970s, Elliott Burch did everything a great trainer from a great training family could have possibly accomplished—everything except write his own book.

10. *Frank Whiteley Jr.*

Frank Whiteley Jr. was a tight-lipped, old-school trainer who began his remarkable career during the late 1950s. Based in Maryland, Whiteley was feared and respected by the best horseman in the country for his exceptional, patient handling of some of the best horses who ever lived.

Whiteley, whose son, David, also became a successful trainer, was the man behind 1967 Horse of the Year Damascus as well as 1965 Preakness winner and champion 3-year-old Tom Rolfe, and he also trained the great gelding Forego to a Horse of the Year title in 1976. But Whiteley is best remembered as the man who trained the great filly Ruffian, who suffered a fatal injury while seeking her 11th consecutive victory in a match race on July 6, 1975, with 1975 Kentucky Derby winner Foolish Pleasure. Perhaps this story about Ruffian's first race will shed some light on Whiteley's training style and acumen.

On May 21, 1974, a day before Ruffian was going to make her career debut in a 5 ½-furlong maiden race at Belmont Park, I received a telephone call from Gerry Strine, a great racing reporter for *The Washington Post* and a phenomenal football handicapper. Strine had been teaching me his football-betting methods, which had produced seasonal profits in print for several years, and he was calling me in an excited voice that was many decibels above his usual low-keyed conversational tone.

"Steve, I just came back from Aiken, South Carolina, where I had a chance to talk with Frank Whiteley Jr. about the stock he's coming north with this year. He was more excited than I ever have seen him about this filly in his barn, a filly named Ruffian who's going to start in a maiden race tomorrow."

Strine continued, "Whiteley swore me to secrecy but said she's the fastest horse he's ever seen, an F-R-E-A-K if there ever was one. She's so fast, he's scared to death he's going to ruin her. He said she's already outrun older horses in trial races at Aiken and could have gone five furlongs in about 55 if he hadn't told the rider to strangle her all the way. Get a bet down."

Strine had a special relationship with Whiteley, having lived in Maryland and spent considerable time with the great trainer through the years. I respected Strine and fully expected Ruffian to win at 6–5 or so, especially with the word out on her. The bookie I was dealing with at the time didn't care for horse bets and only accepted a $40 maximum play. Otherwise, the 400-mile round-trip drive from Columbia, Maryland, to Elmont, New York, for 6–5 had no appeal. This was at a time when there was no simulcast wagering and the only off-track betting was in New York.

The next evening, while listening to the nightly radio broadcast of racing results sponsored by the "National Armstrong Daily," a scratch sheet that provided a service to bookmakers and horseplayers, I was not surprised when Ruffian's name was read as the winner of Belmont's third race. But I was stunned when the announcer, in his gruff horse-racing voice, said that Whiteley's filly had paid $10.40!

The following morning, the Belmont Park result charts added this fact: Ruffian had won the race by 10 lengths, equaling the track record for the 5 ½ - furlong distance!

If you wanted to know how close to the vest Frank Whiteley Jr. operated, this was a great peek into his mind. Here he had the fastest filly of the 20th century in his barn, ready to roll against a field of unsuspecting maidens, a filly that he took to South Carolina to get ready, a filly who, with Whiteley's guidance, would slip through the cracks in New York where secrets were not easily kept, especially secrets about fast and fit young horses.

Whiteley's career began in 1958 and spanned a little more than two decades, during which he annually won more than 25 percent of all starts and regularly ranked among the top 15 money-winning trainers despite saddling fewer horses than any trainer who ranked above him. He was a master horseman, a "horse whisperer" before the world would ever hear the term, a man so in touch with his horses that he was often called the Fox, or the Old Fox from Maryland. Whiteley made few mistakes, but at the same time, he was stricken by the death of Ruffian in a race that he had resisted until the public clamored to see Ruffian perform against a top colt.

Ruffian aside, Whiteley did extraordinary work with the sore-legged, gallant Forego, who ran some of the best races in history under heavy weight assignments during the three years Whiteley handled the aging gelding after Sherrill Ward developed him into a top-flight 4-year-old.

Still, the 3-year-old colt Damascus probably was Whiteley's biggest disappointment and his greatest triumph. Whiteley thought he had a cinch Kentucky Derby winner in Damascus, who finished an uninspiring third in the 1967 Derby with no apparent excuse. But that was the last bad race this horse would turn in as he won nine of the next 11, including the Preakness, the Belmont, the Travers (by 22 lengths), and three of the nation's most prestigious stakes for older horses, including a dramatic 1967 Woodward, in which Damascus defeated 1966 Horse of the Year Buckpasser by 10 lengths with his arch rival Dr. Fager third, another half-length farther back.

Whiteley never would win the Kentucky Derby, but his sharp handling of so many good and great horses, young and old, on dirt and turf, left no doubt that he was one of the truly great horsemen who ever lived.

9. *Billy Mott*

One of the realities of Triple Crown racing is that an out-of-the-money finish usually gets little notice, even when the horse ran as hard as he could and the jockey did nothing wrong. The same goes for the trainer—most of the time.

In the weeks and months leading up to the 1984 Kentucky Derby, trainer Billy Mott was an unmistakable presence at the Fair Grounds in Louisiana and at Keeneland and Churchill Downs in Kentucky as he tried to harness the abundant natural speed of Taylor's Special, hoping to prepare him to compete in Triple Crown races. Mott nearly pulled off the trick, getting Taylor's Special to win the 1 1/16-mile Louisiana Derby and then the 1 1/8-mile Blue Grass Stakes before his sixth-place finish in the Kentucky Derby and fourth in the Preakness.

Moreover, Billy Mott's work did not escape the notice of his peers. Trainer Neil Howard, himself an accomplished horseman who would train 1990 Preakness winner Summer Squall, made it a point to identify Mott's talent, as did many veteran horsemen based in Kentucky.

"If you want to see a future star, there he is," Howard said, pointing away from a Derby horse pulling up after a workout and indicating Mott, 500 feet away, next to the outside fence in the Churchill Downs one-mile chute. Mott had been sitting still on Taylor's Special for almost 30 minutes, treating him as if he were a stable pony. He was just giving the high-strung horse a chance to take in the surroundings in a relaxed mode.

Born in 1953 in Mobridge, South Dakota, the son of a veterinarian, Bill Mott owned and trained his first horse, a $320 mare named My Assets, when he was 15. After running her in several races at unrecognized South Dakota tracks, he won his first official race with her during the Fort Pierce County Fair meet at Park Jefferson in 1969 and used the $2,000 in winnings to buy Kosmic Tour, whom he trained to win the South Dakota Futurity at Park Jefferson.

"He worked under Bob Irwin for a while and then Jack [Van Berg] for three years," Howard continued. "That's like going to trainers' college and graduate school too. Billy smashed the meet record for wins here last year," Howard added, referring to Mott's 52 wins. "He's going to do better than that this year. He's a great talent." Mott did do better, with 54 winners.

Mott, an intelligent, introspective man who has always carried himself with a quiet grace, dominated Churchill trainers in the 1980s, winning nine out of a possible 12 fall and spring meets, surging past nine-time national leading trainer Van Berg and Calumet Farm's Henry Forrest in 1986 to become the all-time leading trainer at Churchill, a distinction that he retains by a significant margin over D. Wayne Lukas. (Mott had 561 Churchill wins to Lukas's 416 through 2005). Also in 1986, Mott passed Calumet's immortal Ben A. Jones as the leading stakes-winning trainer at Churchill.

That year, Mott's work was also noticed by the prominent breeder-owners Bertram and Diana Firestone, who raced 1980 Kentucky Derby winner Genuine Risk and other top horses. Mott did well for the Firestones until the stable was dispersed in 1992, getting seconds in two Breeders' Cup races and winning purses in excess of $20 million. But when the Firestones scaled down their operation, owner-breeders Allen and Madeline Paulson bought a few of the better Firestone horses, and made an even better decision to hire Mott to train their expanding high-class stable.

For the next decade, Mott would win five Breeders' Cup races for the Paulsons, including the 1995 Classic with the great Cigar, Horse of the Year in 1995 and 1996, who retired the richest winner in North American racing history with $9,999,815 in earnings.

"He's the best horse I've ever trained. He may be the best horse anyone has ever trained," said Mott.

Cigar, who won just two of his first nine career starts, including one out of seven races on the turf when trained by Alex Hassinger on the West Coast, was winless in his first four outings for Mott in New York, also on grass, when the light bulb went on prior to his 14th career start, on October 28, 1994.

"I remembered the way John Henry turned his career around when he was moved from dirt to turf, so I decided to try the reverse approach," Mott explained. "He was bred for turf, yes, but he always trained extremely well on dirt."

So it was that Cigar would win his first attempt on dirt for Mott, making Cigar 2 for 3 lifetime on dirt with only one race left in his 4-year-old season, the prestigious NYRA Mile. He won by seven lengths, earning a 115 Beyer Speed Figure.

"I didn't know he would go on a winning streak that would continue into the summer of 1996," Mott said. "But he was such a different horse on dirt, amazing, really."

With Cigar winning 16 races in succession, including all 10 in 1995 and the Dubai World Cup in 1996, Mott was voted the nation's top trainer both years, and in 1998, at 45, became the youngest trainer ever elected to the Hall of Fame. Always modest, Mott cited Hall of Fame jockeys Pat Day and Jerry Bailey for important roles in his success.

"We had great communication," Mott said. "Pat won a lot of races for me at Churchill, and when I moved to New York, Jerry got to know my horses firsthand, knew what they wanted to do and how they should be ridden. We won quite a few races together and that was no accident."

Mott also trained Ajina, 3-year-old filly champion in 1997; Escena, the 1998 champion older filly or mare; Theatrical, turf champion in 1987; and Paradise Creek, champion male turf horse in 1994. He was leading trainer at Belmont Park 10 times and Saratoga eight times in addition to his Churchill titles and the titles he earned at Gulfstream Park in South Florida.

While Mott never has had a highly regarded contender for Triple Crown races, he did train 54–1 shot Vision and Verse to a second-place finish in the 1999 Belmont Stakes. From a handicapping perspective, few trainers in my lifetime have been so reliable with grass horses in allowance races and stakes, or with layoff runners, which Mott quietly prepared for competition at the pastoral Payson Park training facility in Florida and/or the Saratoga training track.

With much more of his training career ahead, Mott's horses had already earned more than $140 million through 2005, third best behind D. Wayne Lukas and Bobby Frankel. He also has won almost 3,500 races from fewer than 16,000 attempts, a win percentage in excess of 22 percent.

As Neil Howard predicted, Billy Mott was headed for stardom.

8. *Shug McGaughey*

Shug McGaughey has been an important trainer on the New York and national racing scene for more than 20 years. Among his 12 Eclipse Award and/or Breeders' Cup winners are the 1988 and 1989 2-year-old champions Easy Goer and Rhythm, both of whom became important 3-year-olds, winning the 1989 and 1990 Travers Stakes. McGaughey also trained 1989 Breeders' Cup Sprint winner Dancing Spree; two-time Breeders' Cup Mile winner Lure (1992–93); 2-year-old filly champion Storm Flag Flying (2002) and 1995 Juvenile Fillies winner My Flag; 3-year-old filly champs Heavenly Prize (1994) and Smuggler (2005); plus three champions in the older filly or mare division—Inside Information (1995), Queena (1991), and the undefeated Personal Ensign (1988).

While Personal Ensign deserves special mention as the only major horse with a multiseason career to retire undefeated since Colin won all 12 of his races as a 2- and 3-year-old in 1907–08, it was Vanlandingham, the first champion of McGaughey's stellar career, who woke up the racing world to his unbridled talent. Vanlandingham was a promising 3-year-old in 1984, a lightly raced son of the long-winded Cox's Ridge, the foundation sire for Loblolly Stable, for whom McGaughey was training in the early 1980s.

Although McGaughey privately confided that he believed Vanlandingham might need more time to develop, Loblolly was intent upon aiming for the Kentucky Derby. Unfortunately, Vanlandingham went lame with a career-threatening leg injury in the 1 1/4-mile race and was an extreme longshot to return to competition at all, much less to return 12 months later in 1985 to win four stakes as a 4-year-old, including the

Suburban Handicap, the Jockey Club Gold Cup, and the Washington, D.C., International in his first career start on grass.

The performance vindicated McGaughey's belief in the colt and confirmed the potency of his training style, which was to be conservatively patient with horses needing extra care and extremely aggressive with horses that were approaching peak condition. This was the balanced approach McGaughey learned working for David Whiteley in the 1970s and it would be his personal stamp for the rest of his career.

"Vanlandingham put me on the radar screen," McGaughey said shortly after he was hired to train the Phipps family's horses on November 11, 1985.

The following year, while dealing with the 2-year-old filly Personal Ensign, McGaughey relied on his experience with Vanlandingham's stop-and-go career by showing the same degree of patience with this extraordinary talent.

Personal Ensign was a homebred, as so many of the Phippses' horses were, dating back to the 1960s when Mrs. Henry Carnegie Phipps's Wheatley Stable dominated the sport with a legion of top class 2-year-olds sired by Bold Ruler, the 1957 Horse of the Year who reigned as a supreme stallion into the 1970s.

Personal Ensign, who raced in the colors of Ogden Phipps, was bred in Kentucky at Claiborne Farm and was by Private Account out of Grecian Banner. She showed speed in her workouts, but McGaughey believed she would mature into a solid 3-year-old, so he patiently waited until September of her 2-year-old season to put her in a maiden race. Somewhat surprised that she won by nearly 13 lengths, he stepped Personal Ensign up sharply in class for her next start, a victory in the one-mile Frizette Stakes at Belmont. She was all set to go in the 1986 Breeders' Cup Juvenile Fillies at Santa Anita when she suffered two fractures to her left hind leg.

Screws were inserted to assist in healing and there was serious doubt that Personal Ensign ever would race again. But, under McGaughey's patient handling, Personal Ensign did indeed return 11 months later, reeling off four consecutive victories, including the Beldame against older fillies and mares. Next stop Breeders' Cup Distaff? Not quite.

"We thought the trip to California and the level of stress that she would be under might undo all the work we put into her," McGaughey explained, referring to the fact that the Cup would be run at Hollywood Park that year. "She did a lot coming back winning those four races, so we put her away and thought about next year."

As a 4-year-old in 1988, Personal Ensign made her return in the Shuvee in May, and from there to the Breeders' Cup Distaff at Churchill Downs on November 5, she racked up six more victories, giving her 12 wins in 12 career starts leading into one of the greatest races ever run.

Given that Personal Ensign had narrowly beaten 1988 Kentucky Derby winner Winning Colors in the Maskette Handicap at Belmont in September, many horseplayers believed that her stiffest challenge would instead come from the Charlie Whittingham-trained Goodbye Halo, a multiple Grade 1 winner in top form. Although Goodbye Halo did run strongly in the 1988 Distaff, finishing a close third, Winning Colors put in a sensational front-running effort and seemed a surefire winner approaching the final furlong. With her regular jockey Randy Romero aboard, Personal Ensign was struggling with the muddy track and was slow to get rolling, nowhere near the lead as she had been in virtually every prior start.

At the top of the stretch, mired in fifth place and lagging eight lengths behind the leader, the unbeaten filly suddenly responded to Romero's prodding and unleashed a sustained, almost devastating rally that brought her within four lengths of Winning Colors with a furlong to run. Still, it seemed impossible that she would make up the difference; Winning Colors had won the 10-furlong Kentucky Derby on this same racetrack and she was still going strong heading toward the finish line of this historic nine-furlong race.

But an equine miracle was in progress, the kind of miracle that stays in your mind's eye for the rest of your life. Personal Ensign just kept coming, relentlessly digging in for every once of power she could muster, running out of time as the Breeders' Cup crowd screamed her name, watching in awe what they might never see again. Still almost a length behind with 30 yards to go, Personal Ensign exerted her indomitable will and reached out with one last lunge forward, finishing off her rally, catching Winning Colors by an inch at the wire, pulling out a most improbable victory, the last of her unblemished career.

"You can't be more proud of a horse than I felt that day," McGaughey said. "She was not going to lose; she was not going to let any horse beat her. That was a tremendous performance. By both horses. But if you want to know what a great Thoroughbred looks like, I don't think you could go wrong looking at Personal Ensign. They should put a photo of her in the dictionary."

Likewise, should you need to see what a great Thoroughbred horse trainer looks like, try a photo of Shug McGaughey. Not many trainers in my lifetime were any better than this man who made it into the Hall of Fame exactly 20 years after he came into view.

7. *Allen Jerkens*

I was still in college when "Tommy," my bookie friend at the New Brunswick cab company, told me about Allen Jerkens.

"That's the best trainer in America," Tommy said. "He's only been around for a couple of years, but he's already upset Kelso three times and won races with horses nobody else probably could."

Allen Jerkens's reputation as the "Giant Killer" of American racing is no hyperbole. Beginning with his three upsets of Kelso by Beau Purple in the early 1960s, continuing through to his two upsets of the mighty Secretariat in 1973 and so many other improbable victories over high-profile horses, Allen Jerkens would have to do very little more to make a list such as this. But it is worth pondering the enormity of his lifelong resume of outstanding trainer feats, accomplished mostly with moderate-quality stock.

* Leading trainer in New York in 1957, 1962, 1966, and 1969.
* Leading trainer at Saratoga in the 1970s, winning four meet titles and setting the record for most wins—19, in 1972—during an era when the Saratoga meet was four weeks long, not 5 ½.
* Upset three-time filly champion Cicada in the 1963 Black Helen Handicap at Gulfstream with the little-known Pocasaba.
* Defeated 1966 Horse of the Year and 1967 handicap champion Buckpasser with Handsome Boy, who emerged from the allowance ranks to win four straight $100,000 races in an era when there were fewer than 75 such races nationwide.
* Was voted the Eclipse Award-winning trainer of 1973, the year he upset Secretariat with two different horses, the sprinter Onion (see

the chapter on greatest upsets) and Prove Out, who also upset two-time champion Riva Ridge the same year. During that amazing season, Jerkens also took a $25,000 claiming filly named Poker Night and improved her sufficiently to win the Hempstead Handicap and Bed o'Roses over the nation's best older fillies and mares.

Two years later, at 45, Jerkens became the youngest trainer elected to the Hall of Fame, a distinction he kept until Billy Mott was inducted in 1998, also at 45, beating Jerkens by a few months.

After a relatively slow decade in the 1980s for Hobeau Farm, Jerkens reached new heights while adding a few new clients in the 1990s. In 1993, Jerkens won New York's Triple Tiara for 3-year-old fillies with Sky Beauty, who came back the next year to win five of her six races and was the 1994 champion older filly.

While Jerkens won five meet titles in New York during in the mid-1990s, he was back to his old tricks, defeating Horse of the Year Skip Away and the top horse Gentleman in the 1998 Jockey Club Gold Cup with the modestly accomplished Wagon Limit.

During nearly 60 years of training, Allen Jerkens has been a home-body, focusing almost exclusively on New York racing, spending his winters in Florida, returning to New York in late March, rarely venturing far out of town with any of his horses. Yet few trainers are as admired throughout the country more than the man his peers call the Chief.

Among his specialties, the Chief has trained an exceptional list of high-class sprinters to numerous New York stakes wins and track-record performances, including Third Martini (1964); Beaukins (1969); Duck Dance (1970); Onion (1973); King's Fashion (1980); Believe the Queen (1984); Belong to Me (1992); Classy Mirage (1993–95); Kelly Kip (1996–98); Limit Out (1998); Put It Back (2001); Smokume (2003–05); and Swap Fliparoo and War Front (2006).

Jerkens also trained a long list of major winners of major Eastern stakes at distances beyond a mile, starting with Beau Purple, who, in addition to his three victories over Kelso, was the winner of the 1 $\frac{1}{2}$-mile Man o' War stakes on turf, another Jerkens specialty through the years.

Others he developed to win important stakes at a distance of ground include Handsome Boy, Mac's Sparkler, Never Bow, Poker Night, Group

Plan, Sensitive Prince, Hechizado, Dance Caller, Missy's Mirage, November Snow, Devil His Due, Virginia Rapids, Choker, Shiny Band, Puzzlement, Passing Shot, and Society Selection.

On the turf, Jerkens has always been a formidable presence, winning numerous allowance races and minor stakes with relatively modestly bred colts and fillies, most of them Hobeau Farm homebreds that outperformed their pedigrees. In fact, that is what is most telling about Allen Jerkens, master horse trainer. Rarely has he had blue-blooded racing stock, or high-priced yearlings in his barn.

The Chief won his races the hard way, with long hours of dedicated effort to bring out performances that most trainers who compete against him admit they probably would not have achieved. He also has recognized the talents of excellent barn help, including his sons Jimmy and Steve Jerkens, who have followed in his footsteps.

Said Nick Zito, elected to the Hall of Fame in 2005: "Forget about the national rankings and the huge amounts of money other trainers have won, forget about the Triple Crown races he hasn't won, or the Breeders' Cup races either. The Chief has been doing miracles with racehorses in New York for as long as I can remember. Sometimes I wonder what [Jerkens] might have done if he had been bankrolled to buy his share of high-priced yearlings. Forget about it. He's not a giant killer, he's just a *giant!*"

Hail to the Chief, who has won stakes in six decades and more than 3,600 races on one of the toughest racing circuits in the world.

6. *Laz Barrera*

Lazaro S. Barrera had been a highly regarded trainer in his native Cuba before he emigrated to America in the early 1970s.

Although he did not hit the ground running, he held his own, moving steadily up the New York trainer standings each season until a horse of great speed was sent to him from Puerto Rico in July 1975. The horse was Bold Forbes, a grandson of Bold Ruler who had won all five of his Puerto Rican races by many lengths during the winter and spring of his 2-year-old season.

Under Barrera's tutelage, Bold Forbes not only won his first two sprint stakes in New York, the Tremont and Saratoga Special, but also continued to develop slowly into a good miler during the winter at Santa

Anita, taking the San Jacinto Stakes at that distance on February 28. Shipped to New York with the rest of Barrera's stable, Bold Forbes won the seven-furlong Bay Shore when ridden for the first time by the great Angel Cordero Jr., himself a native of Puerto Rico.

After the Bay Shore, Cordero and Barrera agreed that Bold Forbes had matured enough to handle the 1 ⅛ miles of the Wood Memorial, which he won so easily that a trip to the Kentucky Derby was no longer a far-fetched adventure, but a realistic spot. This despite the presence of the LeRoy Jolley-trained Honest Pleasure, another grandson of Bold Ruler.

Honest Pleasure, held at 2–5 odds in this Derby, was the 2-year-old champion of 1975 who had been favorably compared to Secretariat by *Sports Illustrated* after nine consecutive victories, including the Flamingo, the Florida Derby, and the Blue Grass Stakes.

Still considered a miler by most, Bold Forbes was a lukewarm 3–1 second choice in a small Derby field that lacked depth beyond the top two. Barrera was convinced he was training the Derby winner, telling everyone who would listen that the general public and the racing press completely missed the significance of the Wood Memorial.

"I wasn't sure I could train him to go a distance," he explained a week before the Derby. "I had trouble training horses for distance since I been in New York." At the time, Barrera had a very low win percentage stretching horses out in distance. "But my brother Luis reminded me of how I used to train horses for stamina in Cuba and it helped a lot. Bold Forbes won the Wood so easy, I know he will win the Derby. That other horse will never catch him."

That is exactly what occurred in the 1976 Kentucky Derby, but it was only a prelude to the amazing victory Bold Forbes would score in the 1 ½-mile Belmont Stakes, a race in which Cordero showed all of his skill holding Bold Forbes together at a distance that was at least two furlongs beyond the colt's true distance limitations.

"I get lots of credit for that ride and I am proud of that," Cordero said. "But it was Laz who trained that horse from a sprinter. He was simply awesome."

My friendship with Laz Barrera was forged during that remarkable spring and would grow closer during the 1978 Triple Crown, one year after Billy Turner Jr. had taken me under his wing while he trained Seattle

Slew. Nine days before the '78 Derby, Laz asked me to clock Affirmed's 1 ⅛-mile workout around *three turns.*

I clocked the workout from ground level in the Churchill Downs infield with Barrera standing alone, 30 yards away. Affirmed began his work on the clubhouse turn under a tight hold and went in successively faster quarter-mile splits to get nine furlongs in a deceptively slow 1:56 ⅕, galloping out the full 1¼-mile Kentucky Derby distance in 2:09 with energy to spare. Affirmed was just galloping when he came past us midway down the backstretch and was under a hold every step of the way while completing his final half-mile in a strong 48 ⅘ seconds.

The next morning at his barn, Barrera explained in great detail how he had battled against time to get this outstanding racehorse ready for his epic battles with the extremely gifted Alydar.

"We missed 40 days of training during the winter [on the West Coast] because of heavy rains," Laz explained. "I had to rush Affirmed into four prep races to get him ready; he thrives on competition. But," he added, "I still needed to put a long work into him yesterday and I'll need to work him again [during Derby Week] to be sure he's really ready."

Barrera respected Alydar, who was trained by John Veitch and his very able assistant, Charlie Rose. Barrera knew that Affirmed would have to be at his best to win, but he also knew what kind of horse he had brought to Louisville. "Alydar is a very good horse," Barrera said. "But Affirmed is a truly *great horse.* If I give him the work he needs, he will never lose another race."

When Affirmed defeated Alydar by a diminishing 1 ½ lengths in the Kentucky Derby, many experts stated unequivocally that Alydar would reverse the verdict in the Preakness. After Alydar worked six furlongs in a rapid 1:10 ⅖ during Preakness Week, it looked as if his supporters might be right. But Affirmed toyed with Alydar in that Preakness, even though the margin at the wire was closer than in the Kentucky Derby. The front-running Affirmed literally waited for stretch-running Alydar to catch up at the top of the lane. Once joined by his rival, Affirmed refused to let Alydar gain a single inch through the final run to the finish as the pair ran the fastest final three-sixteenths of a mile in Preakness history.

Despite the two impressive wins in the first two legs of the Triple Crown, Laz Barrera knew he was in trouble for the 1 ½-mile Belmont.

"Look at him," Barrera lamented. "He's lost weight, he's tired, he could use a couple of months to get ready for the Belmont, but we only have three weeks. I can't train this horse for the Belmont," he said. "I can only feed him for it."

Affirmed, in fact, spent many of the 21 days between the Preakness and the Belmont walking the shed row and jogging or galloping lightly, working only a slow mile in 1:40 on June 1 and a slow five furlongs in 1:01 on June 7, three days before the 1 1/2-mile classic. Meanwhile Alydar was able to work three times during the final nine days, including a full 1 1/2-mile training drill in 2:43 on June 1, a solid six furlongs in 1:12 3/5 on June 5, and a snappy three-eighths of a mile in 35 seconds flat on June 9, the morning before the race.

Affirmed won, of course, as the history books verify, but the drama of the race was in the details, which matched these two great rivals through the final six furlongs, shadow to shadow, nose to nose, as jockey Jorge Velasquez sent Alydar up to challenge Affirmed on the backstretch and did everything he could to wrest the lead away through one of the great stretch battles in racing history.

Alydar might even have taken a narrow advantage outside Affirmed in the upper stretch, only to have Affirmed instantly match the bid. But the race was not really won until the young jockey savant Steve Cauthen switched his whip to the left hand to get one last spurt of reserve energy from the horse who would be the last to win the Triple Crown in the 20th century.

For his expert work, Barrera was voted his third of four straight Eclipse Awards as the nation's top trainer, and the following year he was elected to the Hall of Fame, forever sealing his place among the greatest trainers in modern racing history, a man who trained dozens of important winners until he passed away in 1993.

On a personal level, I consider Laz Barrera to be one of the most decent human beings I have ever met, a man who taught me a lot about horse racing and a whole lot more about life while I was going through a divorce and raising my young son, Bradley.

"Being a single parent is hard," he said. "But you can help each other, as father and son, as son and father. Help him be a man by you being a man."

Wise advice from a wise man who made a difference on and off the track.

5. *Bobby Frankel*

The first time anyone in racing learned about Bobby Frankel, he was an assistant to three-time national leading trainer Buddy Jacobson during the mid-1960s.

Frankel began by walking hots—a term that describes the act of leading a horse around in circles while cooling down after a morning workout or a race. He graduated to the status of a groom, in charge of feeding, brushing, washing, and applying leg bandages to three or four horses for the principal trainer, who relies on his grooms to report every important detail. No trainer wins races without good help, and the Brooklyn-born Bobby Frankel learned his chores quickly and had a lot in common with the streetwise Buddy Jacobson. To a point.

Shortly after Frankel decided to go out on his own in 1966, Buddy Jacobson's career took some bad turns. First, he violated New York claiming rules with a horse that had raced in Maryland, then led a 1969 horsemen's boycott against the New York Racing Association that resulted in a suspension of his training license.

Within a decade it got worse, much worse, as Jacobson invested wildly in New York real estate, started a modeling agency, and built a Manhattan apartment building that he used to attract young models and stewardesses. One of those models was Jacobson's live-in girlfriend, Melanie Cain, who left him in the summer of 1978 and moved in with another tenant, Jack Tupper. When Tupper's body was found in a burning crate in the Bronx a week later, Jacobson was convicted of murder and sentenced to 25 years to life in prison, where he eventually died with few friends in this world.

One of those friends was Frankel, who still credits Jacobson for teaching him what the horse business was like and how to go about every aspect of training and caring for horses.

"When I knew him, he was a cocky, but extremely knowledgeable, very entertaining guy," Frankel said when the subject was brought up in an extensive interview prior to the 2003 Kentucky Derby.

"Buddy did teach me a lot about the horse-racing business—the smallest details of what a trainer does, how to get the horse ready to perform on race day. I'm grateful for that, but he took some really bad turns in his life. It was really sad to see. Terribly tragic. I still feel bad for what happened to him and for all the people he hurt."

On his own, Frankel took a completely different, positive path, winning a high percentage of claiming and low-grade races in his first season—just as Jacobson had done—expanding his horizons step by step, winning stakes with horses he bought cheaply and improved dramatically. Frankel even managed to win a 1970 training title at Saratoga, a rare feat for a claiming-horse trainer at the hallowed summer meet generally dominated by high-class stakes runners and blue-blooded 2-year-olds. Moving west in 1972, Frankel quickly emerged as a prolific winner of races at all three major tracks in Southern California.

Frankel led the trainers standings at Hollywood Park in his first season, 1972, setting a record with 60 victories. The following year, he led the Del Mar and the Santa Anita (Oak Tree) meets, hinting at things to come.

During the early '70s into 1982, Frankel racked up a total of 25 of his 28 meet titles at Hollywood, Santa Anita, and Del Mar, before the quality of his stock improved dramatically through owners Edmund Gann, Bert Firestone, Stavros Niarchos, and the Juddmonte Farms of Khalid Abdullah, all of whom were committed to racing fewer horses, but at the highest levels.

The transition from a claiming-horse trainer to a dominant trainer of graded stakes winners was seamless beyond anything previously seen in the sport. Frankel didn't just win at the same 20 to 25 percent rate he had established with his cheaper stock, he improved upon it, reaching 30 percent some years while breaking national records for money won and victories in Grade 1 stakes.

With no Breeders' Cup winners until 2001 and no winners of a single Triple Crown race until Empire Maker won the 2003 Belmont, Frankel still ranked among the national leaders in money won every year since 1971 and trained more than two dozen winners of $1 million races through 2005, including six runnings of the Pacific Classic (four in a row) and two editions of the Arlington Million.

In 1993, when he won his first of five Eclipse Awards as top trainer while leading the nation in purse earnings for the first time, Frankel trained the first of his seven champions—Bertrando, who was voted the top older horse. Two years later, he was elected to the Hall of Fame and began a string of three straight Eclipse Awards for three different champion older turf fillies: Possibly Perfect in 1995, Wandesta in 1996, and Ryafan in 1997.

Improving his stakes-winning totals almost every year, Frankel took another leap forward in 2000, winning a second Eclipse Award as the nation's leading trainer, the first of four straight. In 2002, he trained 60 stakes winners, including 43 in graded stakes from only 213 starters to win his second consecutive earnings title and third since 1993. In 2003, Frankel outdid himself, earning his fourth straight Eclipse, winning $19.1 million in purses from a moderate 413 total starts, breaking D. Wayne Lukas's seasonal-earnings record. (This record was broken again by Todd Pletcher in 2005, who racked up $20.8 million, but from 1,039 starters.) Even more impressive, Frankel won 25 Grade 1 stakes in 2003, breaking the world record held by Ireland's Aidan O'Brien (23 Group 1 wins).

That also was the year that Frankel surpassed the legendary Charlie Whittingham's career record for most wins at Hollywood Park (860) and the year his Empire Maker won the Florida Derby and Belmont Stakes (over Funny Cide), losing the Kentucky Derby and a probable 3-year-old championship when the after-effects of a foot bruise apparently hampered Empire Maker's ability to perform at his best.

Because Empire Maker had defeated Funny Cide in the Wood Memorial with jockey Jerry Bailey barely asking for Empire Maker's best run and because he easily handled him in the Belmont when 100 percent sound, Frankel still shakes his head when the 2003 Derby is discussed.

"That was a tough week," Frankel admitted. "He really was physically fine. We had the bruise under control, with no heat, no pain, but he did miss two days of important training. I debated with myself all week whether I should run him. The Derby is a hard race to win, but you're taking the worst of it when you have any setbacks leading up to it. He tried hard, but Funny Cide was just at his best that day."

In 2004, Frankel did not have a viable contender for the Triple Crown chase but he did have Ghostzapper, an outstanding performer who was a dominant winner of his four engagements, including the Breeders' Cup Classic, the biggest victory of Frankel's high-powered career. The progress of Ghostzapper somewhat resembles the progress made by

Frankel through the years. After three wins in four starts in 2003—all at sprint distances—Ghostzapper was presumed to have too much speed to go a mile or more. This impression was reaffirmed by a terrific win in the seven-furlong Tom Fool Handicap at Belmont on July 4, 2004, a race that earned a world-class 120 Beyer Speed Figure. Yet, Frankel saw something that many others did not.

"For a while I wasn't sure he would go a distance either. But I really liked the way he relaxed," he said, referring to Ghostzapper rating in third position behind the leader in the Tom Fool. "That race made me think he definitely would go a lot farther than seven furlongs."

A son of 1998 Breeders' Cup Classic winner Awesome Again, Ghostzapper next won the nine-furlong Iselin Breeders' Cup Handicap at Monmouth Park on August 21, 2004, by 10 ½ lengths, earning a sky-high Beyer fig of 128! This was followed by a gutsy, hard-fought, roughly run victory in the nine-furlong Woodward over Saint Liam. Saint Liam was no slouch. In 2005, he would come back to win the Woodward and Breeders' Cup Classic and be voted 2005 Horse of the Year. Finally, in the 2004 Breeders' Cup Classic, Ghostzapper overpowered a strong 13-horse field to clinch Horse of the Year.

Frankel's correct read on Ghostzapper was similar to his accurate assessment of his own potential training talents many years earlier. Not only did he believe in his ability to train at the highest levels, he believed that Ghostzapper was the fastest horse in America, destined to be the best.

As for the Kentucky Derby, considering Frankel's upward curve of success, it is hard to imagine him ending his career with that trophy missing from his very crowded shelf.

"A lot of very good trainers never win the Derby," Frankel pointed out. "I just don't want to be one of them."

4. *Bob Baffert*

Bob Baffert practically burst onto the Thoroughbred-racing scene in 1992 when he brought a well-rested Thirty Slews to Gulfstream Park for the Breeders' Cup Sprint.

Thirty Slews was in fact the first Thoroughbred Baffert bought at auction for a partnership that included a longtime friend, Quarter Horse owner Mike Pegram. Born in Arizona in 1953, Baffert had been a star in Quarter Horse racing, just as D. Wayne Lukas had been before his switch over to Thoroughbreds in the late 1970s.

Thirty Slews won the '92 Sprint at 18–1 over Meafara, a gallant 3-year-old filly who set the pace all the way until Thirty Slews wore her down in the final strides under Eddie Delahoussaye. The eventual Eclipse Award-winning sprinter Rubiano was third and the 1991 Sprint winner, Sheikh Albadou, was a close fourth in one of the strongest Breeders' Cup Sprints ever.

On the thrust of that success, Baffert quickly attracted plenty of eager owners for his public stable, which was anchored by Pegram's investment. A sensational career was sent flying into motion, a career that definitely is going to put the silver-haired, accessible, oft-quotable media darling Bob Baffert into the Hall of Fame the first year he becomes eligible.

Consider just this partial list of Baffert's accomplishments, which rival those of any trainer in history:

* From 1995 through 2005, Bob Baffert won more than two dozen training titles at the three major Southern California racetracks and led the nation in purse winnings three times (1997–99), simultaneously winning three Eclipse Awards as the nation's top trainer.
* His first Kentucky Derby starter, Cavonnier, just missed winning the 1996 Run for the Roses, losing by a nose to the D. Wayne Lukas-trained Grindstone.
* The following year, he brought Silver Charm to the Triple Crown chase and not only won the Derby, but also took the Preakness and just missed sweeping the Triple Crown, finishing a close second to Touch Gold in the 1997 Belmont Stakes.
* In 1998, Baffert was back, winning the Derby and Preakness with Mike Pegram's Real Quiet, who had a four-length lead in mid-stretch, only to lose the Belmont in the final stride when Victory Gallop rallied late to deny another desperately close Triple Crown bid by a nose.
* Earlier that year, Baffert won the Dubai World Cup with Silver Charm, and in the fall he took his second Breeders' Cup race—the Juvenile Fillies—with Silverbulletday, who was a champion that year as well as the next.

* In addition to Silverbulletday's 3-year-old title in 1999, Baffert won another Eclipse Award with Chilukki, who was voted the nation's top juvenile filly.
* In 2001, Baffert would miss winning the Kentucky Derby with the Point Given, owned by the Thoroughbred Corporation of Saudi Arabian prince Ahmed bin Salman. Point Given, however, won the Preakness and Belmont, then added the Haskell Invitational and the Travers (giving him a total of six Grade 1 victories), which would be his final race. Point Given was voted 2001 Horse of the Year.

In 2002, Baffert bought Illinois Derby winner War Emblem for Thoroughbred Corporation less than a month before the Kentucky Derby and promptly upset the 18-horse field at 20–1 in a wire-to-wire performance. Two weeks later, War Emblem won the Preakness, but once again Baffert was denied a Triple Crown sweep when War Emblem stumbled at the start in the Belmont and never fully recovered. Later that year, however, the Baffert-trained Vindication won the Breeders' Cup Juvenile and was voted champion 2-year-old.

All this certainly assures Bob Baffert his standing among the modern giants in the game. *Modern* is the right word.

Among other things, Baffert uses walkie-talkies to convey split-second instructions to his exercise riders during workouts. He works 2-year-olds hard enough to get them ready for their debuts and builds their bones and stamina through the best vitamins and nutritional supplements money can buy. He ships cross-country and back again for the richest stakes and regularly runs his second-stringers in softer spots with big purses at far-flung tracks.

Unlike many in his profession who wish to be left alone, Baffert loves the limelight and shines in its glare, rather than shrinks from it, and never seems to lose his sense of humor under pressure. Bob Baffert does not train horses in the dark. "Why bother," he says. "No one else is there except other horse trainers and the stable help. A grown man does need his sleep."

Baffert seldom misses a trick.

"I work [horses] hard enough so they'll be ready to deal with tough races and I watch everything they do when they come off the track and every day after they work to see if they're going north or south on me," Baffert said. He was specifically discussing a six-furlong work in 1:11 for

Silver Charm less than a week before that colt would score a hard-fought victory over Captain Bodgit and Free House in the 1997 Derby.

"Training is not rocket science," he added, "but it's not something everybody on the street can do either. The horses are fun to work with. They have their own personalities, their own quirks, and you have to see them—really see them—to get their best out on the track. It's not really hard work, just a lot of details, and it does beat the heck out of stocking peach cans at a supermarket. But, it can be very hard on you emotionally when things don't go right, or when you lose one to injury or illness. That's always the worst part. When it happens it hits you in the gut. I've had a few that will stick with me forever. We all have and you never get used to it."

Baffert also says that he sometimes feels like he's "managing a baseball team of four-legged players," or a college football team "with new freshmen recruits each year."

Through 2005, Baffert-trained Thoroughbreds had earned more than $115 million, fifth best in history. He had trained seven different horses to nine Eclipse Awards, won two dozen Southern California meet titles in less than a decade, and was voted the top trainer in 1997, 1998, and 1999.

"The Triple Crown, that's something I'd like to win before I'm done," he said.

Baffert is the only trainer in history to come so close three different times.

3. *Woody Stephens*

Woodford Cefis Stephens was holding court outside his barn at Belmont Park, under the large 100-year-old tree that provided some protection from the rain to several dozen reporters who were scrambling to write down every word he spoke. It was early June 1986, a few days before the Belmont Stakes, and Woody Stephens deserved the audience.

Not only was Stephens a legendary horse trainer with a long resume of accomplishments, including Kentucky Derby winners Cannonade (1974) and Swale (1984), five champion 2-year-olds, including the freakishly fast 1983 juvenile champion, Devil's Bag, plus 1960 handicap champion Bald Eagle and 1982 Horse of the Year Conquistador

101

Cielo, not only did Stephens have stories to tell about his early association during the 1940s with "Julie" Fink, one of the great horseplayers of the 20th century, but Stephens was carrying himself and all those within earshot back to the scene of his greatest triumphs, right here at Belmont Park, where he had won four straight runnings of the Belmont Stakes, the longest and toughest race in the Triple Crown series. Now he was bidding to do what no trainer in history had accomplished, win five in a row.

For many of the reporters on the scene that day, it was just a courtesy call, another chance to listen to Stephens recount his successes as he so often seemed inclined to do. It was an easy opportunity to get the needed material for the next day's obligatory Stephens piece. You see, the horse he was running in that Belmont really did not look like he had much chance.

Yes, Danzig Connection had won the Peter Pan Stakes over the Belmont track on May 25, but he was overshadowed by Kentucky Derby winner Ferdinand and by the lightly raced Johns Treasure, who won a fast allowance race on the same day as the Peter Pan. Many handicappers also expected a big race from Arkansas Derby winner Rampage, who had finished a flying fourth in the Kentucky Derby after being stopped cold at the top of the Churchill Downs stretch.

Even Mogambo, second in the Jersey Derby on May 28 to Preakness winner Snow Chief, was rated a stronger Belmont contender than Danzig Connection, a colt who had not matured into a top-class 3-year-old in time to make either the Derby or the Preakness. Three days before the 1986 Belmont, he still seemed a step behind the division leaders.

Listening to Stephens that morning, you could not tell if he was confident, or just pointing out that he was the man who had won those four Belmonts.

"They didn't think Conquistador could go a mile and half or win this race five days after he won the Met Mile," Stephens pointed out, referring to Conquistador Cielo, who started the streak in 1982. "A lot of people thought I was crazy running him back a mile and half in five days. But they should look up the record books, Arts and Letters won the Met and the Belmont in a week [in 1969] and I would've worked [Conquistador] a good mile for the Belmont anyway."

The thin, 73-year-old Kentucky-born horse trainer with emphysema and a weather-beaten face took a few moments to tell an assistant to check the equipment on a young horse. Turning back to the crowd of reporters, Stephens picked up where he had left off as if he had bookmarked the page.

"Caveat was almost knocked over the inside rail and he still won," Stephens continued, remembering the 1983 Belmont. "Swale, now Swale, he was just too good for them, what a shame, never took so much as an aspirin, but what a shame. . . ." Swale, the 1984 Derby-Belmont winner, had died suddenly and inexplicably at Stephens's barn after returning from a light gallop one morning. "Just like that. A week after he won so easily; I thought he could have gone around again.

"They studied him in Pennsylvania, at the New Bolton Center, and couldn't find out what killed him. A good horse, maybe a great one, and he ran as fast in the last three quarters as ran his first three quarters [1:13 ³/₅ and 1:13 ³/₅]. Not even Secretariat did that. You don't see that in a mile-and-a-half race."

Very few questions were needed to keep Stephens in gear, sharing his insights, his memories, and why he did what he did with what horse in what race. Some had tuned in to similar soliloquies over the years—at Churchill Downs, or at Saratoga, or whenever Woody Stephens had a serious horse in a serious race. But there was never an arrogance in his tone, nor did it seem to grate on the senses when his recitations went a bit over the top. Woody Stephens was easy to be around, sharp as a tack, a man who enjoyed his moments in the sun, a man who was a walking, talking encyclopedia of racing knowledge, especially facts pertaining to Woody Stephens. Who could blame him: He was a part of racing history, a big part.

Standing there at Belmont Park, outside his barn *that morning* before the 1986 Belmont, it felt as if we were all standing at the center of the known universe.

I, for one, could not move from my spot until Stephens was out of breath. It was Arthur Rubinstein playing piano at Carnegie Hall. It was Ted Williams describing how he hit an Allie Reynolds fastball over the wall at Fenway Park. It was Roger Bannister describing the first four-minute mile. You don't turn away from such stuff. Suddenly, in the midst of it all, the thought began to dawn that Danzig Connection just might win the race on Saturday because this wise old owl of a horse trainer obviously had something special on the game.

"We ran 1–2 last year," Stephens continued. "Crème Fraiche was a better horse than a lot of people realized; he sure gave that Spend a Buck [the 1985 Kentucky Derby winner] all he could handle in the Jersey Derby, so it was no surprise he could beat Stephan's Odyssey. They made Chief's Crown the favorite, didn't they. But both my horses beat him.

"Danzig Connection? We'll see on Saturday, but they tell me that Charlie [Whittingham] thinks his horse [Ferdinand] is a perfect Belmont Stakes horse. I love Charlie, but somebody should tell him that the buildings get mighty tall when you cross the Hudson River. We'll see on Saturday."

Saturday, June 7, 1986, was more than a horse race. It was a Woody Stephens celebration, an immortal achievement, a coronation.

With Chris McCarron riding his first winner in a Triple Crown race, Danzig Connection chased Mogambo for almost a mile before he sloshed his way to the front on a rain-drenched track and outgamed both Johns Treasure and Ferdinand in a hard-fought three-way battle through the final half-mile to give Stephens his fifth straight Belmont victory by 1 ½ lengths.

Danzig Connection was the fifth betting choice at 8–1. Rampage, the favorite, was far back in seventh.

"Woody, Woody, Woody," the crowd roared as Danzig Connection was ushered into a jubilant winner's-circle celebration that spilled out onto the track. "WOOD-EE, WOOD-EE, WOOD-EE," the chant continued for several minutes. The sound of it still resonates in the ears of many who shared the moment.

Stephens was king of New York. A great chapter in a legendary career was written, but it was not the only chapter, and there were some that he might have regretted, even though he never let on.

For many years, Stephens and D. Wayne Lukas squared off in a personal battle of wits that became one of the most intense training rivalries of all time.

There were many small irritation points as both men clashed on the Triple Crown circuit and in a few cases during the early years of the Breeders' Cup. But after the Lukas-trained filly Winning Colors scored a narrow wire-to-wire victory over Stephens's Forty Niner in the 1988 Kentucky Derby, Stephens publicly displayed uncharacteristic venom while vowing he was going to change tactics for the Preakness.

"We're not going to take back next time," he said. "We're never going to let that filly get away with an easy lead in the Preakness. I don't care if my horse finishes last, as long as another horse [Winning Colors] finishes next to last. "

Forty Niner's rider, Pat Day, followed Stephens's orders to a fault, sending Forty Niner right from the gate, herding Winning Colors and jockey Gary Stevens wide on the first turn and bullying the filly with repeated brushes on the backstretch. Winning Colors did well to hang on for third in that Preakness, while Forty Niner was seventh in the worst finish of his career.

Stephens's words came back to haunt him from coast to coast, as editorial writers, including the publisher of *Daily Racing Form*, Michael Sandler, castigated Stephens for his unsportsmanlike behavior.

"It was a black eye for the sport," Sandler wrote. "The people need to believe every horse is trying to win, not trying to beat one particular horse."

The great horse trainer had made a public mistake and it did affect the way he was perceived by casual racing fans during the final years of his career. However, when Stephens passed away in 1999, even Lukas went out of his way to heap praise on the man he had fought so hard a decade earlier.

"Woody Stephens was a wonderful horseman and I personally enjoyed knowing him and competing against him as he enjoyed competing against me. He did a lot of great things to promote the game and as long as they run races at Belmont Park, his record might never be broken and he certainly will never be forgotten."

2. *D. Wayne Lukas*

Trainer D. Wayne Lukas has been an inescapable, powerful force on the national racing scene ever since he left a successful career as a Quarter Horse trainer in 1979. By many yardsticks, he is the Babe Ruth of racing.

Through more than a quarter-century, Lukas has set historic standards that are hard to match. A four-time Eclipse Award winner as the nation's top trainer, a 14-time national leader in purses won, the winner of an astonishing 65 different meet training titles in New York, California, and Kentucky, Lukas has trained 23 horses to 28 Eclipse Awards, including 1986 Horse of the Year Lady's Secret, 1990 Horse of the Year Criminal Type, and 1999 Horse of the Year Charismatic. He also trained a record 18 winners of Breeders' Cup races and 13 Triple Crown race winners—four in the Kentucky Derby, five in the Preakness, and four in the Belmont Stakes, equaling the winning Triple Crown output of the legendary Ben A. Jones.

Through 2005, his 24,000-plus starters had earned more than $245 million, about $55 million more than any other trainer. During one remarkable stretch, Lukas won an unprecedented six straight Triple Crown races, beginning with Tabasco Cat's 1994 Preakness and Belmont, running through Thunder Gulch's Derby and Belmont Stakes in 1995, which were sandwiched around Timber Country's 1995 Preakness, and finishing with Grindstone's 1996 Kentucky Derby.

The scope of his accomplishments is breathtaking. No one could possibly develop so many important stakes winners with mirrors. Indeed, no trainer in history has had a higher public profile or bought as many expensively bred horses for his clients, and none has won as much money or developed as many divisional champions or tutored more winning trainers, including Dallas Stewart, Kiaran McLaughlin, Randy Bradshaw, Mark Hennig, Rebecca Maker, and the extraordinary Todd Pletcher, who is setting records of his own in the 21st century.

Scaling his operation down a bit since 2001, Lukas continued to maintain an immaculate barn, complete with beautiful plants and flowers watered on a tight schedule, just as his horses are fed and washed down to perfection every day. To describe his training regimen as efficient and businesslike is to underestimate his attention to minute detail. Yet there have been instances when his approach has been borderline callous.

Seeking to quickly identify top stakes prospects and cull those that might not stand up to the stress of high-class racing, Lukas frequently put his young horses through rigorous training regimens. When one failed to make the cut or went lame, Lukas knew he had several highly fancied horses waiting in the wings to occupy the same stall space.

It also is true that D. Wayne Lukas projected a Dr. Jekyll image to those who watched him through the years, attracting a steady stream of media criticism for a significant number of top horses that broke down or left the racing scene a mere shell of their best form. Many were heavily bet on the assumption they were fit to race; others were seriously injured in full public view. It is this side of his ledger that limits his placement below

106

the very top of this list, a ranking he surely would deserve if accomplishments were the only criteria.

The list of fallen horses started with 1980 Preakness winner Codex, Lukas's first Triple Crown race winner, who came back lame after finishing a weak seventh in the Belmont Stakes. The list also includes some of the most gifted horses of the modern era: Tank's Prospect, winner of the 1985 Preakness, who also broke down in the Belmont; Marfa, the 1983 Kentucky Derby favorite, whom Lukas opted to run in the Preakness with a quarter-crack patch that was applied after a Preakness Week workout; Stalwart and Saratoga Six, considered by Lukas to be among the best juveniles he ever trained, who both suffered career-ending leg injuries in training drills; Landaluce, the undefeated 1982 champion 2-year-old filly, who died from a mysterious virus; and Capote, the 1986 champion 2-year-old colt, who went lame in the 1987 Kentucky Derby.

In addition, there was Charismatic, winner of the 1999 Kentucky Derby and Preakness, who broke down in the Belmont Stakes; High Yield, winner of the 2000 Blue Grass Stakes, whose form fell apart in the Derby and Preakness and was never recovered; Jump Start, winner of the 2001 Saratoga Special, who was vanned off the track after he was injured in the Breeders' Cup Juvenile; Scorpion, winner of the 2001 Jim Dandy Stakes at Saratoga, who went off form immediately thereafter and was beaten a total of 49 lengths in his final two starts; Scrimshaw, upset winner of the 2003 Lexington Stakes in April, who immediately went off form and was beaten a combined 61 lengths in his final four starts before he had to be removed from training.

In a bizarre example of this negative pattern, the Lukas-trained Lady's Secret—a daughter of Secretariat, and the 1986 Horse of the Year—evidently went sour on training and racing the next season. She was beaten 32 ½ lengths in her first start of 1987, then failed to win another stakes and eventually bolted to the outside fence on the clubhouse turn in an allowance race at Saratoga.

The most dramatic occurrence involved Union City, who went to the 1993 Derby starting gate as the 5–1 second betting choice. But there were hints of physical issues and rumors of unsoundness that circulated through the Churchill Downs backstretch during Derby Week, so when Union City finished a distant 15th, several astute observers watched the awkward steps he took while walking back to the barn.

"That horse didn't look good leaving the track," Churchill Downs clocker Mickey Solomon told me the next day. "I doubt he'll do much in the Preakness."

Despite a groundswell of similar negative opinions during Preakness Week, Lukas publicly attested to the colt's soundness and saddled Union City in the 1 $^3/_{16}$-mile classic at Pimlico. He was noticeably stricken with grief when he saw the colt break down during the race.

On the other side of this coin, Lukas can point to his many trophies and Eclipse Award winners as well as several horses that seemed to be going the wrong way and were ambitiously placed, yet proved the trainer's judgment correct by rising to the occasion at long odds.

* Thunder Gulch won the 1995 Kentucky Derby at 24–1 after seemingly going off form in the Blue Grass Stakes.
* Cat Thief won the 1999 Breeders' Cup Classic at 19–1 after a succession of defeats followed by 10 more losses the following year.
* Charismatic, a loser in a $65,000 claiming race during the winter, won the 1999 Kentucky Derby at 31–1.
* Commendable won the 2000 Belmont Stakes at odds of 18–1 after finishing a dismal 17th in the Kentucky Derby and failing to win another race for the rest of his life.
* Spain won the 2000 Breeders Cup Distaff at 55–1 despite overall good form because no one other than Lukas really believed that this frequent bridesmaid was up to such a high-powered performance.

Lukas's awards and his Ruthian records notwithstanding, it is possible that the trainer's single greatest achievement was linked inexorably to the worst moment in his life.

In December 1993, Lukas's son and trusted assistant, Jeff, nearly was killed when he was run over by the fiery 2-year-old Tabasco Cat, the top Derby prospect in the Lukas barn. The colt had broken loose and run over Jeff as he stood in Tabasco Cat's path, waving his arms in the traditional manner that usually helps to convince a loose horse to come to a stop.

Now put yourself in the place of the father who had worked closely with his son for 15 years and was forced to look the very horse in the eye who put Jeff Lukas in a sustained coma within an inch of his life. It is far beyond my ability to comprehend how Wayne Lukas could have chosen the path he did.

Shuttling between Jeff's bedside and the Santa Anita backstretch for 12 weeks, Lukas quietly came to grips with the earliest impulses that brought him to train racehorses in the first place.

Standing in the winner's circle after Tabasco Cat won the 1 ½-mile Belmont Stakes to go along with his victory in the Preakness, Lukas revisited Union City's death and gave moving testimony about how sad he felt that day at Pimlico and how he had rediscovered what it felt like to be a true horse trainer while sitting in introspective silence at his son's bedside.

Lukas talked about how he had gone into the stall with Tabasco Cat and closed the door to personally tell this wildly nervous horse how he would make something special out of him and that he was not to blame for the accident that had left his son fighting for his life.

Lukas shunned any talk about his success that did not involve Jeff's recovery. He brushed aside praise for his efforts to help Tabasco Cat become a professional racehorse, a dual winner of Triple Crown races, partially reversing the sickening feeling Overbrook Farm had endured the year before. Yes, the same people who owned Union City also owned Tabasco Cat.

"It was a horrible experience for everyone in the barn," Lukas admitted. "It's hard to take, but things like that do happen in racing. You have to be prepared for it in your gut or you couldn't go back to the barn and do justice for the rest of the horses. . . . That's why we treat our horses with the best feed, the best veterinary care every single day. We want them to be as healthy as possible and as fit as we can make them. I know I take a lot of criticism in the media, but the public should know that we never would run a horse if we believed something like that was going to happen," he said. "I'm still sick about it."

I have to confess that I never witnessed a more stunning training achievement than the one this man pulled off in getting the dangerously excitable Tabasco Cat to relax kindly for the pressure-packed Triple Crown races. It was beyond extraordinary. Lukas did an amazing job caring for Jeff while simultaneously working with this horse that had nearly killed his son. No horse trainer in my lifetime ever did anything more difficult or more honorable.

1. *Charlie Whittingham*

Charles Whittingham's work with Ferdinand was detailed in an earlier chapter, and Whittingham would win another Kentucky Derby (and Preakness) in 1989 with Sunday Silence, but that was mere icing on a very tall cake. In a storied career that began shortly after Word War II, when Whittingham and his mentor and pal, Horatio Luro, barnstormed together, he would write some of the most amazing chapters of training success in the history of the sport.

During an era when million-dollar stakes were just becoming the norm for the highest-class races, Whittingham trained 20 different horses that earned at least $1 million. "The Bald Eagle," as he was affectionately known for his lack of hair, trained 10 different national champions to win 15 Eclipse Awards, including Ack Ack, Ferdinand, and Sunday Silence, each of whom was voted Horse of the Year (in 1971, 1987, and 1989, respectively).

This tall, proud man cast a large shadow on Southern California racing for 46 years until his death in 1999, orchestrating many upsets over Hall of Fame horses. Among them were victories over Swaps with his first good horse, Porterhouse, in the 1956 Californian Stakes at Hollywood Park, and over Nashua with the miler Mister Gus in the 1956 Woodward Stakes at 1 ¼ miles on Nashua's home track, Belmont Park. He also handed Bold Ruler his first career defeat with the short-winded Nashville in a six-furlong sprint on the straightaway course at Belmont (which was in use until the early 1960s) and he trained Exceller, who defeated Seattle Slew in one of the great races of all time, the 1978 Jockey Club Gold Cup.

Beyond those singular triumphs, Whittingham was best known for winning just about every Southern California stakes at one mile or longer, some many times each:

An astounding 14 times, Whittingham won the prestigious San Juan Capistrano at 1 ¾ miles on the Santa Anita turf.

Eleven times each he won the San Bernardino Handicap at 1 ⅛ miles at Santa Anita; the Carleton F. Burke Handicap at 1 ½ miles on the Santa Anita turf; and the Californian at Hollywood Park at 1 ⅛ miles. He also won the Sunset Handicap at 1 ½ miles on the Hollywood Park turf 11 times, including six years in succession.

Nine times each he won the famous Santa Anita Handicap at 1 ¼ miles for 4-year-olds and up on the main track at Santa Anita; the Oak Tree Invitational at 1 ½ miles on the turf; and the San Luis Rey Stakes—a marathon at Santa Anita for older turf horses—as well as the Inglewood Handicap at varying distances.

Eight times he won the Beverly Hills Handicap for fillies and mares at 1 ⅛ miles on the Hollywood Park turf course and the Hollywood Gold Cup at 1 ¼ miles on the main track at Hollywood.

Seven times Whittingham won the Del Mar Oaks for 3-year-old fillies and the Ramona Handicap for fillies and mares, the latter two at 1 ⅛ miles on the Del Mar turf course. *Seven times* he also won the Santa Barbara Handicap for fillies and mares at 1 ¼ miles on the Santa Anita turf.

Whittingham also won the Hollywood Oaks for 3-year-old fillies *six times*, the Del Mar Handicap on the turf *six times*, the Goodwood Handicap for 3-year-olds and up at 1 ⅛ miles at Santa Anita *five times*, plus more than 800 other stakes races during his career, including the 1982, 1986, and 1990 Arlington Million; the 1987 and 1989 Breeders' Cup Classic; the 1986 and 1989 Kentucky Derby, and the 1989 Preakness.

Whittingham's style was old school, similar to Frank Whiteley Jr.'s approach, close to the vest, keeping his own counsel with little to say whenever he could avoid having to reveal his plans. He was highly competitive, but never mean and was content with his place on the racing map. Whittingham knew his skill, knew racehorses and was able to teach other men how to train them, some by osmosis, others by example, including former assistants Neil Drysdale, Dick Lundy, Joe Manzi, Alex Hassinger, Chris Speckert, and his son, Michael Whittingham, who trained Skywalker, winner of the 1986 Breeders' Cup Classic.

Charlie Whittingham was patient, always thinking long term with his horses, some of whom were imported from Europe and South America, where stamina was their strong suit. But he also knew more about how to use workouts to get a horse ready for a difficult race than any trainer I have ever seen, perhaps better than anyone in history.

His handiwork with Ferdinand, discussed in the section on jockey Bill Shoemaker in the previous chapter, was a textbook example of that, as were the works he put into Cougar II to get that 1972 grass champion ready to win the 1 ¼-mile Santa Anita Handicap on dirt in Cougar's first outing of 1973 after a five-month layoff. Cougar, by the way, was 7 years old when he won that Big Cap.

A further illustration was something I witnessed at Pimlico racecourse the day before and the day of Sunday Silence's hard-fought victory over the outstanding Easy Goer in the memorable 1989 Preakness.

The day before the race, the sun was barely in view when Sunday Silence was galloping on the track. Whittingham was cursing under his breath as he stood on the porch of the grandstand next to Bob Summers of *The Buffalo News* and me, as we watched Sunday Silence practically pulling his exercise rider's arms out of their sockets.

"Going to have to do something with him tomorrow," Whittingham said twice. "He's jumping out of his skin."

Shortly after dawn on the morning of the Preakness, Summers and I were back on the porch, as Sunday Silence was back on the track, but not for a light jog or a short gallop, which many trainers use on the morning of a race. No, Sunday Silence was sent on a remarkable two-mile gallop—twice around the one-mile track, the last half-mile at a good clip—an exercise that would have left many horses empty for the race itself.

"He's ready now," Whittingham said as he took Sunday Silence back to the barn to get reshod for the race of his life.

Whittingham had called an unbelievable audible to fine-tune this racehorse at a crucial, risky moment. But there is no doubt that it was just one of many extraordinary decisions he made during a career that ranks among the greatest of all time.

Charlie Whittingham was elected to the Hall of Fame in 1974, a legend in his own time. Yet, it is simple fact that most of his greatest accomplishments occurred after that when he overcame more than 30 years of personal disdain for the hype that surrounds the American Triple Crown and proved that he could win the Kentucky Derby (twice) and almost swept the Triple Crown. Putting it as simply as possible, Charlie Whittingham was the best trainer of racehorses I have ever seen.

The Star-Crossed Trainer

In doing this book of the "best and worst" accomplishments and failures in Thoroughbred racing, I could have made a separate category for "the best individual training feat and the worst one" as well. Fact is, such a list would include the most notable achievements and failures by many of the sport's greatest horsemen as already outlined in previous pages. But instead of recapitulating what already has been cited, it would be a major omission if I did not include the story of one trainer whose work during the Triple Crown chase of 1983 ranks alongside the very best training jobs of modern racing history and yet, in my opinion, also symbolizes the very worst. Indeed, David Cross's work with 1983 Kentucky Derby winner Sunny's Halo demonstrates the sheer brilliance of a trainer striving to reach the top whose singular triumph quickly deteriorated into a fall from grace.

One week before the 1983 Derby, Cross was explaining to me and Steven Crist (at that time a reporter for *The New York Times*) that he had run Sunny's Halo with minor fractures in his legs during the colt's 2-year-old season. While rain drained from the roof of the Derby horses' barn, Cross said that "Sunny" probably should not have been in the Laurel Futurity or the Young America the previous fall.

"I was stupid; I thought he would win anyway," recalled Cross. "But, God gave me another chance, I don't know why; but if I ever make another freakin' mistake like that with him they should take him away from me."

Sunny's Halo did win the Kentucky Derby, mostly due to Cross's brilliant training, which included extended swimming sessions in a pool in California to assist in the colt's healing, followed by two scintillating prep races at Oaklawn Park in Arkansas.

The limited training regimen defied the fact that no horse in modern times had managed to win the Derby with less than three prep races. Another key component was an amazing one-mile workout that Sunday morning, six days before the Kentucky Derby, a crucial maneuver scheduled on the fly when Cross looked up to the sky and saw an impending monsoon headed for the track.

"I have to train him this morning, *right now*," Cross said emphatically. "With the rain on its way, the track might not be good enough 'till Wednesday. And if I wait the weather out, the distance will be wrong. He's only had those two races and he needs a mile, a good mile. If I wait, I won't even be able to train him six furlongs so close to the Derby."

Cross was right. His horse desperately needed a long, strong workout to compensate for his light racing schedule. All winter and spring, Sunny's Halo had been making up for lost training time. The two-race prep campaign was Cross's only choice, given the problems the colt had to overcome. The rain was forcing his hand again. He had to go now. The weather forecasters were predicting an ominous storm and they were going to be the best handicappers in Louisville. The rain was coming down hard that Sunday morning, but it would continue for 36 hours straight. Some residents near Churchill Downs would have to be evacuated by helicopter from their rooftops. The track was going to be closed for training on Monday and the racing surface would remain a gooey, sloppy mess until midweek.

With the impromptu one-mile workout behind him—a strong mile with a solid finish—Cross was releasing all his demons, all the pent-up energy of the previous six months as he passionately told his story to us. Cross was confident that he had walked through the raindrops to get Sunny's Halo ready to deliver a peak performance in the 109th Kentucky Derby.

Sunny's Halo won convincingly over a good field that included major stakes winners Desert Wine, Caveat, Slew o' Gold, Marfa, and Play Fellow, becoming only the second Canadian-bred to take the Derby. He did it with such authority that he seemed a potential Triple Crown winner, a superstar in the making. So, on the Monday morning after the Derby, I went out to a deserted Churchill Downs with my 35-mm camera to take photographs of a jubilant Cross grazing the new Kentucky Derby winner. It didn't take long to notice that Cross was in a terrible mood and his horse had a raging case of hives all over his chestnut coat.

"I can't even enjoy the greatest victory of my life," Cross said between a dozen curse words. "Look at the freakin' horse. If we can't get control over this skin rash, there's no way he'll ever be fit enough to run in two weeks."

Despite the circumstances, despite his earlier vow not to run Sunny's Halo in any race if he was not 100 percent healthy, David Cross headed to Pimlico for the Preakness Stakes.

Having gone to Belmont to see Slew o' Gold work six furlongs on the day Sunny's Halo was scheduled to work seven-eighths at Pimlico, I asked

Maryland track officials to videotape the Derby winner's drill for dissemination to the media.

It was an awesome training move, clocked in a sensational 1:23, possibly the fastest seven-furlong workout in Pimlico history. Just a day earlier, however, the skin rash had been so severe, so annoying to the colt, that Cross had trouble keeping Sunny still while he tried to secure his saddle for a morning jog. Cross tried everything—medication, wood shavings instead of straw bedding, a soft sheepskin cover for the girth to protect against irritation—but the rash persisted.

Two days before the Preakness, in the middle of another driving rainstorm, I confronted Cross near the barn where Sunny's Halo was standing quietly in the corner of his stall as if he wanted to take a nap and forget the whole thing.

"You promised that you would never run this horse if he was not 100 percent, and you know he's not really ready to run in this race," I said. "Look at him, the rash is still there."

Cross exploded into a tirade. "This is a Triple Crown race, don't you know that?" he yelled "Get the hell outa here, leave me alone."

Sunny's Halo finished sixth on a sloppy track in the Preakness and then lost his next three starts while racing in Illinois and New York. Meanwhile, the problematic skin rash continued, and kept him out of the Queen's Plate, Canada's premier race for 3-year-olds. Even worse, for Cross, Sunny's Halo tested positive for prohibited antihistamines and decongestants while he was in Illinois. Although the Illinois stewards originally gave Cross only a token five-day suspension, the Illinois Racing Board reopened the case when Sunny's Halo was retired to stud at the end of the 1983 season. Following a probing investigation, Cross was suspended for six months.

A year later, Cross, who had given up many of his clients in 1983 while concentrating on Sunny's Halo, was struggling to put a small racing stable together, including a few Quarter Horses. I ran into him at Hollywood Park, site of the 1984 Breeders' Cup.

"It probably would have been a small fine if the same thing happened in Kentucky or California," he said. "I just got caught at the wrong time in the wrong state. I guess the [Ilinois Racing] Commission had been getting heat from members of the media to clean up things in Chicago. Then my horse tests positive and the next thing you know they've got a

Derby-winning trainer to trot out to the public as an example. Going through this legal mess is just about taking me out of the game."

The next day, in virtually the same spot in the Hollywood Park barn area, a voice spoke out softly from behind. It was David Cross.

"I suppose I can't blame anybody but myself for what happened," he said. "I never should have run him in the Preakness. . . . I made a mess of things and can only hope this time I will get past it and move on with my life."

A few years later, David Cross was given another training opportunity. He even succeeded in developing the 3-year-old colt Quintana into a legitimate 1991 Kentucky Derby starter. While Quintana could only finish sixth in that Derby, the media attention lavished on Cross brought out his brilliant work with Sunny's Halo prior to the 1983 Derby and led to Cross gaining a few more horses, including Diane's Halo, who finished third in the 1995 Kentucky Oaks. In 2006, Cross was inducted into the Canadian Horse Racing Hall of Fame.

Nevertheless, I believe that Cross's handling of Sunny's Halo after the Kentucky Derby tainted his career. Indeed, his story is a cautionary tale for all horse trainers, one not always heeded. Not only is the trainer the man behind the horse, not only does he bask in the glory of the horse's accomplishments, but the trainer is also the key person ultimately responsible for its health and welfare.

4 THE MOST ACCOMPLISHED OWNERS

THE BEST RACEHORSE owners are those who appreciate the necessity to roll with the punches while dealing with major setbacks over the long haul. They may be actively involved in the management of their stable, but defer to expert trainers in charge of the day-to-day decision making and long-term planning of racing goals.

Many of the best owners also breed the horses they race, while others have a trained eye for bargain claims, or for well-proportioned yearlings and private purchases. In the modern age, owning one or two Thoroughbreds still can be relatively inexpensive, especially in group partnerships, but the ownership of a string of racehorses at any level of competition requires an ample bankroll to cover all expenses.

In fact, the majority of the most successful owners have had to invest considerable sums before they found a horse or two that made the effort worth the trouble. Yet, there is one owner who defied all the odds and jumped from obscurity to the biggest stage with his first horse. Far from a flash in the pan, Fred W. Hooper outlasted virtually every other horse owner who made this list.

12. *Fred W. Hooper*

After his first horse, Hoop Jr., won the 1945 Kentucky Derby, Fred W. Hooper was an active owner until he passed away at 102 years old in 2000. Hooper also bred and raced the three-time Eclipse Award-winning filly Susan's Girl (1972, 1973, and 1975), plus numerous high-class stakes winners, including 1963 Santa Anita Handicap winner Crozier, 1974 Whitney Handicap winner Tri Jet, and the versatile Precisionist, who not only won the 1985 Breeders' Cup Sprint and an Eclipse Award, but also won several graded stakes at 1 ¼ miles and earned in excess of $3.4 million.

Renowned for his contributions to the Florida breeding industry, Hooper also was one of the best jockey talent scouts of all time. His specialty was recruiting Panamanian riders, most of whom developed into meet leaders and nationally ranked stakes performers. Among his best protégés were four Hall of Famers: Braulio Baeza, Laffit Pincay Jr., Jacinto Vasquez, and Jorge Velasquez.

11. *Greentree Stable*

Established in 1912 by Payne Whitney of the socially prominent Whitney family, Greentree's racing stables were primarily based in Red Bank, New Jersey, and Saratoga Springs, New York, with their breeding operation in Kentucky.

Under Whitney family management, Greentree had its greatest years prior to the modern age. Among their best horses were 1931 Kentucky Derby-Belmont-Travers-Jockey Club Gold Cup winner Twenty Grand; 1943 champion handicap horse Devil Diver; and 1953's champion handicap horse and Horse of the Year, Tom Fool, unbeaten in 10 starts that year.

Greentree also won the 1942 Kentucky Derby and Belmont Stakes with Shut Out as well as the 1949 Preakness with Capot, but also enjoyed success in the modern era, winning the 1968 Belmont with Stage Door Johnny and the 1979 Washington, D.C., International with turf champion Bowl Game, to name just a handful of their top-class horses, most of whom were homebreds.

With such a classy legacy, it seemed unlikely that the Greentree banner would disappear from American racing, but after the passing of Joan

Payson, daughter of Helen Hay Whitney, the properties were sold off and racing operations dwindled, then eventually ceased. Similar story arcs can be found in the rise and disappearance of other highly esteemed breeding and racing operations, including Paul Mellon's Rokeby Stable and storied Calumet Farm, which appear on this list of the top racing stables of the modern era.

10. *Marion H. Van Berg*

Father of Hall of Fame trainer Jack Van Berg, Marion H. also is a member of the Hall of Fame for his accomplishments as the owner-trainer of a large, very mobile stable that dominated modest-grade Midwest racing from the early 1950s through 1970. In fact, Marion H. Van Berg led the national owners' list 14 times—three times in the 1950s and 11 straight years from 1960 through 1970.

While son Jack led the national trainers' standings in 1968, 1969, and 1970, it was his father who pioneered the multidivision racing stable that was copied and improved upon in the 1980s and 90s by D. Wayne Lukas and his protégés after jet transportation for racehorses became so accessible in the 1970s.

In Marion H. Van Berg's time, training horses at multiple racetracks was nowhere near as convenient, yet Van Berg horses regularly won 200 to 390 races every year, shipping by van from track to track throughout the Midwest. Given that Van Berg dealt mostly in claiming and lower-grade allowance horses, it is most impressive that he managed to be the leading money-winning owner in 1965, 1968, 1969, and 1970.

9. *Robert and Beverly Lewis*

The Lewises were an endearing married couple who turned their personal joy into a joint love affair with racing. Easy to work with and ever trusting in their high-class training talent, they began investing in royally bred yearlings and 2-year-olds in the 1990s and were rewarded with a succession of major winners.

Among their best horses were 1995 champion 3-year-old filly Serena's Song and 2002 champion sprinter Orientate and a pair of 3-year-old colts—Silver Charm and Charismatic—who each fell one race shy of sweeping the elusive Triple Crown when they respectively lost the 1997 and 1999 Belmont Stakes.

While enduring these two heartbreaking Belmont losses, especially the defeat suffered by an injured Charismatic, Bob and Beverly Lewis projected their love for the sport, their love for their horses, and the love they shared.

Bob Lewis passed away in 2006, but his wife continues to be an active owner.

8. *Juddmonte Farms*

This powerful international stable is owned by Prince Khalid Abdullah of Saudi Arabia, whose devoted interest in horse racing began when his family lived in England in the 1960s.

With high-class breeding and racing operations established first in Europe, Juddmonte began to slowly impact American racing in 1992 with the first few of more than three dozen Grade 1 stakes winners, including Eclipse Award-winning female turf runners Wandesta in 1996 and Ryafan in 1997.

In the young 21st century, Juddmonte has raised its profile to become one of the most effective racing and breeding stables in modern American racing history. Already, Juddmonte has won the 2002 Arlington Million with Beat Hollow; the 2003 Belmont Stakes with Empire Maker; and a pair of Breeders' Cup races in 2001 and 2005 with the Eclipse Award-winning turf fillies Banks Hill and Intercontinental. Since 1995, Juddmonte has been named leading American breeder four times (1995, 2001, 2002, and 2003) and top owner twice (1992 and 2003).

7. *Frank Stronach*

The Austrian-born, Canadian-based chairman of Magna Entertainment Inc., Frank Stronach has become an important track owner, buying and selling properties across America. While the jury is still out on Stronach's track stewardship, few can match his excellent track record as a horse owner-breeder. Consider this partial list of his accomplishments:

* Stronach was leading owner in New York in 1999 and 2000.

* Leading money-winning owner in America four times: 1998, 1999, 2000, and 2002.
* Sovereign Award-winning owner in Canada 10 times between 1993 and 2003, missing only 1996.
* Eclipse Award-winning owner in 1998, 1999, and 2000, and Eclipse Award-winning breeder in 2000, 2004, and 2005.
* Bred and owned 2004 Horse of the Year Ghostzapper and the 1980 Eclipse Award-winning filly or mare, Glorious Song, as well as a pair of 2000 Eclipse Award winners, the 2-year-old colt Macho Uno and the turf filly Perfect Sting.
* Bred and owned Awesome Again, winner of the 1998 Breeders' Cup Classic, a race also won in 2004 by Stronach's Horse of the Year, Ghostzapper.
* Owned 2000 Preakness winner Red Bullet and 1997 Belmont Stakes winner Touch Gold, among more than 30 Grade 1 winners.

6. *Allen Paulson*

Founder of the Gulfstream Aerospace Corporation, Allen Paulson was a passionate horse owner-breeder who enjoyed enormous success during the 1980s and 1990s.

In 1986, Paulson campaigned the champion turf mare Estrapade, who is the only female to have won the Arlington Million. In 1987, Paulson had another national champion: Breeders' Cup Turf winner Theatrical. In 1989, Blushing John was voted champion older male; in 1991, Arazi won the Breeders' Cup Juvenile in his first American start and was voted champion 2-year-old colt.

The following year, Paulson's Eliza won the Breeders' Cup Juvenile Fillies and was voted 1992 champion 2-year-old filly, while in 1995 and 1996 he campaigned Horse of the Year Cigar, winner of 16 straight races including the 1995 Breeders' Cup Classic and the 1996 Dubai World Cup. In 1997 and 1998, Paulson won the Breeders' Cup Distaff with Ajina, voted champion 3-year-old filly, and then Escena, who was voted champion older filly or mare.

In both 1995 and 1996, Paulson was the Eclipse Award-winning owner, while in 1995 and 1997 he was leading money-winning owner.

After Allen Paulson died in 2000, his wife, Madeleine, and his son,

Michael, were unable to agree on many issues involving the stable and went their separate ways. The Allen E. Paulson Living Trust, managed by Michael, assumed control of the high-class filly Azeri, winner of 11 Grade 1 stakes, including the 2002 Breeders' Cup Distaff, the year she was voted Horse of the Year.

5. *Rokeby Stable*

Owned by philanthropist and art collector Paul Mellon, Rokeby Stable was a major force in racing from the early 1950s until Mellon decided to end his racing operations in 1995, at the age of 87, when his Hall of Fame trainer MacKenzie Miller announced his retirement.

Miller gave Rokeby its only Kentucky Derby winner, Sea Hero, in 1993, and also trained 1987 Travers winner Java Gold. But it was another Hall of Fame trainer—Elliott Burch—who was responsible for Rokeby's greatest success.

Burch, whose tenure lasted until the late 1970s, developed the Rokeby-bred 1964 Belmont and Travers Stakes winner, Quadrangle; the 1969 Horse of the Year and Belmont Stakes winner, Arts and Letters; 1967 and 1970 turf champion and Horse of the Year Fort Marcy; 1971 turf champion Run the Gantlet; and the 1972 champion 3-year-old, Key to the Mint, among many major stakes winners.

On the international front, Rokeby's Mill Reef was the 1971 winner of the Epsom Derby, trained by Ian Balding.

4. *Darby Dan Farm*

A once-powerful racing and breeding operation, Darby Dan Farm was started in 1935 by John W. Galbreath, who also owned the Pittsburgh Pirates baseball team from 1934 through 1985.

Galbreath, born in Derby, Ohio, in 1897, was a sportsman in the highest tradition of Thoroughbred horse owners until his death in 1988 when the stable won its last Eclipse Award with turf champion Sunshine Forever.

Galbreath actually acquired the farm from the estate of the legendary Colonel E. R. Bradley, who bred and raced four Kentucky Derby winners—Behave Yourself (1921), Bubbling Over (1926), Burgoo King (1932), and Brokers Tip (1933)—when the property was known as Idle

Hour Stock Farm. Following in that tradition, Galbreath bred and raced horses for stamina, horses who could compete in classic races. Galbreath was in fact the first person to breed and own winners of the Epsom Derby (Roberto, 1972) and the Kentucky Derby (Chateaugay, 1963), a feat that would be matched by Paul Mellon's Rokeby Stable.

Also in the modern era, Darby Dan bred and raced Primonetta, the 1962 champion filly or mare; the aforementioned Chateaugay, champion 3-year old colt of 1963, who also won the Belmont Stakes; Proud Clarion, who defeated Damascus in the 1967 Kentucky Derby; Roberto, who defeated the outstanding Brigadier Gerard in that memorable 1972 Epsom Derby; 3-year-old champion Little Current, winner of the 1974 Preakness and Belmont Stakes; 1978 champion 3-year-old filly Tempest Queen; and Proud Truth, upset winner of the 1985 Breeders' Cup Classic.

Darby Dan Farm continues to operate into the 21st century as a popular breeding and boarding facility on magnificent grounds in Lexington, Kentucky, standing a roster of promising young stallions that includes 2003 champion sprinter Aldebaran. The reduced racing operation, managed by Galbreath's grandson, John Phillips, and his mother, Joan Phillips (Phillips Racing Partnership), won an Eclipse Award with Soaring Softly, the top female turf performer in 1999, and campaigned 2004 Grade 1 winner Wonder Again.

3. *Claiborne Farm and the Hancock family*

Under the astute management of the legendary Arthur B. "Bull" Hancock Jr., Claiborne Farm was a breeding dynasty in the 1940s, 1950s, and 1960s. When Bull Hancock passed away in 1972, the executors of his estate turned things over to the younger of his two sons, Seth, who was just learning the family business.

First crack out of the box, the 23-year-old Seth arranged for a record $6 million syndication of Secretariat at the request of Penny Tweedy, and further managed the farm brilliantly through the next three decades while Claiborne continued to make a positive impact in high-class racing.

In the modern era, Claiborne raced 1965 champion 2-year-old filly and Horse of the Year Moccasin; 1984 Kentucky Derby-Belmont winner and 3-year-old champion Swale; 1987 juvenile champion Forty

Niner; 1992 and 1993 Breeders' Cup Mile winner Lure; plus several dozen other graded stakes performers.

Intertwined with the story of Claiborne Farm is that of Seth's older brother, Arthur Hancock III, who independently developed Stone Farm, a strong breeding and racing operation not far from Claiborne in Paris, Kentucky.

At Stone Farm, Arthur Hancock bred and raced 1982 Kentucky Derby winner Gato del Sol, and foaled and raced 1989 Kentucky Derby-Preakness-Breeders' Cup Classic winner and Horse of the Year Sunday Silence, who was sold for a princely sum to become the foundation stallion of the modern Japanese breeding industry. Arthur Hancock also bred 1988 Preakness-Belmont winner Risen Star and 2000 Kentucky Derby winner Fusaichi Pegasus, who sold for $4 million as a yearling in 1998.

Like the horses bred and raced by Bull Hancock, his two sons had it in their genes.

2. *Calumet Farm*

The most famous racing colors in history may be the devil's red and blue silks of Calumet Farm, the most prominent and most successful racing operation in America for more than three glorious decades, most of which occurred before the modern (television) age began in the early 1950s.

During the 1940s, when owned by Warren Wright, Calumet bred and raced two Triple Crown winners—Whirlaway in 1941 and Citation in 1948—plus a long list of champions and top-class racehorses in every division, all developed and trained by "the Jones Boys," Ben A. Jones and his son H. A. "Jimmy" Jones.

From the 1950s through the 1970s, when owned by Warren Wright's widow, Lucille Parker Wright (who married Eugene Markey in 1952), Calumet still was a prominent breeding and racing operation, winning the Kentucky Derby with Hill Gail (1952), Iron Liege (1957), Forward Pass (1968), and Tim Tam, who also won the Preakness (1958), and winning major stakes with the 3-year-old filly champions Our Mims in 1977 and Davona Dale in 1979.

Calumet, of course, also bred and raced Alydar, a six-time Grade 1 winner who became a leading sire after giving the great Affirmed all he could handle in the latter's 1978 Triple Crown sweep.

Following Mrs. Markey's death in 1982, Calumet had several good years under the management of J. T. Lundy, winning one last Horse of the year title in 1990 with Criminal Type, but Lundy overextended the farm's financials and led Calumet into bankruptcy following the suspicious death of Alydar in November 1990. The farm was acquired at auction in 1992 by Henryk de Kwiatkowski, a flamboyant owner-breeder who had raced the first and last of Woody Stephens's five straight Belmont Stakes winners—Conquistador Cielo (Horse of the Year in 1982) and Danzig Connection (1986)—as well as future sire of sires Danzig and many other top-class horses.

De Kwiatkowski pledged to save the property from dismemberment, and Calumet briefly was brought back into mainstream racing. But with de Kwiatkowski's passing in 2003, his heirs have concentrated on maintaining the property as a facility for boarding, breaking, and training, while consigning a modest number of yearlings at auction and maintaining the fabled farm as an immaculate shrine to the sport.

1. *The Phipps family*

Ogden Mills "Dinny" Phipps and his sister, Cynthia Phipps, are part of the living legacy that was begun by their grandmother, Gladys Mills Phipps, when she and her brother established Wheatley Stable in the 1930s—a legacy that grew and gained strength through their father, Ogden, as Phipps-owned horses became a dominating force during the 1950s and 1960s.

Wheatley bred and raced the great Bold Ruler, who not only was Horse of the Year in 1957, but also was one of the most prolific sires of top-quality horses in racing history. In fact, many of Bold Ruler's sons and daughters were Wheatley- and/or Phipps owned champion 2-year-olds during the 1960s. These included Bold Lad, Queen Empress, Successor, Queen of the Stage, and Vitriolic.

The best horse anyone in the family ever raced was probably Ogden Phipps's 1966 Horse of the Year, Buckpasser, a son of Tom Fool out of the Phipps mare Busanda, but the list of high-class runners also includes Reviewer, who was a multiple stakes winner in 1969, 1970, and 1971, and sired the great Ruffian; 1972 champion 2-year-old filly Numbered Account; the unbeaten Personal Ensign, champion older filly or mare in

1988; Easy Goer, champion 2-year-old colt in 1988 and winner of the 1989 Belmont and Travers Stakes; 1994 champion 3-year-old filly Heavenly Prize; and Breeders' Cup winners Dancing Spree (1989 Sprint) and My Flag (1995 Juvenile Fillies).

Mrs. Ogden Phipps, by the way, also was involved in the family stable, breeding and racing steeplechase champions Ancestor, in 1959; Top Bid, in 1970; and Straight and True, in 1976.

In the mid-1960s, Dinny Phipps began to race horses in his own name, and has had more than two dozen Grade 1 winners, including 1989 2-year-old champion Rhythm, winner of the Breeders' Cup Juvenile; Inside Information, winner of the 1995 Breeders' Cup Distaff and champion older filly or mare that year; 2002 champion 2-year-old filly Storm Flag Flying, winner of that year's Breeders' Cup Juvenile Fillies; 2005 champion 3-year-old filly Smuggler; and the 2005 Breeders' Cup Distaff winner, Pleasant Home.

Dinny's sister, Cynthia Phipps, also has continued in the family tradition, breeding and racing seven Grade 1 winners, including 1982 champion 3-year-old filly Christmas Past.

Like father, like mother, like son and daughter too.

HONORABLE MENTION

Below are 12 more highly successful stables, many of which ceased operations or enjoyed their best days a few decades ago. They are listed in alphabetical order with at least two of their best horses or greatest accomplishments. Several other dozen well-run stables could have made this list with similar accomplishments.

Dale Baird: A very big fish in the smallest of ponds, Dale Baird has compiled an amazing record while training and owning large numbers of low-priced claiming horses in West Virginia since the late 1960s. Still active through the summer of 2006, Baird was the national leading owner in races won 17 different years, including 11 in succession (1990–2000). As owner-trainer, Baird also led the national trainers' list for most victories 15 different years during the 1970s, 1980s, and 1990s, scoring at a win percentage between 20 and 30 percent in both categories. Baird never has had a horse to train for nationally important stakes, but is not really envious of those who have played on that high-profile stage.

"Sure, a Derby horse would be great," he said in a 1998 interview. "I think I could handle that. But, if it never happens, I know I'll be able to look back at my work and feel I did the most with what I got."

Dogwood Stable: Under the innovative management of W. Cothran "Cot" Campbell, Dogwood helped usher in the era of racing partnerships, as Campbell bought yearlings for $150,000 or less and sold shares to interested parties, retaining management of the racing operations. The formula was copied by dozens of other enterprising owners and opened up racehorse ownership to thousands of investors throughout the country.

Among Dogwood's best horses were 1990 Preakness winner Summer Squall; Grade 1-winning sprinter Trippi; Hopeful Stakes winner Wild Escapade; Super Derby winner Wallenda; and two Eclipse Award winners, 1987 steeplechase champion Inlander and 1996 2-year-old filly champion Storm Song.

Dubai ruling family: The Godolphin, Shadwell, and Darley stables are all part of the far-flung racing operations of Sheikh Mohammed bin Rashid al-Maktoum and his family. They are a worldwide presence, with increasing success in America, including 2006 Preakness-Travers-Jockey Club Gold Cup winner Bernardini, Belmont Stakes winner Jazil, and Pimlico Special-Whitney Stakes-Breeders' Cup Classic winner Invasor, among other Grade 1 winners. The immensely talented Discreet Cat appeared poised to join that group as of late 2006.

John Franks: Modeling his operation after the Marion H. Van Berg approach to large-volume, modest-quality horse ownership, Franks was five-time leading money-winning owner (1983, '84, '86, '93 and '94) and six-time leading owner in races won (1983, '84, '86, '87, '88, and '89). He also raced 1998 2-year-old champion and Breeders' Cup Juvenile winner Answer Lively.

Frances A. Genter Stable: Mrs. Genter, who passed away in 1992 at the age of 94, is best known as the owner of 1990 Kentucky Derby-

Breeders' Cup Classic winner Unbridled. She also raced 1959 champion 2-year-old filly My Dear Girl; 1986 sprint champion Smile; and Rough'n Tumble, the sire of 1968 Horse of the Year Dr. Fager.

Hobeau Farm: In 1962, Beau Purple upset the mighty Kelso twice, and then did it once more in the Widener Handicap at Hialeah the following winter. A decade later, Hobeau Farm's Onion and Prove Out both upset Triple Crown winner Secretariat in the 1973 Whitney and the Woodward Stakes, respectively. Prove Out also defeated 1973 champion older male Riva Ridge in that year's Jockey Club Gold Cup. Beyond those historic upsets—orchestrated by Hall of Fame trainer Allen Jerkens—Hobeau has bred and raced dozens of stakes winners in New York and was the nation's leading money-winning owner in 1967.

Ethel Jacobs, daughter Patrice Jacobs and Louis Wolfson's Harbor View Farm: During the modern era, Ethel and Patrice Jacobs bred and raced 1960 juvenile champion Hail to Reason, while Ethel, wife of the late Hall of Fame trainer Hirsch Jacobs, bred and raced 1965 sprint champion Affectionately and 1970 Preakness winner and 3-year-old champion Personality. In 1964, Patrice Jacobs married Louis Wolfson, owner of Harbor View Farm, who had bred and raced Raise a Native. Together, under the Harbor View Farm banner, Jacobs and Wolfson raced the 1965 Horse of the Year, Roman Brother, and bred and raced 1978 Triple Crown winner Affirmed. Harbor View was leading owner in money won in 1977, '78, and '80 and voted the nation's top breeder in 1978. Through 2006, Harbor View remains a prominent breeding and racing operation based in Florida.

Eugene V. Klein: A former owner of the San Diego Chargers football team, Klein got into Thoroughbred racing in the early 1980s, hiring D. Wayne Lukas as his trainer. Among his best runners were 1984 champion 3-year-old filly Life's Magic; 1985 juvenile filly champion Family Style; 1985 Preakness Stakes winner Tank's Prospect; 1986 champion older filly and Horse of the Year Lady's Secret; Open Mind, a champion at 2 and 3 in 1988 and '89; and 1988 Kentucky Derby winner and 3-year-old filly champion Winning Colors.

Dan Lasater: Took the Van Berg model of large-volume, multitrack ownership to another level, winning more races in 1973, '74, '75, and '76, while also winning more money than any other owner in 1974, '75, '76, and '77. Was the Eclipse Award-winning owner in '75, '76, and '77 while not owning a single national champion.

Meadow Stable: The racing operation of owner-breeder Christopher Chenery, who was succeeded by his daughter, Penny Tweedy. Meadow Stable's best horses include 1958 juvenile champion First Landing; 1961 champion juvenile filly Cicada, who also was the 1962 champion 3-year-old filly; 1971 champion 2-year-old and 1973 champion older horse Riva Ridge; and 1973 Triple Crown winner and two-time Horse of the Year Secretariat.

Overbrook Farm: Things really took off for owner-breeder W. T. Young when he hooked up with trainer D. Wayne Lukas in the 1980s. Their most successful horses included 1994 Breeders' Cup Juvenile Fillies winner and 2-year-old champion Flanders; 1994 Breeders' Cup Juvenile winner and champion Timber Country, who also won the 1995 Preakness; 1995 juvenile filly champion Golden Attraction; 1996 Breeders' Cup Juvenile winner and 2-year-old champion Boston Harbor; 1996 Kentucky Derby winner Grindstone; 1996 Belmont Stakes winner Editor's Note; and 2000 champion 3-year-old filly Surfside.

Young also bred and raced Storm Cat, runner-up in the 1985 Breeders' Cup Juvenile, who went on to become the world's hottest sire. Young died in 2004, and Overbrook is now under the leadership of his son, Bill Young Jr., and grandson, Chris Young.

Tartan Stable: Tartan Farm was started by William McKnight, chairman of the 3M corporation, and continued under his son-in-law, James Binger, until the late 1980s. Under the astute management of Hall of Fame trainer John Nerud, Tartan bred and raced some of the best horses in history, most notably 1959 sprint champion Intentionally; 1968 Horse of the Year Dr. Fager; and 1969 and '70 sprint champion Ta Wee. Tartan also bred 1980 Preakness winner Codex and 1990 Kentucky Derby-Breeders' Cup Classic winner Unbridled, who was sold at auction as a weanling when the majority of Tartan's horses were dispersed in 1987.

129

5

CHAMPIONS:

The Best of the Best in Every Division

NO MATTER WHICH horses you or I select as the best of the past 50-odd years, this much is going to be true: We are all going to overrate some and miss a few completely, *all of us*, for two reasons that rarely get serious play when anyone attempts to put together a Top 10 or Top 50 list—in any sport.

* All top athletes excel in one or a few special skills, but no athlete is the best in all things.
* Performances are extremely difficult to compare under different rules and different playing conditions, much less in different eras, given the changes in training techniques, facility maintenance, nutrition, and use of drugs, both legal and illegal.

How do we compare the mid-20th-century boxing champion Joe Louis to the 1970s' Muhammad Ali, or four-time middleweight champion Sugar Ray Robinson to either one?

Is it fair to say that 1980s quarterback Joe Montana was a better football player than 1950s running back Jim Brown? Playing two different positions with different responsibilities in different eras certainly complicates things. Similarly, who can really say where Montana and/or Brown rank against defensive linebacker Lawrence Taylor of the 1990s?

Regarding horses, how do we know if Man o' War was faster than Secretariat? Would it be any surprise if one was superior at one distance and the other better at another? Do we really know how fast horses actually were in eras that preceded the use of precise speed figures, which factor in the relative speed of racing surfaces?

Basic intellectual honesty commands that we make our lists with a wink or two and supplement them with additional lists that pertain to the differences between the sexes, between 2-year-olds and older horses, and between horses who did their best racing on turf rather than dirt and/or over different distances.

Beyond researching hundreds of past-performance records and various historical accomplishments, I do have one advantage over most who would venture an opinion. I was lucky to see the majority of the best horses in person.

Identifying the nation's best sprinters, 2-year-olds, fillies, turf horses, and long-distance runners has been part of my thinking since the early 1960s. As a budding handicapper, I realized that familiarity with the pecking order in each division helped identify important drops in class in various maiden races, allowance races, and stakes. In the 21st century, when the game is played across regional barriers via simulcasting and phone-betting accounts, such knowledge is even more productive. As for assessing qualitative differences between eras, part of this game is just plain good fun.

SPRINTERS

Among almost two dozen winners of the Breeders' Cup Sprint and about three dozen other very fast horses who made positive impressions through the years, the weakest, or slowest, national sprint champion probably was Cardmania, winner of the 1993 Breeders' Cup Sprint on his home track, Santa Anita.

A European import with 42 productive starts on the turf in France, Cardmania came into the 1993 Sprint with only one victory from his last 15 North American races. That lone victory was in the Ancient

Title Handicap at Santa Anita three weeks earlier, so Cardmania certainly was in career form the day the '93 Sprint was run. Yet, the slow-breaking 7-year-old gelding still needed a severe pace meltdown to get the job done, as the first quarter-mile was clocked in a sizzling 21 seconds flat, and the half-mile in a scorching 43 $^4/_5$.

This brutal pace sapped the reserve energy from the game front-running filly Meafara and the pace-pressing Gilded Time, winner of the 1992 Breeders' Cup Juvenile, who turned in a remarkable performance in his first start in 12 months.

Apparently this victory by Cardmania was sufficient to earn the 1993 Eclipse Award, but he could not repeat the triumph in 1994 and 1995, winning only one race from his last 10 starts through his 9-year-old season. A durable, very willing horse; but probably the slowest sprint champion of modern times.

Below are the 10 sprint champions that I believe were better horses than all the other top sprinters of the past 50-odd years—the modern era of sports, the era that inaugurated national television coverage of major sporting attractions, including Thoroughbred racing. Missing from the list are some who may have run just as fast, or even faster—horses such as 1987 champion sprinter Groovy, who lost the '87 Breeders' Cup Sprint, and Phone Trick, who was never a champion but was a very fast horse. Another who just missed the list was 1959 sprint champion Intentionally. Each of the horses on my list possessed a rare combination of speed, weight-carrying ability, and heart. Some were even stronger at longer distances.

10. *Orientate*

He was ineffective as a middle-distance stakes horse, but once trainer D. Wayne Lukas decided to accent his sprint form, Orientate was a powerful performer. He won his last five career starts at six and 6 ½ furlongs, posting consecutive Beyer Speed Figures of 115, 115, 112, and 116, then closed out his career with a 114 Beyer while winning the 2002 Breeders' Cup Sprint at Arlington Park to clinch an Eclipse Award. Among the top sprinters Orientate defeated in that final race were Aldebaran, champion sprinter of 2003; Swept Overboard, winner of the 2002 Met Mile with a 122 Beyer; and Xtra Heat, the champion 3-year-old filly of 2001, who finished second in the 2001 Breeders' Cup Sprint and was a sprint specialist who almost made this list

9. *Gulch*

LeRoy Jolley developed and managed this son of Mr. Prospector until he was turned over to D. Wayne Lukas for his 4-year-old campaign in 1988. His debut for Jolley as a 2-year-old on June 2, 1986, at Belmont Park was one of the most impressive five-furlong races I have ever seen. Loping along in fifth through the first three furlongs, Gulch accelerated powerfully approaching the eighth pole to win by 7 3/4 lengths with jockey Jerry Bailey attempting to gear him down near the wire. Even so, Gulch's last furlong was clocked in an excellent 11 2/5 seconds. By the time he reached the next furlong past the finish line, Gulch was 20 lengths in front of the closest horse to him. From that moment through the rest of his career, Gulch was a horse I followed closely.

At six to seven furlongs, Gulch won 8 of 11 attempts, including the 1988 Breeders' Cup Sprint on a sloppy track at Churchill Downs in his final career start for Lukas, defeating, among others, 1985 Sprint winner Precisionist and 1987 Sprint winner Very Subtle. Gulch also was able to carry his form well beyond sprint distances, winning the 1 1/8-mile Wood Memorial for Jolley at 3 and back-to-back runnings of the prestigious Metropolitan Mile Handicap at 3 and 4, first for Jolley, then for Lukas in 1988, Gulch's championship season.

Amazingly, Gulch also finished third to Bet Twice in the 1987 Belmont Stakes at 1 1/2 miles and was in the money eight times while going 1 1/16 miles or longer. He retired with $3 million in career earnings and was out of the money only six times in 32 career races, three of them at 1 1/4 miles.

8. *Housebuster*

The Eclipse Award-winning sprinter of 1990 and 1991, Housebuster was a terror at seven furlongs, winning six of his nine attempts at that distance, and he was even better at six furlongs, winning four of his five attempts before he unfortunately went lame as the 2–5 betting favorite in the 1991

Breeders' Cup Sprint, his final career start. While Housebuster won 15 of his 22 career starts, his Beyer Speed Figures generally ranged from 113 to 118, the latter figure earned when he defeated the high-class sprinting filly Safely Kept in the $300,000 Frank J. DeFrancis Memorial Dash Stakes at Laurel in 1991.

7. *Safely Kept*

This well-traveled miss won 20 of her 24 attempts at six furlongs at nine different tracks and also won the seven-furlong Test at Saratoga as a 3-year-old and the Budweiser Breeders' Cup at that distance at Arlington Park when she was 5. Three of her losses at six furlongs were against males, as she finished fourth twice and second to Dancing Spree in the 1989 Breeders' Cup Sprint at Gulfstream Park. Her other Breeders' Cup Sprint appearance, in 1990, resulted in a bizarre victory when the British invader Dayjur jumped a shadow nearing the finish line, seconds after he had taken the lead away. Dayjur was champion sprinter in Europe and might have made this list had we seen more of him.

6. *Decathlon*

Champion sprinter at 3 and 4 years old in 1956 and '57, the son of Olympia out of a Bull Dog mare was quintessentially bred for high speed and lost the only two times he tried to go longer than seven furlongs. Decathlon won 25 of his 42 sprints, including 17 of 25, with six seconds, during his two-year reign as national sprint champion. I saw him only on film—in the Library Room at Monmouth Park, where he impressively won four of six races and set track records for five and six furlongs that lasted more than a decade. Interestingly, this strong-bodied horse seemed to reach out for more ground by using a circular, natural swinging motion with his leading front leg, virtually the same unusual stride that Seattle Slew would employ two decades later. Decathlon was quite a horse, a bulldog.

5. *Artax*

He was force-fed into the 1998 Triple Crown mix as a 3-year-old with moderate success in Southern California prep races, but tired badly in the Kentucky Derby and did not win another race until he clicked in the seven-furlong Vosburgh one year to the day later while earning a sky-high 123 Beyer Speed Figure. Artax was kept sprinting thereafter and put it all together in his final three career starts in 1999, repeating his score in the '98 Vosburgh and winning two more stakes with 123 and 124 Beyer figures, among the fastest of the modern age. He won the 1999 Breeders' Cup Sprint over hard-charging Kona Gold, who would win that race the next year.

4. *Ruffian*

Undefeated in 10 career starts until her tragic breakdown in the match race with Foolish Pleasure in July 1975. As a precocious 2-year-old in 1974, Ruffian won her first seven starts at 5 ½ to seven furlongs, and indisputably was one of the fastest 3-year-olds in racing history. Even so, she was able to project her talent far beyond the usual sprint distances, winning the one-mile Acorn, the 1 ⅛-mile Mother Goose, and the 1 ½-mile Coaching Club American Oaks in 1975 to complete the New York version of a Triple Crown for fillies. Few horses of any age or sex were as fast as she was at any distance, even as a 2-year-old.

3. *Kona Gold*

This California-based gelding raced at the highest levels for six seasons. He finished third in the 1998 Breeders' Cup Sprint and second in 1999 before winning the 2000 Sprint, then finished an unlucky fourth in the same $1 million race in 2001. Kona Gold was a consistent, highly tenacious battler who won 14 races with seven seconds from 30 career tries, all at 5 ½ to seven furlongs, earning $2.2 million. As a testament to his high class and consistency, Kona Gold carried top weight in most of his engagements while scoring Beyer Speed Figures of 112 to 123 in 16 different races from 1998 through 2002.

2. *Ta Wee*

This remarkable filly was sprint champion in 1969 and 1970, winning 15 of her 20 sprint races, including back-to-back runnings of the Fall

Highweight Handicap against older males in 1969 while carrying top weight of 130 pounds and then 140 pounds in the same race in 1970. At the time, there were no $100,000 sprint races in America, and the Fall Highweight was one of the two most prestigious sprint stakes on the East Coast. The other was the $58,000 Vosburgh Handicap—the richest sprint stakes in the country—which Ta Wee also won as a 3-year-old while carrying top weight of 123 going seven furlongs against 10 older males.

Developed and trained by John Nerud through her first 10 starts and trained by Flint "Scotty" Schulhofer thereafter, Ta Wee was not a one-dimensional speedball—she won most of her races from slightly off the pace with final quarter-miles regularly clocked in 24 seconds, or faster. At six furlongs, she was 10 for 11, finishing second to the high-class 4-year-old male Distinctive while carrying 134 pounds, spotting the winner 20 pounds. In her final career start, Ta Wee successfully carried an unbelievable 142 pounds in the Interborough Handicap, spotting her female rivals as much as 30 pounds!

While some would argue that others might have been the fastest sprinter of modern times, at six furlongs my money would have been on Ta Wee against any other horse, in any era, male or female.

1. *Dr. Fager*

One of the few horses who truly fits among the best horses in several categories, winning major stakes from seven furlongs to $1\frac{1}{4}$ miles, on dirt and turf, Dr. Fager was named champion sprinter in 1967 and '68 and also was voted 1968 Horse of the Year for his thorough dominance of the handicap division.

As a sprinter, Dr. Fager won all six of his career races from $5\frac{1}{2}$ furlongs to seven furlongs, including his amazing career finale, when he carried 139 pounds to a six-length victory in the 1968 Vosburgh Handicap at seven furlongs while setting a track record that stood until Artax broke it 31 years later in 1999.

At one mile, Dr. Fager was 5 for 6, including a world record of $1:32\frac{1}{5}$ at Arlington Park, a clocking that never has been surpassed on dirt. At $6\frac{1}{2}$ furlongs to one mile, I would have taken Dr. Fager against any other horse in this category. At $6\frac{1}{16}$ furlongs, a race that never could have been run, I would have given Dr. Fager a split-hair's edge over Ta Wee, and that is the only reason he is listed first.

2-YEAR-OLD MALES

Although Favorite Trick was voted 1997 Horse of the Year after winning the Breeders' Cup Juvenile to complete a notable undefeated 2-year-old season for trainer Patrick Byrne, I thought the voting was way off. Favorite Trick, who died in a tragic New Mexico fire in 2006, certainly was a good youngster, but the 2-year-olds competing in 1997 were way below the usual standards. In my judgment, this was the poorest Horse of the Year choice since the Eclipse Awards were created in 1971. Preference should have been given to either Kentucky Derby-Preakness winner Silver Charm, or Breeders' Cup Classic winner Skip Away. Moreover, on my own personal list of top 2-year-old male horses of the past half-century, I can name two dozen champions and near champions who ran faster than Favorite Trick and were more impressive on numerous occasions.

These include WARFARE, a Western-based 2-year-old winner who shipped east to win the Cowdin, Champagne, and Garden State Stakes in 1959; NEVER BEND and NORTHERN DANCER, who dominated 2-year-old races in 1963; RIVA RIDGE, who dominated the top 2-year-old stakes of 1971; BOLD FORBES, who won all seven of his starts in 1975 as a 2-year-old, including two very fast wins in New York stakes; AFFIRMED and ALYDAR, whose rivalry began in 1977, with both horses winning important stakes over each other; and SPECTAC-ULAR BID, who developed slowly at 2 in 1978, but closed out his juvenile campaign with five straight wins in fast clockings. All three—Affirmed, Alydar, and Spectacular Bid—were much better than Favorite Trick and easily could be included in a rational list of Top 10 juveniles (and certainly developed into all-time greats as they matured). In addition, ROVING BOY also was a stronger juvenile champion, having won his last five starts in 1982 at one mile or more, including three straight graded stakes over the high-class Desert Wine.

The same is true of CHIEF'S CROWN, winner of the 1984 Saratoga Special, the Hopeful, and three other Grade 1 stakes that year, including the first Breeders' Cup Juvenile at Hollywood Park, in which he defeated future Triple Crown race winners Tank's Prospect and Spend a Buck. ARAZI, a European import who made a strong visual impression while rallying from back in the pack to win the 1991 Breeders' Cup Juvenile, also seemed faster than Favorite Trick; so did TIMBER COUNTRY, an impressive stretch-running winner of the 1994 Champagne Stakes and Breeders' Cup Juvenile; likewise VINDICATION, unbeaten in his four career starts including the 2002 Juvenile at 1 ⅛ miles before he was forced to retire due to injury in 2003; and DECLAN'S MOON, unbeaten in his four races as a 2-year-old in 2004, including a victory in the Hollywood Futurity over future Kentucky Derby winner Giacomo.

My Top 10 appear below.

10. *Johannesburg*

He only raced once in America, but what a race it was. Unbeaten in six races on grass in Europe, Johannesburg never had been on dirt, never raced beyond six furlongs, but rallied strongly between horses to win the 2001 Breeders' Cup Juvenile at Belmont over a deep field of high-class youngsters that included Repent, Siphonic, and Officer, all of whom had, or would have, productive careers.

Said Officer's trainer, Bob Baffert, "To come over here and beat a very good group of our top-class 2-year-olds in such style was amazing and you didn't need to see anything else to know this was a tremendous young horse."

As a footnote to this performance, there have been two other Europeans who have come to America to win the Breeders' Cup Juvenile: Arazi made an eye-catching move on the far turn to pull away and win easily in 1991, and in 2004, Wilko took advantage of an exceedingly hot pace while Afleet Alex, the future 2005 Preakness and Belmont Stakes winner, could not overcome a difficult trip and finished third. In my judgment, neither Arazi nor Wilko was as strong or as fast as Johannesburg.

9. *First Landing*

He would sire 1972 Kentucky Derby-Belmont Stakes winner Riva Ridge and was himself the favorite to win the 1959 Derby and Preakness, but did not win either race and was a much better 2-year-old in 1958. First Landing won nine of his 11 juvenile starts, including the Hopeful, the Champagne, and the $297,000 Garden State Stakes, the second-richest race in America that year, defeating the future 1959 Derby winner, Tomy Lee, and Sword Dancer, the '59 Horse of the Year. Few racing fans of today have any idea how good he was. Fact is, I had no idea until I studied his past performances closely and watched his Garden State Stakes victory on film.

8. *Foolish Pleasure*

Better known for winning the 1975 Kentucky Derby and for his empty victory over Ruffian in their 1975 match race, this son of the top-class sprinter What a Pleasure was brilliantly managed by LeRoy Jolley as he went unbeaten in seven starts as a 2-year-old in 1974, winning six graded stakes, including the Grade 1 Sapling, Hopeful, and Champagne, all clocked in fast time. Foolish Pleasure had great tactical speed and a good, smooth finish. Probably the most underrated 2-year-old in my lifetime.

7. *Devil's Bag*

This son of Halo was undefeated in five starts as a 2-year-old in 1983, and trainer Woody Stephens was so excited that he prematurely called him the best horse he had ever trained. Devil's Bag won the seven-furlong Cowdin by three lengths in 1:21 $^2/_5$, the one-mile Champagne by six in 1:34 $^1/_5$ and the 1 $^1/_{16}$-mile Laurel Futurity by 5 $^1/_4$ lengths in 1:42 $^1/_5$, the fastest clocking in that race since Spectacular Bid posted a time of 1:41 $^3/_5$ in 1978.

While Devil's Bag did win three of his four starts as a 3-year-old, he did not improve on his 2-year-old form and was retired two days after the 1984 Kentucky Derby, which he had skipped. (Stephens won that Derby anyway with Swale.) X-rays had revealed a knee chip, but the premature retirement of Devil's Bag, which was viewed as a tactic to protect his stud value, disappointed many who were expecting this colt to do wondrous things as a mature horse. Some still would rank Devil's Bag much higher than this among the 2-year-olds of the modern era.

6. *Hoist the Flag*

Would have been undefeated in six career starts had he not been disqualified from a three-length score in the 1970 Champagne Stakes at Belmont after crossing in front of a tiring rival in a 16-horse field. We never had the chance to see what kind of 3-year-old he would develop into after his career-ending ankle injury following the Bay Shore Stakes as a young 3-year-old, an injury similar to the one suffered by Kentucky Derby winner Barbaro in the 2006 Preakness.

As a 2-year-old, Hoist the Flag was awesome, finishing first in all four of his juvenile starts in fast clockings while jockey Jean Cruguet kept him under wraps. Won the seven-furlong Cowdin Stakes in 1:22 $^2/_5$ over a solid field with a last-to-first move, and despite his DQ, was much the best in the Champagne Stakes, clocked in 1:35 $^2/_5$ on a relatively dead track. Fortunately, Hoist the Flag survived his severe ankle injury to become a successful sire.

5. *Seattle Slew*

Raced only three times as a 2-year-old, but was devastating in all three, winning a six-furlong maiden race by five lengths under a hard pull by jockey Jean Cruguet, who, as noted above, also rode Hoist the Flag in 1970. Also won a seven-furlong allowance race under no urging at all in 1:22 flat and completed his brief but spectacular 2-year-old campaign by winning the one-mile, Grade 1 Champagne by 9 $^3/_4$ lengths in 1:34 $^2/_5$ as Cruguet admired the infield scenery. At 3 and 4, Seattle Slew would become a horse for the ages.

4. *Native Dancer*

Unbeaten in nine starts as a 2-year-old, including a track-record-equaling performance in the 1952 Belmont Futurity. While my first racing experience was Native Dancer's only career defeat—the 1953 Kentucky Derby (see Chapter 1)—I did see films of three of his 2-year-old races, including his Hopeful score, in which he broke first, dropped back to last, and rallied around the field with consummate ease. In fact, all of Native Dancer's victories—including a pair of five-furlong races at the start of his career—were stretch-running efforts. He is another horse who seems underrated by modern racing enthusiasts who know his name but not his accomplishments.

3. *Bold Lad*

One of several Phipps family 2-year-old champions trained by Eddie Neloy during the 1960s. By Bold Ruler out of a Princequillo mare (a breeding nick that would be employed to produce Secretariat in 1970), Bold Lad won 8 of 10 starts as a 2-year-old in 1964, including four important stakes: the Sapling at Monmouth, the Hopeful at Saratoga in track-record time, and the Futurity and Champagne Stakes at Aqueduct (while Belmont was being rebuilt).

With breeding that suggested he would be a force on the Triple Crown chase, Bold Lad was injured in the 1965 Kentucky Derby and did not race again until his 4-year-old season in 1966, when he won 4 of 5 starts, including the Met Mile under top weight of 132 pounds.

2. *Buckpasser*

One of the top horses of modern times, Buckpasser was a sensational 2-year-old, winning 9 of 11 outings, including the Sapling at Monmouth, the Hopeful at Saratoga, and the $335,000 Arlington Washington Futurity—the richest race in America at the time. Two weeks later, Buckpasser was narrowly upset in the Futurity at Aqueduct by the high-class juvenile filly Priceless Gem, but came back three weeks later to score a decisive victory in the Champagne Stakes to earn his first of three seasonal championships.

1. *Secretariat*

Lost his first race by 1 ¼ lengths after a poor start and severe traffic problems, then reeled off eight straight mind-numbing performances in 1972 to foreshadow what he would do in 1973 as a 3-year-old.

Was handed a defeat in the Champagne Stakes by the Belmont stewards for crossing in front of the useful Stop the Music. But other than that miscue, Secretariat was a fluid-moving, very fast, dominating performer, who would get better with age. All of his races were exciting and interesting to watch. For example, in the Hopeful Stakes at Saratoga, Secretariat was in last place for the first four furlongs of the 6 ½-furlong race, but circled all eight rivals on the final turn with no special urging by jockey Ron Turcotte to enter the stretch in complete control of the contest. Among the reasons that I believe Secretariat was the best 2-year-old of the modern age is the fact that he not only toyed with a good crop of 2-year-olds, he ran faster than older horses at the same distance on the same day, more than once.

2-YEAR-OLD FILLIES

The problem with evaluating many of the best 2-year-old fillies of the modern age is the lack of a true championship race until the Breeders' Cup came along in 1984. Where the juvenile colts had five truly important stakes—the Hopeful at Saratoga, Arlington-Washington Futurity at Arlington Park, the Garden State Stakes, Champagne at Belmont, and the Laurel Futurity—2-year-old fillies did not get the same acclaim for winning the Spinaway at Saratoga and/or the Arlington-Washington Lassie, the Frizette at Belmont, the Selima at Laurel, and/or the Gardenia at Garden State Park. Of those races, the Gardenia was perhaps the best and most important, because it not only was the richest, it regularly attracted top-quality juvenile fillies from every region in the country.

As for the least impressive juvenile filly champion, I had no trouble settling on Regal Gleam in 1966. She did win the Frizette (run at Aqueduct that year) and the Selima, but she was trounced in the Spinaway, trounced in the Gardenia, trounced in the Colleen at Monmouth, and trounced in the Polly Drummond at Delaware Park to give her one of the least convincing records for a divisional champion. When Regal Gleam was good—and that did not happen often—she was good enough to win two important stakes. More often she was nowhere near good, losing 8 of her 13 starts, finishing sixth or worse six times. As a 3-year-old in 1967, it was more of the same as Regal Gleam lost her next 12 races.

Here are my top 10 Juvenile Fillies.

10. *Halfbridled*

This daughter of 1990 Kentucky Derby-Breeders' Cup Classic winner Unbridled was unbeaten in her four starts as a 2-year-old in 2003, but her career was aborted after two losing races and assorted minor injuries as a 3-year-old in April 2004. As a juvenile, though, Halfbridled made a most positive impression with powerful finishes under Hall of Fame jockey Julie Krone. In her maiden victory at 5 ½ furlongs at Del Mar, Halfbridled was last at the top of the stretch and a 4 ½-length winner at the wire, getting her last sixteenth of a mile in a shade under six seconds. In her second career start, the Grade 1 Del Mar Debutante at seven furlongs, Halfbridled won by five lengths over Hollywood Story and the unbeaten 3–5 shot Victory U.S.A, despite overcoming tight quarters while making an initial bid on the far turn.

After winning the Oak Leaf at 1 ¹⁄₁₆ miles, Halfbridled overcame a very wide trip from post 14 in the 14-horse Breeders' Cup Juvenile Fillies to rally from seventh for a convincing 2 ½-length victory over future two-time champion Ashado in 1:42.75, almost a full second faster than Breeders' Cup Juvenile winner Action This Day would run later on the card.

9. *La Prevoyante*

The Canadian-based daughter of Buckpasser was unbeaten in 12 starts at seven different tracks in 1972, the same year Secretariat was being discovered. Did not run nearly as fast as that champion colt, but she did win three stakes in Canada; the Schuylerville and Spinaway at Saratoga; the Matron and Frizette at Belmont; the Selima at Laurel; and the Gardenia at Garden State Park to complete a tour of the era's most important juvenile-filly stakes without a close call.

La Prevoyante also might have been the most versatile 2-year-old champion of modern times. She won on fast tracks, slow tracks, sloppy and drying-out "good" tracks; she won at 5 ½ furlongs on the dirt and turf and she won at distances from six furlongs to 1 ¹/₁₆ miles. Although she was a good filly for the rest of her career, winning 13 races from her final 27 starts, she had no graded stakes victories and never developed into an immortal, while being favored in all but two of her 39 career starts.

8. *Silverbulletday*

This popular Bob Baffert-trained miss improved steadily throughout an excellent 2-year-old season in 1998 and well into her 3-year-old campaign as well.

She won her career debut by 11 lengths in a 5 ½-furlong maiden race at Churchill Downs one month after Baffert's Real Quiet won the 1998 Kentucky Derby, then came back 14 days later to post a victory in the Debutante Stakes over the same track and distance. Mike Pegram, Baffert's longtime friend and original Thoroughbred sponsor, was ecstatic. Pegram owned both Real Quiet and Siverbulletday. From there, Silverbulletday shipped thousands of miles, winning the Sorrento Stakes at Del Mar, the Alcibiades at Keeneland, and the Breeders' Cup Juvenile Fillies at Churchill Downs by a half-length over her talented stablemate Excellent Meeting, a multiple stakes winner in her own right.

Silverbulletday completed this ambitious 2-year-old campaign by winning the Golden Rod at Churchill by 10 lengths with a 104 Beyer Speed Figure, the second-best Beyer for any 2-year-old filly at one mile or longer since 1992.

7. *Flanders*

Had almost the same performance record as the 1970 juvenile champion colt, Hoist the Flag, in that she would have completed an unbeaten season in 1994 were it not for a disqualification in an important stakes at Belmont when she was much the best. As with Hoist the Flag, Flanders never had a chance to deliver on the promise she showed at 2. Her career ended when she pulled up lame after winning a breathtaking wire-to-wire duel with her D. Wayne Lukas-trained stablemate Serena's Song in the 1994 Breeders' Cup Juvenile Fillies.

In her brief five-race career, Flanders won a five-furlong maiden race and immediately jumped into the 1994 Spinaway, which was now being run at seven furlongs, and won with speed to spare. Next she won the Matron at one mile in 1:35 flat, with a 101 Beyer Speed Figure.

Flanders then turned in one of the most dominating victories of the modern era by winning the Frizette by 21 lengths with a Beyer of 102, while jockey Pat Day was easing her up in the final sixteenth. But of course, Flanders topped that in many ways with her amazingly courageous win by a head over Serena's Song in aforementioned Breeders' Cup. (Serena's Song would develop into the 3-year-old champion filly of 1995.) Just as Hoist the Flag was saved for stud duty, so was Flanders saved to be a productive mare, giving birth to Surfside, champion 3-year-old filly of 2000, also trained by Lukas.

6. *Cicada*

This outstanding filly was a superstar from the moment she began her career by winning three-furlong races at Hialeah in 1961. The winner of three straight national championships—as top 2-year-old filly in 1961, top 3-year-old filly in 1962, and top handicap mare in 1963— Cicada was right there with Tosmah as one of the best fillies I saw in the 1960s.

From the same Meadow Stable that produced First Landing, Riva Ridge, Secretariat, and the ill-fated but outstanding Sir Gaylord, Cicada won her races from off the pace or on the lead, as the situation commanded. The first time I saw her in person, she moved from fifth to first on the first turn en route to 10-length score in the 1 1/16-mile Gardenia Stakes on a sloppy track that was a front-runner's paradise. This impressive victory completed a run of six straight stakes victories at four different tracks in 11 weeks, including the Spinaway at Saratoga and the Frizette at Belmont. At 2, Cicada never was worse than third in 16 starts, including 11 victories, two seconds and three thirds.

5. *Sweet Catomine*

As in the case of several of the best 2-year-old fillies of the modern era, this daughter of Storm Cat had a brief career that included only four starts at 2 and a pair of races at 3. Unlike most 2-year-olds, Sweet Catomine was not a speed horse, not a front-runner. She was instead a powerful finisher who telegraphed her style when she closed relentlessly from back in the pack after missing the break from the gate to win the Del Mar Debutante at seven furlongs while still a maiden in her second career start.

In her next engagement, the 1 1/16-mile Oak Leaf, Sweet Catomine was resting comfortably in sixth position, about six lengths back at the top of the stretch, when Corey Nakatani pointed her to the outside for a clear run and felt her surge to a four-length victory over highly regarded Splendid Blended, who would become a multiple Grade 1 winner in her own right. Next stop was Lone Star Park for one of the best performances in the history of the Breeders' Cup Juvenile Fillies.

Breaking slowly and blocked three times during the first seven furlongs, Sweet Catomine unleashed a furious rally to not only win the race, but also score by 3 1/2 widening lengths, posting a 102 Beyer Speed Figure for her magnificent effort. Frankly, I doubt many horses on this list could have defeated her in this race, which is why she is in this spot on my Top 10 roster.

4. *Numbered Account*

This Roger Laurin-trained daughter of Buckpasser (who also sired 1972 juvenile filly champion La Prevoyante) was a sensational 2-year-old filly for Ogden Phipps in 1971, winning 8 of her 10 starts in fast clockings by decisive margins while rarely pressed for her best.

Among her string of stakes wins, Numbered Account won the Schuylerville and the Spinaway at Saratoga; the Frizette and Matron at Belmont; and the Selima and Gardenia, all in a seven-week onslaught, and came back one week later to finish a gallant fourth to the eventual 1972 Kentucky Derby-Belmont Stakes winner, Riva Ridge, in the Garden State Stakes. Until Ruffian came along in 1974, I did not think there could be a better 2-year-old filly, and in the years since, very few approached her talent.

3. *Meadow Star*

Unbeaten as a 2-year-old in seven starts in 1990 for trainer LeRoy Jolley, this daughter of freakishly fast Meadowlake had the same basic unbeaten record and running style as Jolley's 1974 juvenile champion colt, Foolish Pleasure. Both Foolish Pleasure and Meadow Star were 7 for 7; both were midpack runners who employed very good finishing kicks to win going away.

Meadow Star won at five furlongs, 5 ½, six furlongs twice, seven furlongs, a mile, and 1 1/16 miles in a beautifully managed progression that LeRoy Jolley learned while a teenage apprentice trainer to his father, Moody Jolley. In 1961, both father and son co-trained the sharp 2-year-old Ridan, who defeated the eventual 1961 champion 2-year-old, Crimson Satan, twice in succession that year.

LeRoy Jolley, a most difficult man to get close to at times, is a cerebral horseman who always seems in deep, don't-come-near-me concentration, whether he is or not. I can laugh about it now, but he did get the best of a young reporter at Churchill Downs in 1976, when he was training the heavily favored Honest Pleasure for the Kentucky Derby.

Jolley brushed off dozens of requests for interviews and answered every reporter with short, cryptic yes or no answers, barely looking up from the ground when he spoke except when he chose to give you a searing glare. But one morning after he spent more than five minutes pointing things out on the training track to anyone who would listen, I figured I could get what I needed from him.

"LeRoy, I'd like to ask you a question about Honest Pleasure."

To my surprise, Jolley stopped and said, "Yes, what do you want to know?"

"How do you compare his physical condition to the way Foolish Pleasure was a week before last year's Derby?"

"They're two different horses and there is no comparison to be made," he answered. To which I said, "What makes them so different?" Or, at least I tried to ask, but before I completed the question, Jolley interrupted,

"You said you wanted to ask *a* question—that's one question, not two," and he walked away without saying another word.

2. *Landaluce*

Hall of Fame trainer D. Wayne Lukas has developed more than two dozen champions, including 1986 Horse of the Year Lady's Secret and seven juvenile filly champions, but if you pin him down, he will always say that this Seattle Slew filly had more talent than any of them.

Unbeaten in her five career starts in 1982 before she became ill and tragically died, Landaluce never was threatened, never seriously challenged while winning each race by open daylight in fast fractions and fast final-time clockings. She won her maiden race in 1:08 $\frac{1}{5}$; her second start—in the Hollywood Lassie—by 21 lengths in 1:08 flat; her third start, the Del Mar Debutante, by 6 $\frac{1}{2}$ lengths in 1:35 $\frac{3}{5}$ for the mile, an exceptional clocking for a 2-year-old filly going two turns. She won the seven-furlong Anoakia by 10 lengths at Santa Anita in 1:21 $\frac{4}{5}$, and the Oak Leaf at 1 $\frac{1}{16}$ miles at 1–20 odds in 1:41 $\frac{4}{5}$, after setting the six-furlong pace in 1:09 $\frac{4}{5}$. Those are clockings that would put most older horses to shame.

Landaluce never had the opportunity to prove herself as a 3-year-old and the Breeders' Cup did not exist in her 2-year-old season. But anyone who saw her perform or compares her past performances with other highly accomplished juvenile fillies must realize that she was one of the very best of all time.

1. *Ruffian*

As stated previously, this amazing filly was faster than all but a few horses—male or female, young or old—at sprint distances, and she would carry her speed through much longer races as a 3-year-old. But, as a juvenile filly, I can only tell you about her Spinaway Stakes to give some perspective as to who she really was.

I was at Saratoga for the entire 1974 meeting and had never seen Ruffian in the flesh until the Spinaway. As a horseplayer, I am always looking to beat heavily hyped favorites and am quick to spot any chink in their armor. Ruffian looked vastly superior on paper, having won her maiden race by 15 lengths and three stakes by large margins in very fast clock-ings. But there was another filly in the Spinaway who had impressed me—Laughing Bridge, the 10-length winner of a division of the Schuylerville Stakes on opening day, a filly who had finished second to Ruffian in a prior stakes appearance at Belmont.

At first I was not going to bet against Ruffian in the Spinaway, but when she came out on the racetrack for the post parade looking washy, extremely fractious, and hard to manage, something seemed amiss. I decided that she might not be on her game this day and might even fin-ish off the board. Great sums were wagered on Ruffian. She was an unplayable 1–5 in the win pool and commanded 85 percent of all the money wagered in the place pool, a circumstance that can lead to box-car payoffs when a heavily backed favorite finishes out of the money.

At the same time, there seemed little risk betting Laughing Bridge to place in this four-horse field (there was no show betting permitted). Even if Ruffian went on to win, as everyone in the grandstand expected, Laughing Bridge looked sharp as a tack and was likely to finish second, thus almost guaranteeing the return of my bet and at least a minimum profit of five cents on the dollar.

I wagered every dollar in my pocket on Laughing Bridge to place and then watched in complete amazement as Ruffian continued to act like a nut case all the way to the starting gate. "Ruffian, what a phony," I said to myself as I saw the nervous sweat dripping from her loins onto both rear legs as jockey Vincent Bracciale Jr. struggled to maintain control. What happened next was hard to believe.

The moment Ruffian turned and saw the starting gate, her ears went straight up in the air like they were coiled springs. Almost robotically, she moved powerfully into stall number 2. A few seconds later, she broke like a shot, getting to the lead instantly, opening up a quick two-length mar-gin on the speedy Laughing Bridge. My mouth dropped at this display of amazing speed as Ruffian ran a hole in the wind all the way to the wire. She won by 12¾ lengths in stakes-record time of 1:08⅗ for six furlongs, more than a full second faster than older, experienced winning colts and geldings needed to complete the same distance earlier on the card.

Laughing Bridge, a good young filly in her own right, did finish sec-ond, but was in another zip code and never again would be matched against Ruffian. I collected my five cents on the dollar and, along with about 25,000 fans, departed Saratoga in complete awe of the fastest 2-year-old filly of the modern age.

That was Ruffian, and we would see more of her at 3.

3-YEAR-OLD FILLIES

In addition to the top 3-year-old fillies listed below, Open Mind and Mom's Command did not quite make the list, but deserve special mention for different reasons.

Open Mind won the Breeders' Cup Juvenile Fillies of 1988 to be named champion 2-year-old filly for that year, one of many for trainer D. Wayne Lukas. As a 3-year-old, Open Mind was similarly outstanding, winning eight straight, including five Grade 1 races—the Kentucky Oaks, Acorn, Mother Goose, Alabama, and the Coaching Club American Oaks (via disqualification). But Open Mind never did beat older fillies in three attempts toward the end of her 3-year-old campaign, which placed her slightly outside the Top 10. In fact, she never won another race; she was soundly defeated twice as a 4-year-old in 1990 before Lukas stopped on her. Had he done so a few races earlier, her record would have been among the best in history.

Mom's Command, a major 3-year-old filly force in 1985, also ranks just outside my Top 10. But any mention of this filly brings with it a story that expresses the full spectrum of highs and lows in the racing game.

A winner of three stakes as a 2-year-old in 1984, Mom's Command was a homebred owned by Peter Fuller, the Massachusetts automobile dealer who enjoyed and suffered through the ups and downs of winning and losing the Kentucky Derby with the same horse. Dancer's Image won the 1968 Kentucky Derby, but that victory was nullified by the Kentucky State Racing Commission and various courts that upheld the verdict to disqualify Dancer's Image for a positive postrace test for phenylbutazone (Bute), an analgesic that can reduce pain and inflammation in an affected joint. At the time, it was a prohibited substance for racing purposes, but it is now legal in almost every racing state.

Despite his public embarrassment and several years of expensive legal battles, which he lost, Fuller continued to operate a modest stable after the 1968 Derby. He simply loved racing with a deep passion and refused to sour on the sport. Then along came Mom's Command, the filly who would provide a delicious year of recouped status and an opportunity for his daughter, Abigail Fuller, to share in the family's public vindication.

Abigail Fuller was already 25, a jockey who was not viewed seriously by most of her male riding rivals, a woman rider who rarely got the opportunity to compete in major stakes. Yet through the grace of her father, who believed in his daughter's talent and in their combined belief in Mom's Command, Abigail Fuller rode the champion filly to all seven of her victories in 1985, including a sweep of the New York Filly Triple Crown. Two months later, in the final race of the filly's career, the Fullers scored a climactic victory in the prestigious Alabama Stakes at Saratoga. The moment was not lost on the Saratoga crowd who cheered for Mom's Command, Abigail Fuller, and her father to the wooden rafters.

Fuller had been regarded as an enemy by numerous racing insiders who openly rooted against the success of his stable, his horse, and his daughter. But the race-going public seemed to be following a different compass, sympathizing with his travails. In the end, Fuller's triumph—his family's triumph—completed a real-life story arc that could well have been made into a pretty good movie.

There also was one other filly who might have been included among the top fillies in the previous list, but certainly deserves mention for being the most disappointing 3-year-old filly of all time. Her name was Moccasin, the 2-year-old champion filly of 1965 who won all eight starts as a juvenile in 1965 and simultaneously was voted Horse of the Year in one of the two co-existing polls at the time.

Similar to 1997's unbeaten 2-year-old colt, Favorite Trick, there probably were better candidates for 1965 Horse of the Year than Moccasin, including Roman Brother, the top older horse and perhaps even Buckpasser, the extraordinary 2-year-old colt who could have run rings around Moccasin if they had ever met. Nevertheless, Moccasin did plenty of good things to earn her 2-year-old championship, even though her clockings did not appeal to astute handicappers who were waiting to take advantage of her when she was likely to meet stiffer competition as a 3-year-old.

After winning the 1965 Spinaway under a snug hold by 3 ½ lengths, the Matron by six without any urging from jockey Larry Adams, and the Alcibiades by 15 with no betting allowed because Moccasin was sure to create a minus win pool, costing the track thousands of dollars, Moccasin went on to win the Selima at Laurel by five, also with no betting allowed for the same reason. She concluded her excellent 2-year-old campaign winning the Gardenia by 2 ½ over Lady Pitt, who would be the champion 3-year-old filly the following year.

All that raised expectations for a solid 3-year-old season, but Moccasin's lack of true speed and further development finally caught up with her, as she only was able to win three races from 13 attempts through the next two seasons, falling hard from grace. Nevertheless, Moccasin was among the top dozen 2-year-olds of my lifetime and deserves to be a Hall of Famer strictly on what she did as a juvenile in 1965.

Moving on to the 3-year-old fillies who did distinguish themselves, it should be no surprise to find that some of the top-class juvenile fillies on the previous list developed into stronger and faster 3-year-olds. A few were even more productive at 4. What may be surprising is how many of the very best of the modern age were on the scene in the 1960s and '70 s. Here are my Top 12:

12. *Ta Wee*

As mentioned previously, Ta Wee was a match for any horse of either sex at the precise distance of six furlongs. At 3 years of age and again at 4, she was a bona fide horse for the ages at her specialty and deserves to be considered among the best of her sex to appear in competition in America.

11. *Winning Colors*

After she won her second of two starts as a late-developing 2-year-old in 1987, some of the grooms and stable help who worked for trainer D. Wayne Lukas made a trek to Las Vegas with one purpose in mind: to bet several hundred dollars on Winning Colors to win the 1988 Kentucky Derby at 100–1 odds. Nice bet!

The stable personnel knew that Lukas was going to point the oversized, sleek-moving roan daughter of French-bred Caro to America's most famous race. They also knew that she had won two sprints in fast time with no pressure at all, an important clue to her abundant talent because she was built and bred to improve significantly beyond sprint distances.

Up to that point in his career, Lukas had been compiling a losing record in the Derby that was beginning to get embarrassing. Then he broke through with Winning Colors and went on a Triple Crown rampage that would equal the 13 Triple Crown wins set decades earlier by Sunny Jim Fitzsimmons.

To get Winning Colors ready for the 1 ¼-mile Derby, Lukas boldly put her in against colts in the 1 ⅛-mile Santa Anita Derby. Expertly ridden by Gary Stevens, Winning Colors went right to the front and improved her position to win the Santa Anita Derby by seven lengths. The identical tactics were utilized in the Kentucky Derby when she extended her early lead on the far turn and had just enough left to hold off fast-charging Forty Niner to score a historic Derby victory.

After the rough-and-tumble Preakness (detailed in Chapter 3, under "Woody Stephens"), Winning Colors looked cooked for the year when she fell far back out of contention in the Belmont Stakes after chasing a relatively fast pace. But Lukas did one of his best training jobs that summer, bringing the filly back to top form with a good second-place finish to unbeaten Personal Ensign in the Maskette at Belmont in September, which served as a prelude to the stern test she would give Personal Ensign in their amazing Breeders' Cup Distaff at Churchill Downs six weeks later.

As a 4-year-old in 1989, Winning Colors never reached similar heights, winning only two of her seven starts. Where she really ranks on the list of great fillies is open to question, but there is no doubt Winning Colors performed at an ultra-high, historic level at least twice in her racing life, a level beyond the capabilities of all but a few.

10. *Tosmah*

After an excellent 2-year-old campaign in 1963 in which she lost only one race, the Gardenia Stakes, Tosmah improved significantly as a 3-year-old in 1964, winning 10 of 14, including a victory over good males in the Arlington Classic. That kicked off a six-race winning streak to the end of the year that included victories over older mares in the Maskette and Beldame at Aqueduct.

Given her fine form at 2 and 3, as well as an important victory over older male horses as a 4-year-old in the 1965 John B. Campbell

Handicap at Bowie, Tosmah should be remembered as one of best fillies of modern times.

9. *Gallant Bloom*

A good 2-year-old who did win the 1968 Gardenia Stakes, Gallant Bloom was an awesome performer at 3, finishing first in seven of her eight starts in 1969, and being officially credited with an unbeaten season when Pit Bunny was disqualified for interference in the Delaware Oaks.

As a 4-year-old in 1970, Gallant Bloom would extend her winning streak to 12 with two stakes victories at Santa Anita before she went off form in two races against top-class males at Belmont and Aqueduct. She was retired in July 1970 as one of the best horses bred and raced by legendary King Ranch.

8. *Desert Vixen*

With only one win in five tries as a 2-year-old, Desert Vixen was a major surprise at 3 and a continuing championship presence at 4. After a second-place finish in her seasonal debut at Belmont in May 1973, Desert Vixen won nine of her next 10, all in stakes, all by dominating margins, several in very fast clockings. In successive order she won the Monmouth Oaks, Delaware Oaks, Test, Alabama, and Gazelle, finishing her 1973 campaign with an eight-length victory in the Beldame over the Allen Jerkens-trained Poker Night and three-time champion Susan's Girl.

At 4 years of age, Desert Vixen got off slowly, losing four straight before she turned that around with four straight graded stakes victories. But it was her final race of the year, a sharp second-place finish in the Washington, D. C., International against world-class males at 1 ½ miles on the grass—not only her first try on grass, but also her first attempt at 12 furlongs—that may have been the finest performance of her career.

7. *Davona Dale*

This Calumet Farm filly won both of her starts as a 2-year-old in 1978, but trainer John Veitch packed her away to give her more time to develop into a top 3-year-old. After a fair fourth against colts in the Tropical Park Derby to start her 1979 campaign in January and a second to Candy Éclair, Davona Dale reversed the loss to Candy Éclair in the Bonnie Miss at Gulfstream Park, then won the Debutante at the Fair Grounds; the Fantasy at Oaklawn Park; the Kentucky Oaks at Churchill Downs; and the Black-Eyed Susan at Pimlico. This was followed by victories in the Acorn, Mother Goose, and Coaching Club American Oaks at Belmont Park—before she was upset by the Laz Barrera-trained West Coast shipper It's In the Air in the Alabama at Saratoga.

One week later, in an ill-advised attempt to recoup lost glory, Davona Dale struggled to finish fourth to the LeRoy Jolley-trained colt General Assembly in the Travers and was only able to recover her top form once in her final four career starts into the summer of 1980. Still, Davona Dale had accomplished a feat unmatched by any other filly in history, before or since: She won both the traditional filly triple crown of the three companion stakes to the Kentucky Derby, Preakness, and Belmont Stakes (the Kentucky Oaks, Black-Eyed Susan, and Coaching Club American Oaks) and the New York Filly Triple Crown of the Acorn, Mother Goose, and CCA Oaks.

6. *Chris Evert*

A very good 2-year-old in 1973, this filly, named to honor the great tennis champion—in her prime at the time—swept the New York Filly Triple Crown one year before Ruffian would do the same. She then was invited to a "winner-take-all" $350,000 match race on July 20 at Belmont Park, against the best in the West, Miss Musket.

Result: A 50-length victory—yes, a 50-length victory—clocked in 2:02 for the 1 1/4 miles, a race followed 20 days later by a hard-luck second-place finish in the 1 1/4-mile Alabama at Saratoga on August 10. One week later, she ran a very good third in the Travers to Monmouth Invitational winner Holding Pattern and Preakness-Belmont winner Little Current on a rain-drenched, soupy track.

With four months off from such a grueling series of races at classic distances, Chris Evert returned to win a six-furlong sprint stakes at Aqueduct on December 31 and then shipped to California to run in Santa Anita's La Canada Stakes in an all-out, wire- to-wire duel she would win by a desperate nose, the last victory of her adventurous career. As many of us who started in this game during the 1960s are prone to say, they really do not make horses like this tough gal anymore.

5. *Genuine Risk*

The first filly to win the Kentucky Derby since Regret in 1915, Genuine Risk won all four of her 2-year-old races in 1979 and her first two as a 3-year-old in 1980 before trainer LeRoy Jolley reluctantly agreed with owners Bert and Diana Firestone that she should try the best 3-year-old colts in America to see if she belonged in the Kentucky Derby.

The third-place finish in the Wood Memorial at Aqueduct led Jolley to believe that Genuine Risk should run in the Kentucky Oaks, but the Firestones saw enough in the performance to exercise their prerogative to enter her in the world's most famous race.

This was one time when an involved horse owner had it right, as Genuine Risk not only won the Derby, she but also finished a courageous second in the roughly run Preakness Stakes (described in Chapter 2, under "Angel Cordero Jr.") and then turned in an extremely game second-place effort to Temperence Hill on a muddy track in the Belmont Stakes. This completed one of the most remarkable series of performances by a filly in racing history.

After a three-month vacation to recapture her strength, Genuine Risk returned to lose the Maskette Handicap by a nose to Bold 'n Determined, a sensational filly who probably deserved a piece of the 3-year-old championship for her seven Grade 1 stakes victories. Genuine Risk did win the title, though, mostly on the strength of her Triple Crown run and her final win of the year in the Grade 1 Ruffian against older fillies and mares.

4. *Bold 'n Determined*

As hinted above, this Neil Drysdale-trained 3-year-old was a victim of circumstance not to be voted a championship. In fact, no other sophomore filly ever won so many Grade 1 races in one season (seven), and she had the talent and credentials to rank alongside Genuine Risk at 3 years of age in 1980, as well as Lakeville Miss, champion 2-year-old filly in 1977, and Relaxing, the champion filly or mare of 1981. Bold 'n Determined was unbeaten in four starts at 2; won those seven Grade 1 stakes at 3—the Santa Susana, Fantasy, Kentucky Oaks, Acorn, Coaching Club American Oaks, Maskette, and Spinster—and finished second by a nose in the Mother Goose.

In 20 career starts, Bold 'n Determined won 16 races, with two seconds, including wins in all three races as a 4-year-old to become the first top-quality horse developed by future Hall of Famer Neil Drysdale. It was a hair-splitting decision between her and Genuine Risk in the public mind at the time, and so it remains a hair-splitting choice which filly should rank higher long after they did battle. The deciding point for me is that Bold 'n Determined beat Genuine Risk fair and square while carrying four more pounds in their lone meeting.

3. *Cicada*

This extremely game miss gave the talented 3-year-old colt Ridan one of his toughest races, dueling with him in a gritty wire-to-wire battle in the 1 ⅛-mile Florida Derby, losing only in the final stride by less than an inch.

While Cicada was entered with her highly regarded stablemate Sir Gaylord in the 1962 Kentucky Derby, Meadow Stable elected to run her instead in the Kentucky Oaks the day before the Derby, even though owner Christopher Chenery found out upon arrival in Kentucky that Sir Gaylord was injured and would have to be scratched from the Derby. Chenery was torn between running Cicada in the Derby or the Oaks, but reasoned that the Oaks would be the proper target and watched with mixed emotions as his prize filly scored a dominating three-length victory. In retrospect, many observers, including myself, believe that Cicada had a realistic chance to win the Derby that year by taking a line through Ridan. Ridan finished a solid third in the Derby and went on to lose a tight photo finish to longshot Greek Money in the 1962 Preakness two weeks later.

For the rest of her 3-year-old campaign, Cicada won the Acorn and the Mother Goose over her own age group and then took the Beldame over older fillies and mares while edging closer to a record she would claim the following year as the richest mare in history, with $783,674 gleaned from 23 wins, 8 seconds, and 6 thirds in 43 starts, an extremely rich bankroll at that time when Cicada only competed in five races with purses of $100,000 or more.

2. *Go for Wand*

The tragic breakdown in the 1990 Breeders' Cup Distaff that cost this special 3-year-old filly her life shocked the many thousands who witnessed it at Belmont Park and millions more on the NBC network telecast. It was further played out in brutal detail in all-too-vivid photographs published in *Sports Illustrated* magazine the following week. The breakdown took place just as Go for Wand seemed to edge to a half-length lead over the defending 1989 Breeders' Cup Distaff winner, Bayakoa, as both of these great female Thoroughbreds were on the verge of completing one of the best stretch duels in Breeders' Cup history.

In the winner's circle, Bayakoa's Hall of Fame trainer, Ron McAnally, was sick with dismay over what had happened and never would be able to enjoy the victory. Go for Wand's trainer, Bill Badgett, a former assistant to Woody Stephens, never would train another horse anywhere near as talented, or enjoy much more about the game until his retirement.

"Some things you get over, some things you don't," Badgett said simply and eloquently several years later.

What Badgett and all those who appreciated Go for Wand have to fall back on is the great performances she gave us. After winning three races in four outings as a 2-year-old, including the 1989 Breeders' Cup Juvenile Fillies at Gulfstream Park, Go for Wand won seven of eight starts prior to the fateful Distaff, including six Grade 1 stakes—the Ashland, Mother Goose, Test, Alabama, Maskette, and Beldame, the last two over older mares.

Go for Wand ran fast—very fast. She covered seven furlongs in 1:21 flat in the Test; ran 1 1/8 miles at Belmont in a scorching 1:45 4/5, just two-fifths of a second off Secretariat's track record; and she went 1 1/4 miles in the Alabama on a drying-out "good" track at Saratoga in 2:00 4/5, the fastest clocking in that historic race. We were blessed to see her run and we were cursed to see her fall.

1. *Ruffian*

As in the case of Go for Wand, we were blessed to see this amazing filly perform and we were shaken to the core to see her tragic fall in the infamous match race with Foolish Pleasure on July 6, 1975.

Ruffian simply was the fastest filly of modern times, perhaps of all time, scoring all 10 of her victories while always in front, always in command, never seemingly in any danger of finishing second, much less losing a race. Her lone serious challenge was in the Sorority at Monmouth, a Grade 1 stakes at the time. This was Ruffian's fourth career start in her 2-year-old season and her obvious opponent was the unbeaten Hot N Nasty, a speedball who had turned in a few very fast races of her own. For the first half-mile they ran as a team, but Ruffian always was at least a head in front and when the two fillies turned into the stretch, there was little doubt about the outcome. Ruffian pulled away to a comfortable 2 ½-length victory in a swift 1:09 flat, the smallest winning margin of her life.

Ruffian in fact tied the track record for 5 ½ furlongs in each of her first two starts at Belmont Park; won her third start under wraps by nine lengths, one tick off the 5 ½-furlong track record at Aqueduct; won the Sorority as described above; and won the six-furlong Spinaway by 12 ¾ lengths in 1:08 ⅗, as previously described in her 2-year-old resume.

She came back for her 3-year-old campaign in April 1975 with a perfunctory 4 ¾ -length allowance win at Aqueduct; followed that with a 7 ¾-length romp in 1:21 ⅕ for seven furlongs in the Comely; took the one-mile Acorn by 8 ¼ in 1:34 ⅖ while being geared down in the final sixteenth of a mile; won the 1 ⅛-mile Mother Goose around two turns at Aqueduct in 1:47 ⅘ while jockey Jacinto Vasquez never cocked the whip; and took the 1 ½-mile Coaching Club American Oaks by 2 ¾ lengths under a tight rein in 2:27 ⅘. That was on June 21, just 11 days after Avatar and Foolish Pleasure finished noses apart in the Belmont Stakes on a similar racing strip in 2:28 ⅕.

Sixteen days later, there were no real words to describe the feeling of watching such a gifted horse fall victim to her own speed and the intrinsic fragility of the Thoroughbred breed.

In 2006, we saw Kentucky Derby winner Barbaro break his right hind ankle in three places barely 100 yards out of the starting gate in the Preakness Stakes. We also saw a team of talented veterinary surgeons put that colt's splintered ankle together with metal plates and 27 screws. Yet, that is not what gave Barbaro his chance to survive the tragedy of his accident.

What gave Barbaro a fighting chance was what was learned when Ruffian was unable to keep sufficiently still after she came out of anesthesia from the operation that was performed trying to save her at a nearby emergency equine facility. When Ruffian awoke from her operation, she did what came naturally—she moved her legs in the manner she always did, as if she were still running in the race that ended less than a furlong after the start. While no one knows for sure if she would have avoided infection, or if she would have healed properly, Ruffian never had a chance, kicking loose all the good work that had been performed on the operating table. It was a sad, inevitable outcome in 1975. But she did not die in vain. Veterinary surgeons who studied her case gave hope to many horses with seemingly catastrophic injuries.

This was explained best after the operation on Barbaro by Dr. Dean Richardson, director of equine surgery at the University of Pennsylvania Large Animal Hospital at the New Bolton Center for Equine Research: "Because of what happened to Ruffian coming out of anesthesia, it was a logical thing to develop a specially designed rubber harness, sort of a body raft with rubber legs that we can put the horse into after an operation. Once in the body raft, while still under anesthesia, we can lower the patient into a pool. The apparatus keeps the legs dry and when the patient starts to come out of anesthesia, the pool gives just enough resistance to slow the leg movements so that he can't thrash about and hurt himself. If Ruffian had that, we don't know if it would have saved her, but she would have had a chance."

Thus, Ruffian, one of the most admired and appreciated Thoroughbred racehorses in the 20th century, made a contribution to the endangered lives of injured Thoroughbreds who came after her. She is reverently buried in the Belmont infield.

3-YEAR-OLD COLTS AND GELDINGS

No division has had more high-quality horses than 3-year-old colts and geldings. Likewise, no division receives more attention from fans and the media, due to the popularity and historical importance of the Kentucky

Derby, Preakness, and Belmont Stakes. The three races have all existed for more than 130 years, but were not labeled the Triple Crown until *Daily Racing Form*'s Charles Hatton linked them together when Gallant Fox became the second horse in history to win all three in 1930.

During the 50-odd years spanned by this book, only four champion 3-year-olds never ran in a Triple Crown race, while two extremely high-class 3-year-olds were not voted championships after missing the spring classics.

Kelso, Buckpasser, Tiznow, and Wajima were the 3-year-old champs who did not appear in a Triple Crown race. Dr. Fager and Java Gold were the two who lost out because there were solid performers in the Triple Crown that beat them at the polls.

Kelso, a five-time Horse of the Year, was champion 3-year-old in 1960 partly by default when no horse emerged from that year's Triple Crown with any hold on the title. Six late-season victories, including the Jockey Club Gold Cup over older horses, gave Kelso the 1960 title and his first Horse of the Year Award. Realistically, Kelso's best form would come as an older horse during the next four seasons.

Wajima surfaced in August to win five straight races, including the Monmouth Invitational, the Travers, the Governor Stakes by a head over Kentucky Derby winner Foolish Pleasure, and the Marlboro Cup over reigning Horse of the Year Forego, with Foolish Pleasure a tired fifth after his arduous campaign.

Dr. Fager in 1967 and Java Gold in 1987 were both outstanding 3-year-olds who were unable to outpoll the deserving Damascus and Alysheba, respectively, after Damascus won the 1967 Preakness and Belmont and Alysheba won the '87 Derby and Preakness. All four of these were great horses.

Damascus actually clinched his 3-year-old championship and 1967 Horse of the Year Award with a series of extraordinary performances during the summer and fall, including a resounding 10-length triumph in the 1967 Woodward over reigning Horse of the Year Buckpasser, with Dr. Fager third. With that cast of great horses, the 1967 Woodward was one of the top races of my lifetime, as was Damascus's dominating performance.

Alysheba, for his part, built up a lot of equity winning the 1987 Kentucky Derby after a severe stumble off the heels of Bet Twice in midstretch—an incident that was as dramatic and as dangerous as Afleet

Alex's stumble when bothered by Scrappy T at the top of the stretch in the 2005 Preakness.

But after Bet Twice defeated Alysheba in the Belmont Stakes and Haskell Invitational in June and July, and Java Gold beat them both in the Travers Stakes in August, it seemed Java Gold had gained a slight advantage in the 3-year-old rankings. The Rokeby Stables homebred, who also won the Whitney at Saratoga and the Marlboro Cup at Belmont against older horses that year, eventually lost his claim when beaten by the 5-year-old Creme Fraiche in the 1987 Jockey Club Gold Cup. He came out of that race with a broken bone in his foot and never raced again, while Alysheba recovered to win the Super Derby at Louisiana Downs and was an inch shy of defeating Ferdinand in a dramatic running of the Breeders' Cup Classic three weeks after Java Gold suffered his ill-timed loss.

The Breeders' Cup Classic, in fact, became as important as Triple Crown races in deciding 3-year-old championships, which explains why Tiznow won the 3-year-old title and 2000 Horse of the Year despite missing the Triple Crown. Tiznow, the best California-bred since Swaps, had very unusual campaigns that bypassed many of the most prestigious stakes. As a 3-year-old, he won a maiden race at Hollywood Park in his third career start on May 31, 2000. He would win only one stakes through the summer, but took the Super Derby in September, the Goodwood over older horses at Santa Anita in October, and then narrowly won the 2000 Breeders' Cup Classic at Churchill Downs in a gripping performance over the highly ranked European challenger Giant's Causeway.

In 2001, Tiznow was champion older horse, but did not win Horse of the Year. That honor went to the talented 3-year-old Point Given, who won five Grade 1 races that season—the Preakness, Belmont, and Travers Stakes, along with the Santa Anita Derby and Haskell Invitational—before he was retired in September because of a strained tendon in his leg. But Tiznow did win the San Fernando and Santa Anita Handicap during the winter and returned to Belmont on October 27, 2001, to score another thrilling, extremely close victory in the Breeders' Cup Classic over another high-class European—Sakhee, winner of Europe's most important race, the Prix de l'Arc de Triomphe. Frankly, I believe Tiznow was a slightly better 3-year-old than Point Given, but not by much.

During the 1950s there were no Triple Crown winners, but there was Native Dancer, who won the 1953 Preakness and Belmont and suffered his only career loss in the Kentucky Derby. There also was Nashua, who won the 1955 Preakness and Belmont after losing the Derby to the ultrafast Swaps, whom Nashua would defeat in a historic match race later that summer.

Beyond Damascus and Dr. Fager in 1967, that decade produced more than its share of very good and truly great 3-year-olds: 1969 Horse of the Year Arts and Letters and four horses that took two legs of the Triple Crown—Carry Back (1961 Derby and Preakness); Chateaugay (1963 Derby and Belmont); Northern Dancer (1964 Derby and Preakness); and Majestic Prince (the 1969 Derby and Preakness winner, who lost the Belmont to Arts and Letters).

Realistically, Northern Dancer's stock rose appreciably after his racing career was over when he became one of the leading stallions in Thoroughbred history. While I personally fell in love with Carry Back's amazing rallies, he too was a cut below Top 10 caliber, as was Chateaugay. But Majestic Prince was every bit as good as Arts and Letters, having defeated him twice before Arts and Letters turned the tables on a subpar Majestic Prince in the Belmont, which proved to be that colt's only career loss and his final race.

In the 1970s, there were three winners of the elusive American Triple Crown—Secretariat, Seattle Slew, and Affirmed. All were freakishly talented members of the Thoroughbred breed who certainly were among the best horses of modern times. Then there was Spectacular Bid, who almost won a Triple Crown in 1979, failing, as his trainer Buddy Delp insists, because the colt stepped on a safety pin in his stall the morning of the race. While that is debatable, jockey Ronnie Franklin did not exactly give this Hall of Fame horse a Hall of Fame ride.

What of Alydar, who lost the 1978 Triple Crown races to Affirmed, yet ran so gallantly and pushed his arch rival to levels of performance that did them both proud? Or Sunday Silence and Easy Goer, who staged such memorable battles in the 1989 Triple Crown and Breeders' Cup? Where do they rank in a division loaded with great and near-great horses?

In the aftermath of Affirmed's Triple Crown sweep in 1978, a remarkable 17 different horses won two-thirds of the Triple Crown through 2006 without one completing the sweep:

Spectacular Bid (1979); Pleasant Colony (1981); Swale (1984); Alysheba (1987); Risen Star (1988); Sunday Silence (1989); Hansel (1991); Tabasco Cat (1994); Thunder Gulch (1995); Silver Charm (1997); Real Quiet (1998); Charismatic (1999); Point Given (2001); War Emblem (2002); Funny Cide (2003); Smarty Jones (2004); and Afleet Alex (2005). All but Tabasco Cat were voted champion 3-year-old of their respective years and there is no question that we did not see enough of the prematurely retired Smarty Jones, or Afleet Alex, to really know how good they might have become.

In addition, there were great performances by Bet Twice against Alysheba in 1987; Holy Bull against Tabasco Cat in 1994; Touch Gold against Silver Charm in 1997; Victory Gallop against Real Quiet in 1998; and Empire Maker against Funny Cide in 2003.

Spend a Buck was awesome winning the 1985 Kentucky Derby and Monmouth Handicap, the latter against older horses; Fusaichi Pegasus was a powerhouse winning the 2000 Derby; Unbridled was first-rate winning the 1990 Kentucky Derby and Breeders' Cup Classic; and who knows how many more impressive victories Barbaro would have earned after his effortless Kentucky Derby victory in 2006. The same has to be said for Bernardini, who was every bit as impressive as Barbaro while winning the 2006 Preakness, Jim Dandy, and Travers. In fact, Bernardini seemed even better than Barbaro by the time he cruised to an embarrassingly easy victory in the Jockey Club Gold Cup, and only needed to complete his 2006 campaign with a victory in the Breeders' Cup Classic to crack the top dozen listed below.

The bottom line is that the pecking order of the best 3-year-olds of modern times is beyond anyone's ability to firmly establish without leaving out several great horses. My personal favorites for assorted reasons are:

12. *Easy Goer*

Ogden Phipps's homebred son of Alydar was a powerful winner of the Belmont Stakes over his nemesis, Sunday Silence, and was a solid winner of the Wood Memorial and Travers during the spring and summer, as well as an impressive winner over older horses in the Whitney, the

Woodward, and the Jockey Club Gold Cup before he lost to Sunday Silence in their fourth and final meeting, the Breeders' Cup Classic at Gulfstream Park. The massive chestnut colt was still was 8 for 11, with three second-place finishes to Sunday Silence, in a 3-year-old campaign that was both exciting and frustrating for those who believed he was the best 3-year-old of that year.

11. *Sunday Silence*

This Charlie Whittingham trainee owns Eclipse Awards for 1989's top 3-year-old and Horse of the Year, by virtue of his three victories in four tries over the hard-hitting Easy Goer. He was 7 for 9 that year, including victories in the Kentucky Derby, Preakness, Santa Anita Derby, Super Derby, and Breeders' Cup Classic, and deserves the narrowest of edges in this rivalry of two great horses.

10. *Native Dancer*

But for bad racing luck and the unheralded Dark Star, this fabulous horse would have been undefeated in 22 starts, which simply would have been the greatest career in racing history.

9. *Arts and Letters*

He earned the 1969 Horse of the Year title with successive wins in the Metropolitan Mile, Belmont Stakes, Jim Dandy, Travers, Woodward, and the Jockey Club Gold Cup—the latter two over older horses.

8. *Majestic Prince*

Was undefeated until he was beaten by Arts and Letters in the Belmont Stakes while not 100 percent healthy. He had defeated Arts and Letters in the Kentucky Derby and Preakness fair and square when the latter had dead aim through the length of the stretch in Louisville and Baltimore. Nothing I saw said that he could not have done it again if he had been at his best.

7. *Alydar*

Just as Easy Goer pushed Sunday Silence to his best, so too did Easy Goer's sire, Alydar, push Affirmed to sky-high limits of performance every time they met. For his part, Alydar won everything in sight except the Triple Crown races and probably would have been a Triple Crown winner himself in all but a few years.

6. *Spectacular Bid*

Was a monster at 4 years of age, but almost as good at 3, winning 11 of 13 starts, losing only the 1979 Belmont Stakes and the Jockey Club Gold Cup, won by defending 1978 Horse of the Year Affirmed.

5. *Seattle Slew*

Unbeaten through the Triple Crown series, Seattle Slew nevertheless was underrated as a 3-year-old by many observers, including the great jockey Eddie Arcaro and my good friend and much respected handicapper-columnist, Andrew Beyer. Both stated in the media after Seattle Slew won the 1977 Kentucky Derby that "Slew" was just a good horse who had the good fortune to beat a bad lot.

The following year, when Seattle Slew ran several astonishing races, all the critics changed this tune, yet hedged their bets by pointing out that Seattle Slew had improved dramatically. While he did improve at 4, he already had established himself as a freakishly talented 2-year-old, and his victories during the spring of 1977 were extraordinary in their own right. It still gives me goose bumps when I see Seattle Slew knifing his way through the whole Kentucky Derby field like a blur in the first quarter-mile after he broke dead last.

4. *Damascus*

Lost the one-mile Gotham to Dr. Fager early in his 3-year-old season, and Dr. Fager would prove to be a better 4-year-old, but at 3, Damascus was one of the truly great horses of all time, winning 11 stakes (10 of them under Bill Shoemaker), including the Preakness and Belmont with devastating rallies; the Travers by 22 lengths; and the Aqueduct, Woodward, and Jockey Club Gold Cup over older horses before losing the 1 ½-mile Washington, D. C., International by a nose to turf champion Fort Marcy in Damascus's only career attempt on turf.

3. *Affirmed*

No horse had stronger competition to earn a sweep of the Triple Crown and no horse ever showed more athletic talent, more gears, more resolve, more heart. As detailed in prior chapters, Affirmed was brilliantly trained by Laz Barrera, brilliantly ridden by Steve Cauthen, and was better than Alydar, which took some doing.

2. *Buckpasser*

Indisputably, one of the best horses of all time from his juvenile season in 1965, when trained by Bill Winfrey, through his 3- and 4-year-old seasons, when trained by Eddie Neloy.

As a 3-year-old, Buckpasser was unable to make the 1966 Triple Crown chase due to injury, but already had won the Everglades and Flamingo Stakes at Hialeah in February before returning in June to win his final 10 starts of the season—nine of them stakes. Among them were the Arlington Classic in world-record time for the mile; the Brooklyn Handicap at 1 ¼ miles while spotting weight to older horses; the nine-furlong American Derby at Arlington in track-record time; the Travers over Belmont Stakes winner Amberoid; the 1 ¼-mile Woodward, and the two-mile Jockey Club Gold Cup, both over older horses.

Beyond the winning streak that would reach 15 straight through the early stages of Buckpasser's 4-year-old campaign in 1967, this handsome son of Tom Fool was one of the most entertaining, exciting 3-year-olds of modern times, a crowd-pleasing stretch-runner who performed on the razor's edge of defeat. Usually slow to get into his best gear, Buckpasser invariably responded to jockey Braulio Baeza's smooth urging to get up in the final strides to defeat whomever was in front with a sixteenth of a mile to go.

In his 12 straight victories during his memorable 1966 racing season, Buckpasser won four photo finishes and five other races by exactly three-quarters of a length, providing thrills to the legion of fans that made him the odds-on betting favorite in every start that year—except for the two races in which Hialeah track management refused to permit betting.

One of those nonbetting races, the $139,000 Flamingo Stakes, was not only the richest race Buckpasser would compete in during his 3- and 4-year-old seasons, it was dubbed the Chicken Flamingo by members of the press, ridiculing Hialeah's decision to bar win betting in the race. As it turned out, the 1966 Flamingo was a race that Buckpasser had to pull out of the fire with an amazing last-gasp effort to reclaim the lead from Abe's Hope on the finish line after he seemed beaten.

That was Buckpasser, always leaving racing fans gasping for breath and (when betting was allowed) with more money in their pockets. Buckpasser won 25 out of 31 career races, with four seconds and one third, finishing worse than third only once, in his career debut.

1. *Secretariat*

No horse ever ran the Kentucky Derby with succeedingly faster quarter-mile splits. No horse except Secretariat, who not only did that, but also set the Churchill Downs track record for 1 1/4 miles in 1:59 2/5 and ran his fifth and final quarter-mile in a shade over 23 seconds. No horse in my lifetime ever made a last-to-first move on the first turn at Pimlico like the one he made in the Preakness. No horse I have ever seen could have matched Secretariat's 31-length Belmont Stakes victory, clocked in 2:24, breaking Gallant Man's 1957 track record by 2 3/5 seconds, a significant difference.

No other Triple Crown winner ever set track records in all three Triple Crown events, which Secretariat definitely did, even though Pimlico officials and the Maryland Racing Commission did not acknowledge it. No other horse could have won the Marlboro Cup over a top-flight field of older runners in the manner that Secretariat won that race, in hand, setting a world record for nine furlongs. No other horse could have dusted the top grass horse Tentam so easily when the latter challenged Secretariat three different times during the 1 1/2-mile Man o' War Stakes. Secretariat was scary that day. Making his debut on grass, he posted nearly the same clocking as he did in the Belmont Stakes while proving he was not only the best 3-year-old dirt horse, but also the best grass horse in America.

Still, as great as he was, Secretariat was not invincible, losing the Wood Memorial to his slower stablemate Angle Light due to a reported toothache; losing the Whitney to the Allen Jerkens-trained Onion when he was reportedly recovering from a fever; and losing to the Jerkens-trained Prove Out when that horse was loose on the lead in soft fractions of 50 seconds for the first half-mile and 1:13²/₅ for six furlongs in a tactical nightmare. The moral of this story is that very few horses can achieve perfection, not even the best 3-year-old of modern times.

OLDER FILLIES AND MARES

Excluding fillies and mares who were better horses at 3 years of age and excluding fillies and mares who were at their very best on turf, most of the best female racehorses in the 4-year-olds-and-up division had flaws in their resumes.

Affectionately, a sprinter of high quality, won 11 stakes on both coasts as a 4- and 5-year-old in 1964–65, but lost three of her four races against males and won only one race in seven tries at one mile to 1 ⅛ miles. Berlo, a very good 3-year-old filly in 1960, was a dud at 4; Bowl of Flowers, very good at 2 and 3, never raced at 4. Cicada, an all-time great at 2 and 3 in 1961 and '62, was good, but not great, as a 4-year-old in 1963.

Tosmah continued to be a serious contender in all of her starts through her retirement as a 5-year-old in 1966, but actually won only one major race in 1965, the Maskette Handicap over Affectionately at one mile, plus one more in 1966—the John B. Campbell Handicap over male rivals, one of the richest victories of her career.

Bold 'n Determined, a great 3-year-old in 1980, raced but three times as a 4-year-old in 1981, winning all three against relatively weak opposition. Christmas Past, a very promising 3-year-old filly champion in 1982, was even more promising in her only two starts at 4 in 1983, winning both, including a strong stretch-running victory against older males in the

Grade 1 Gulfstream Park Handicap, after which she was prematurely retired due to injury.

Shuvee, champion handicap mare as a 4-year-old in 1970, won 16 races in a solid career, including consecutive runnings of the Jockey Club Gold Cup, but lost 28 times. Old Hat, champion handicap mare in 1964 and '65, was even more durable, winning 35 races in 80 starts through 1966. But both Shuvee and Old Hat seemed a cut below the very best of the modern age.

10. *Princess Rooney*

Undefeated through her 2-year-old season and through her first four starts at 3, she nevertheless had to wait until her 4-year-old season in 1984 to win an Eclipse Award as champion older filly or mare.

Princess Rooney lost her first race in 1984—a turf experiment by trainer Joe Pierce in a minor stakes at Hialeah—but then won six of her last eight for Neil Drysdale, including three Grade 1 events, all in extremely fast time. These included a decisive seven-length victory over 1984's champion 3-year-old filly, Life's Magic, in the inaugural Breeders' Cup Distaff to point out her superiority. Princess Rooney finished her career with an excellent record of 17 wins, two seconds and a third from 21 starts.

9. *Ta Wee*

This truly great sprinter was sensational in 1970 at 4, just as she was at 3. In my opinion, no list of top older fillies and mares can be complete without Ta Wee, even though she had clear-cut distance limitations that would have left her vulnerable to many very good fillies and mares who did not make this list. She was that outstanding.

8. *Late Bloomer*

This smooth-moving daughter of 1968 Belmont Stakes winner Stage Door Johnny certainly lived up to her name, saving all of her eight stakes victories for her 4- and 5-year-old racing seasons. Trained by John Gaver Jr., whose father trained Tom Fool in the 1950s, Late Bloomer took over the female handicap division in 1978, winning seven straight stakes as a 4-year-old, including three straight Grade 1 races—the Delaware Handicap, Ruffian, and Beldame. She was just as effective on dirt and turf and continued in respectable form as a 5-year-old in 1979 with two wins and two sharp seconds in six outings.

7. *Gamely*

A top 3-year-old filly who won a division of the 1967 Test and the prestigious Alabama Stakes at Saratoga, Gamely won six stakes in her 13 starts as a 4-year-old. She handled top-quality males in the Inglewood Handicap at Hollywood after finishing strongly for a solid second to the overpowering Dr. Fager in the $1\,^1/_{16}$-mile Californian Stakes.

As a 5-year-old, in 1969, Gamely was co-champion with Gallant Bloom while winning four more stakes, but her best performance of the year may have been her fast-closing second to male handicap champion Nodouble in the Santa Anita Handicap.

6. *Susan's Girl*

Fred Hooper Jr.'s homebred filly was a champion at 3 in 1972, with seven wins from 10 starts that year; won five Grade 1 stakes as a 4-year-old in California, Delaware, Kentucky, and New York; and took four more Grade 1's in 1975 to maintain a high level of performance that ranks above all but a few fillies and mares in the last half-century or so.

5. *Inside Information*

Ogden Mills Phipps's filly was never out of the money in 17 career starts, with 14 victories, one second, and two thirds while going to the post as an odds-on favorite in all but three of those races. Won seven of her eight starts as a 4-year-old in 1995, including five Grade 1's, the most important and most impressive of which was a $13\,^1/_2$-length wire-to-wire romp on a muddy track in the Breeders' Cup Distaff at Belmont over her stablemate Heavenly Prize, champion 3-year-old filly of 1994.

Inside Information was a very fast, extremely reliable racehorse whose outstanding career record might even have been better, had she not encountered problems at the starting gate in two of her three career defeats.

4. *Lady's Secret*

A solid stakes performer as a 3-year-old in 1985, when she beat divisional champion Mom's Command in the Test at Saratoga and finished second to fellow D. Wayne Lukas trainee and two-time champion Life's Magic in the Breeders' Cup Distaff, Lady's Secret won eight Grade 1 stakes as a 4-year-old in 1986. These included the Whitney Handicap over males in August and the Breeders' Cup Distaff in November, both of which sealed her Eclipse Award as champion filly or mare and also led to her being named 1986 Horse of the Year.

3. *Azeri*

With a record of 17 for 24 lifetime, including four seconds, Azeri was champion filly or mare for three straight years (2002 through 2004) and Horse of the Year in 2002 to compile one of the most impressive resumes by a female racehorse in history.

Unraced as a 2-year-old and just 1 for 2 the next year, Azeri was expertly developed by Laura de Seroux. As a 4-year-old in 2002, Azeri won seven straight Grade 1 stakes, finishing off that spectacular campaign with a dominating five-length victory in the Breeders' Cup Distaff. Picking up where she left off in 2003, Azeri won the Grade 1 Apple Blossom at Oaklawn Park with a desperate rally and added three more victories to extend her winning streak to 11 before she was interfered with while finishing third in Grade 2 Lady's Secret Stakes at Santa Anita, her final race of the year.

Trained by D. Wayne Lukas in 2004, the 6-year-old Azeri won three Grade 1 events and was second in two others, finishing out of the money for the first time in her career in the Metropolitan Mile at Belmont and two other races, including an ambitious try against Horse of the Year Ghostzapper in the Breeders' Cup Classic to close out her popular career.

2. *Bayakoa*

She raced in Argentina as a 3-year-old and was trained by Ron McAnally for her 31 starts in America. Bayakoa was not a major stakes winner as a 4-year-old, but was nothing short of a truly great racemare through the next two seasons, winning an astonishing 12 Grade 1 stakes, including back-to-back runnings of the Breeders' Cup Distaff—the last one at the expense of the fatally injured Go for Wand. In 21 starts as a 5- and 6-year-old, in 1989 and '90, Bayakoa won 15 races, with four seconds, at seven different tracks and earned two richly deserved Eclipse Awards.

1. *Personal Ensign*

Ogden Phipps's homebred daughter of Private Account won her seven starts as a 4-year-old to complete one of the few unbeaten careers by a major stakes winner in racing history and, as previously discussed in Chapter 3 (in the section on trainer Shug McGaughey), she was a near miraculous winner of the 1988 Breeders' Cup Distaff by a nose over 1988 Kentucky Derby winner Winning Colors in a truly great performance. But it was not her only great performance as a 4-year-old. It wasn't even her first victory over Winning Colors, who put up a good battle in the Maskette stakes six weeks earlier.

Personal Ensign dominated her competition in all other starts that year, including a historically important win over the high-class 4-year-old colt Gulch and the durable King's Swan in the nine-furlong Whitney Handicap at Saratoga, clocked in 1:47 4/5, only four-fifths of a second off the track record set by Tri Jet in 1974.

While even Secretariat was unable to use his amazing talent to remain undefeated, and both Native Dancer and Man o' War lost one race during their immortal careers, Personal Ensign was absolutely perfect. You can't do better than that.

TURF HORSES

Turf racing is the natural form of racing in Europe, where horse racing began informally on undulating grass courses near London in 1174 and progressed into more formal races with specific prizes for the top three finishers in the 16th century. At the turn of the 18th century, entry fees, richer prizes, basic breeding rules, distances, number of heats, and weight assignments were codified by Queen Anne, the unheralded

Mother of Thoroughbred racing. Of course, the good queen's fastest horse, Star, won the first race under her new rules.

Grass racing is still the dominant form of the sport in England, France, Germany, Italy, South Africa, South America, New Zealand, and Australia, while in North America, it came into vogue in the early 1950s. As a novelty and as a follow-up to steeplechase (hurdle) racing, which had been conducted on the grassy infields of many American tracks since the turn of the century, grass courses for flat runners were installed in 1953 and '54 at Atlantic City Racecourse, Arlington Park, Hialeah Park, Laurel Racecourse, Belmont Park, Santa Anita, and Hollywood Park.

The first national grass-horse champion was the Chilean import Iceberg II in 1953, primarily for his victory in the inaugural running of the United Nations Handicap at Atlantic City and his second-place finish to the European invader Worden in the inaugural Washington, D.C., International at Laurel. Iceberg II was not exactly a highly accomplished champion, winning only three of his 13 grass starts that year, but he was the best we had.

The quality of grass racing improved quickly, primarily through the efforts of John Schapiro of Laurel Racecourse, who paid the shipping and stabling costs for several top foreign-based horses to compete against America's best in the Washington, D.C., International. In many ways, the D.C. International was a planted seed that would grow into the Breeders' Cup Turf, 30 years later.

Mighty Kelso never was comfortable on grass, but ran in the D.C. International four times and finally won it in his last attempt as a 7-year-old in 1964. Mongo was a popular winner of that race; so was the Mack Miller-trained Hawaii, who was imported from South Africa in 1969 and won the three most important grass races on the American continent that year—the United Nations Handicap at Atlantic City, the Man o' War at Belmont, and the D.C. International.

The following year, the Elliott Burch-trained Fort Marcy completed the same three-race sweep and was voted 1970 Horse of the Year, while two years later that outstanding trainer replicated the feat with the 3-year-old Run the Gantlet, who was named grass champion of 1971, losing Horse of the Year to Charlie Whittingham's Western-based handicap horse Ack Ack.

In 1981, Arlington Park's Richard Duchossois went one better than

Schapiro, creating the Arlington Million, the richest race in America at the time. The inaugural running was a spectacular success as the immortal gelding John Henry was perfectly ridden to a last-gasp victory by Bill Shoemaker over the British invader The Bart. Such close finishes were typical of most grass races, and fans loved the large fields they attracted as much as the stunning beauty of sleek racehorses with their colorful jockey silks set against the plush backdrop of a lush green grass course.

While the grass-racing game was becoming more popular, astute handicappers found manna from heaven through the power of two basic principles of turf-race handicapping that still have potency. "Class on the Grass" was a bromide that actually meant something. Horses that had performed well against top company on the turf were great bets against slightly weaker competition. "Breeding counts" was an equally powerful notion. Horses that had not previously started in a grass race could be expected to run well if they came from sire lines that had produced previous grass winners.

In the 50 or so years that grass racing has been in play in America, we have seen all but a few tracks build turf courses to satisfy the demand, with no end in sight. We also have seen many great champions, male and female, milers and long-distance runners, including several who were dual champions on dirt and turf. Here are the best grass horses I have seen since Iceberg II was declared the first American grass champion in 1953.

In 1960, '62, and '64, there were no grass champions named, and the 1965 champ, Parka, was a "compiler" rather than a sterling star. T.V. Lark, the 1961 grass champion, did win the 1960 U.N. Handicap on grass over Round Table and the 1961 D.C. International over a stubborn Kelso, while also finishing a close second to Mongo in the '62 U.N. Handicap, but overall was just 5 for 17 on grass during his well-traveled 3-, 4-, and 5-year-old campaigns to the end of his career in 1962.

Of the early grass champions, Mongo probably was best. A versatile runner and champion grass horse of 1963, Mongo defeated Kelso in the 1963 D.C. International on grass and in the '64 Monmouth Handicap on dirt. He also defeated the older Carry Back on dirt in the 1962 Trenton Handicap and beat him again on turf in the '63 United Nations.

In the 1970's, 80s, 90s, and through the early years of the 21st century, the quality of top grass performers in America rivaled the best in the world. This was clearly demonstrated in the premier distance races on the grass prior to the start of the Breeders' Cup in 1984, and the trend continued through the succeeding decades.

Here are my Top 12 distance performers on the turf, followed by a smaller list of milers and female grass performers.

LONG-DISTANCE TURF HORSES

12. *Round Table*

Was champion grass horse as a 3-year-old in 1957 after winning his only three turf races—an allowance race and two stakes—during a four-week period from August 20 to September 14, including the United Nations Handicap by a nose under a brilliant front-running ride by Bill Shoemaker.

As he matured, Round Table would win 11 of his next 13 grass races through his 5-year-old season in 1959, the last victory under 136 pounds.

Round Table may have been at his best on turf, but he was versatile enough to win 29 out of his 50 races on dirt to go along with his 14 career wins and a pair of seconds in 16 tries on grass. In 1958, the son of Prince-quillo was voted champion grass horse for the second of three consecutive years and also was named 1958 champion handicap horse on dirt and 1958 Horse of the Year. To this day, Round Table remains one of the most prolific grass champions in American racing history.

11. *Mac Diarmida*

Outstanding 3-year-old grass performer in 1978, won 12 of his 13 grass attempts, losing only the Man o' War to the high-class 4-year-old filly Waya (who won six of her nine turf races in 1978). Following that defeat, Mac Diarmida rebounded to beat older rivals in the Canadian International and then got his revenge on Waya in the Washington, D.C., International with a final quarter in 23²/₅ despite a horrible start.

10. *Fantastic Light*

This Godolphin stable runner failed to win a stakes at 2 and 3 years old in 1998 and '99 while performing in top European company. He began to turn his career around on his home course in Dubai, winning the 2000 Dubai Sheema Classic as part of the ultrarich Dubai World Cup program instituted by the Maktoums, the ruling family of Dubai. The Maktoums ordered the creation of the world-class Nad Al Sheba racecourse and own Godolphin.

After winning the Sheema Classic, Fantastic Light was a good second in a pair of important Group 1 stakes in England before shipping to America to win the Man o' War Stakes. He was unable to win either the Turf Classic at Belmont or the Breeders' Cup Turf while enduring poor racing luck, but did win the Hong Kong Cup in his final start of 2000 to raise his earnings to $4.5 million for the year.

In 2001, as a 5-year-old, this world traveler was second by a nose in the Dubai Sheema Classic and then won three Group 1 races over the best in Europe before returning to America to overpower a world-class field in the 2001 Breeders' Cup Turf with a 117 Beyer Speed Figure. It was that performance that put him on this list.

9. *Bowl Game*

Almost a forgotten performer, the gelded son of 1965 Preakness winner Tom Rolfe was an amazing long-distance turf horse. A strong finisher who could handle any course condition, Bowl Game won his first two turf stakes in 1978 at 1 ½ miles—the Pan American at Gulfstream on a firm course and a division of the Dixie on a soft course at Pimlico.

In 1979, Bowl Game won four straight long-distance turf stakes in a spectacular late-season championship run—two on firm grass, two on very soft turf. They were: the 1 ½-mile Arlington Handicap; the 1 ³/₈-mile Man o' War at Belmont; the 1 ½-mile Turf Classic at Aqueduct; and the 1 ½- mile Washington, D. C., International at Laurel. Trained for stamina by John Gaver Jr., Bowl Game also was second twice and third once in his only other tries at 1 ³/₈ miles or longer.

177

8. *Run the Gantlet*

One of the least-appreciated champions trained by the great Elliott Burch, who developed Sword Dancer, Arts and Letters, and Key to the Mint. This son of Tom Rolfe was a promising 2-year-old winner of the 1970 Garden State Stakes on dirt, but really came into his own in July of his 3-year-old season when Burch put him on the grass.

Run the Gantlet, who later would sire 1982 champion turf filly April Run, won his last five outings in 1971—all on turf—including a remarkable sweep of the United Nations, Man o' War and Washington, D. C., International, the three most important turf races in America during the 50s, 60s and 70s.

7. *Theatrical*

An Irish import who was unable to win a stakes while trained in the West by Bobby Frankel in 1986, Theatrical benefited a great deal when shifted east to Billy Mott for his 4-year-old campaign in 1987. He won seven of eight starts that year for Mott, including six Grade 1's, losing only to Manila in the Arlington Million and defeating Prix d l'Arc de Triomphe winner Trempolino in the $2 million Breeders' Cup Turf in a triumphant final return to Hollywood Park. Mott, as previously pointed out in Chapter 3, is one of the most productive stakes-winning trainers with older horses in modern America racing history.

6. *Fort Marcy*

Another top horse developed by Elliott Burch, who quickly established himself during the 1970s as a turf master. This one was a two-time winner of the D.C. International, but they were not consecutive. In fact, one of Fort Marcy's D.C. victories was as 3-year-old in 1967 and the other came when he was 6 years old in 1970, when he was the first turf horse voted Horse of the Year.

In between, Fort Marcy was third in the '68 and '69 runnings of the D.C. International, while winning 18 of his 48 starts on grass. He set the standard for his stablemate Run the Gantlet by winning the 1970 United

Nations, Man o' War, and D.C. International, as stated, the three most important turf races of the pre-Breeders' Cup era.

5. *Kotashaan*

He was a French import who was very slow to acclimate to American grass racing after arriving in California as a 3-year-old in 1992, winning only an allowance race at Santa Anita before losing five straight stakes through late January 1993. As is so often the case with a naturally gifted runner in the hands of a master—in this case, Hall of Famer Dick Mandella—it was only a matter of time before this long-winded horse would figure things out.

Kotashaan won six of his next eight (five of them Grade 1's), including the 1993 Breeders' Cup Turf with a sustained drive from ninth on the final turn. Kotashaan was so good at the end of that campaign that Mandella opted to send him to Japan to compete in the world-class, $2.5 million Japan Cup, which he most definitely would have won had Hall of Fame jockey Kent Desormeaux not misjudged the finish and settled for second. With his outstanding late-season turf form, Kotashaan was voted 1993 Horse of the Year.

4. *Secretariat*

Secretariat only ran twice on grass, but he was amazing in both outings. He beat the defending 1972 turf champion, Tentam, with speed to spare in course-record time for $1\frac{1}{2}$ miles in the Man o' War Stakes. Then, in his final career start, Secretariat cruised to a $6\frac{1}{2}$-length triumph over multiple Grade 1 grass winner Big Spruce in the Canadian International to close out the most brilliant career of my lifetime.

3. *Daylami*

As a 4-year-old, this Godolphin star won the 1998 Eclipse Stakes in England and the Man o' War at Belmont Park. As a 5-year-old in 1999, Daylami was even better, winning the Coronation Cup; the King George VI and Queen Elizabeth Diamond Stakes; and the Irish Champion Stakes in

Europe, before he returned to America to win the 1999 Breeders' Cup Turf by 2 ½ lengths with a powerful stretch kick that compares favorably with any in the history of the race. He also clinched an Eclipse Award as 1999 champion turf horse on the strength of that sole American appearance.

2. *John Henry*

After 17 starts on dirt for trainer Phil Marino, and one for Harold Snowden Jr., the legend of John Henry began with his 14-length grass win in a $35,000 claiming race at Belmont in June 1978, when John Henry was 3 years old.

He did not score his first Grade 1 victory until 1980, when he was 5, but over the next four years John Henry would win 14 Grade 1 turf stakes, including the 1980 San Juan Capistrano at Santa Anita; the Arlington Million twice ('81 and '84); the San Luis Rey at Santa Anita twice ('80 and '81); the Hollywood Invitational three times ('80,' 81, and '84); the Oak Tree Invitational three times ('80,' 81, and '82); plus the 1983 Hollywood Turf Cup, the '84 Sunset Handicap, and the '84 Turf Classic at Belmont, the last two when he was 9 years old. This to go along with 12 other rich grass stakes at seven different tracks across the country.

John Henry was strictly mediocre as a dirt runner early in his career, but his confidence grew with every grass victory to the point that he won several important dirt stakes, most notably the 1981 Jockey Club Gold Cup at Belmont and back-to-back runnings of the Santa Anita Handicap in '81 and '82—the latter via the disqualification of Perrault, a versatile Charlie Whittingham trainee who won the second Arlington Million later that year and was named grass champion.

John Henry may have been a compiler, but unlike most who build positive resumes through long careers, he was a brilliant performer who held his form past the point when most horses tend to be in steep decline. At 4 through 9 years of age, John Henry was a match for any grass horse in the world.

1. *Manila*

Another great horse developed by the enigmatic but exceptionally talented trainer LeRoy Jolley, and quite probably his best. Manila lost his three races as a 2-year-old in 1985, all on dirt, and was strictly raced on grass as a 3-year-old in 1986 and as a 4-year-old in 1987, when he won 12 of 15 grass starts with three seconds.

He won six grass stakes in succession during his strong 3-year-old season, including three Grade 1's, and capped his campaign with a victory in the Breeders' Cup Turf over the next year's grass champion Theatrical, with the high-class turf mare Estrapade finishing third and the European champion Dancing Brave fourth. With those four plus others in the field, the 1986 Turf may have been the strongest grass race in Breeders' Cup history. Frankly, there are no American turf horses in my lifetime that I would have favored to beat this outstanding performer at a classic distance.

TURF MILERS

As stated previously, there were no turf races in America until the early 1950s, and the popularity of the one-mile grass race did not begin until the advent of the Breeders' Cup in 1984. Several winners and near winners of the Breeders' Cup Mile rank among the best at that special distance, including two-time winner Da Hoss (1996 and '98); Cozzene, winner in 1985 after his third-place finish the previous year; plus the fillies Royal Heroine in'84, Ridgewood Pearl in '95, and Six Perfections in 2003.

Likewise, the strong finishers War Chant in 2000 and Val Royal in 2001 certainly could fill out a Top 10 list, and there would be some argument to include 2005 Breeders' Cup Filly and Mare Turf winner Intercontinental, whose best distance really was a mile. But, after a long review of *Daily Racing Form* past performances, result charts, and privately compiled videotapes, I believe the five turf milers listed below were a cut above them all, even though one was unable to win the Breeders' Cup Mile due to circumstances beyond his control.

5. *Royal Academy*

This British import was a serious miler throughout his limited career, winning the Group 1 July Cup and finishing second in the Irish 2000 Guineas prior to his adventurous, stout victory in the 1990 Breeders' Cup

Mile at Belmont Park when he was ridden by aging British legend Lester Piggott.

In that Mile, Royal Academy was forced to drop back toward the rear of the 13-horse field, then circled very wide through the turn while holding his position in move that usually saps the strength of most horses. In the stretch, Royal Academy continued on with a last-quarter surge from eighth position to get up in the final strides to beat the hard-hitting and versatile Itsallgreektome, subsequently voted 1990's champion turf horse. Although the Beyer Speed Figure for the race was 111, which was topped by several other Breeders' Cup Mile winners through the years, this was a visually impressive, if not underrated, performance by a colt who seemed several lengths better than Itsallgreektome, especially at one mile.

4. *Steinlen*

The only one of trainer D. Wayne Lukas's many champions who excelled on grass, Steinlen finished a respectable second to Miesque in the 1988 Breeders' Cup Mile, then won the '89 Mile the following year despite a series of bumps and changes in direction that might have stopped many other horses. He finally got clear very late to win going away in a sparkling performance. The 1989 Breeders' Cup Mile completed a streak of five straight important turf victories that included the 1 1/4-mile Arlington Million. In his final career race as a 7-year-old in 1990, while below his best form, Steinlen still managed to finish a respectable fourth to Royal Academy, one of the better Breeders' Cup Milers I have seen.

3. *Rock of Gibraltar*

Finished a strong and very unlucky second to a lucky Domedriver in the 2002 Breeders' Cup Mile after winning seven straight Group 1 stakes in Europe. Attempting to rally from ninth in the field of 13, Rock of Gibraltar was forced to check while in his best gear, regrouped under jockey Michael Kinane, and angled out to the middle of the track to launch a furious late rally that was too late. Although defeated, Rock of Gibraltar seemed clearly best of this field and probably would have been favored to defeat all but the top two Breeders' Cup winners listed below.

2. *Lure*

Claiborne Farm's Lure was a spectacular repeat Breeders' Cup Mile winner in 1992 and '93, and won 11 of his 18 grass races, with six seconds and a fifth in his final career start in the 1994 Mile. During his two-year run as the best turf miler in the world, Lure was unfortunate not to win an Eclipse Award. In 1992, the long-distance grass runner Sky Classic was voted turf champ by a slim voting margin without winning either the Arlington Million or the Breeders' Cup Turf. In 1993, Lure won six of eight, with two seconds, losing both races to Star of Cozzene at distances beyond Lure's range. That also was the year Kotashaan won the Eclipse Award as the nation's top turf performer and Horse of the Year, an award Kotashaan deserved.

1. *Miesque*

As a 3-year-old in 1987, this French-based filly trained by Francois Boutin won four Group 1 stakes at one mile in Europe and then easily won the 1987 Breeders' Cup Mile in near-world-record time by open lengths over high-class male rivals at Hollywood Park.

As a 4-year-old in 1988, Miesque raced only four times, winning a pair of Group 1 events in France before she turned in an extraordinary stretch-running triumph in the 1988 Mile that impressed as much as Personal Ensign's outstanding late run in the Breeders' Cup Distaff to kept her unbeaten record intact.

Frankly, I doubt there was a better turf miler, male or female, since grass racing began in this country. Miesque is the only grass miler in the Hall of Fame, which seems quite an oversight or an indictment of the voting procedure, given that Da Hoss and Lure each won the Breeders' Cup Mile twice and Cozzene, an Eclipse Award winner, was the first Mile winner bred and raced in America.

LONG-DISTANCE TURF FILLIES AND MARES

Some champion fillies and mares on the turf were better than the champion turf males of the same year. The miler Miesque, for example, was superior to Sunshine Forever, champion turf horse of 1988. The same is true for at least half of the 11 fillies and mares on the list below, who were more effective at distances beyond a mile, eight of whom have been disgracefully ignored by the Hall of Fame through the years.

11. *Waya*

This French import, trained by David Whiteley, was voted top turf filly in 1978, the year she won six of her nine starts with two seconds, beating males in the Man o' War and Turf Classic and finishing third to Mac Diarmida in the Washington, D.C., International.

10. *Ryafan*

A high-class European import who was 3 years old when she made her three U.S. starts in 1997—all Grade 1 grass victories, including two against older fillies and mares. She was voted champion turf filly that year because there was no doubt whatsoever that she was too good to deny, despite such a limited campaign. Ryafan was developed and trained by John Gosden until Bobby Frankel took over for her last career outing.

9. *Royal Heroine*

This Irish-bred filly was also trained by John Gosden, who took over from fellow Englishman Michael Stoute when Royal Heroine arrived in California. Gosden continued to train her for a full year in America beginning in November 1983, continuing to November 1984, when she retired with six stakes victories from her 10 starts in America. Among those triumphs were three over male rivals, including a division of the Hollywood Derby as a 3-year-old in 1983 and the inaugural Breeders' Cup Mile at Hollywood Park in 1984. That race, in which future Mile winner Cozzene finished third, proved just how good she was, considering that all of Royal Heroine's other victories and three second-place finishes in America were at longer distances. One of those second-place finishes was to John Henry in the 1984 Arlington Million.

8. *Pebbles*

This popular British-based filly was a Group 1 winner over 3-year-old fillies in 1984 and then won a pair of Group 1 stakes over males in England before shipping to New York for a sensational stretch-running victory in the 1985 Breeders' Cup Turf at Aqueduct.

Pebbles went from 13th on the far turn to first entering the stretch and held off the good Australian import Strawberry Road to the wire in her only American start. That single powerful performance over accomplished older males was enough for Pebbles to be voted the 1985 Eclipse Award as champion turf female. It was one of the best in Breeders' Cup Turf history.

7. *Flawlessly*

A high-class homebred daughter of Harbor View Farm's Triple Crown winner Affirmed, she originally was trained by Dick Dutrow through her 2-year-old campaign in 1990, which included only one turf race, a dominating win in the less important Gardenia Stakes now run at the Meadowlands after a rebuilt Garden State Park was shut down. She bled badly to start off her 3-year-old season in 1991 and was shipped west to the care of Charlie Whittingham, who wisely raced her on grass for the rest of her career.

From 1991 through 1994, Flawlessly won 14 of her 22 grass races, all stakes, including nine Grade 1's, eight of them at exactly nine furlongs, plus four seconds and a third, all in stakes. In 1993, as a 5-year-old mare, Flawlessly raced only five times, winning four Grade 1 races, including a DQ victory when she was bothered late when second by a nose in the $1\,^3/_{16}$-mile Beverly D at Arlington Park, the most prestigious grass race for fillies and mares in an era when there was no Breeders' Cup Filly and Mare Turf race. Flawlessly was elected to the Hall of Fame in 2004.

6. *April Run*

A filly with truly international connections, this daughter of 1971 grass champion Run the Gantlet was bred in Ireland, owned by Diana Firestone of Genuine Risk fame, and trained by Frenchman Francois Boutin.

April Run won two Group 1's as a 3-year-old in 1981 and was a very close third in the Prix d l'Arc de Triomphe before winning the Turf Classic at Belmont and finishing a good second in the Washington, D.C., International. She also finished a close fourth in the 1982 Arc before returning to America to win the Turf Classic a second time and taking the D.C. International by 6 ½ lengths over the good turf horse Majesty's Prince. She made one more international trip—to Tokyo—for the Japan Cup, where she finished a close third, a neck behind future Horse of the Year All Along, with John Henry 13th.

5. *Ouija Board*

She was third in the 2004 Prix de l'Arc de Triomphe at 1 ½ miles after winning a pair of Group 1 races in England and Ireland, then won the 2004 Breeders' Cup Filly and Mare Turf at Lone Star Park with speed to spare. Ouija Board competed actively in high-class stakes company in 2005 and was a solid second to Intercontinental in the 1 ¼-mile Filly and Mare Turf at Belmont. She was still going well in 2006, with a strong second to 2005 Breeders' Cup Turf winner Shirocco in the Coronation Cup at Ascot in June 2006 and a pair of victories in Group 1 stakes during the summer before winning the Filly and Mare Turf a second time.

4. *Estrapade*

One of many outstanding older grass horses—male and female—trained by Charlie Whittingham, this daughter of Vaguely Noble was a stakes winner in Europe as a 3- and 4-year-old in 1983 and '84, but came into her best form when owner Allen Paulson shipped her to Whittingham on the West Coast in 1985. As a 5- and 6-year-old, Estrapade won six Grade 1 races, including the '86 Arlington Million and the Oak Tree Invitational against males, while finishing third to the outstanding Manila and future 1987 Eclipse Award winner Theatrical in the 1986 Breeders' Cup Turf.

3. *Typecast*

Although Cougar II was a lukewarm choice as 1972 turf champion, the real turf champion that year was the 6-year-old mare Typecast. In those days, there only was only one turf award, and Typecast beat Cougar and other male rivals in the 1 ½-mile Hollywood Turf Invitational Handicap and then beat most of the same group in the two-mile Sunset Handicap at Hollywood.

In her final start of 1972, Typecast put an exclamation point on her season, completing her rampage over males with a sharp win at Belmont in the prestigious Man o' War stakes. Typecast is another major omission from the Hall of Fame.

2. *All Along*

For six weeks in 1983, this French import compiled one of the most astonishing series of performances in turf-racing history.

Trained by Patrick Biancone throughout her career, All Along won Europe's most prestigious race, the Prix de l'Arc de Triomphe at Longchamp on October 2, 1983. She then was shipped to North America, where she continued to run exclusively against male rivals, winning three straight Grade 1 events—the Rothmans Invitational at Woodbine on October 16; the Turf Classic at Aqueduct on October 29; and the Washington, D.C., International at Laurel on November 12. In other words, All Along won all four of the highest-class stakes in three countries in five weeks! The performances not only earned the 4-year-old All Along an Eclipse Award as America's top female grass horse, but also the Horse of the Year title.

The following year, as a 5-year-old, All Along did not win in her four starts, all against males, but did finish third in the Arc and was a sharp second to British import Lashkari in the inaugural Breeders' Cup Turf at Hollywood Park, the final race of her meteoric career. All Along was elected to the Hall of Fame in 1990.

1. *Dahlia*

Those who saw it will never forget the electrifying stretch kick this great 3-year-old filly, trained by French-based Maurice Zilber, turned in to win the 1973 Washington, D. C., International.

Already the winner of four Group 1 stakes in Europe, including the prestigious King George VI and Queen Elizabeth Diamond Stakes over older male rivals at Ascot, Dahlia went from last to first with a final quarter clocked in 23 ³⁄₅ on a soggy Laurel turf course to win the D.C. International by 3 ½ lengths over multiple Grade 1 winner Big Spruce. It was a performance that made one wonder if Secretariat could have handled her that day.

Returning to Europe for another top-notch campaign as a 4-year-old in 1974, Dahlia won three more Group 1 races, including a repeat triumph in the King George and Queen Elizabeth.

Back in America that fall, Dahlia promptly beat male rivals two more times, in the 1974 Man o' War and the Canadian International, before she was a fast-closing third behind an extremely slow pace in the D.C. International. Dahlia had some high and low points late in her extended American career through 1976, but she did beat males once more in the Grade 1 Century Handicap at Hollywood Park as a 6-year-old, while under the care of Charlie Whittingham. At her best, Dahlia was out of this world. She was the first female turf horse elected to the Hall of Fame, in 1981.

THE BEST OLDER HORSES

In the early 1950s through the late 1970s there were four characteristics that identified the best of the older horses: winning important stakes at classic distances; running exceptionally fast; beating other worthy opponents; and successfully carrying significant weight.

In recent decades, Beyer Speed Figures have become an important tool for comparing the relative speed of contemporary horses, but there have been few major stakes in which weight-carrying ability has been an issue. Also, aside from the extremely rich Breeders' Cup races and perhaps a dozen other nationally prominent stakes, it is rare to see multiple matchups of top horses in the same events.

Comparing the performances of horses under heavy weight assignments also is a thing of the past, because the stakes calendar has become so rich with options that trainers have learned to effectively bargain with racing officials in different jurisdictions to keep the weight assignments down, or they go elsewhere. At first, the intimidation issue was discounted by racing secretaries, but when champion horse "A" went to a different track that was willing to assign 122 pounds instead of 125 for a similar purse, the concept of handicap racing was undermined to the point where weight assignments became minimal factors at the championship level.

This is bad for the game. The ability to tote significant weight was and should be an important handicapping consideration for mature horses traveling a distance of ground.

"The longer the race, the more important weight can be," says Hall of Fame trainer Allen Jerkens, who has won his share of distance races using apprentice jockeys who get five pounds reduced from the assigned weight for their inexperience, in all races except stakes. (Very inexperienced riders can get seven or 10-pound reductions.) While I personally can argue that weight assignments that range between 112 to 119 pounds have virtually no impact on horses' performance at any distance, numerous studies on the subject say that some attention should be paid to large shifts in weight from one race to another and that a discernible effect on performance can be seen with weights in the high 120s and above.

The diminishing importance of weight as a factor in matching horses also is seen in the Breeders' Cup races, in which all horses are assigned specific weights according to their respective ages. Older male horses in the Breeders' Cup Classic carry 126 pounds, while 3-year-olds get in with 121 and fillies and mares get three pounds fewer. This is as it should be for championship races, simply because we want to find out who the best horse is on a level playing field that gives no special concession to any horse.

But the idea that handicap races provide an unfair test during the rest of the year is countered by the fact that we have always been thrilled by the horse who can overcome an obstacle, or win despite having to do more than his principal rivals. Moreover, several dozen of the richest races in the country, such as the Whitney Handicap at Saratoga, the Metropolitan Mile at Belmont, and the Hollywood Gold Cup still are contested under handicap conditions. But that is in name only. I doubt you will see a single horse asked to carry 130 pounds in any of these races during the foreseeable future. You might not even see 127.

Another and equally important issue that interferes with good comparisons across the decades is the number of races—or rather, the reduced number of races—that contemporary horses compete in compared to the lengthy campaigns that were customary in years gone by.

In today's world, the owner of a fast Grade 1 horse is likely to be offered millions of dollars to retire him for stud duty, rather than risk a hard race or two, or three.

In the meantime, here are the top 13 older horses I have seen using all the tools and comparisons I would make if they all were entered in a 1 1/4-mile race on dirt around two turns on a fast track. Some very strong performers fell just below my cut line, including 2003 Horse of the Year Mineshaft, who earned Beyer Speed Figures of 114 to 118 in seven straight outings; Nashua, who was a great 3-year-old in 1955 and a near-great 4-year-old; Exceller, who won five Grade 1 races on turf and two Grade 1's on dirt during the late 1970s, including his memorable stretch-running victory in the mud over an extremely game Seattle Slew in the 1978 Jockey Club Gold Cup; and Lava Man, who won the Sunshine Millions Classic, Santa Anita Handicap, Hollywood Gold Cup, Pacific Classic, and Goodwood Breeders' Cup Handicap, plus a stakes on the turf during a solid run in 2006. Last but not least, Formal Gold was a championship contender in 1997 and ran 122-126 Beyer figures in four different races that year, including two victories over Skip Away, before that horse reeled off triumphs in the Jockey Club Gold Cup and Breeders' Cup Classic to edge Formal Gold for Horse of the Year and placement on this list.

Top weight in my hypothetical 1 1/4-mile race is 134 pounds. In today's world, it would be close to a mortal certainty that at least 10 of the baker's dozen named below would scratch out of the race to run under lighter assignments against weaker competition.

13. *Skip Away, 120 pounds*

Caroline and Sonny Hine's powerful gray was a good horse at 3 in 1996 with in-the-money finishes in the Preakness, Belmont, and Travers to go along with wins in the Blue Grass Stakes, Woodbine Million, and the Jockey Club Gold Cup, his first outing against older horses.

As a 4- and 5-year-old, Skip Away moved forward at least a notch, winning four stakes, including the Jockey Club Gold Cup and Breeders' Cup Classic to complete his 4-year-old campaign in 1997 while beginning a nine-race winning streak—with seven Grade 1 victories. During that streak, Skip Away posted 120–125 Beyer Speed Figures four times. One of those highly rated victories was a six-length score in the '97 Breeders' Cup Classic, which clinched the Horse of the Year award and established Skip Away as deserving a place in the Hall of Fame.

12. *Cigar, 123 pounds*

The two-time Horse of the Year in 1995 and '96, Cigar was expertly trained by Billy Mott under enormous pressure as he went halfway around the world and back again to equal Citation's record of 16 straight victories. The streak began in October 1994 and continued midway through 1996, but the most interesting win wasn't the 1996 Dubai World Cup, or the '95 Breeders' Cup Classic at Belmont, both of which showed his grit and abundant class—it was victory number 4—the '95 Donn Handicap.

Carrying a paltry 115 pounds despite having won the NYRA Mile by seven lengths (subsequently renamed the Cigar Mile), Cigar was a lukewarm 4–1 shot in the nine-furlong Donn, meeting the reigning 1994 Horse of the Year, Holy Bull, who was on a winning streak of six straight since his dismal 12th-place finish in the 1994 Kentucky Derby. Holy Bull was the prohibitive 3–10 wagering favorite under 127 pounds against Cigar. But Cigar took the lead from the start and was in complete command, while Holy Bull, in obvious distress, pulled up lame in what turned out to be his final race.

Holy Bull survived to sire 2005 Kentucky Derby winner Giacomo and many other stakes winners, while Cigar continued on from that moment to build his own historic streak in a symbolic passing of the torch from one Horse of the Year to another, unlike any in racing history. Cigar, in fact, won 10 straight during his unbeaten 1995 campaign. Mott was elected to the Hall of Fame in 1998, Cigar in 2002.

11. *Ghostzapper, also 123 pounds*

He won 3 of 5 in sprints as a 2- and 3-year-old without attracting much attention, but trainer Bobby Frankel suspected he had a world-class distance performer on his hands and was anxious to test that thesis after Ghostzapper effortlessly won the seven-furlong Tom Fool at Belmont with a 120 Beyer Speed Figure to begin his 4-year-old season in July 2004. Frankel chose the Iselin Handicap at Monmouth Park and was blown away by what the son of Awesome Again did on a sloppy track in his first two-turn race.

"I knew he was good, but I don't think anybody realized how good; he was great, not good," Frankel said.

Ghostzapper won the Iselin by 10 3/4 lengths and earned a sky-high Beyer Speed Figure of 128 for that performance and proceeded to win the nine-furlong Woodward and 10-furlong Breeders' Cup Classic to be a landslide choice for Horse of the Year despite having only four races. Returning in May 2005, Ghostzapper won the Metropolitan Mile Handicap by 6 1/2 lengths under the absurdly light weight of 122 pounds, but there was nothing absurd about the horse he trounced—Silver Train—who would win the 2005 Breeders' Cup Sprint later in the year and the 2006 Met Mile as well.

Ghostzapper never had another chance to show how good he was, as he was retired prematurely due to a training injury. But during his brief stay in the limelight, he gave sufficient hints that he was one of the best horses of the modern age, earning Beyer Speed Figures of 124 and 122 in his last two races to go along with his lofty 128 in the Iselin. One can only wonder how he would have fared under heavier burdens and through a longer campaign.

10. *Bold Ruler, 125 pounds*

Wheatley Stable's homebred son of Nasrullah won the 1957 Preakness and earned Horse of the Year over one of the best 3-year-old crops of all time via his overall consistency. Ironically, Bold Ruler did not win Horse of the Year, or even champion handicap horse as a 4-year-old in 1958, despite some of the best performances of the decade.

Bold Ruler won the seven-furlong Carter Handicap under 135 pounds; finished second in the '58 Met Mile under 135 pounds to '57 Belmont winner Gallant Man (130); won the nine-furlong Stymie Handicap by five lengths under 134 while spotting his principal rivals 21 and 25 pounds; won the 1 1/4-mile Suburban Handicap under 134 pounds, 25 and 24 pounds more than the second- and third-place finishers; and he won the 1 1/4-mile Monmouth Handicap under 134, spotting as much as 29 pounds to prime contenders.

While there were no accurate speed figures during the 1950s, Bold

Ruler did set stakes-record clockings in his three longest races of the year—the Stymie, Suburban, and Monmouth Handicaps, and was judged properly to be the fastest horse in America, the champion sprinter of 1958.

Although he was trained by Hall of Famer Sunny Jim Fitzsimmons and ridden in all but a few of his starts by Hall of Famer Eddie Arcaro, somehow it took the Hall of Fame voters until 1973 to elect Bold Ruler— and then probably only because of the media attention he got that year through Secretariat.

9. *Ack Ack, 126 pounds*

This cleverly named son of Battle Joined was a useful 3-year-old in 1969, winning three moderate stakes in Florida, Kentucky, and Illinois, but developed into a great 4- and 5-year-old in 1970 and '71 under the patient care of the venerable Charlie Whittingham. Ack Ack won 10 of 13 during those two years, the last seven in succession. He was fast and extremely versatile, winning from 5 1/2 furlongs to 1 1/4 miles, and posting clockings in near track-record time in all of his starts as an older horse, including a pair of victories on the turf, one at six furlongs, one at 1 1/8 miles.

He defeated his versatile stablemate Cougar II in the 1971 Santa Anita Handicap under 130 pounds, while Cougar had 125, and finished his career with three more victories in handicap stakes, carrying 130–134 pounds. Ack Ack was the champion sprinter, handicap champion, and Horse of the Year in 1971, and was inducted into the Hall of Fame in 1986.

8. *Affirmed, also 126 pounds*

Beyond his great battles with Alydar to become the last Triple Crown winner of the 20th century, Affirmed was a repeat Horse of the Year as a 4-year-old in 1979 by virtue of seven straight victories to the end of his career, all under Laffit Pincay Jr., who took over for the struggling Steve Cauthen.

Among them were six Grade 1 triumphs, including the Santa Anita Handicap under 128 pounds, the Californian under 130, the Hollywood Gold Cup under 132, and the Jockey Club Gold Cup under weight-for-age conditions when he gave the imposing 3-year-old Spectacular Bid his last defeat before that superstar went on a 10-race winning streak to the end of his career.

Affirmed was an incredibly athletic colt, with superior speed that he successfully carried the classic 1 ¼-mile distance on four occasions as a 4-year-old, including the Santa Anita Handicap, in which he set a stakes-record clocking of 1:58 ³/₅ that has yet to be equaled. When he won the Hollywood Gold Cup carrying 132 pounds, Affirmed covered the 10 furlongs in 1:58 ²/₅, only a fifth off the existing track record. Superbly trained by Laz Barrera, Affirmed won 22 of 29 starts, with five seconds and a third. He was elected to the Hall of Fame in 1980, one year after Barrera.

7. *Seattle Slew, 127 pounds*

The 1977 Triple Crown winner was developed brilliantly by Billy Turner Jr. but also was well handled as a 4-year-old in 1978 by young Doug Peterson after this great horse was near death due to a serious infection during the winter. Seattle Slew also was forced to the sidelines for another three months following a winning allowance sprint at Aqueduct in May.

He returned at Saratoga in August 1978 with a victory over allowance-class sprinters and promptly followed that with a sharp second-place finish to co-sprint champion Dr. Patches in the nine-furlong Paterson Handicap under the lights at the Meadowlands. In a strange turn of events, that very good, albeit losing, effort in the Paterson somehow convinced jockey Jean Cruguet to jump ship, telling members of the press that he believed Seattle Slew was "not the same horse."

"He's game, but he's through," Cruguet said. Ironically, Dr. Patches' jockey, Angel Cordero Jr., saw things differently, as he lobbied enthusiastically to ride "Slew" in his next outing, the Marlboro Cup Handicap.

Score one for Cordero, who rode Seattle Slew to an impressive wire-to-wire, four-length victory under 128 pounds over 1978 Triple Crown winner Affirmed (who carried 124 as a 3-year-old)—the first meeting of Triple Crown winners in racing history.

Seattle Slew then won the Woodward by four over Exceller, lost the Jockey Club Gold Cup to Exceller by an inch in an amazingly brave performance (battling back after being passed) and completed his career as a world-renowned superstar of the highest magnitude with a very easy wire-to-wire win at 1–10 odds in the Stuyvesant Handicap under 134 pounds, spotting his overmatched rivals as many as 21 pounds. Seattle Slew was elected to the Hall of Fame in 1981.

6. *Tom Fool, 128*

Greentree Stable's bay colt was just another useful 2- and 3-year-old in 1951 and '52, but was one of the very best horses of the modern age as a 4-year-old, winning all 10 of his starts that year to extend a winning streak that began in his final race in 1952 and reached 11 straight. Trained hard and often by John Gaver, who toughened up his better horses as if they were going to run three races a month, Tom Fool was a horse who could take it and dish it out.

During his magical year, Tom Fool won at 5 ½ and six furlongs; equaled the seven-furlong track record at Aqueduct in the Carter Handicap under 135 pounds; won the Met Mile under 130; the 1 ¼-mile Brooklyn Handicap under 136; and in his final career start, set the 1 ³/₁₆-mile track record in the Pimlico Special to complete his unbeaten Horse of the Year campaign. Tom Fool finished with 21 wins, seven seconds and a third from 30 career starts, all with Hall of Famer Ted Atkinson aboard.

Tom Fool, 1953's champion sprinter, champion handicap horse, and Horse of the Year, was a fast weight-carrier and it is unfortunate that he never met the great 3-year-old of 1953—Native Dancer. Tom Fool was elected to the Hall of Fame in 1960, Gaver in '66.

5. *Swaps, 130 pounds*

Although Nashua proved to be a better 3-year-old in their historic match race at Washington Park in 1955, Swaps was one of America's greatest 4-year-olds, winning eight of his 10 starts, with one second, finishing out of the money only once—in a turf race.

Swaps carried 130 pounds successfully *six times*; set or equaled six track records, four at Hollywood Park; set a world record for 1 ¹/₁₆ miles (1:39 ³/₅) at Gulfstream Park in April; and broke his own world record for that distance at Hollywood (1:39 flat) 14 days after he broke the world record for the mile (1:33 $\frac{1}{5}$), a record that would stand until Dr. Fager broke it 12 years later at Arlington Park.

Bill Nack, the turf writer and biographer of Secretariat, is firm in his personal view that Swaps was "the best older horse I have ever seen." As stated earlier, it is hard to prove or disprove such opinions, even when they are voiced by bona fide expert observers, but I would not have wagered against Swaps on his best day on a lightning-fast track.

4. *Forego, 131 pounds*

This great gelding was fourth in Secretariat's record-breaking 1973 Kentucky Derby while still growing into his huge frame, but won his final two outings that year—both stakes—to foreshadow his emergence as one of the best handicap horses of the modern age.

Early in 1974, Forego extended his modest winning streak to five, winning the three premier winter handicap stakes in Florida—the Donn, the Gulfstream Park Handicap, and the Widener—and then he made it six straight, winning the seven-furlong Carter on his arrival back at Belmont Park in May. After two seconds under 129 pounds in the Met Mile and the Nassau County, Forego won four of his next seven under 126 to 131 pounds to earn the first of four championships as America's top handicap horse and the first of his three consecutive Horse of the Year titles.

Trained by Sherrill Ward through his 5-year-old season in 1975 and thereafter by Frank Whiteley Jr., Forego won 12 Grade 1 stakes at 4, 5, 6, and 7 years of age and was only out of the money three times in the 37 starts he made during those years. As a modern-age weight carrier, no horse can match his record, and few his versatility. Consider that Forego successfully carried 130–137 pounds in 12 handicap stakes victories, spotting his nearest rivals as much as 26 pounds. Forego won under those heavy burdens at seven furlongs, at one mile, 1 $\frac{1}{8}$ miles, 1 $\frac{3}{16}$ miles, 1 $\frac{1}{4}$ miles, and 1 $\frac{1}{2}$ miles. He also won several prestigious weight-for-age stakes, the most important of which was his only start in the two-mile Jockey Club Gold Cup in 1974 under scale weight of 126 pounds.

Yet, there is no question that Forego will forever be remembered by those who had the pleasure of witnessing his dramatic, almost desperate rally to victory in the final stride of the 1976 Marlboro Cup when he caught the fleet and fit 3-year-old Honest Pleasure on the wire. While good stretch runs occur every day at every track in America, I can count on one hand the number of comparable, seemingly impossible victories that other truly great Thoroughbreds have scored with such determination: Personal Ensign's 1988 Breeders' Cup Distaff; Buckpasser's victory over a free-running Ring Twice in the 1967 Suburban under 133 pounds; Kelso running down front-running All Hands under 130 pounds despite serious traffic problems in the 1961 Met Mile; and John Henry's gut-wrenching nose victory over The Bart in the 1981 Arlington Million.

It is hard to rank those races, just as it is hard to confidently rank all of these great horses who accomplished so much. But no horse on this list was carrying 137 pounds while trying to catch a world-class rival at 1 ¼ miles while simultaneously overcoming a speed-favoring, sloppy track. Forego was elected to the Hall of Fame in 1979, one year after both of his trainers preceded him into the same shrine.

3. *Dr. Fager, also 131 pounds*

Dr. Fager may not have been quite as good as Damascus as a 3-year-old in 1967, and he did expose an Achilles heel when pressed into red-hot fractions by Damascus's stablemate Hedevar in the 1968 Brooklyn Handicap. But aside from that single defeat in eight starts that year, Dr. Fager was an imposing 4-year-old who would have been a match for any horse on this list at any distance from six furlongs to 1 ¼ miles.

Not only did he set the world record for one mile at Arlington Park during the summer of 1968, he also carried 130 or more pounds in each of his outings that year, winning seven. These included the 1 ¼-mile Suburban, while tying the track record in 1:59⅗ under 132 pounds. He finished off his career with victories in the United Nations Handicap on the Atlantic City turf course (under 134 pounds) and a mind-numbing track-record victory in the seven-furlong Vosburgh Handicap at Aqueduct, clocked in 1:20 ⅕ while carrying a staggering 139 pounds!

2. *Spectacular Bid, 132 pounds*

"The Bid" lost his bid for a Triple Crown sweep in the 1979 Belmont Stakes and also was beaten by 1978 Triple Crown winner Affirmed in the

'79 Jockey Club Gold Cup. But Spectacular Bid never lost another race, finishing his 3-year-old season with a victory in the Meadowlands Cup as a prelude to one of the great campaigns in racing history.

In 1980, Spectacular Bid was indeed spectacular, winning six straight on the West Coast, including a track-record performance in the seven-furlong Malibu Stakes (clocked in 1:20 flat, a record still intact through 2006). Spectacular Bid won the Santa Anita Handicap under 130 pounds, the Mervyn LeRoy under 132, and the Californian under 130 before he shipped to Illinois to win the Washington Park Handicap under 130 en route to his score in the Haskell Handicap at Monmouth Park under 132.

Finally in the 1 1/4-mile Woodward at Belmont, the true quality of Spectacular Bid was reflected in a most unusual way. No owner or trainer was willing to run against him! In a classic walkover, one of the few in major stakes-racing history, Spectacular Bid breezed around Belmont Park unopposed to complete one of the few undefeated seasons at the championship level. Spectacular Bid was elected to the Hall in 1982. Trainer Buddy Delp, a successful claiming-horse trainer in Maryland most of his career, was voted in 20 years later.

1. *Kelso, 134 pounds*

If somebody offered me a million dollars to pick one horse to win one race at 1 1/4 miles against the best older horses of the past 50-odd years, Kelso might not be the choice. But if the offer was to pick the horse to win five or more races out of 10 against the same group, Kelso would be a cinch play, even if they piled 134 pounds on his back.

Kelso, who was gelded in 1959 following a modest 2-year-old campaign, did not have an undefeated season in his lengthy career, but he did win 11 in succession during one streak and seven in a row during another. Kelso did not set a bushel of track records from seven furlongs to 1 1/4 miles, but he did set the Aqueduct track record for 1 1/4 miles; tied Whisk Broom's 1 1/4-mile mark at Belmont Park; and tied Man o' War's 1 5/8-mile mark at the same track. Kelso also set the two-mile track record at Aqueduct while winning the Jockey Club Gold Cup for the first time in 1960 and he set it again as a 7-year-old in 1964 when he won that signature race for the fifth straight year in world-record time. That performance led to another record, one that probably will stand forever. Kelso won his fifth straight Horse of the Year Award.

Kelso set still another track record when he won the 1964 Washington, D.C., International on the Laurel turf course in his fourth attempt 11 days after his world-record clocking in the Jockey Club Gold Cup. As a horse who never was all that comfortable on grass, Kelso won that D.C. International in a sizzling 2:23 $^4/_5$ for 1 $^1/_2$ miles, a course record that never would be broken while Laurel ran the D.C. International through 1984.

Kelso carried 130–136 pounds successfully 12 times, won 39 of his 63 races (18 for 34 while ridden by journeyman jockey Ismael Valenzuela), and finished second 12 times and third twice. After one final race as a 9-year-old in 1967, Kelso retired as the world's leading money winner with a $1.9 million bankroll during an era when the richest race he competed in was worth $144,000.

Kelso was a fighter, a champion over five generations of horses, or approximately 130,000 Thoroughbreds of racing age in North America during his career. Hall of Fame jockey Eddie Arcaro, who rode Kelso to 11 wins in 12 races and retired in 1961, called Kelso the best horse he ever rode—this despite the fact that Arcaro rode two different Triple Crown winners (Whirlaway in 1941 and Citation in 1948). That is good enough for me.

Trainer Carl Hanford, who did such excellent work managing the career of this great gelding, finally was elected to the Hall of Fame in 2006.

STEEPLECHASERS

Steeplechase horses run far and carry high weights over obstacles. To some, that is the ultimate test of the Thoroughbred.

The popularity of steeplechase and hurdle racing has remained very high in Great Britain through the centuries, but it is nowhere near as prominent in America. Yet, its devotees are a passionate group of sportsmen who breed, own, train, and/or ride at a variety of short meets at a handful of major tracks and in a few states such as South Carolina and Tennessee where parimutuel racing does not exist.

In Camden, South Carolina, the Colonial Cup has been an important hurdle stakes since it was inaugurated with a purse of $100,000 in 1970. Same goes for the $150,000 Iroquois at the Nashville Tennessee course since the mid-1980s.

Some other major races that have played a role in deciding hurdle championships include the $75,000 Temple Gwathmey in Middleburg, Virginia (formerly run at Belmont Park), and the $150,000 New York Turf Writers Cup at Saratoga, one of only 10 tracks offering a limited schedule of parimutuel hurdle races in the 21st century.

The Grand National, run at Belmont Park and Fair Hill in Maryland until discontinued in the late 1990s, rivaled the Colonial Cup for its importance, but the premier hurdle stakes has been the $200,000 Breeders' Cup Steeplechase since it was created in 1986.

Through the past half-century, there have been some wonderful hurdle performers, including the versatile Neji, a three-time Eclipse Award winner in the 1950s; Bon Nouvel, a three-time champion in the 1960s; Quick Pitch, a stakes winner on the flat and over the jumps in the 1970s; Café Prince, a two-time Eclipse Award winner in 1977 and '78; Zaccio, winner of three straight titles in 1980 through '82; and the unusual Morley Street, who was champion in 1990 and '91 after having raced only once in America in each year—winning the 1990 Breeders' Cup Steeplechase by 11 lengths and the 1991 BC Steeplechase by 9 3/4 lengths (along with his numerous victories in Ireland and Great Britain). Another impressive hurdle performer was Flat Top, a winner of an Eclipse in 1998 who came back to win it in 2002. But the three best steeplechase horses I have seen during the past 50-odd years were:

3. *McDynamo*

During his 2003 championship season at the age of 6, he won all five of his hurdle races to follow up a 5-year-old campaign when he was 4 for 6 when competing in hurdle races for the first time. He continued to race in high form through 8 years of age. Among his most important victories, McDynamo won the Breeders' Cup Steeplechase four straight years, 2003–06, and the Colonial Cup in 2003 and 2005.

2. *Lonesome Glory*

Won 17 steeplechase and hurdle races during a remarkable, extended career that included five Eclipse Awards spread out over eight seasons (1992 and '93, '95, '97, and '99). He was seldom dominant and his longest winning streak was five in 1995, one of which was a victory in a hurdles race at Sandown in England to replicate a previous win in England at Cheltenham in 1992.

Those two winning trips to England certified Lonesome Glory's special place in American steeplechase history as much as his three victories in the Colonial Cup or his two wins in the Carolina Cup or his dominating eight-length victory in the 1993 Breeders' Cup Steeplechase.

1. *Flatterer*

This gelding by Mo Bay was a $40,000 claiming horse through his 3-year-old season in 1982, but became steeplechasing's version of Kelso and John Henry rolled into one when Hall of Fame trainer Jonathan Sheppard converted him to the jumps in 1983. Flatterer won the Colonial Cup four straight times (1983–86) when that race was the dominant championship forum for steeplechase horses in America. He also won the Temple Gwathmey twice (1983 and '84); the Grand National in '83; the 1986 Georgia Cup; the 1987 Iroquois Steeplechase in Nashville; the 1984 New York Turf Writers Cup at Saratoga; and was voted champion steeplechase horse four straight times, from 1983 through 1986. He was the best I saw, but there is room to argue the point.

6

CROWD PLEASERS:

The Most Consistent, Versatile, and Popular Horses, and the Best Rivalries of the Modern Era

---

ULTRACONSISTENT HORSES

Aside from the very best Hall of Fame horses who compiled sensational career records, there have been a handful of near-great horses, including several champions, and the less famous who were so reliable, so consistent that they deserve special mention. More than a few on this list should be in the Hall of Fame.

12. *Silver Charm*

1997 Kentucky Derby-Preakness winner trained by Bob Baffert also won the 1998 Dubai World Cup in an underrated career of 24 races in which he was out of the money only three times, including his final two starts when well past his best form. Won 12, was second seven times and third twice, with separate in-the-money streaks of 14 and seven races, respectively.

11. *Chief's Crown*

1984 Breeders' Cup Juvenile and 1985 Travers winner was fourth in his career debut and fourth in the 1985 Breeders' Cup Classic, the final start of his 21-race career. In between, Chief's Crown won 12 races and was in the money in 18 of 19 starts. It would have been 19 in succession had he not been disqualified from a win in a turf race at Saratoga, his only attempt on grass.

10. *Bold Forbes*

Laz Barrera-trained Kentucky Derby-Belmont Stakes winner of 1976 won 13 races in Puerto Rico and the U.S. and never finished out of the money in 18 career starts. I find it hard to believe this horse is not in the Hall of Fame.

9. *Queen Empress*

Juvenile filly champion of 1964 when trained by Bill Winfrey; started her career with 18 straight in-the-money finishes, including all 14 of her starts at 2! Her streak was broken in her fifth outing as a 3-year-old, when she was injured in the '65 Alabama Stakes at Saratoga. As a 4-year-old in 1966 for trainer Eddie Neloy, Queen Empress also raced 14 times with 11 in-the-money finishes. From 33 career starts, the daughter of Bold Ruler had 15 victories, 10 seconds, and four thirds.

8. *Heavenly Prize*

Champion 3-year-old filly of 1994 trained by Shug McGaughey, never finished out of the money in 18 well-spaced career starts from 1993 through '96, winning nine, with six seconds and three thirds.

7. *Old Hat*

Champion older mare in 1965, won 35 races from 80 starts, from 1961 to 1965, with 18 seconds and nine thirds. Had in-the-money streaks of 11 races, seven, nine, 15, and seven while taking only brief winter breaks between her six racing seasons.

6. *Bowl Game*

Was out of the money only once in 23 career starts. Started career with 12 straight in-the-money finishes on dirt and turf as a 3- and 4-year-old in 1977 and '78. Finished out of the money in a dirt sprint to begin his 4-year-old campaign in 1979, then reeled off 10 straight in-the-money finishes en route to his Eclipse Award as turf champion, a streak that continued to his final start as a 6-year-old in 1980.

5. *Dave's Friend*

Maryland-based sprinter had 35 wins from 76 career starts from 3 years of age through 10 (1978–1985). Was second 16 times, with nine thirds, and recorded separate in-the-money streaks of seven races, eight, nine, 10 and 12 during his popular career.

4. *Banshee Breeze*

Champion 3-year-old filly of 1998 trained by Carl Nafzger; raced 18 times as a 3- and 4-year-old, winning 10, with five seconds and two thirds. Indeed, the only time she was out of the money was in her career debut, her lone start as a 2-year-old in 1997.

3. *Safely Kept*

Champion sprinter of 1990, won 24 of her 31 career races, with two seconds and three thirds. Began her career with five starts as a 2-year-old and never was out of the money until midway through her 4-year-old season, finishing 1-2-3 in 19 straight starts. Also finished her career with eight straight in-the-money finishes.

2. *Cougar II*

Kept out of the Hall of Fame until 2006, Cougar was in the money in eight of 10 starts in Chile as a 3- and 4-year-old in 1969 and '70 and continued to perform with the same precision in America to the end of his career as a 7-year-old in 1973. Finished in the money 36 times from 40 starts in California, New Jersey, and New York, with 16 victories. Was 1-2-3 in the final 20 starts of his career while competing in high-class stakes on dirt and turf.

1. *Xtra Heat*

Champion 3-year-old filly of 2001 was a pure sprinter with 26 wins, five seconds, and two thirds in 35 starts. Strung together 24 consecutive in-the-money finishes after suffering her first career defeat in her seventh start. That was in the 2000 Breeders' Cup Juvenile Fillies which, at 1 1/16 miles, was well beyond her scope. Finished out of the money only one other time.

THE MOST VERSATILE HORSES

Very few horses are great performers at disparate distances and/or on radically different racing surfaces. The following half dozen took versatility to another level. All won stakes under three or more distinctly different circumstances, such as turf, dirt, sprints, and routes.

6. *Ancient Title*

Became an important fan favorite in Southern California while winning 24 of 57 career starts, with 11 seconds and nine thirds from his 2-year-old season in 1972 through 8 years of age in 1978. Won at nearly every distance from 5 1/2 furlongs to 1 1/4 miles on dirt and turf and surpassed Native Diver as the leading Cal-bred money winner when he retired in 1978 with $1.25 million in career earnings. Although all but three of his starts were in Southern California, Ancient Title did ship across the country to win the 1975 Whitney Handicap at Saratoga under top weight of 128 pounds and was third in two Grade 1's at Belmont in September.

5. *Dance Smartly*

Eclipse Award-winning 3-year-old in 1991, won dirt sprints, dirt and turf routes against males and older mares on the highest level. Probably the best overall performer to come out of Canada since Northern Dancer won two-thirds of the 1964 Triple Crown.

4. *Precisionist*

Eclipse Award-winning sprinter in 1985 won stakes at 2, 3, 4, 5, 6, and 7 years of age through 1988, including a turf stakes at one mile as a 2-year-old in 1983. Won Grade 1 stakes at 1 1/4 miles and set the one-mile track record at Del Mar in 1:33 1/5 around two turns, while all other one-mile clockings faster than that on dirt tracks in America since the 1950s have been run around one turn.

3. *Dr. Fager*

Set several track records on dirt from seven furlongs to 1 1/8 miles, including the 1:32 1/5 world record for one mile at Arlington Park in 1968 that stood for more than three decades. Won his only turf race, the '68 United Nations Handicap, and successfully carried 139 pounds.

2. *Secretariat*

Yes, him again! Secretariat won major stakes from six furlongs to 1 5/8 miles on dirt and turf and set several track and world records in the process. I seriously doubt there ever has been a more versatile championship performer on the flat in racing history.

1. *Quick Pitch*

Unsung stakes performer of the 1960s won on dirt at six furlongs and won turf stakes from one mile to 1 1/4 miles on firm and soft footing through his 6-year-old season in 1966. Was converted into a hurdle performer in '67 and promptly won seven straight hurdle stakes to be named steeplechase champion. That is taking versatility to a whole other level.

THE MOST POPULAR HORSES

Although there have been many outstanding horses who were obviously quite popular—including five-time Horse of the Year Kelso, three-time Horse of the Year Forego, and Cigar, who won 16 straight in 1995 and '96—popularity in racehorses often goes beyond their accomplishments.

In fact, there is a horse, Zippy Chippy, who never won a race in 100 starts and received fan mail well past his retirement at age at 13 in 2004. Zippy Chippy fell just five races short of the futility record set in the 1950s by Thrust, another gelding, but Zippy Chippy's awful run turned him into a celebrity, attracting widespread press coverage as well as letters that still reach his owner-trainer, Felix Monserrate.

The horses below were nowhere near that futile; most, actually, were outstanding performers. They just inspired extraordinary fan allegiance.

10. *Carry Back*

A much-loved horse in the early 1960s, Carry Back was labeled the people's horse in print many times, mostly because the $2 bettors appreciated his lunch-pail career, which began with a relatively obscure mating. Carry Back's sire was the little-known Saggy, whose claim to fame was that he was the last horse to beat Citation before that historic champion went on a 16-race winning streak in 1948. As a sire, Saggy essentially was a dud bred to cheap mares, including the mating with a $600 Florida-based mare named Joppy.

Carry Back's owner and trainer, Katherine and Jack Price, also struck a popular chord as the loving couple who lived out a dreamlike fantasy while bringing Carry Back to the 1961 Triple Crown. In an era dominated by the mighty Kelso and by a string of blue-blooded 2-year-old champions, many of which were owned by members of high society, Jack Price raced Carry Back 21 times as a 2-year-old, winning a three-furlong sprint in February and three stakes in October—the Cowdin, the rich Garden State Stakes, and the Remsen at Aqueduct—all with crowd-pleasing rallies from far back in the pack.

Going toward the 1961 Kentucky Derby, Carry Back raced seven times, including victories in the Everglades and Flamingo Stakes at Hialeah and the Florida Derby at Gulfstream. Carry Back not only won the '61 Derby, making up 13 lengths in the final quarter of a mile, he made up 15 lengths to catch loose, front-running Globemaster to win the Preakness two weeks later. After failing to show similar form in the '61 Belmont Stakes, Carry Back returned that summer with three wins in six outings.

As a 4-year-old, Carry Back raced in New York, New Jersey, Louisiana, Florida, Maryland, and France in an ambitious campaign that included stakes victories in the Metropolitan Mile, Aqueduct Handicap, and Monmouth Handicap (over Kelso) and in-the-money finishes in nine other stakes. An adventurous trip to France for the Prix de l'Arc de Triomphe was not so fruitful, resulting in a 10th-place finish, but Jack Price only saw the brighter side, pointing to the 14 horses the American-based Carry Back beat.

At the end of that season, Carry Back went to stud, but midway through '63, Katherine and Jack noticed a restlessness in Carry Back on the farm. So Price took his overweight, overfed Carry Back to the track for training and got him reasonably fit to run on August 17, in a minor stakes at Randall Park in Ohio, which he lost.

Next came a moderate allowance victory on the grass at Atlantic City Racecourse, but Carry Back could do no better than third to the top grass horse Mongo in the United Nations Handicap one week later. A distant fourth-place finish to Kelso in the Woodward, followed by a dismal performance in the Manhattan Handicap, led to widespread criticism in the press and in the grandstand for Price's decision to continue with Carry Back's racing career.

Retirement seemed prudent. Carry Back was being embarrassed. Even Jack and his wife wondered if they had done something horribly wrong for the horse they loved. For the next two weeks, Price spoke of retirement and backed off. Every time he looked at Carry Back on the training track, he seemed physically fine.

The decision to run Carry Back again in the Trenton Handicap at Garden State Park on November 2, 1963 was met with considerable derision throughout racing. But Price had not given up hope and had an ace up his sleeve. For all of Carry Back's best races as a 3-year-old, the jockey had been Johnny Sellers, who lost favor with the Prices after the colt lost four straight to kick off his 4-year-old campaign in 1962. So for the colt's final career start, Jack Price ate some humble pie and asked Sellers to climb aboard one last time.

In addition, and most remarkably, the Prices knew they owed an explanation to the public that had supported their horse with so much affection through his 61-race career. So they bought a full-page ad in the *Daily Racing Form* on race day for an open letter that clearly stated three things: Carry Back's defeats in this second career should not be held against the horse, but against the people who had brought him back to race; Sellers deserved to be aboard the horse in his final appearance; and win or lose, this would be Carry Back's final race, no ifs, ands, or buts.

I was there at Garden State Park that day, and along with many of his fans, I wondered if Carry Back would hit the board. What more than 18,000 fans saw that day still ranks as one of the most emotionally invigorating experiences of my racetrack life. Carry Back was a dominant winner of that Trenton Handicap, rallying effortlessly from midpack on the far turn to take control of the race entering the stretch to win by 2 ½ lengths in 2:01 ⅘.

From the moment the crowd realized that he actually was going to win this race, there were sustained cheers and a standing ovation that lasted well past 10 full minutes as he was led out of the winner's circle and guided off the track by Jack Price and his wife. No expression of appreciation for any horse, not even Secretariat after his resounding Belmont Stakes triumph, can match what was seen and felt that day.

Years later, Jack Price sent me a letter of encouragement after I wrote a column mentioning how that Trenton Handicap was such a stirring experience for so many.

"I'll bet everybody who saw that race became a racing fan for life," the letter said. I would bet the same.

9. *Fourstardave*

A Saratoga institution for his popularity with the public and for having won at least one race at Saratoga in eight straight seasons through 1994. Bred in New York, the son of Compliance was given a special farewell at Saratoga when he led the post parade for the Fourstardave Handicap in 1996, a year after he was retired.

As part of his sentimental retirement ceremony, Fourstardave even received an edible key to the city of Saratoga Springs at Siro's restaurant, the popular gathering place outside the clubhouse gates, and also had a small lane named in his honor there (Fourstardave Way). The Fourstardave Handicap, a graded stakes at 1 $^1/_{16}$ miles on the turf, was renamed for him in 1996; he had won the race in 1990 and 1991 when it was called the Daryl's Joy.

In the 1991 running of the Daryl's Joy, Fourstardave set a course record for the 1 $^1/_{16}$ miles on the turf in 1:38 $^4/_5$, a record that still stands. Fourstardave raced 100 times, earning $1.6 million for 21 victories, 18 seconds, and 16 thirds, and is buried at Saratoga.

8. *Native Diver*

This California-bred was a durable, extremely popular performer who started 81 times in the mid-1960s and won 37 races for more than $1 million in career earnings.

Native Diver equaled the world record of 1:20 for seven furlongs in the 1965 Los Angeles Handicap at Hollywood Park; won three straight runnings of the San Diego Handicap at Del Mar (1963–65), and three straight Hollywood Gold Cups from 1965 through 1967, turning in faster clockings as he ripened with age. Carefully handled throughout his fine career by trainer Buster Millerick, Native Diver shipped to Northern California for the Bay Meadows Handicap in peak condition but died suddenly from a severe case of colic. He was buried beneath a monument at Hollywood Park.

7. *Smarty Jones*

Winner of the Arkansas Derby, Kentucky Derby, and Preakness, "Smarty" attracted huge crowds to his workouts at Philadelphia Park as he was adopted by casual racing fans as one of their own, a blue-collar horse owned by a local automobile dealer whose stable was wistfully called Someday Farm. Someday was 2004, when Smarty Jones looked to be a sure-fire Triple Crown winner until 36–1 shot Birdstone caught him in the final yards in what proved to be Smarty Jones's final race.

6. *Go for Wand*

A great filly locked in a stirring battle with a champion rival breaks her leg inside the final furlong of the 1990 Breeders' Cup Distaff. The horror and the anguish that followed made racing look bad in the media, but it also served to heighten people's appreciation for Go for Wand's talent and inherent courage, as such accidents tend to do.

5. *Silky Sullivan*

He was called the Eighth Wonder of the World by those who could not fathom how any horse could come from so far back so often to win stakes in California.

Trained by Reggie Cornell, who later would train for Calumet, Silky Sullivan attracted huge crowds to tracks that brought him back for post-parade displays a dozen years after he came from 47 lengths back to win a 6 ½-furlong race by daylight.

Third betting choice in the 1958 Kentucky Derby, Silky Sullivan was exposed as a horse who had been defeating much weaker competition, yet that did nothing to dim his popularity among those who saw him at his best. Veteran California horseplayers and racing officials still talk about Silky Sullivan's patented rallies a half-century later.

4. *Genuine Risk*

In 1980, she became the first filly since Regret in 1915 to win the Kentucky Derby. While that was a good reason for her popularity, especially among women in an era when Billie Jean King played Bobby Riggs in a "Battle of the Sexes" tennis match several years earlier to make a statement about women in professional sports, Genuine Risk became a cause celebre in the Preakness when she was the victim of Angel Cordero's intimidating riding tactics aboard the D. Wayne Lukas-trained Codex.

Codex won the race, but the result was challenged in a highly publicized hearing before the Maryland Racing Commission, and the verdict against Genuine Risk only contributed to her popularity to the end of her excellent career.

3. *Ruffian*

The undefeated champion filly breaks down on the backstretch of her match race with 1975 Kentucky Derby winner Foolish Pleasure. Ruffian was an exceedingly popular racehorse before that tragedy and is remembered by many in the 21st century as probably the greatest filly ever to race in America. Books have been written about her and the people who were close to her still get fan mail many times a year.

2. *Secretariat*

He not only won the Triple Crown to break a 25-year drought, he took the nation by storm, making the cover of *Newsweek, Time* and *Sports Illustrated* in the same week, temporarily wiping out the depressing Watergate scandal as the big news in the spring of 1973. Secretariat was not racing's first television star, Native Dancer was, but he was the biggest television star—the sport's version of Muhammad Ali and Mickey Mantle. He is far from forgotten.

1. *Barbaro*

After watching him win the 2006 Kentucky Derby so effortlessly, to complete six wins in six career starts, a horrified public, along with his emotionally devastated owners and trainer, endured a life-and-death struggle to repair severely broken bones in Barbaro's right hind leg, incurred in the Preakness. To make things worse, Barbaro soon developed a case of laminitis in the opposite hind leg. Laminitis, a frequently fatal hoof disease, occurs when the bone pushes through to the hoof's supporting tissue because the horse cannot put equal weight on all fours.

Daily updates and medical bulletins came from the University of Pennsylvania's Large Animal Hospital at New Bolton Center in Kennett Square, Pennsylvania, to satisfy the public demand for news. Dr. Dean Richardson, who performed the operation and supervised all aspects of Barbaro's case, contributed many nuances about how veterinary medicine has advanced to attempt such complicated treatment. This not only muted the public's distaste for what had occurred at Pimlico, it also helped millions of people see how much care is in the hearts of racing people for their horses. Not yet out of the woods in October 2006, Barbaro became the most popular horse of the modern era through his touching saga.

THE GREATEST RIVALRIES

Throughout racing history, there have been heavily promoted confrontations and multirace rivalries that have captured the public's imagination. Some were spawned by controversial events, others by hard-fought photo finishes and the sheer brilliance of their relative performances. Some even put the glare of media attention on high-profile jockeys and trainers, whose extreme competitiveness transcended the horses involved. The 10 rivalries listed below all sparked the extra media attention that heightened public interest in the game.

10. *Secretariat vs. Sham*

Sham was a strong second to Secretariat in the Kentucky Derby and the Preakness, shocking his trainer, Frank "Pancho" Martin, who was almost 100 percent sure he was training the best 3-year-old in the country until he saw his horse beaten handily in both races.

Vowing to turn the tables, Martin trained Sham hard for the Belmont and instructed jockey Laffit Pincay Jr. to go after Secretariat early, stay with him, and make him run as hard as he could. Pincay followed orders to a T, sending Sham from the gate to engage Secretariat, who uncharacteristically broke quickly to the lead in the 1 ½-mile race.

The Belmont would be Sham's last-ditch attempt to beat Secretariat. The two set red-hot fractions in their head-to-head duel before Sham finally cracked approaching the far turn in the grueling 1 ½-mile climax to the Triple Crown. A normal horse probably would have backed off a bit too, slowing down appreciably through the final half-mile, but it was in this race that Secretariat proved conclusively that he was not a normal horse.

On the turn, into the stretch, Secretariat continued to hold his stride together, slowing down only slightly while extending his lead on the field to 10, 12, 15, 20 lengths en route to his unbelievable 31-length victory and the first Triple Crown sweep since 1948. A champion for the modern era was being crowned to thunderous applause; Sham was drifting back to the rear of the field, completely spent, never to race again.

This was a rivalry that was a whole lot better than the result conveyed. Without Secretariat, Sham certainly would have won the Kentucky Derby and Preakness with brilliant clockings a shade above or below the 1 1/4-mile Churchill Downs track record and the 1 3/16-mile track mark at Pimlico. Moreover, Sham's all-out, gut-wrenching attempt to take the lead away from Secretariat during their intense early duel in the Belmont Stakes pushed the great champion to the best performance of modern times.

9. *Real Quiet vs. Victory Gallop*

After Real Quiet defeated Victory Gallop in the 1998 Kentucky Derby and did it again in the Preakness, most everyone on the planet believed that a Triple Crown winner was going to be unveiled in the Belmont Stakes, when the two would meet again.

At the top of the Belmont Park homestretch, Real Quiet certainly looked as if he was going to close the deal, as he held a sizeable lead under Kent Desormeaux and seemed to be traveling well enough. But Victory Gallop was picking up momentum. Closing the gap slowly at first, and then with a bold late rush, he caught the Derby-Preakness winner with heads bobbing up and down at the wire. It was too close for anyone to call without a good look at the finish-line photograph.

Where this Triple Crown sweep seemed wrapped up one stride before the wire, the photo said otherwise as Victory Gallop reversed his two defeats by less than an inch. This instantly set up a rivalry of gigantic proportions, but the rivalry only existed in the press and the public consciousness, because every time a prospective meeting seemed imminent—in the Travers, for example, or the Breeders' Cup—injuries prevented it. Actually, they never faced each other again. Real Quiet did not even return to the races until 1999 and Victory Gallop did not win until March at Gulfstream, when he began a limited but effective campaign as the best older horse in training. As much as the racegoing public wanted to see them mix it up again, this was an unrequited affair with no satisfying outcome.

8. *Alysheba vs. Bet Twice*

After overcoming Bet Twice's interference and a near-catastrophic stumble in the 1987 Kentucky Derby, Alysheba also won the Preakness by a measured half-length over his rival while seemingly tons the best. Yet, in the Belmont Stakes, Bet Twice made a quick move on the backstretch to break the 1 ½-mile race open and put an end to Alysheba's Triple Crown bid.

In the Haskell Stakes at Monmouth in early July, Bet Twice beat Alysheba once more to even the box score at two wins apiece, adding fuel to the rivalry—a rivalry that saw both finish out of the money in the Travers Stakes but nevertheless carried over into their 4-year-old seasons.

Regaining his top form, Alysheba nearly won the 1987 Breeders' Cup Classic and was a dominant Horse of the Year performer the next year en route to his victory in the 1988 Classic. But there were two more meaningful meetings between the two horses who dominated the 1987 Triple Crown. Bet Twice won the Pimlico Special with Alysheba fourth at 3–5 odds, while Alysheba had the last word, winning the Iselin Handicap over his arch rival at Monmouth Park, Bet Twice's home track. Alysheba, in fact, never lost another race.

7. *Nashua vs. Swaps*

The California-based Swaps was a very fast horse, as he would aptly demonstrate many times over as a 4-year-old en route to his 1956 Horse of the Year campaign. But as a 3-year-old, Swaps burst on the national scene with a wire-to-wire Kentucky Derby victory over favored Nashua, the pride of the East.

Owner Rex Ellsworth and trainer Mesh Tenney had no interest in going on to Pimlico or Belmont Park for the Preakness and/or Belmont Stakes, which stirred up a hornet's nest of controversy among fans and horsemen east of the Rocky Mountains.

Ellsworth was satisfied to ship east, win the Derby, and take his horse back home on the next train. "If they want to meet us again they can come out west," he pointed out. Those were fighting words that inspired headlines and talk of a rematch, perhaps even a match race.

The clamor for another confrontation gained momentum when Nashua went on to Pimlico to win the Preakness and then to Belmont Park to take the third jewel in the Triple Crown. Nashua's owner, William Woodward Jr. of Belair Stud, and trainer Sunny Jim Fitzsimmons were dead-set against facing Swaps on one of the speed-favoring California tracks. Ellsworth and Tenney were dead-set against shipping 3,000 miles to Belmont or Saratoga. But from the moment the Belmont Stakes result became official, it seemed inevitable that the two horses would meet, and Washington Park in Illinois—neutral ground for both parties—came up with the guaranteed $100,000 purse.

The die was cast, and so was this historic rivalry that would only last as long as it took Nashua to jump into the lead unexpectedly at the start under cagey Eddie Arcaro en route to Nashua's front-running win over Swaps, which avenged his Derby defeat. While a minor foot injury to Swaps may have compromised his training for the race, Arcaro's bold, preemptive strike proved to be the winning tactic.

6. *Jockeys Eddie Arcaro, Bill Hartack, and Bill Shoemaker*

Eddie Arcaro's lifetime record in the Triple Crown events always cast a large shadow over Bill Hartack and Bill Shoemaker, but the trio invariably measured themselves against one another in their overlapping careers.

By the time Arcaro retired in 1961, he had a record 17 victories in Triple Crown races and was the standard for success in Triple Crown competition. Shoemaker, a contemporary of Arcaro's for the last decade of "the Master's" career, also was a contemporary of Hartack's for another full decade. Combined, the three great Hall of Fame jockeys accounted for 37 Triple Crown victories and frequently competed against each other for the best horses. There was mutual respect, but no quarter given.

As the table below shows, Hartack equaled Arcaro's Derby success and had three Preakness wins to Shoemaker's two. Shoemaker had his moments in both the Derby and Preakness, while also ranking a close second to Arcaro in the Belmont Stakes with five wins.

	Derby	*Preakness*	*Belmont*	*Triple Crown Wins*
ARCARO	5	6	6	17
HARTACK	5	3	1	9
SHOEMAKER	4	2	5	11

Beyond the above summary, here are their most meaningful matchups in the Triple Crown series, all of which took place between 1955 and 1965.

1955 Kentucky Derby: Bill Shoemaker was aboard Derby winner Swaps when Arcaro was aboard heavily favored second-place finisher Nashua. Arcaro got his revenge later that summer in the famous match race at Washington Park that catapulted Nashua to the 1955 Horse of the Year title.

1957 Kentucky Derby: Hartack was aboard upset winner Iron Liege when Bill Shoemaker stood up in the saddle before the finish and had to settle for second aboard Gallant Man. Although the Derby result may have been flawed by Shoemaker's miscue, the 1957 Triple Crown was to become a compelling series despite the fact that it would be won by three different horses, each ridden by one of the three Hall of Fame riders who dominated Triple Crown racing in the 1950's and 60s.

1957 Preakness: Eddie Arcaro rode a well-paced, front-running race aboard Bold Ruler to defeat Hartack aboard Derby winner Iron Liege by two full lengths.

1957 Belmont Stakes: Shoemaker got important vindication early in his career, riding Gallant Man to a track-record triumph in this race as the Arcaro-ridden Bold Ruler finished third. Both horses went to the post at less than even money odds.

1959 Kentucky Derby: Shoemaker was aboard the British-bred Tomy Lee when he won the Kentucky Derby as favored First Landing, ridden by Arcaro, finished a close third.

1960 Kentucky Derby: Shoemaker had his pick of the top 3-year-olds for this Derby and chose Tompion, the 11–10 betting favorite, who finished fourth while Hartack was scoring a 6–1 upset victory aboard Venetian Way.

1960 Belmont Stakes: Hartack rides stretch-running Celtic Ash to victory at 8–1, while Arcaro is second aboard Derby winner Venetian Way and Shoemaker is fourth aboard odds-on favorite Tompion.

1962 Belmont Stakes: Shoemaker rides gritty Jaipur to a hard-fought victory over Admiral's Voyage, as Hartack is fourth aboard Derby winner Decidedly.

1964 Kentucky Derby and Preakness: Prior to the 1964 Kentucky Derby, Shoemaker went back and forth before making his final decision to ride Derby favorite Hill Rise, as Hartack was the second choice of trainer Horatio Luro to ride the Canadian-bred Northern Dancer. Hartack won the Derby and Preakness, while Shoemaker narrowly missed with Hill Rise in Kentucky and gave ground late to finish third with Hill Rise in the Preakness.

1965 Derby: Shoemaker, riding third choice Lucky Debonair to a wire-to-wire victory, got the best of Hartack, whose mount Bold Lad made only a brief bid before finishing 10th of 11 as the 2–1 betting favorite.

Throughout this decade and beyond, there were dozens of instances when these three great jockeys rode against each other in major stakes throughout the country as air travel came increasingly into play in the modern racing game. Having Arcaro, Shoemaker, and/or Hartack involved, two or three at a time in any prestigious stakes, heightened public interest, as each usually performed at his very best when the money was on the line.

5. *Trainer D. Wayne Lukas vs. Bob Baffert*

The rivalry between D. Wayne Lukas and Bob Baffert may or may not have more chapters to play out in the early stages of the 21st century, but their accomplishments in the sport's most prestigious races say these two had something special going that has not been fully resolved.

Baffert followed Lukas out of Quarter Horse racing into Thoroughbreds, racking up a phenomenal run of Triple Crown and Breeders' Cup winners during the late 1990s into the early 2000s. After winning his first Breeders' Cup race with the sprinter Thirty Slews in 1992, Baffert astonishingly won two-thirds of the Triple Crown four times from 1997 through 2002, with Silver Charm, Real Quiet, Point Given, and War Emblem.

He also won two more Breeders' Cup races with Silverbulletday in 1998 and Vindication in 2002. Meanwhile, Lukas won six of his record 18 Breeders' Cup victories during the same time frame, and after his Grindstone defeated Baffert's first Kentucky Derby horse, Cavonnier, by a nose in 1996, Lukas proceeded to win the 1999 Derby and Preakness with Charismatic and the 2000 Belmont with Commendable.

While the competition between these two nationally prominent trainers always was highly respectful, it reached an artificial intensity courtesy of the modern media, which regularly extracted sound bites from their lengthy Triple Crown and Breeders' Cup daily press conferences. Both Baffert and Lukas were more than professional horse trainers, they were skilled in the art of public relations, artfully using their daily press briefings to explain their strategies and promote their relative positions as the best and/or most famous trainers in the game. Each seemed to outdo the other in presenting his image to the public, while solidifying their efforts to recruit owners with deep enough pockets to invest in the expensive yearlings that would fill their barns with Triple Crown and Breeders' Cup horses of the future.

Baffert was the common-sense, grass-roots quipster with a great eye for a good horse. Lukas was the serious-minded professor of horsemanship who had a brief fling as a basketball coach in Wisconsin, where he also learned about the care and feeding of horses and other animals.

Baffert was the white-haired, California-based free spirit who took pride in the fact that he rarely arrived at the track before 8:00 a.m. Lukas was the meticulous worker who obsessed over minute details and began his day at 4:30 or 5:00 a.m. Baffert trained his horses fast and often; Lukas trained them sparingly, relying on long, strong gallops for their primary exercise. Both were stout believers in expert help, advanced nutrition, and the best feed and veterinary care money could buy.

Both seemed to attract nearly equal amounts of newsprint and TV time and both had no fear challenging each other in far-flung major stakes with their classy racing stock. The rivalry may have been a media creation, but it was boosted by both men's willingness to get into the spotlight and was reinforced by their extraordinary ability to compete on equal terms at the highest levels the sport has to offer.

4. *Trainer Woody Stephens vs. D. Wayne Lukas*

If we compare their relative performances in the Triple Crown and/or Breeders' Cup races, it would be no contest. While both D. Wayne Lukas and Woodford Cefis Stephens were actively training horses in the 1980s, Lukas was well on his way to winning 13 Triple Crown races to Stephens's eight. Lukas also was beginning to rack up several Breeders' Cup wins while Stephens never would get one. Yet, the raw numbers do no justice to the seething intensity that existed between these two great trainers.

Stephens was at the pinnacle of his lengthy career when he won five consecutive Belmont Stakes from 1982 through 1986, and Lukas was just beginning to get untracked, having won the 1980 Preakness with Codex. He remained blanked with 12 Derby starters and zip for three in the Belmont Stakes until his star filly Winning Colors won the 1988 Kentucky Derby. It was that very race and the Preakness that followed two weeks later that defined this rivalry.

Stephens was very much aware of Lukas's rising popularity and enormous success, but he saw it mostly as a function of Lukas's army of well-bred, expensive horses. When pressed, Stephens would point out his success with far fewer horses and seemed confident that others viewed him as the better horseman.

Stephens took immense pride in the fact that he had learned his craft from the legs of a Thoroughbred on up, through lean years with modest talent. Lukas had learned his skills working with Quarter Horses and was the first to convert his championship form with that breed into similar success with Thoroughbreds. Lukas, in fact, took the art of training champion horses to unprecedented levels, shipping from coast to coast for important stakes and operating efficient stakes-winning operations at several tracks simultaneously. Lukas dominated the annual money list and was the top trainer at a half dozen meets each year.

While both Stephens and Lukas successfully launched the training careers of many able assistants through the years, Lukas's businesslike methods became the working model for the most ambitious trainers in the early 21st century.

Stephens, a pure, old-school horseman, sensed the tide of his craft turning toward polished men in dapper suits such as Lukas, men who catered to an eager clientele hungry for the limelight. As successful as he was in his own right, Woody Stephens's resentment of Lukas bordered on jealousy.

In 1988, a self-confident Stephens was still on top, seeking his second Derby winner of the decade as Lukas was seeking his first after 12 failures. Stephens came to Louisville with Forty Niner, a Claiborne Farm homebred, and Lukas had Eugene V. Klein's filly Winning Colors ready to try a front-running theft in the 1 1/4-mile classic.

Winning Colors went to the front immediately from post 11 under Gary Stevens, while Pat Day backed off aboard Forty Niner after breaking right behind her from post 17. Winning Colors took control of the race through realistic fractions of 23 and 46^4/$_5$ for the half-mile, opening up to a four-length advantage approaching six furlongs in 1:11 ^{2}/$_5$ as Forty Niner dropped from fourth to fifth position at the mile mark.

From the top of the stretch to the wire, Winning Colors held a clear, seemingly insurmountable lead, but Forty Niner, with Day gathering him up for a big late surge, closed the gap steadily to just miss by a diminishing neck in a historic outcome.

Lukas, naturally, was ecstatic, but Stephens was not only convinced his colt had been victimized by the way the race was run, he also vowed that he would never let "that filly" get loose on the lead in the Preakness.

As previously described in Chapter 3, the 1988 Preakness was a roughly run race—orchestrated by Stephens's desire to defeat the Lukas-trained filly more than he wanted to win the race himself. For his part, Lukas was furious over the tactics that Pat Day had used under instructions from Woody Stephens.

"He tried to do more than get my filly beat," Lukas said with obvious anger. "I know this game isn't for the faint of heart, but I don't believe there is place for what they did, either."

The significance of the way the 1988 Preakness unfolded stretched far beyond the black mark it gave Stephens. It set up an undercurrent of enmity between Lukas and Stephens that played itself out every time the two men had horses entered in any race until Stephens retired due to his recurring emphysema in the early 1990s. While a mutual respect between them did grow slowly through the rest of Stephens's training years, the old-school trainer always took extra pleasure when one of his horses defeated a Lukas-trained horse—even in a maiden race.

3. *Sunday Silence vs. Easy Goer*

Easy Goer ended Sunday Silence's Triple Crown bid with a resounding eight-length victory in the Belmont Stakes. But Sunday Silence won the other three meetings, without ever satisfying the supporters of Easy Goer that he had proven his superiority. It may seem ironic, but Easy Goer, a son of Alydar, was a great horse who was doomed to play the same role as his sire—to be the horse that pushed another champion to his greatest triumphs.

2. *Damascus vs. Dr. Fager*

Damascus was 3 for 4 as a 2-year-old; Dr. Fager was 4 for 5 as both were rated slightly behind Successor, the Champagne Stakes winner. In the great 3-year-old season of 1967, Dr. Fager beat Damascus in the Gotham at one mile but was forced to miss the spring classics due to a minor training setback. Damascus lost the Kentucky Derby to Proud Clarion, but reclaimed his top form by winning seven of his next eight, including two-thirds of the Triple Crown; the Travers (by 22 lengths); and the Aqueduct Handicap while spotting older horses significant weight.

After his Gotham victory, Dr. Fager won another one-mile stakes, the Withers, before he finished first by more than six lengths in the Jersey Derby, but was disqualified for ostensibly crossing over on the field entering the first turn. This would prove to be Dr. Fager's only defeat in his six starts leading up to a rematch with Damascus in the 1 1/4-mile Woodward Stakes at Aqueduct in September, a race that had every dramatic element a horse race can bear.

Damascus was a powerful finisher, Dr. Fager was a horse with nearly unparalleled speed. The field also included the Allen Jerkens-trained Handsome Boy, a winner of four straight $100,000 races, and Buckpasser, the 1966 Horse of the Year, who had won four of six races in 1967, but was making his final career start after dealing with minor physical problems through the summer.

Of equal import, the Woodward also included Damascus's stablemate Hedevar. Realizing the significance of the contest, Damascus's cagey trainer, Frank Whiteley Jr., thought he spotted an Achilles heel in Dr. Fager and was set to exploit it. Whiteley believed correctly that Dr. Fager sometimes became overanxious, overly competitive when pushed early, so he entered the sprinter-miler Hedevar to press or make the pace.

The battle plan worked to perfection as Hedevar alternated in setting and pressing the pace with Dr. Fager through six furlongs in 1:09⅕ as Damascus rallied from 12 lengths back to score a resounding 10-length victory. The gritty Buckpasser, still dealing with the effects of his summer injuries, gamely caught a weary Dr. Fager for second.

The victory ended the debate for 1967. Damascus was the best 3-year-old; Buckpasser was still good enough to be declared handicap champion in one poll, Damascus in the other, while Dr. Fager was clearly the best sprinter, if not the best "miler," even though no such award has ever been tendered.

In 1968, the decks were cleared for the next round of confrontations, and trainer John Nerud still believed that Dr. Fager was fully capable of beating his arch rival at a classic distance. On July 4, 1968, Dr. Fager proved Nerud's point, taking the 1¼-mile Suburban Handicap at Belmont by two lengths in 1:59⅗, equaling the track record under 132 pounds before a crowd in excess of 54,000. Bold Hour was second; Damascus third. Dr. Fager carried 132 pounds, Bold Hour 116, and Damascus 133. But the most important detail was that Hedevar was not in the race.

Fans did not have to wait long for the rematch, as these two great Thoroughbreds met 16 days later in the 1¼-mile Brooklyn, with Damascus winning by 2½ lengths and setting a new track record of 1:59⅕, after his stablemate Hedevar did his thing pushing Dr. Fager out of his relaxed stride into a suicidal pace. As if he needed it, Damascus also got a break in the weights, carrying 130 to Dr. Fager's 135.

From that point forward, Dr. Fager was unbeatable, setting the world record for one mile at Arlington, carrying as much as 139 pounds while

setting a track record for seven furlongs in the Vosburgh, and leaving little doubt that he was better than Damascus as a 4-year-old.

1. *Affirmed vs. Alydar*

They battled each other 10 times from their 2-year-old campaign through
the Triple Crown and Travers Stakes. The Derby was close, the Preakness was closer, and the Belmont was one of the most compelling races
ever run. Affirmed was better, but not by so much that Alydar did not
have a realistic chance of turning the tables any time they met.

Affirmed was discernibly superior, winning four of their six meetings
as a 2-year-old and all three Triple Crown races before he won the Travers and was disqualified for interference. But the measure of this rivalry
can be found in these few powerful facts:

* Affirmed and Alydar completed the exacta in all 10 of their meetings at six different tracks at seven different distances: 5 $\frac{1}{2}$ furlongs
  twice; 6 $\frac{1}{2}$ furlongs; one mile; 1 $\frac{1}{16}$ miles; 1 $\frac{1}{4}$ miles twice; 1 $\frac{3}{16}$
  miles; and 1 $\frac{1}{2}$ miles.
* Alydar repeatedly pushed Affirmed to historic performances.
* Without Alydar, Affirmed would not have run as brilliantly, and without Affirmed, Alydar certainly would have been a Triple Crown winner.

There was no better rivalry, no matchup of two horses that captured
the public's imagination nearly as well or on so many occasions. No
rivalry was as close, yet so far away.

BLOODSTOCK:

The Best Sires, Sire Lines,

Broodmares, Bargains, and

Foal Crops—and the Biggest Duds

THE GREATEST SIRES

It is not my intention to discount the potency of Northern Dancer, who is often listed first by breeding authorities as the most influential sire of the modern era. But, even though Northern Dancer sired many top-class stakes winners—especially European stakes winners, such as Lyphard, El Gran Senor, Nureyev, and many others—his greatest contribution at stud was as a sire and grandsire of prepotent sires.

For example, Northern Dancer's son Storm Bird carried his valuable genes forward through the third-generation sire Storm Cat. That is why Northern Dancer's most potent grandson, Storm Cat, is on this list of the three greatest sires of the modern era, while Northern Dancer himself is reserved for a special place as the wellspring of a great *sire line*. The top three sire lines appear below the following list, reserved for the top three sires.

3. *STORM CAT*
(1983, Storm Bird—Terlingua, by Secretariat)

Storm Cat, the leading sire in 1999 and 2000, remains one of the most influential stallions of the modern era. A high-class racehorse who finished second in the 1985 Breeders' Cup Juvenile, Storm Cat has sired more than 130 stakes winners worldwide through 2005.

Included among his successful offspring are 10 horses with earnings in excess of $1 million and more than two dozen Grade 1-winning horses. Among the most prominent are: 1992 Alabama winner November Snow; 1994 Kentucky Oaks winner Sardula; Tabasco Cat, winner of the 1994 Preakness and Belmont Stakes; 1995 Breeders' Cup Sprint winner Desert Stormer; 1999 Breeders' Cup Classic winner Cat Thief, who earned $3.9 million; 2000 European 3-year-old champion Giant's Causeway; 2002 juvenile filly champion Storm Flag Flying; and 2004 juvenile filly champion Sweet Catomine.

As will be seen in subsequent material on the top sire lines, Storm Cat's immediate influence on high-class racing sons and daughters was to be exceeded by his potency as a sire of sires and as a broodmare sire.

Very few stallions in racing history can match Storm Cat's record, and he is still a highly attractive sire in the 21st century who commands an industry-leading $500,000 stud fee. One of the reasons for that price tag is the fact that Storm Cat has had more yearlings who sold at public auction for $1 million or more than any other sire.

2. *MR. PROSPECTOR*
(1970, Raise a Native—Gold Digger by Nashua)

Certainly another of the greatest, most influential sires in racing history, Mr. Prospector sired numerous sons who were successful sires, and whose influence can be felt in the 21st century. But strictly on his merits as a sire of outstanding racehorses, Mr. Prospector ranks extremely close to the very best.

Among more than 180 stakes winners, Mr. Prospector sired dozens of champions and near champions, including 1982 Belmont Stakes winner and Horse of the Year Conquistador Cielo; Eillo, the 1984 sprint champion; Gulch, the 1988 sprint champion and two-time

Metropolitan Mile winner who earned $3 million; Woodman, the 1985 Irish champion 2-year-old; 1985 Preakness winner Tank's Prospect; 1987 juvenile champion Forty Niner; 1990 juvenile champion and 1991 Travers winner Rhythm; $2.3 million winner Seeking the Gold; 2000 Kentucky Derby winner Fusaichi Pegasus; 2000 Arlington Million winner Chester House; Ravinella, the champion filly at 2 and 3 in Europe; It's In the Air, 1978 champion 2-year-old filly; Gold Beauty, 1982 champion sprinter; Golden Attraction, the 1995 champion juvenile filly; and Queena, 1991 champion older filly.

As described in the material below on great sire lines, Mr. Prospector's status as a positive gene carrier into the next generation is unparalleled. On that basis alone, some might prefer his overall stud record as the best of the modern era.

1. *BOLD RULER*
(1954, Nasrullah—Miss Disco, by Discovery)

Bold Ruler, Horse of the Year in 1957, was, I believe, the most successful sire of top-class horses in the modern era, if not in racing history. While this point of view may spark disagreement, my reasoning is based on the following facts.

Not only was Bold Ruler the leading North American sire eight times, including seven in succession (1963–69), but no other horse in American breeding history comes close to that record. (Bull Lea and Nasrullah—Bold Ruler's sire—each led the list five times.)

A long list of Bold Ruler's stakes-winning sons and daughters dominated the sport during the 1960s and 70s. The best of them was of course the great Secretariat, Horse of the Year as a 2-year-old in 1972 and again at 3, when he swept the Triple Crown and beat older horses in major stakes on grass and dirt, while setting world and track records.

Among Bold Ruler's other stakes-winning sons and daughters were five more juvenile champions: Bold Lad, Queen Empress, Queen of the Stage, Successor, and Vitriolic. Only Mr. Prospector comes close to such a record of potency with top-flight juvenile racehorses.

Bold Ruler also sired several near champions. These included Hopeful Stakes winners Bold Hour (1966); What a Pleasure (1967), and Irish Castle (1969). He sired multiple stakes winner Chieftain and Bold and

Brave, who each won stakes three straight years. Bold Ruler also sired Raja Baba, a multiple sprint stakes winner; Reviewer, a track-record holder and six-time stakes winner at 2 and 4 years of age; as well as Bold Bidder, champion handicap horse in 1966.

There's more: Bold Ruler sired the 1975 champion 3-year-old, Wajima; the 1963 champion 3-year-old filly, Lamb Chop; the 1968 champion older mare, Gamely; and several productive sires and brood-mares, including some named here and detailed in the sire-line section that follows this list.

Bold Ruler also sired 1969 Spinaway Stakes winner Meritus; 1970 Brooklyn Handicap winner Dewan; and What Luck, a disappointing runner who nevertheless sired 39 Thoroughbred stakes winners, including What a Summer and 1983 champion older filly Ambassador of Luck, plus 17 Quarter Horse stakes winners.

In other words, Bold Ruler was an awesome sire of racehorses, certainly one of the best in racing history. Yet with all his high-class sons and daughters, it is surprising that the potency of his bloodlines fell sharply in influence past the second generation. The fact is, there are few of his grandsons and great-grandsons at stud who seem capable of maintaining his place in the pedigrees of the best horses of the 21st century. That may be one reason why he has slipped in the minds of breeding experts, who tend to favor Northern Dancer and/or the deserving Mr. Prospector over Bold Ruler in their own lists. Frankly, I think they do Bold Ruler a disservice by forgetting how prolific his stallion record really was.

THE WIN, PLACE, AND SHOW OF SIRE LINES

3. *NEARCO—NASRULLAH*

Nearco sired Nasrullah, who sired Nashua, Never Bend, and Bold Ruler, among many other horses of the highest class. Bold Ruler, cited earlier as one of the top three sires of the modern era, was very well represented by many successful sons at stud. One of the most interesting was the ever-present Secretariat.

Secretariat was slow to be recognized as a high-class sire after expectations were in the stratosphere and early tests suggested a low sperm count. But he did sire a top-notch filly in his second crop, Terlingua, who would prove to be a world-class broodmare several years later.

In addition, Secretariat began to gain favor late in his stud career, siring 1986 Horse of the Year Lady's Secret and the 1988 champion 3-year-old Risen Star before a long list of his daughters lifted him to an elite status among the best broodmare sires of the modern era. Unfortunately, Secretariat contracted the frequently deadly hoof disease laminitis and died in October 1989.

The aforementioned Terlingua produced Storm Cat, one of the most prolific sires in racing history. Another daughter of Secretariat, Six Crowns, produced the 1984 juvenile champion, Chief's Crown.

Some of Bold Ruler's best racing sons also were solid sires. Irish Castle sired 1976 Kentucky Derby-Belmont Stakes winner Bold Forbes; Chieftain sired 1977 filly champion Cascapedia; What a Pleasure sired 1975 Kentucky Derby winner Foolish Pleasure and multiple stakes winner Honest Pleasure as well as Ecstacion, who would become a successful broodmare, producing, among others, the 1985 juvenile champion, Tasso.

Bold and Brave sired Bold 'n Determined, nearly a champion 3-year-old filly in 1980; Raja Baba sired Sacahuista, the 3-year-old filly champion of 1987; Reviewer sired 1976 champion 3-year-old filly Revidere as well as the great Ruffian; and Bold Bidder sired the great Spectacular Bid.

Among Bold Ruler's most productive mares were King's Story, who produced 1972 handicap champion Autobiography; Meritus, who produced the 1976 juvenile filly champion, Sensational; and Yule Log, who produced Christmas Past, champion 3-year-old filly of 1982.

While the Bold Ruler line reached its zenith with his many outstanding sons who proved to be solid sires into the next generation, it has been carried forward mostly on the female side, through Secretariat's productive daughters. Indeed, as pointed out earlier, very few of Bold Ruler's second-generation sires carried his line successfully into the 1990s or the 21st century.

One prominent and hopeful exception is the strain that traces through Bold Ruler's son Boldnesian, who sired Bold Reasoning, who sired Seattle Slew. Seattle Slew, the Triple Crown winner of 1977, became a potent sire of several major stakes winners, including 1984 Kentucky Derby and Belmont Stakes winner Swale and 1992 Horse of the Year A.P. Indy, who was produced by a daughter of Secretariat, Weekend Surprise.

While Swale died mysteriously after a routine light gallop at Belmont Park eight days after his scintillating Belmont victory, A.P. Indy has sired eight millionaires through 2005, including 2003 Horse of the Year Mineshaft. Most importantly, A.P. Indy is showing signs of becoming a sire of sires, which is countering fears that the once prepotent Bold Ruler line might be nearing its end.

A.P. Indy's son Malibu Moon sired 2004 juvenile champion Declan's Moon; Stephen Got Even sired 2005 juvenile champion Stevie Wonderboy; and A.P. Indy's sons Aptitude, Pulpit, and Jump Start have shown similar promise at stud.

2. *NATIVE DANCER—RAISE A NATIVE*

The once-beaten Native Dancer, one of the best horses in racing history, sired Raise a Native, who sired Majestic Prince, Exclusive Native, Alydar, and Mr. Prospector, among other terrific horses and sires. By any standard, Raise a Native was one of the best sire of sires in racing history.

His son Exclusive Native sired 1978 Triple Crown winner and Horse of the Year Affirmed, who became a successful sire of grass horses even though Affirmed never raced on turf. Affirmed's best offspring were 1992-93 filly grass champion Flawlessly and 2006 Arlington Million winner The Tin Man.

Raise a Native sired the near champion Alydar, who pushed Affirmed so hard throughout their historic rivalry. Moreover, at stud, Alydar was even more productive than Affirmed, siring, among others, Alysheba, the 1987 Kentucky Derby-Preakness winner and 1988 Horse of the Year.

Alydar sired 10 winners of $1 million or more, including the 1988 champion 2-year-old colt, Easy Goer; 1986 champion older male Turkoman; and 1990 Horse of the Year Criminal Type. He also sired the broodmares Winglet and Ivory Idol, who produced Ajina, the champion 3-year-old filly of 1997, and Anees, champion juvenile colt of 1999, respectively.

Alydar was, in fact, the leading sire in 1990, the year he allegedly was killed for insurance money by J. T. Lundy, manager of the struggling and once-glorious Calumet Farm. While Lundy always maintained his innocence, he was convicted of insurance fraud in connection to the case 10 years after Alydar died from a suspiciously broken leg that a judge and jury did not accept as having been caused by accident. (For more information about the Calumet-Alydar-J. T. Lundy case, I can heartily recommend two resources: an award-winning *Texas Monthly* magazine story by Skip Hollandsworth, published in June 2001, and journalist Ann Hagedorn-Auerbach's book *Wild Ride*, which chronicles "The Rise and Tragic Fall of Calumet Farm.")

Even more prolific than Alydar and Exclusive Native at stud was Raise a Native's third prominent son, Mr. Prospector.

Mr. Prospector was a very fast horse with untapped potential, but became North America's leading sire in 1987 and '88 and the leading broodmare sire in 1996 through 2001. His most productive sons at stud were Gulch, who sired 1994 Kentucky Derby-Belmont Stakes winner Thunder Gulch; and Gone West, the sire of more than 75 stakes winners through 2005 and two leading sires in Europe, Zafonic and West Man. In addition, Gone West's son Elusive Quality sired 2004 Kentucky Derby-Preakness winner Smarty Jones.

Mr. Prospector also sired Fappiano, a Met Mile winner who not only sired 1990 Kentucky Derby winner Unbridled (sire of 2003 Belmont Stakes winner Empire Maker) but also the good European performer Woodman, who sired 1991 Preakness and Belmont Stakes winner Hansel. Fappiano also sired Kingmambo, sire of 1999 Belmont Stakes-Travers winner Lemon Drop Kid, whose daughter Lemons Forever won the 2006 Kentucky Oaks.

Two of Mr. Prospector's better sons were Seeking the Gold, winner of $2.3 million; and Forty Niner, champion 2-year-old colt of 1987. These two were rivals on the track and each has had a successful career at stud, with Seeking the Gold siring 1994 champion 3-year-old filly Heavenly Prize as well as the outstanding 1994 juvenile filly champion Flanders, who in turn produced Surfside, champion 3-year-old filly in 2000. Forty Niner is the sire of Distorted Humor, sire of 2003 Kentucky Derby-Preakness winner Funny Cide as well as more recent Grade 1 winners Flower Alley, Commentator, and Awesome Humor.

Mr. Prospector's daughters were almost as strong on the racetrack as they would prove to be in the breeding shed. His best were Queena, champion filly or mare in 1991, and Golden Attraction, champion juvenile filly of 1995. Indeed, daughters of Mr. Prospector produced more than 180 stakes winners, which parallels the numbers of stakes winners he sired.

The most prominent stakes winners produced by Mr. Prospector mares were Hollywood Wildcat, who won the 1993 Breeders' Cup Distaff and was the dam of Breeders' Cup Mile winner War Chant; Dayjur, 1990 Horse of the Year in England; Dancehall, Golden Opinion, Green Tune, and Fasiliyev, each of whom won Group 1 stakes in Europe; Maplejinsky, the Alabama Stakes winner in 1988, who was the dam of 1993 Alabama winner Sky Beauty; and 1997 Blue Grass Stakes winner Pulpit.

Placing all of this in perspective, Mr. Prospector's offspring and grandsons and broodmare daughters have been so important that the jury is still out on where he may rank in another generation or two. It is conceivable that he may yet push the Native Dancer—Raise a Native—Mr. Prospector line to the top of a list such as this by the end of the next decade.

1. *NEARCTIC—NORTHERN DANCER LINE*

This is a powerful, potent breeding line that continues to have worldwide influence. Northern Dancer, the Canadian-bred Kentucky Derby-Preakness winner of 1964, was North America's leading sire in 1971, but is most respected for having sired European champion Nijinsky II, who sired 1989 Breeders' Cup Sprint winner Dancing Spree; 1986 Kentucky Derby winner Ferdinand; and 1992 champion turf male Sky Classic, among several champions in Europe and America.

Beyond Nijinsky, Northern Dancer sired dozens of top-quality European stars who flourished on a regimen of wall-to-wall turf racing. Even more important, Northern Dancer proved to be a prolific, prepotent sire of successful sires on both sides of the Atlantic.

Among his most notable sons were: Nureyev, sire of the two-time Breeders' Cup Mile winner Miesque; El Gran Senor, sire of 1996 Breeders' Cup Sprint winner Lit de Justice; Sadler's Wells, who sired 2003 turf champion High Chaparral; Storm Bird, sire of Summer Squall and the prepotent Storm Cat; and Vice Regent, sire of Deputy Minister, a leading broodmare sire in 2002 and 2003. Among many others, Northern Dancer also sired Lyphard, Danzig, and Dixieland Band.

Danzig, the leading sire in 1991 and '92, sired Langfuhr, a Grade 1 winner in 1996 and the leading sire of winning performers in 2005. Danzig also sired 1984 juvenile champion Chief's Crown; 1986 Belmont Stakes winner Danzig Connection; 1990 European Horse of the Year

Dayjur; 3-year-old filly champion Dance Smartly, winner of the 1991 Canadian Triple Crown; two-time Breeders' Cup Mile winner Lure; and 2000 Breeders' Cup Mile winner War Chant, among a dozen winners of more than $1 million through 2005. Another of Danzig's sons, Polish Navy, sired 1993 Kentucky Derby winner Sea Hero.

Northern Dancer's son Dixieland Band actually followed in the footsteps of Northern Dancer's grandson Deputy Minister as those two led the broodmare-sire list for two years each from 2002 to 2005.

Tracing Storm Cat directly back to Northern Dancer, as indicated above, the Storm Bird-Storm Cat wing of the Northern Dancer line is establishing a potency of its own into the 21st century. This wing deserves separate mention while it continues to reinforce the Northern Dancer line as narrowly the best of the modern era.

Storm Bird—Storm Cat—Giant's Causeway

Storm Cat, a grandson of Northern Dancer through Storm Bird, was leading sire in 1999 and 2000. Storm Cat's son Giant's Causeway, a star in Europe and second to Tiznow in the 2000 Breeders' Cup Classic, was the second-leading freshman sire in 2005 and among the leaders of all sires in 2006. Thus, it seems safe to say that the Storm Bird-Storm Cat-Giant's Causeway branch of the Northern Dancer line will be a major influence in the years ahead.

HONORABLE MENTIONS

Turn-To—First Landing and
Hail to Reason—Halo—Sunday Silence

Turn-to sired Hail to Reason, who was juvenile champion in 1960 and never raced as a 3-year-old, but did sire the outstanding turf horse Halo, who became an influential sire in his own right. Among several champions Halo sired were: 1980 champion older filly or mare Glorious Song; 1983 Kentucky Derby winner Sunny's Halo; 1983 juvenile champion Devil's Bag; and 1989 Kentucky Derby-Preakness-Breeders' Cup Classic winner and Horse of the Year Sunday Silence, who became one of the world's most successful sires while establishing a classy foundation for a burgeoning Japanese racing industry. Even in 2005, Halo's son Saint Ballado was leading money-winning sire in North America. Turn-to also sired First Landing, who sired Riva Ridge, the 2-year-old champion of 1971 and winner of the 1972 Kentucky Derby and Belmont Stakes.

Man o' War—War Relic—Intent—Intentionally—In Reality

There was exceptional class in the genes of this sire line and it carried through several generations. Man o' War, a high-spirited, very fast champion as a 2-year-old and a horse for the ages at 3, was a strong stamina influence through the first half of the 20th century. One of his sons, War Admiral, was a Triple Crown winner in 1937.

While not quite of that caliber, Man o' War's son War Relic was a good stakes winner in 1941 who also excelled at route distances. War Relic's son Intent also performed best at distances much longer than one mile, winning, among other stakes, the San Juan Capistrano Handicap at Santa Anita in 1952. But when Intent was mated to the nonwinning My Recipe, the resulting foal of 1956 was, strangely enough, Intentionally, one of the fastest sprinter-milers in racing history.

Intentionally was a blur on four feet. I saw him race six times in 1959–61 and he was one of the quickest horses I ever saw, a horse that would have earned sky-high pace and speed figures had they been in use at the time. In 1959 he set the world record for the one-mile distance, a record he would keep until Buckpasser broke it in 1966.

As bloodlines and gene pools go, the turn toward exceptional speed through Intentionally was to yield the outstanding sprinting filly Ta Wee and the good 3-year-old of 1967 In Reality, who sired 1986 champion sprinter Smile. While In Reality was a successful sire of many good horses, Ta Wee produced Great Above, sire of 1994 Horse of the Year Holy Bull.

Ribot—His Majesty and Graustark; and
Tom Rolfe—Hoist the Flag

Undefeated European champion Ribot sired the top-class His Majesty, who in turn sired 1981 Kentucky Derby and Preakness winner Pleasant Colony. Ribot also sired His Majesty's full brother, the outstanding Graustark, who was injured and retired before he could compete in the 1966 Kentucky Derby. Graustark in turn sired Key to the Mint, the 3-year-old

234

champion of 1972; Tempest Queen, 1978 champion 3-year-old filly; Proud Truth, winner of the 1985 Breeders' Cup Classic; and Outward Sunshine, dam of 1988 turf champion Sunshine Forever.

In addition to Graustark and His Majesty, Ribot also sired Tom Rolfe, champion 3-year-old of 1965, who in turn sired Hoist the Flag, the undefeated 2-year-old champion of 1970 who sired 1976 juvenile filly champion Sensational as well as Alleged, winner of the 1977 and '78 Prix de l'Arc de Triomphe. That's a powerful group of Thoroughbreds to come from one family.

Tom Fool—Buckpasser

Tom Fool, unbeaten in 10 starts as a 4-year-old when named 1953 Horse of the Year, sired 1965 Horse of the Year Buckpasser, who sired 1971 juvenile filly champion Numbered Account and 1972 juvenile filly champion La Prevoyante, unbeaten in her five starts as a 2-year-old, all stakes. Buckpasser, known more for the success of his fillies as broodmares, nevertheless sired Buckaroo, sire of the 1985 champion 3-year-old, Spend a Buck. Buckpasser also sired Silver Buck, sire of the 1997 champion 3-year-old, Silver Charm.

THE BEST BLUE-HEN BROODMARES

Sires get the big bucks in stud contracts and mares get 11 months of growing pains—literally so. But high-quality broodmares are stars in their own right, and the best of them, so rare, have equal responsibility in passing on the genes that make great racehorses. The most prolific of these broodmares are treasured by their owners and are affectionately labeled blue hens.

The best blue-hen mares of the modern era did not suddenly appear out of a magic hat. They each came from other successful producers, including a select few that were producing winners and blue-hen daughters before most of us were born.

Frankly, I have never been an expert on breeding and could not have compiled the lists in this section without considerable help from Lauren Stich, breeding columnist for *Daily Racing Form*. It was Lauren who pointed out subtleties I would have missed, and I am grateful for her efforts on behalf of this book.

With her help, here are the best blue-hen broodmare lines that have surfaced in American racing during the modern era, including a few whose dominance began in the 1930s and 40s. The key element here is the quality of the broodmare's offspring as well as the quality of her daughters' and granddaughters' offspring.

16. *Key Bridge*
(1959, Princequillo—Blue Banner, by War Admiral)

Key Bridge produced 1967 turf champion and 1970 Horse of the Year Fort Marcy, 1973 champion 3-year-old Key to the Mint, plus the multiple stakes winners Key to the Kingdom and Key to Content. That is a very good output, but others on this list have done quite a bit better.

15. *Too Bald*
(1964, Bald Eagle—Hidden Talent, by Dark Star)

Too Bald was the dam of 1978 Jockey Club Gold Cup winner Exceller, 1986 2-year-old champion Capote, and stakes winners Baldski, American Standard, and Vaguely Hidden.

14. *No Class*
(1974, Nodouble—Classy Quillo, by Outing Class)

Dam of six stakes winners from just eight foals, the badly misnamed No Class produced four Canadian champions: Sky Classic, Grey Classic, Regal Classic, and the Canadian 3-year-old filly champion Classy 'n Smart, who in turn produced Dance Smartly, champion 3-year-old filly in the U.S. and Canadian Horse of the Year in 1991. No Class also produced stakes winners Always a Classic and Classic Reign.

13. *Courtly Dee*
(1968, Never Bend—Tulle, by War Admiral)

Produced eight stakes winners including the 1984 Arkansas Derby winner, Althea, who in turn was the granddam of stakes winners Arch and

Balletto. The latter filly was a Grade 1 winner as a 2-year-old in 2004 and Grade 1-placed in 2006. Courtly Dee also was the dam of several other producers, most notably the unraced Foreign Courier, who produced the high-class European Green Desert, who became a successful European sire in his own right.

12. *ROUGH SHOD II*
(1944, by Gold Bridge—Dalmary, by Blanford)

This is one of the fillies who was born before the 1950s, but became a formidable broodmare in the late 1950s and 1960s. Rough Shod was, for example, the dam of undefeated 1965 juvenile filly champion Moccasin, who went on to foal five stakes winners. Rough Shod also was the dam of multiple stakes winners Ridan, Lt. Stevens, Thong, and Gambetta.

Rough Shod's daughter Thong was a blue-hen mare who foaled Special, who in turn produced the high-class Nureyev, champion 3-year-old in Europe in 1980. Special also produced Fairy Bridge, the dam of Sadler's Wells, a multiple group winner in Europe who was leading sire in Great Britain 14 times, including 12 in succession. Another daughter of Rough Shod, Gambetta, produced Gamely, 1968 champion older filly or mare in America.

11. *MISSY BABA*
(1958, My Babu—Uvira, by Umidwar)

Dam of 1977 Arlington-Washington Futurity winner Sauce Boat, but most of Missy Baba's potency was revealed through her granddaughters. Missy Baba was the dam of multiple stakes winner Raja Baba as well as Gay Missile, whose daughter Lassie Dear produced Weekend Surprise, dam of 1990 Preakness winner Summer Squall and 1992 Horse of the Year A.P. Indy. Missy Baba's daughter Toll Booth was the dam of several stakes winners, including 1980 champion sprinter Plugged Nickle and the multiple stakes winner Key to the Bridge.

10. *BOUDOIR II*
(1938, Mahmoud—Kampala, by Clarissimus)

Born more than a decade before the modern television age began, Boudoir II has to be included on this list because she was the dam of Your Host. All Your Host did was sire five-time Horse of the Year Kelso (foaled in 1957)!

Boudoir also was the dam of Flower Bed, who produced Flower Bowl (foaled in 1952). Flower Bowl was a champion racehorse and a blue-hen mare who produced the high-class stakes winners His Majesty, Graustark, and Bowl of Flowers, champion filly at 2 and 3 years of age, in 1960 and '61, respectively. Boudoir also was the dam of Your Hostess, who produced Gay Hostess, the dam of 1969 Derby-Preakness winner Majestic Prince.

9. *BEST IN SHOW*
(1965, Traffic Judge—Stolen Hour, by Mr. Busher [who traces back to La Troienne])

Dam of stakes-winning Blush With Pride and Minnie Hauk, whose daughters and granddaughters produced several high-class stakes winners, including the 1997 Breeders' Cup Mile winner Spinning World; 2003 sprint champion Aldebaran; and 2006 Belmont Stakes winner Jazil, among others. Best In Show also produced the unraced Sex Appeal, who produced the high-class European stakes winner El Gran Senor and Compliance, the sire of multiple graded stakes winners Fourstardave and his full brother Fourstars Allstar.

8. *ASPIDISTRA*
(1954, Better Self—Tilly Rose, by Bull Brier)

One of my favorite broodmares, Aspidistra produced only two horses of high quality, but they were two of the best horses of modern times: 1968 Horse of the Year Dr. Fager, one of the fastest and best horses of the 20th century, and the great female sprinter Ta Wee, who was a match for any horse, male or female, at six furlongs. Unbridled, winner of the 1990 Kentucky Derby and Breeders' Cup Classic, and his full brother, 1991

Wood Memorial winner Cahill Road, as well as 1996 Santa Anita Derby winner Cavonnier, all trace back to Aspidistra.

7. *ALMAHMOUD*
(1947, Mahmoud—Arbitrator, by Peace Chance)

She was the dam of Natalma, dam of Northern Dancer, which by itself would qualify her for this list. But she also foaled Cosmah, the dam of champion Tosmah and the influential stallion Halo, plus two other stakes winners. Cannonade, winner of the 1974 Kentucky Derby, is out of Queen Sucree, one of Cosmah's daughters.

6. *TOUSSAUD*
(1989, El Gran Senor—Image of Reality, by In Reality)

One of America's greatest producers of top-quality stakes winners, Toussaud produced 2003 Belmont Stakes winner Empire Maker, 2000 Arlington Million winner Chester House, multiple Grade 1-winning Honest Lady, 2002 Secretariat Stakes winner Chiselling, and the Grade 2 winner Decarchy. That's a select lineup of top-quality runners.

5. *FALL ASPEN*
(1976, Pretense—Change Water, by Swaps)

Fall Aspen was the dam of nine stakes winners, including 1994 juvenile champion Timber Country and the blue-hen mare Colorado Dancer, who produced the Dubai World Cup winner Dubai Millennium. Fall Aspen also produced Fort Wood, sire of 1998 and '99 South African Horse of the Year Horse Chestnut, sire of the speedy Spanish Chestnut.

4. *SOMETHINGROYAL*
(1952, Princequillo—Imperatrice, by Caruso)

Legendary dam of the great Secretariat and three other prominent stakes winners—Sir Gaylord, Syrian Sea, and First Family—as well as The Bride, who was "won" by the Phipps family in the famous coin toss that also determined who would own Secretariat. The Bride was winless in a brief career and had 15 foals with combined earnings of less than $325,000.

3. *GREY FLIGHT*
(1945, Mahmoud—Planetoid, by Ariel)

The dam of nine stakes winners: Misty Morn, Misty Flight, Misty Day, What a Pleasure, Full Flight, Bold Princess, Gray Phantom, Bold Queen, and Signore. Grey Flight's best son was 1967 Hopeful Stakes winner What a Pleasure, the top-rated stallion in 1975 and '76 who sired 1975 Kentucky Derby winner Foolish Pleasure and multiple Grade 1 winner Honest Pleasure. But it is through Grey Flight's blue-hen daughters, granddaughters, and great-granddaughters that she is rated among the sport's elite producers.

Among the notable horses who trace their bloodlines to Grey Flight's daughters and granddaughters are juvenile champions Bold Lad (1964) and Successor (1966), 1995 champion older filly or mare Inside Information, and 2000 champion sprinter Kona Gold, as well as stakes winners Sunrise Flight, Sovereign Dancer, Time for a Change, Dispute, Adjudicating, Intrepid Hero, Formal Dinner, Quick as Lightning, Pure Profit, Educated Risk, Caller One, Prospect Bay, Pleasant Flight, Cassidy, Priolo, and Flitalong.

2. *KERALI*
(1984, High Line—Sookera, by Roberto)

One of the most influential mares in the modern era, Kerali is the dam of Skiable, who produced multiple-stakes-winning Three Valleys. Kerali also produced Dissemble, the dam of 2005 champion turf horse Leroidesanimaux.

Most notably, Kerali produced the blue-hen mare Hasili, whose five foals included five major stakes winners: Banks Hill, the 2001 female grass champion; Intercontinental, the 2005 female grass champion; multiple stakes winner Cacique (all sired by Danehill); Heat Haze; and the high-class European miler Dansili. In baseball terms that equates to a batting average of 1.000!

240

1. *LA TROIENNE*
(1926, Teddy—Helene de Troie, by Helicon)

Although the intended scope of this book is to cover the best (and worst) of the *modern era* of Thoroughbred racing, La Troienne breaks the mold. La Troienne's profound potency has carried her genes from the late 1920s through the 21st century. She above all other blue-hen mares remains the greatest broodmare of all time. Her imprint on modern bloodlines is so powerful that her descendants continue to win the most important races in the world.

La Troienne herself was the dam of five stakes winners, including Black Helen, Biologist, Big Hurry, Bee Ann Mac, and Bimelech.

Bimelech was champion 2-year-old in 1939 and champion 3-year-old of 1940. Black Helen was the best 3-year-old filly of 1935 before formal 3-year-old filly champions were named beginning in 1939. Her genes were passed on through several generations to include 1992 champion older horse Pleasant Tap and 1994 Kentucky Derby winner Go for Gin.

Big Hurry was the dam of five stakes winners and prominent in the pedigrees of Straight Deal and Regal Gleam. Big Hurry's daughter Marking Time produced the blue-hen mare Relaxing. Both Relaxing's sire, Buckpasser, and her dam, Marking Time, descended from daughters of La Troienne, making her intensely inbred. A terrific multiple Grade 1-winning racehorse, Relaxing was the dam of Easy Goer, his full sister Cadillacing, and their half-sister Easy Now.

Another prominent daughter of the blue-hen mare Big Hurry was Searching, who might have been the very best producing mare to stem from the La Troienne line. Bred to Swaps, Searching produced 1965 champion sprinter Affectionately. Bred to Hail to Reason, Searching produced Priceless Gem, who defeated Buckpasser in the 1965 Futurity and was second-best juvenile filly in 1965 behind undefeated Moccasin. Carrying on this line with considerable power, Priceless Gem also produced one of Europe's all-time great fillies in Allez France, and through a mating with Secretariat, Allez France produced Lady Winborne, the dam of five stakes winners.

Big Hurry's daughter Searching had another foal by Hail to Reason named Admiring, who foaled the blue hen Glowing Tribute, dam of several stakes winners including 1993 Kentucky Derby-Travers winner Sea Hero.

La Troienne's other potent daughters included Big Event, the granddam

241

of several stakes winners including The Axe II, Malicious, Francis S., and Nasomo; Businesslike, the dam of Busanda, who produced Buckpasser, along with stakes-winning Bupers, Bureaucracy, Comic, and Navsup, who produced Polish Navy; Belle of Troy, who produced Cohoes, the sire of Quadrangle; and Baby League, whose descendants include Busher, Harmonizing, and the prolific blue-hen mare Striking.

The list goes on and on. There is no escaping the fact that La Troienne was the best broodmare in American racing history, if not world racing history. Her influence was so powerful through numerous producing blue-hen daughters and granddaughters and great-granddaughters that she began the best broodmare line of the modern era several times over.

THE BEST BARGAINS . . . AND WORST DUDS

Getting lucky or enduring bad luck is part of the breeding game too. Most breeding experts and stud-farm managers live by the credo "Breed the best to the best and hope for the best." But almost anyone involved in breeding or buying yearlings at auction grudgingly will admit that there is no guaranteed method for predicting how great horses will perform in the breeding shed, much less which of their offspring will be bargains or duds.

The Best Yearling Purchase

Some winners of $1 million or more were bought at public auction for less than $10,000. But that notwithstanding, there is no controversy who the greatest bargain was. Seattle Slew, a large-bodied, somewhat awkward, but beautiful nearly-black son of Bold Reasoning was bought for a moderate $17,500 at auction by Mickey Taylor and his wife, Karen, along with their partners and friends Jim and Sally Hill. A Triple Crown winner and major star at stud, Seattle Slew became one of the world's most valuable and sought-after stallions.

The Worst Yearling Purchase

The fate of Snaafi Dancer, purchased by Aston Upthorpe Stud for the princely sum of $10.2 million at the Keeneland July Select Yearling

Sale of 1983, can be summarized in one very painful sentence: Snaafi Dancer never raced and was sterile. No matter how much money is involved, or how risky the speculative yearling game is, you cannot spend $10 million worse than that.

The Biggest Dud at Stud

Breeding a champion horse to high-class mares does not always work. It is patently unfair to include a horse such as Snaafi Dancer in this category, just as it would be to include 1995–96 Horse of the Year Cigar. Both were sterile and never had the opportunity to prove their worth as stallions. But, there is at least one very high-profile champion racehorse with Bold Ruler in his genes who was not sterile, yet never sired a horse that seemed worth the trouble. The horse was, surprisingly, the great Spectacular Bid.

Although Spectacular Bid was syndicated for a then-record $22 million after he retired to Claiborne Farm in Kentucky for the 1981 breeding season, his stud fees plummeted throughout his stallion career, which reflected his disappointing performances.

Eventually moved to a modest breeding farm in upstate New York, Spectacular Bid did sire 44 stakes winners, but none earned close to $1 million, not one was able to contend for any divisional championship, and none raced with any distinction on the Grade 1 level.

The Most Disappointing Broodmare

Genuine Risk, the 1980 Kentucky Derby winner, was the biggest disappointment of all. Genuine Risk was nearly barren, but did have two foals, neither of whom made it to the races and neither of whom was successful at stud.

THE BEST CROPS OF THE MODERN ERA

The depth of talent, the range of accomplishments are the distinguishing characteristics that figure into any evaluation of specific crops of horses born in the same year. The following are the best of the modern age, and the 2003 crop is the only one to crack this list so far in the 21st century.

7. *1986*

This crop produced the dominant 3-year-olds Sunday Silence and Easy Goer, plus With Approval, Prized, Twilight Agenda, and Safely Kept.

6. *1994*

The best of these were four very impressive 3-year-olds who dominated the 1997 Triple Crown—Silver Charm, Touch Gold, Free House, and Captain Bodgit—plus the 1998 Breeders' Cup Classic winner, Awesome Again, and the durable champion sprinter Kona Gold.

5. *2003*

Stevie Wonderboy was a very good 2-year-old champion who was injured and unable to participate in the Triple Crown chase. Barbaro was an extraordinary winner of the 2006 Kentucky Derby after a seven-week layoff to remain unbeaten in six career starts, before he was severely injured in the Preakness. The Preakness was only one of several excellent performances turned in by Bernardini, who surpassed Barbaro with his performance in the 2006 Travers. Bluegrass Cat was a good winner of the Haskell Invitational and was second in the Derby, Belmont, and Travers before he was retired. Discreet Cat defeated the solid older horse Invasor in the $2 million UAE Derby in Dubai in March and was a superb-looking winner of the Jerome at Belmont in October. The 3-year-old fillies included Pine Island and Bushfire. On the turf, Showing Up was an impressive stakes winner. Other good horses in this crop included Santa Anita Derby winner Brother Derek, plus the high-class sprinters Henny Hughes and Too Much Bling.

4. *1964*

Some of the best horses of the modern era were in this very strong crop: Damascus, Dr. Fager, Successor, Fort Marcy, In Reality, Proud Clarion, Bold Hour, plus the champion fillies Gamely, Furl Sail, Regal Gleam, and Mira Femme, as well as the high-class stakes winners Amerigo Lady and Princessnesian.

3. *1954*

Considered by many to be the best crop of all time, mostly because of the high quality of the horses that dominated the 1957 Triple Crown, I personally rank it third. The crop included three Hall of Famers—Gallant Man, Bold Ruler, and Round Table—plus Iron Liege, and Gen. Duke, who was injured and forced into retirement before he could start as the probable favorite for the 1957 Kentucky Derby.

2. *1970*

This was a close call. The sheer depth of horses at the highest level of performance is what makes it so tempting to put this crop at the top of my list. There were a handful of dominant performers in several divisions for several years.

The best of them were five Hall of Famers: Secretariat, Forego, Desert Vixen, Dahlia, and La Prevoyante. There was also the very fast Mr. Prospector, who became one of the world's most prolific sires, and the ultradurable and consistent Ancient Title and Sham.

1. *1984*

A very deep crop represented by eight outstanding male horses and three fillies who won Breeders' Cup races against mixed-age competition. The males who excelled were Alysheba, Bet Twice, Java Gold, Gulch, Lost Code, Polish Navy, Demons Begone, and Cryptoclearance.

The top fillies from this crop were Breeders' Cup Sprint winner Very Subtle, Breeders' Cup Distaff winner Sacahuista, and the immortal, undefeated Personal Ensign, who won the 1988 Distaff. The top turf horses from this crop were not American, but the best of them was among the very best turf fillies ever to race in America—the French-based Miesque, a two-time winner of the Breeders' Cup Mile. Another top filly or mare was the two-time Distaff winner Bayakoa, an Argentinian import.

8 Before My Time

Perhaps it is folly to identify the best horses, jockeys, and trainers who performed many decades before all but a few *people* currently alive saw them. But through the miracle of past-performance profiles and eyewitness accounts in severely worn-out newspapers, it is difficult to resist the attempt.

BEST HORSES

3. *Citation*

The best horse bred and raced by Calumet Farm, Citation won 16 straight races, including the 1948 Triple Crown, and was next to invincible during the height of his powers. Jockey Eddie Arcaro, who was aboard Citation in all but one of his 16 straight, ranked him as the second-best horse he ever rode, after five-time Horse of the Year Kelso, whom Arcaro rode before he retired in 1961.

Out of training for the entire 1949 racing season, Citation was sent back to the track in 1950 and '51 in order to become the first horse to win $1 million or more.

Although not the same horse that he was in 1947 and '48, Citation won five races, with eight seconds and two thirds from 16 outings in 1950 and '51, all on the West Coast. Winning his final three career starts, Citation reached career earnings of $1,085,760 in the $157,000 Hollywood Gold Cup, the richest purse of his life and the final race of his historic career.

2. *Count Fleet*

Until Secretariat came along 30 years later, no horse ever dominated the Triple Crown to the extent that Count Fleet thoroughly outclassed his opposition in 1943. Not only did Count Fleet compile fast clockings in all three races, he won under virtually no urging from jockey Johnny Longden, who unequivocally labeled Count Fleet the best horse he ever rode or saw, Secretariat included.

The winner of 16 of his 21 career starts with four seconds and a third-place finish, Count Fleet extended his winning margin in nearly every instance—this while Longden kept him under wraps or was easing him up through the last furlong.

"He had so much reserve power, I know we never got to the bottom of him," Longden said. One can only imagine what Count Fleet might have been capable of had he been sound enough to race as a mature 4- and 5-year-old. He was forced to retire prematurely after he won the Belmont Stakes.

1. *Man o' War*

The star of 1919 and 1920 lost only one race in 21 career starts—to Upset in the 1919 Sanford Stakes at Saratoga. Just as Native Dancer lost the 1953 Kentucky Derby due to a bad start, so did Man o' War lose the Sanford after an equally awkward beginning.

The defeat did nothing to diminish Man o' War's reputation as the best juvenile in the land and he avenged the loss 10 days later with a one-length victory over Upset while being eased up in the final sixteenth of a mile. As a 3-year-old, Man o War was a veritable monster, a horse who never was in any danger of defeat—not when he dominated Upset in the Preakness and Travers (setting the Saratoga track record of 2:01⁴/₅ for 1¼ miles that would stand until 1962); nor when he left Donnacona in the dust in the Belmont Stakes; nor when he won the Lawrence Realization by a staggering 100 lengths, setting a Belmont track record for 1⅝ miles that still stands.

In addition to his record-breaking performances in the Belmont and Lawrence Realization, Man o' War set seven other track records at five tracks, defeating John P. Grier in the nine-furlong Dwyer Stakes; beating Upset for the third time in the 10-furlong Travers; beating the older Damask by 15 lengths in the 12-furlong Jockey Club Stakes; and outclassing Wildaire in the Potomac Handicap while spotting that rival 30 pounds and being eased up in the final furlong.

In Man o' War's final career appearance, he left no doubt about his superiority over 1919 Triple Crown winner Sir Barton, leaving that rival in the dust in the 10-furlong Kenilworth Park Gold Cup when they were the only two horses entered.

Although none of the surviving newsreels and private 16-mm films that show Man o' War in action do him justice, veteran players and racing writers who did have the pleasure of seeing him speak just as reverently about Man o' War as modern observers speak of Secretariat.

Charles Hatton, the columnist for *Daily Racing Form* who most famously labeled the Kentucky Derby, Preakness, and Belmont Stakes as the Triple Crown, saw Man o' War and slightly preferred Secretariat, but Hatton also believed that Citation and Count Fleet belonged in the conversation.

HONORABLE MENTION (IN ALPHABETICAL ORDER):

Colin: Undefeated and probably underrated by modern evaluators, including me, but he did win all 12 of his starts at 2 and his three outings at 3, including the 1908 Belmont Stakes when he beat Man o' War's sire, Fair Play, by a head in a driving rainstorm while being eased up at the wire.

Equipoise: A very consistent performer who finished in the money 12 times in succession to complete an excellent 2-year-old season in 1930 and then had a 10-race in-the-money streak at 3 and 4 years of age in 1932 and '33. Equipoise also finished in the money in 20 straight races from October of his 3-year-old season through his first two starts as a 7-year-old in 1936. He won 25 of 51 career starts, with 10 seconds and four thirds.

Exterminator: The 1918 Kentucky Derby-winning gelding who won 50 of his 100 career starts with 17 seconds and 17 thirds. Exterminator was the Kelso and John Henry of his era, winning races from 1917 through his 9-year-old season in 1924.

Old Rosebud: Won 12 of his first 14 races, including the 1914 Kentucky Derby, and then won 15 more races in 22 subsequent starts as a 3-year-old, all against older horses. Next to Man o' War, he might have been the best of the early-20th-century performers.

Pan Zareta: Certainly belongs on any "Most Durable" list. She won 76 races with 31 seconds and 21 thirds in 151 career starts from 1912 through 1917 while running for purses ranging from $500 to $3,900 at more than three dozen tracks. For some perspective on Pan Zareta's durability, get this: As a 7-year-old, she raced 12 times during the final two months of her career!

Seabiscuit: A rags-to-riches equine hero who was a durable, extremely popular champion in 1937 and '38. More than a movie-made legend, Seabiscuit drew large crowds wherever he appeared and won a historic match race with Triple Crown winner War Admiral at Pimlico in 1938. Then, after a long period of convalescence from a serious leg injury, Seabiscuit came back to win the 1940 San Antonio Handicap and Santa Anita Handicap in his final two starts as a 7-year-old.

Twilight Tear: Champion 3-year-old filly and Horse of the Year in 1944, won 11 straight and 14 of 18 starts that year, including seven victories over male rivals and three over older horses. Certainly one of the best fillies of all time.

War Admiral: Despite his loss to Seabiscuit as a 4-year-old in the 1938 Pimlico Special (run as a match race), this son of Man o' War was one of the great 3-year-olds in history. He won all eight starts in 1937, including the Triple Crown, and was not too shabby as an older horse either, winning 10 of his final 12 starts.

Whirlaway: The 1941 Triple Crown winner and Horse of the Year also was champion handicap horse as a 4-year-old in 1942 and one of the most reliable and crowd-pleasing stretch-runners of all time. He completed his career with 32 victories, 15 seconds, and nine thirds in 60 career outings. Most remarkably, Whirlaway was in the money in 48 straight races from September of his 2-year-old season in 1940 through his first of two starts as a 5-year-old in January 1943. This is the all-time record for consecutive in-the-money performances by an American racehorse in the 20th and 21st century.

Zev: Kentucky Derby-Belmont Stakes winner in 1923 also defeated the English champion Papyrus in the $105,000 "International" match race at Belmont Park on October 23, 1923. This race did a lot to validate the quality of American horse racing and was one of the most historically significant races ever run in this country.

BEST RACE CALLER

Clem McCarthy

This famous announcer was every American's link to the great races and championship boxing matches of the 1930s through the 1950s. McCarthy's gravelly, low-pitched, emotionally powerful voice set a distinct tone for his profession and seemed especially poignant for racing. In the pre-television era, McCarthy also was the lead voice heard in weekly newsreels produced by Pathe News and RKO that were as popular in the movie houses of the day as the leading feature films.

In the legendary Seabiscuit vs. War Admiral match race, McCarthy's call of the final sixteenth of a mile was reported in a phrase of three clearly descriptive words, repeated in staccato rhythm for emphasis, a phrase that conveyed all the drama and surprise of the event without unnecessary histrionics.

"It's Seabiscuit by three! Seabiscuit by three! Seabiscuit is the winner!"

McCarthy, a near-perfect race caller, was guilty, however, of one of the most famous race-calling mistakes in Triple Crown history.

The faux pas took place in the 1947 Preakness and apparently was caused by a crowd standing on a platform blocking McCarthy's view of the eventual winner, Faultless, moving to the front on the far turn. Thoroughly embarrassed by his miscue, McCarthy apologized immediately to his large radio audience, and that act of contrition earned him as much praise as if he had never made the error in the first place.

A true pioneer in his field, McCarthy also is credited with having been the first full-time public-address announcer at a major U.S. racetrack, Arlington Park in 1927.

GREATEST UPSETS

3. *Man o' War Loses to Upset in the 1919 Sanford Memorial Stakes.*

While this historic upset usually is mentioned at the top of most lists citing shocking race results, it might not have been as surprising as a few others in racing history, including the modern Kentucky Derby upsets posted by Dark Star, Canonero II, and Giacomo, or the two upsets on this list of three that occurred before the television age.

Man o' War certainly was a highly regarded 2-year-old when he came to Saratoga with five straight victories, all accomplished in dominating fashion in relatively fast clockings. When he won the U S Hotel Stakes at 11–20 odds, most racing observers labeled him the best 2-year-old in the land. Only the talented Golden Broom was expected to give Man o' War a serious battle in the Sanford Memorial on August 13. Both were assigned 130 pounds for the race that many expected would decide the juvenile championship.

Upset was no slouch, having finished a respectable second to Man o' War in the U S Hotel Stakes 11 days earlier. He was also in the Sanford with 115 pounds, which a scattering of players believed would put him in the mix.

Essentially, the race was won a few beats after the tape fell to signal the start. Man o' War was unprepared, caught in a tangle, due in part to jockey James Loftus's difficulties in getting set for the break. Barely after completing the first 50 yards, Upset was in front by more than three lengths, while Golden Broom had an advantage over his slow-breaking rival in the ensuing chase.

Upset prevailed by a diminishing half-length, with the hard-charging and unlucky Man o' War beating Golden Broom by three lengths, gaining enormous respect for his performance.

Indeed, the most significant fact gleaned from the running of this historic race was that Man o' War was seen unanimously as the class of 1919's juveniles as well as a colt who seemed destined for greatness at 3.

To prove the point, Man o' War reversed the verdict in his next outing, beating Upset by a length in the Grand Union Hotel Stakes at the same 11–20 odds he went to the post in the Sanford. As the world knows, Man o' War would never lose another race, winning his next 14, all stakes, and would be remembered forever as one of racing's greatest champions.

2. *Count Turf Wins the 1951 Kentucky Derby.*

Count Turf, owned by New York restaurateur Jack Amiel, was a most improbable winner of the world's most famous race. After he failed to perform well enough in the Everglades and Flamingo Stakes at Hialeah and the Wood Memorial at Aqueduct, his trainer, Sol Rutchick, was convinced that the horse should not even go to Louisville to clutter up the Derby field.

Amiel was insistent, however, and actually arranged for Count Turf to be shipped to Churchill Downs against the recommendation of his trainer. Count Turf, a son of the brilliant 1943 Triple Crown winner Count Fleet, was lumped into a four-horse mutuel field as one of the least-likely winners of the race.

Ridden by Conn McCreary, Count Turf outperformed all expectations, even those of the persistent Amiel, rallying from midpack in the field of 20 to take the lead in the upper stretch to win by four lengths over the very lightly regarded Royal Mustang. The latter, dismissed at 53–1, completed a most improbable exacta in an era when there was no such betting pool. Had Count Turf been a single betting interest and not part of the mutuel field, he probably would have gone to the post at much higher odds than Royal Mustang.

Count Turf did not win another stakes at 3 and managed only one victory in 10 tries as a 4-year-old in 1952 and one more win in 11 outings the following year. Aside from Canonero II's amazing upset in the 1970 Kentucky Derby, it is hard to top Count Turf's astonishing reversal of form in a Triple Crown race.

1. *Jim Dandy Defeats 1930 Triple Crown Winner Gallant Fox at 100–1.*

Ten months after the 1929 stock-market crash, the country was heading deep into a prolonged economic depression when the 1930 Travers was being run at Saratoga before an estimated crowd of 30,000 in intermittent rain. Although the tenor of the moment was to believe that no icon was sacred, the defeat of 1930 Triple Crown winner Gallant Fox was beyond improbable, especially by 100–1 Jim Dandy, a proven loser of historic proportions.

In 20 career starts prior to the Travers, Jim Dandy had won just twice, with two other in-the-money finishes. He frequently finished last or next to last, as he had in his only start of the current season, 12 days earlier in a six-furlong handicap, his first start since he completed nine poor races in Agua Caliente, Mexico.

The mighty Gallant Fox was being offered at 50 cents on the dollar; Whichone, considered to be a serious contender, was 8–5; while Sun Falcon, who finished second to Whichone in the Saranac Handicap, was seen as a marginal longshot possibility at 30–1.

Jim Dandy? According to reports that have filtered down through the years, at least one bookmaker in the ring was willing to raise his price from 100–1 to 500–1 for New York-based construction magnate Sam Rosoff, a well-known horseplayer with a bent toward playing unrealistic longshots. Rosoff took $500 to win on Jim Dandy at the 500–1 odds that would produce a $250,000 payoff in an era when $1,000 was an excellent annual salary.

Under jockey Sonny Workman, Whichone jumped to the lead, bidding for a front-running upset, while Gallant Fox moved up to challenge before the first turn under Earl Sande. Jim Dandy took up a good stalking position under jockey Red Baker, 3 ½ lengths behind the dueling leaders.

The fractional splits were slow enough not to worry Workman or Sande as they continued 1–2 through the first seven furlongs. But Jim Dandy was much sharper today, and relishing the rain-moistened, muddy track, he rallied resolutely along the rail coming out of the final turn while Gallant Fox was being carried out a bit by a tiring Whichone, both weakened by their ill-advised duel on the tiring track.

Jim Dandy glided to the lead and improved his position through the stretch run to score by eight widening lengths without much urging from Baker. The crowd was stunned to silence, and the losing owners, trainers, and jockeys all regarded the performance as a fluke of gigantic proportions. But there was some evidence that it was nothing of the kind.

Consider this: Jim Dandy's trainer, James B. McKee, had entered Jim Dandy in an allowance race on the card, but scratched to run in the Travers when he saw the rain turn the racing strip into slick, sticky mud. McKee had reason to believe that his colt was many lengths better on a wet surface than dry. Jim Dandy's only prior winning race of any consequence was in the Grand Hotel Stakes over the same Saratoga racing strip as a 2-year-old in August 1929. The track that day was muddy and Jim Dandy paid 50–1 as the longest shot on the board. Jim Dandy was not quite a fluke; he was a world-class mudder with a special fondness for wet footing at Saratoga.

Undaunted, Gallant Fox's trainer, Sunny Jim Fitzsimmons, sent his tarnished Triple Crown winner out for a winning romp against older horses in the Saratoga Cup two weeks later, at 1–5 odds. During the next month, Gallant Fox completed his career with victories in the Lawrence Realization and Jockey Club Gold Cup at Belmont Park, the latter race as the overwhelming 1–20 betting favorite. For his part, McKee started Jim Dandy 141 times during his 11-year racing career, winning only seven, including the Travers. But his horse would never be forgotten for pulling off one of the most astounding upsets in any sport at any time.

BEST HORSEPLAYERS

There was nothing wrong with Sam Rosoff's $500 winning bet at 500–1 odds on Jim Dandy in the 1930 Travers, and there are many other famous winning bets and bettors who might deserve mention. But the legendary Pittsburgh Phil has to be regarded as the best horseplayer of the early 20th century.

In his hard-to-find, out-of-print, ghost-written book, *The Maxims of Pittsburgh Phil,* the great horseplayer explains how he made his fortune by utilizing professional clockers and stable informants on his payroll. Inside information was Phil's edge on the bookmakers of his day and he spared no effort or expense to obtain it. Phil also understood something akin to "track bias," taking notes about the way some horses needed deep and tiring tracks to succeed, while others could be eliminated from consideration when rain fell on the racing ground.

Operating in the era of the legal bookmaker, Phil also had a few tricks up his sleeve. For instance, he regularly had some of his associates make modest, misleading wagers on horses he really did not like, in order to drive up the odds on horses he truly preferred.

Phil's success as a player may have been somewhat exaggerated through the decades and there is no formal record of his picks, his plays, or his bankroll. But he definitely conveyed several workable handicapping angles in his published works to reinforce the notion that he was one of the great horseplayers who ever lived.

Arthur Rooney also deserves some special mention in this category for one dramatic season of horseplay at Saratoga in the 1940s. It seems that Mr. Rooney parlayed a very small bankroll into more than $80,000, which he used to help buy the Pittsburgh Steelers Professional Football Club, the NFL team still owned by the Rooney family that has won a record five Super Bowls and has an estimated book value of $600 million.

JOCKEYS

3. *Isaac Murphy*

Murphy was an African American jockey star in the 19th century, when young blacks were regularly employed as all-around stable help, exercise riders, and, in some cases, as jockeys. In fact, 11 different African American jockeys rode 15 winners of the Kentucky Derby during the first 30 years of America's most famous race.

They were: Oliver Lewis, who rode Aristides to the first Derby win in 1875, Babe Hurd, George Lewis, Erskin Henderson, Jimmy Winkfield, Willie Simms, William Walker, Alonzo Clayton, Jimmy Perkins, Isaac Lewis, and Murphy.

Murphy was an extraordinary rider by any standard. Not only did he become the first jockey to win three Kentucky Derbies (Buchanan in 1884, Riley in 1890, and Kingman in 1891), he rode numerous stakes at his home track, Churchill Downs. Even more impressively, Murphy won with an astounding 44 percent of his mounts throughout his riding career, which is the singular reason why an award bearing his name honors the jockey with the highest winning percentage each year. An original 1955 inductee into Racing's Hall of Fame, Murphy died of pneumonia at the age of 35 in 1896.

In the years prior to the 20th century, Murphy's only serious rival for supremacy in the saddle was James McLaughlin, who won six Belmont Stakes in addition to the 1881 Kentucky Derby aboard Hindoo. McLaughlin also rode 1885 Preakness winner Tecumseh and led the national jockey standings four consecutive years, from 1884 through 1887.

2. *Johnny Longden*

Not only did Longden ride Count Fleet to his spectacular Triple Crown sweep in 1943, but he also led the national earnings list that year and repeated the feat in 1945. Longden also won more races than any other jockey in 1937, '47, and '48, and passed England's Sir Gordon Richards in 1956 with his 4,681st victory to become the winningest jockey in racing history, a distinction he would keep until Bill Shoemaker passed him in 1970. A 19 percent lifetime winner of 6,032 races, Longden was a keen judge of pace and a polished performer on any surface at any distance, but he became an early turf master when races on grass increased in popularity on the West Coast during the 1950s. Well past his prime and riding tentatively, Longden finally decided to call it a career at the age of 59, when he made one of the most memorable exits from the saddle, an exit no Hollywood script writer could have dreamed up.

The scene was the 1966 San Juan Capistrano Handicap at Santa Anita, in which Longden was sentimentally assigned to ride an off-form George Royal, as he had ridden that horse to victory in the 1965 running of this 1 ³/₄-mile turf event. Rallying through the stretch to thunderous applause and shocked disbelief, Longden guided George Royal to a nose victory in the final stride over Plaque to post his final career win in his 32,413th and final career race. Observers who were among the 60,000 fans in attendance insist that it was among the most emotional, most satisfying races ever run in California.

As a footnote to his Hall of Fame riding career, Longden would later utilize his expert horsemanship as the trainer of 1969 Kentucky Derby-Preakness winner Majestic Prince, whom Longden reluctantly ran in the Belmont Stakes at the insistence of owner Frank McMahon—this despite the fact that Longden strongly urged rest for the colt, who did not fully recover from the Derby-Preakness experience. Unbeaten after the Preakness, Majestic Prince gallantly finished second to Arts and Letters in the Belmont and never raced again.

"That was my one regret as a jockey or trainer," he said a few years later. "He shouldn't have run in that race; he should have gone out as I did, with a win."

1. *Earl Sande*

Winner of more than 26 percent of his career mounts, Earl Sande was the regular jockey for 1930 Triple Crown winner Gallant Fox. He also won the 1923 Kentucky Derby aboard Zev and the 1925 Derby aboard Flying Ebony, as well as four other runnings of the Belmont Stakes during the 1920s. Unrivaled as a money rider during the 20s and early 1930s, Sande was in high demand to ride the best horses in the country, and among his numerous stakes winners were five of the 10 Jockey Club Gold Cup winners from 1921 through 1930.

Few jockeys in any era had Sande's skill as a true horseman. He frequently rode without using his whip while still getting plenty of response from his mounts by whistling and singing in their ears. Of the pre Arcaro-Shoemaker era, the only jockeys who rivaled Sande on any measurable level were George Woolf and James Stout, the dominant money riders in the 1930s.

TRAINERS

3. *Ben A. Jones and H. A. "Jimmy" Jones*

This famous father-and-son team is credited with training eight Kentucky Derby winners from 1938 through 1958. All but Lawrin in '38 were owned and bred by Calumet Farm, which "the Jones Boys" helped to prominence through their abundant skills in judging and developing natural racehorse talent and potential matings.

While Ben A. Jones is given credit for six of those victories, including Calumet's two Triple Crown winners, Whirlaway and Citation, the Joneses worked together on virtually all of their horses, including 1944 filly champion and Horse of the Year Twilight Tear. Thus it is impossible to label either Ben or Jimmy Jones better than others on this list, given their tag-team advantage.

2. *Hirsch Jacobs*

A prolific winner of 3,593 races, most on the claiming level in New York, Jacobs also was the national leader in races won a record 11 times during a 12-year period from 1933 through 1944. Jacobs is best known for claiming the gelding Stymie in 1943 for $1,500 in his third lifetime start. Stymie went on to win 35 races, with 33 seconds and 28 thirds from 131 starts for career earnings of $918,485, the world record for a brief time in 1948.

Jacobs also trained the brilliant 1960 juvenile champion Hail to Reason and the equally talented filly Affectionately, champion sprinter of

1965, the year Jacobs and his stable of very few stakes horses and numerous claimers won more money than any other trainer in America. Along with Marion H. Van Berg, who owned and effectively trained an army of cheap horses, Hirsch Jacobs was one of the few horsemen of his era to win a high percentage of lower-level races while developing a handful of top-flight horses.

In Jacobs's case, he set the upwardly mobile tone for the stable of his wife, Ethel D. Jacobs, to become a national presence. Eventually, the Jacobs stable would morph into Harbor View Farm when daughter Patrice Jacobs married Louis Wolfson and the pair would breed and race 1978 Triple Crown winner Affirmed, among many other notable runners.

1. *Sunny Jim Fitzsimmons*

Although Fitzsimmons made one of the biggest blunders in racing history by giving up on Seabiscuit, he expertly trained numerous champions including Bold Ruler, Nashua, Granville, Vagrancy, High Voltage, Misty Morn, and two Triple Crown winners, Gallant Fox and Omaha. Indeed, Fitzsimmons's Triple Crown resume is extraordinary: He won three Derbies, four Preaknesses, and six Belmonts, for a total of 13 Triple Crown-race victories, a record only matched by the modern era's D. Wayne Lukas.

The venerable Sunny Jim was a keen strategist, as he proved with his method of training Nashua for a front-running win in his match race against Kentucky Derby winner Swaps. No spring chicken, Sunny Jim was able to maintain his place in the New York Racing Association trainers' standings well into his 80s. Few trainers in any era had his acumen for good horses and/or how to prepare them.

THE WORST ASPECT OF EARLY-20TH-CENTURY RACING

The fact that African Americans were good enough to be used as jockeys in America's greatest races during the post-Civil War years all the way through the early 20th century leaves mixed emotions about the sport's failure to help promote their true citizenship in everyday American life.

Riding horses was and is dangerous work for any man, and it is racing's shame that it was a sport dominated by wealthy and influential people who employed African Americans, yet did not fight harder for equal rights for the black riders and their families when they were truly taken advantage of in so many ways by society in general, for so many years.

Fact is, the African American jockey virtually disappeared from the sport in the 1920s and remains an extreme rarity in modern-day racing. The root causes of this are difficult to pin down, but this much remains true: The opportunities for African American athletes and trainers are nowhere near as lucrative as opportunities in other professional sports.

9

RACETRACKS, RACE CALLERS, AND HORSEPLAYERS

THE BEST AND WORST
RACETRACKS OF THE PAST AND PRESENT

Since the early 1960s I have visited more than 40 harness tracks, a dozen tracks that feature Quarter Horse racing, and more than 60 tracks where Thoroughbreds are either the dominant racing breed or the only breed in play. I am one of many with a special fondness for Saratoga and Del Mar, but those two summer gems are not the only great racetracks that have a special ambiance worth repeated visits.

There is Arlington Park—the rebuilt Arlington, the modern, beautifully appointed Arlington that hosted the 2002 Breeders' Cup and deserves another Cup Day sometime soon. Very few tracks in America have such a comfortable, stylish grandstand, complete with sparkling tile floors and plenty of spaces inside and out for both casual visitors and expert, dedicated horseplayers.

Old Hialeah was a wonderful place to play the horses and watch flamingos fly about between races. But it has lain fallow for too many years, and the pink-tinted paint that decorated many of its walls is peeling, while the statues dedicated to racehorses look as if Hialeah is a homeless shelter for once-regal animals turned to bronze.

As for Gulfstream Park—lavishly rebuilt Gulfstream Park—the jury is still out after many flaws were observed in the track's reopening during the winter of 2006. Obviously built for future casino expansion and designed to accommodate simulcast players more than live-racing fans, Frank Stronach's newest racetrack had many beautiful touches, but was not completely ready when the gates opened. To his credit, Stronach and his staff seemed to hear customer complaints and promised to rework some of its concepts in time for 2007. Among the scheduled improvements are more grandstand seats. (There were fewer than 1,200 outdoor seats for the 2006 opening.)

On the opposite end of the spectrum is Tampa Bay Downs, a modestly appointed, well-run track on the west coast of Florida that has become famous for its racing surface, which is deeper and slower than most tracks and gives the horses who spend the winter there opportunities to build up their stamina as much as compete for moderate purses before the best of them head north.

Another modestly appointed, sometimes-overlooked track, Colonial Downs in Virginia, accents turf racing six or more times per day, every day, as if it were a European course transplanted in the hills of Virginia.

In the Midwest, historic Churchill Downs also underwent a major face-lift that was completed in time for the 2005 spring meet. The changes drew raves from most visitors, who appreciated the internal creature comforts preserving much of the feel of the track that has hosted the Kentucky Derby since 1875. The Kentucky Derby Museum, which is on the Churchill Downs grounds, remains a great place to visit, especially if you are interested in seeing replays of all the Kentucky Derbies that have been preserved on film and videotape.

The Fair Grounds in New Orleans, burned to the ground in 1993 and severely damaged again by Hurricane Katrina in 2005, has more than 100 years of charm to rebuild its reputation. Indeed, a rebirth of the Fair Grounds is important to the ongoing effort to rebuild the Crescent City. On a personal note, the Fair Grounds used to be an extremely formful track in the mid-1960s, when I played the game professionally and regularly picked horses for entertainer Jimmy Durante when he was in town for scattered weekends. For my services, Durante let me use his private box for the season.

Oaklawn Park in Arkansas also is a pleasant throwback to an earlier era and certainly attracts large crowds several times a season. The "Racing Festival of the South," which features several graded stakes, including the Arkansas Derby, is one of the better closing weeks offered by any track in the country. Oaklawn, plus the Texas-based tracks Lone Star Park and Sam Houston Race Park, all have many pluses, not the least of which are first-rate simulcast facilities that remain open throughout the year.

Canterbury Park in Minnesota also has excellent simulcast facilities and is a well-proportioned, middle-sized racetrack with friendly employees, plenty of information centers, a good turf course, and an accessible paddock. It also has a good if relatively modest-sized poker room, with some additional tables for blackjack, which in my opinion offers a far better marriage with parimutuel racing than a slot-machine parlor. At least poker, and in some cases blackjack, is a game of skill in which the takeout is reasonable compared to the one-armed bandits that racetracks from coast to coast are lobbying to bring into the mix to improve their bottom line. One has to wonder if the executives of these tracks will have any plan to hold off state legislatures when the legislators begin to question the viability of racing compared to the enormous profits gleaned from slots.

Delaware Park, which does have slots, is bent on keeping the well-manicured grounds that made this playground of the DuPont family a great racecourse in the 1960s and 70s. In the current slot era, however, purses may be high, but there are very few racing days when more than 2,000 people bother to watch Thoroughbreds perform at a cavernous racecourse built to hold 40,000 or more.

The same feeling of emptiness can occur on a weekday card at oversized Belmont Park, even though Belmont does not have the distraction of slot machines—at least not yet. Only on Belmont Stakes Day and perhaps three or four other times a year does beautiful Belmont attract enough people to remind a player of the days when large crowds regularly came out every Saturday to watch Kelso and Carry Back and other stars of the 1960s compete against one another.

The California tracks are interesting and somewhat schizophrenic. Santa Anita Park in Southern California has a spectacular stakes schedule, a picturesque mountain backdrop, as well as a great early-morning scene that permits free access to morning workouts. But the main dirt track has been hard on many horses and difficult to manage during the winter rainy season, which is one reason why the California Horse Racing Board has ordered Santa Anita and all the other major tracks in the state to install a synthetic racing surface before the end of 2007. While that seems understandable for Santa Anita, there is nothing wrong that I can detect with the Hollywood Park racing surface, which has been an ideal place to train and race horses for several decades. Hollywood, sold by Churchill Downs to land developers in 2005, is not likely to be given a reprieve after 2008.

In Northern California, Bay Meadows probably could have used an extensive face-lift a decade ago, but now is in the process of being turned over to land developers and is expected to be closed in 2008. The value of Bay Meadows' land, located about 12 miles south of San Francisco, is many times greater than the value of a racetrack on that property.

Golden Gate Fields, across the San Francisco Bay, is not only one of the best-named racetracks in America but also features a beautiful background view of the Berkeley and Albany hills. But at Golden Gate and other Northern California tracks, the majority of play is through intrastate simulcasting. No one in the region has any clue what the future holds, given the state of the facilities, plus the increasing pressure on a diminishing horse population and far too many racing dates throughout the state.

Frankly, the best track in Northern California probably is located at the Sonoma County Fairgrounds in Santa Rosa, which runs a 2 ½ -week annual meet as part of the Northern California Fair summer rotation. Santa Rosa actually is a relic from the past built for the future, having introduced a new turf course in 2005 and generally featuring 13 races each day for mules, Quarter Horses, and Arabians, with seven or more reserved for Thoroughbreds. With Bay Meadows likely to be closed in 2008, most of the county-fair tracks probably will be getting more dates, and Santa Rosa's allotment might double.

If Saratoga and Del Mar were not on the calendar each summer, I would go to Santa Rosa, unless I decided to head east and go to Monmouth Park. Monmouth, on the Jersey shore, is one of the best tracks in America. It has beautiful grounds and a Colonial-style grandstand with comfortable pockets to hang out with friends as well as picnic areas that kindle memories of the old Garden State Park, my favorite track of those that have closed down, burned to the ground, or been long forgotten.

Monmouth is scheduled to host the 2007 Breeders' Cup, which is good for those who may remember or never had the chance to experience Garden State Park when it offered the best fall schedule of 2-year-old racing in the country. Monmouth survived where Garden State (and Atlantic City Racecourse) have not. Monmouth is located in a popular summer resort community, while Garden State—in Cherry Hill, New Jersey, across the Delaware River 15 miles from Philadelphia—was in trouble before a fire burned the place to the ground in 1977.

In the early 1980s, Robert Brennan, an overzealous financial investor and horse owner-breeder (Due Process Stable), decided to rebuild a new and bigger Garden State Park—this despite many consultants forecasting smaller crowds due to a migrating population, in addition to entrenched competition from Philadelphia Park and Delaware Park, which had taken control of Garden State's traditional spring and fall racing dates. Brennan, later convicted for investment fraud for a wide variety of schemes that would crumble his whole financial empire, built his new and extremely expensive Garden State Park as if it were a Taj Mahal.

He also built it with many unforgivable design flaws: It was next to impossible to get from one section of the track to another without taking multiple elevators; it was hard to see the horses in the paddock from the appointed locations 100 to 150 feet away; it was difficult to watch races without an obstructed view in several sections of the grandstand (and completely impossible to see the track from most seats in the press box). There also were too few bathrooms, too few wagering terminals, too many untrained mutuel clerks, and not nearly enough drive paths to enter and exit the undersized parking lots. All in all, it was hard to figure where the friendly ambience of the original Garden State Park had gone, along with $100 million to $150 million in construction costs.

Talk about the best track of the 1960s and 70s turning into the worst!

The new Garden State had a few flashy moments, such as when 1985 Kentucky Derby winner Spend a Buck won a Jersey Derby worth in excess of $2 million by successfully sweeping a series of races that had been set up to attract publicity for the newly reopened track. Spend a

265

Buck had won two Derby preps at Garden State and then also won the Derby itself, making owner Dennis Diaz eligible for a windfall if the colt could also win the Jersey Derby—although running in that race would mean skipping the Preakness. Diaz went for the money instead of a shot at the Triple Crown, and Brennan got $2 million worth of publicity by attracting the Derby winner for his marquee race. He got all the postrace PR he could hope for when the race for the bonus money turned out to be a genuine classic, with Spend a Buck narrowly holding off Crème Fraiche, who would win the Belmont Stakes in his next start.

That moment of glory notwithstanding, Brennan and all his investors in the new Garden State Park should have known that they were wasting their money. They had enough evidence of the likely failure of their Taj Mahal on opening night two months earlier. Attendance that night was well in excess of 25,000, but most of those fans left the building with negative impressions and complaints that never were resolved. In fact, a survey taken by Garden State officials discovered that Jersey Derby Day 1985 was the last time many fans of the original Garden State Park ever set foot in the place.

The new Garden State Park was a disaster. Management eventually had to pare down its ambitious purse structure; eliminate racing dates; switch completely to harness racing; close down portions of the track to conserve electricity; and finally shut the track's doors and knock the building to the ground in order to salvage space for a series of condominiums and other supporting businesses.

In 2006, the empty feeling the place provoked probably felt similar to the reaction Brooklyn residents experienced when they drove past the apartment houses that occupy Flatbush and Bedford Avenues—where Ebbets Field once played host to Jackie Robinson, Duke Snider, Gil Hodges, and all the other daffy Dodgers who moved to L.A.

Saratoga and its history aside, Del Mar and its Pacific Ocean too, the old Garden State Park was the best racetrack I have ever set foot in; the new Garden State Park was the absolute worst.

THE BEST HORSEPLAYERS I HAVE KNOWN

The best horseplayers I know are people who appreciate the difficulty of long-term success at the betting windows, yet are not afraid to step in and aggressively play to the strength of their opinions. They also have grown with the changes in the game from win, place, show, and daily doubles to the exotic world of exactas, trifectas, superfectas, and multiple-choice, multirace bets that frequently produce large payoffs.

In the 1960s and 70s, straightforward handicapping married to sensible money management were the key elements in building a winning game. In the 21st century, it is extremely difficult to win serious money by consistently accenting win, place, and show bets. Horses are more fragile; they do not race as often or retain their form as long, and so much publicity has been given to standard handicapping approaches that the odds have dropped precipitously on clearly identifiable win contenders.

To be successful, the modern horseplayer has to have an arsenal of approaches to the exotic-wagering pools and be much more aggressive when the opportunities for large profits present themselves.

In my lifetime, I have met many winning horseplayers, the majority of whom prefer to be anonymous while they fight their battles against the mutuel machines and the IRS. But I also have circulated through dozens of racetrack grandstands, casino race books, public seminars, and press boxes, sharing handicapping views with hundreds of good players who could be great if they had the time to dedicate themselves professionally to the task.

While it is not rocket science and there is great joy in playing the game well enough to hover at or slightly above even, playing the horses professionally takes a commitment that few with families or good day jobs can make. That notwithstanding, I personally know of nine outstanding horseplayers who not only have day jobs, but also have worked in horse racing—mostly as racing writers, or published handicappers, or some combination of the two.

Andrew Beyer, creator of the Beyer Speed Figures, has been a wonderful racing columnist since the early 1970s. He also has been a major winning player for most of those years.

Steven Crist, publisher of *Daily Racing Form*, was *The New York Times*'s racing writer in the 1980s when he was making his own private figures and was developing his approaches to the expanding "exotic betting" game that is the principal focus of his latest book of the same name.

Jeff Siegel, a syndicated public handicapper in Southern California, was one of the first media horseplayers to capitalize on the opportunities posed by the lucrative pick six. Siegel, in fact, organized numerous winning pick-six plays in the Southern California press boxes that helped him capitalize a stake in a successful racing stable he formed in partnership with Barry Irwin: Team Valor. Among many stakes winners bought and raced by Team Valor since Siegel applied his keen eye for a good horse to the task were Prized, My Memoirs, and Captain Bodgit. In the 21st century, Siegel still publishes his handicapping analysis in several Southern California newspapers while serving as expert commentator for the satellite horse-racing network HRTV. Siegel is one "expert" who really merits the term.

Scott McMannis is a Chicago-based player who wrote for *The Racing Times* in 1991 and has contributed to many handicapping publications. McMannis also has conducted hundreds of handicapping seminars at Sportsman's Park, Arlington, and Hawthorne through the years. Above all else, he is a savvy professional player who utilizes his local expertise to great effect. In fact, McMannis rarely plays anything but Chicago races, except for an occasional shot in Triple Crown and Breeders' Cup events.

Gordon Jones, known as Professor Gordon Jones, was the regular racing writer and handicapper for the *Los Angeles Herald Examiner* during the 1970s and was one of the first winning pick-six players in America. Jones held seminars at nearby hotels in the Southern California market in which his followers chipped in for shares of his pick-six plays, which produced several millions of dollars in hits. Jones also lost his job when he was arrested for violating an obscure, ridiculous law that barred players from transporting wagers from outside gathering places to the track. The fact that the *Los Angeles Herald Examiner* had accepted numerous ads paid for by Jones that regularly pointed out where his seminars were being held shows their hypocrisy in severing their relationship with him when he had to fight this absurd legal battle on his own in court.

The late Ron Cox, who published the excellent *Northern California Report* for several years, was a very strong, long-term winning player. Cox's protégé and partner, Dan Montilion, was nearly as strong when they were together in the early 1990s and has developed into a top-flight professional in his own right since Cox passed away in the late 1990s. The strength of Cox's game, and of Montilion's as well, is focused on astute pace concepts and trainer angles, many of which Cox taught me when I spent almost a year playing with him in the early 1990s.

Bill Stevenson, a former public handicapper at Penn National and Atlantic City Racecourse for *The Philadelphia Inquirer* and a strong public handicapper at several tracks for *Daily Racing Form* in the 1980s, is one of the few winning horseplayers I know who has made his biggest scores in the win pool. Stevenson, a successful businessman and portfolio investor, has almost left the game several times because of the wild changes in form cycles and smaller fields that seem to plague the game in the 21st century. But in the summer of 2006, he was knocking out his usual profit while beginning to expand his game into the exotic realm.

Al Torch, a former harness-horse owner, certainly had a day job in racing while he was learning the Thoroughbred game, but he was a strong tote-board specialist and professional trip analyst when I met him in 1972. Along with his paid assistants and distant relatives, Torch logged all the wagering pools in every race on the NYRA circuit and watched races in the manner of a trip handicapper long before trip handicapping was labeled that by anyone in the game.

Torch was the epitome of a disciplined spot-bet player, who would wait out weeks of inactivity to make sizeable bets on horses he personally knew were much, much better than their records indicated and were attracting subtle betting action. During several meets at Saratoga, I saw Torch score with a high percentage of plays at odds that were amazing, to say the least. Torch did not write up his opinions for all to read and did not like to discuss in depth many of his well-crafted methods. But that was not how Beyer, Crist, and others, including myself, approached the game.

Although the majority of racing writers and public handicappers do not supplement their living through the parimutuel windows (most do not have the time or the dedication), Crist, Beyer, and others who have done so seem to adopt a principle that helps each of us improve our game while we reveal our so-called secrets. The principle can be summarized by this philosophical concept: *You cannot keep a good idea unless you give it away.*

Speaking personally, I learn more about my game when I share insights about track bias and trainer patterns and key races and pace issues and new wagering concepts. Sharing my ideas makes me research them better and apply them with more precision.

As more people inevitably became more aware of track bias and trainer patterns, or Beyer Speed Figures, or the pick-six betting approaches of Steven Crist, Gordon Jones, and Jeff Siegel, we each had to fine-tune our approach to accent nuances that the general public was missing or overinvesting in. The game did become harder, but we realized the need to develop our own interpretations, which is what happens when you pass on to others the basics. As I said, it makes *you* stronger.

Of all the professional players I have known, Andrew Beyer deserves special mention. On one hand, Andy is nowhere near the best handicapper I have ever met. He was, however, born to be a successful horseplayer.

An extremely disciplined man of great personal integrity, Andy had the intelligence and natural curiosity of someone seeking to make an easy living the hard way. Robbing banks was out; so were all the other unethical ways that people choose to avoid a good-paying nine-to-five life. While at Harvard (Steven Crist also went to Harvard), Beyer was more concerned with figuring out the daily double at Suffolk Downs than studying the English classics. (Despite his resistance to paying attention to class work, I rank Andy Beyer among the three best racing writers of the modern era, along with William Nack and the late Pete Axthelm.)

Andy's strength as a horseplayer is simple to spell out, but extremely difficult to master. He is a home-run hitter. He is a player willing to jump into a betting pool that offers a potentially large payoff while barely considering a saver wager, or a straight win bet on a 12–1 shot when a trifecta part-wheel might give him a shot at fifty grand.

Andy may not like me reminding people of this, but he also has poorly evaluated some of the great horses whose exploits appear in this book. Andy hated Seattle Slew; thought Secretariat was in decline before the 1973 Kentucky Derby; completely discounted the chances of Conquistador Cielo in the 1982 Belmont (which he won by 14 lengths) and has publicly picked a high percentage of losers in many high-profile races.

Andy Beyer also has suffered through his share of losing streaks; but he wins, and when he wins, he wins big. That is because Andy watches races like a hawk; takes copious trip notes; creatively uses various exotic-wagering pools; pays attention to trainer trends and biases throughout the country; and has a network of reliable sources that are as interested in talking to him as he is in getting their insights.

Andy is not without sound handicapping skills, either. He is particularly strong on his home tracks in Maryland and has made astute wagers in the Preakness and Belmont Stakes after having made his annual way-off-the-mark public Derby pick in *Daily Racing Form* and *The Washington Post.*

Andy certainly has hit a few well-stocked pick sixes, but the best play I ever saw him make was on the 1984 Belmont, when he virtually conceded the 1 1/2-mile race to Kentucky Derby winner Swale as the logical horse to control the pace (after Swale ran poorly while parked wide in the Preakness). Even more astutely, Andy saw that the stretch-running longshot Pine Circle was a most logical candidate to pick up the pieces after the higher-profile contenders were likely to tire from chasing Swale. Taking a stand against perfect inside trippers Gate Dancer and Play On, who rode the rail to a 1–2 finish in the Preakness, Andy boxed Swale, Pine Circle, and Morning Bob in exactas, keying Swale on top of both for big bucks, and scored a six-figure hit in "the biggest single-race score" of his life from a $125 payoff for every $2 he invested.

"It could have been bigger," Beyer points out. "My three horses ran 1-2-3 but there was no trifecta offered on the Belmont Stakes at that time."

A few years later he used virtually the same reasoning to catch a juicy exacta in the Preakness when Winning Colors was caught up in Forty Niner's multilevel attack that led to the D. Wayne Lukas-Woody Stephens rivalry cited in an earlier chapter. Andy saw the race dynamics perfectly and tipped it to his readers, who despite his poor Derby picks, knew that Beyer was a master handicapper of the Preakness. Andy boxed the three logical stretch-runners in the race and further accented Risen Star as the key to the big hit.

Andy and I have been great friends for more than 35 years. He calls me his mentor, which is very flattering. But it is equally true that I learned a lot from the way Andy Beyer is honest with himself about every aspect of his game and I have adopted some of his approach to crushing races when the situation commands a strong play for a strong opinion. There are not too many better horseplayers in America. Andy Beyer, in fact, is the best I have known.

BEST RACE CALLERS OF THE MODERN ERA

The first race caller of my trackside experience was Fred Capossela, whose simple singsong enunciations of "EET is now POST time" and "THER OFF" were followed by straightforward descriptions with minimal flair or dramatic accent. "Cappy" was the standard in his era on the East Coast, just as Joe Hernandez and Harry Henson and their gruffly deep-toned voices were most preferred in the West. While these three were the best track announcers of the 1950s, 60s, and early 1970s, the art of calling races improved considerably during the mid-1970s and 1980s with the arrival of new voices, new information, and bright, insightful calls that added a positive dimension to the race-track experience.

The first time I really appreciated Trevor Denman's race-calling was when I was stuck in a lavatory at Santa Anita in 1985 and had a $400 bet riding on a 6–1 shot in the fifth race. His race call was an absolute revelation. Not only did I hear where every horse was in the field at every reasonable point of call, but when I came out to watch the replay, I watched in amazement, as if I were now seeing the race *for the second time*. After I cursed to myself a few times while ripping up a handful of parimutuel tickets, I went down to the TV room to see the race and hear the call again. Denman's precise rendering was mesmerizing.

No one I have ever heard drew such an accurate word picture of a complicated, fast-moving horse race that had its share of traffic problems, inside and outside moves on the turn, and a tight stretch battle that was trumped by a last-to-first burst of winning speed. Denman was the only race caller I had ever heard who seemed to appreciate the way some horses were revving up for their run while others were giving hints that they were approaching the bottom of their energy reserves. No one else makes it so easy to see a race so well—even with your eyes closed, or when you step away from the track or television monitor.

Trevor Denman has a few pet phrases ("And away they go" . . ."She's moving like a winner" . . ."They'll have to sprout wings to catch him") just as other announcers have developed their own, and some of the announcers on this list have made consistently great race calls. But Denman is the only race caller who sees horses making their initial moves from fifth or sixth place and alerts the fans in the grandstand that the complexion of the race they are trying to watch is changing.

Trevor Denman calls a horse race in the same manner that Vin Scully calls a ball hit off the right-field wall at Dodger Stadium and instantly informs his radio listeners about the accuracy of the throw while simultaneously describing both the batter's progress toward second base and the potential run streaking toward the plate. This is not to say that Trevor Denman is perfect. In recent years, I have seen and heard some race calls that have lacked his amazing insight. But overall, I rate him the very best I have ever heard and probably the best American-based track announcer who ever lived.

Tom Durkin, however, ranks a very close second and is preferred by many, especially Eastern racegoers. He has been the full-time race caller for the New York Racing Association since 1990 and called every Breeders' Cup race from the inaugural Cup in 1984 until Trevor Denman got the assignment for 2006 when ESPN took over the broadcast rights. Under contract to NBC, Durkin remains the modern-day race caller for Triple Crown races and did not deserve the loss of the Breeders' Cup gig, even though his replacement is so good.

In recent years, in fact, Durkin has sometimes outperformed Denman with journalistically precise race calls that should qualify him for an Eclipse Award for reportage. Indeed, that is Durkin's forte. He is exceedingly accurate, is dramatic when he should be, and has a knack for capsule finishing phrases such as "the unconquerable, the invincible Cigar" when something unusual or spectacular occurs. I love Durkin's work and believe the only advantage Denman has is his uncanny ability to pick up on the key contenders before most observers see them making their moves.

Southern California is lucky to have Trevor Denman; New York is lucky to have Tom Durkin; and we, the race-watching public, are lucky to have both in action at the same time.

Here are my rankings of the best and most famous track announcers I have heard in my travels to more than 60 Thoroughbred racetracks since 1960. Some toward the bottom of the list would have ranked much higher several years ago, but have not maintained the same standard of performance or else have fallen into repetitive patterns that do not do full justice to the races at hand.

1. *Trevor Denman*

The keen-eyed South African-born artist-horseman who draws fully developed pictures with a microphone.

2. *Tom Durkin*

The greatest reporter-announcer of them all. A very classy act.

3. *Chic Anderson*

Precise caller, who caught the drama of the moment without overpowering it. Anderson was the regular track announcer at Churchill Downs from 1960 through 1977, when he took over for Dave Johnson prior to the 1977 Belmont Stakes. In between he also was the regular CBS television voice of the Triple Crown races. Anderson died in 1979, but his quick and powerful vision of Secretariat's amazing victory in the 1973 Belmont probably will live forever. With permission from CBS television network, here is exactly how Anderson described it with less than a half-mile to go:

"They're on the turn, and Secretariat is blazing along! The first three-quarters of a mile in 1:09 and four-fifths. Secretariat is widening now! He is moving like a TREMENDOUS machine! Secretariat by twelve, Secretariat by fourteen lengths on the turn! Sham is dropping back. It looks like they'll catch him today, as My Gallant and Twice a Prince are both coming up to him now. But Secretariat is all alone! He's out there almost a sixteenth of a mile away from the rest of the horses! Secretariat is in a position that seems impossible to catch. He's into the stretch. Secretariat leads this field by eighteen lengths, and now Twice a Prince has taken second and My Gallant has moved back to third. They're in the stretch. Secretariat has opened a twenty-two length lead! He is going to be the Triple Crown winner! Here comes Secretariat to the wire. An unbelievable, an amazing performance! He hits the finish twenty-five lengths in front! It's going to be Twice a Prince second, My Gallant third, Private Smiles fourth, and Sham, who had it today, dropped back to fifth."

After reviewing the tape, Anderson did admit that he might have underestimated the winning margin. It officially took more than 20 minutes for the placing judges to figure that Secretariat had won this Belmont by 31 lengths while running more than five seconds faster than Twice a Prince.

Anderson also called the dramatic Affirmed-Alydar Belmont Stakes ("We'll test these two to the wire!") in 1978 and said it was "the most difficult and best race call" of his life.

4. *Fred Capossela*

The captain of the track announcer's Hall of Fame. Almost invariably kept his race calls to a bare minimum. "Cappy" told you where the horses were, what their margins were between each other, and which horse was on the rail or parked outside. In the style of the time, he never called the horses in their final strides, leaving the outcome to the placing judges. Hard to fault, Capossela also provided excellent prerace announcements and scratch information at the same exact time every day, and his clear, concise approach to his work made him a legend in his own time and forever.

5. *Joe Hernandez*

Beloved by Santa Anita racing fans of the 1960s and 70s, Hernandez's admirers still regard him as no worse than California's second-best race caller of all time (to Trevor Denman). Known for stretching the very restrictive limits of race-calling during an era when any excess was frowned upon by track owners and stewards, Hernandez provided more depth in his calls than any of his contemporaries. Moreover, his deep-toned, distinctive voice was even copied by other Western-based race callers as a tribute to his popularity.

6. *Harry Henson*

The regular race caller at Hollywood Park for 25 years during the Hernandez era at Santa Anita, Henson also had a huge following of devotees who believed he was at least as good as, if not better than, Hernandez. Of equal import, their respective calls sounded very much alike to Eastern visitors unfamiliar with their individual nuances. Both tended to provide dramatic overtones that were suitable to an audience in free-and-easy Southern California, the center of the movie-making universe. Henson was one of the first, if not *the* first, race callers to spike his calls with fractional splits.

7. *Morris Tobe*

The relatively unheralded track announcer at Garden State Park, Atlantic City, and Monmouth Park in the 1960s and early 70s, Tobe had a distinctive gravelly voice similar to television announcer Jack Drees. But where Drees was spare with his running commentary, Tobe was lucid and comprehensive in a manner that foreshadowed Trevor Denman. Tobe also sounded as if he had been born to be a track announcer and seldom made a mistake. As a footnote to his life and dedication to his craft, Tobe literally died at the microphone after calling a race as a guest announcer at Pimlico.

8. *Kurt Becker*

Auto-racing announcer calls horse races only six weeks a year—at Keeneland in the spring and fall. Extremely sharp race caller, with solid awareness of who is running where and how fast they are going. The first and only track announcer in Keeneland history following decades of silence during races in progress, Becker is too good to not have a full-time gig somewhere, but to this point he has preferred to stay with the race-car set most of the year.

9. *Michael Wrona*

Underrated Australian has worked relatively short stints at tracks in Northern California, Chicago, Texas, and other stops along the way. Is an acquired taste for some, but Wrona is sensationally accurate, has a penchant for new phrases to describe familiar situations, and blends in just enough personality with his finely tuned sense of drama to be among the best in the game.

10. *Jack Drees*

Somewhat forgotten if not overlooked race caller for CBS during the 1960s. Drees was best known for his work on the Wednesday Night Fights for two networks and other boxing broadcasts with Russ Hodges from various New York arenas in the 1950s. Still, Drees's race call of Chateaugay's upset victory over Candy Spots in the 1963 Kentucky Derby and some of his other Derby calls were among the most satisfying televised race calls until Tom Durkin came along.

11. *Bob Weems*

The heir to Morris Tobe at the New Jersey tracks, had a similar gravelly voice and was as precise as his predecessor in all but a few instances. Probably provided the best and most consistently discernible prerace announcements about scratches and other handicapping information I have ever heard. Frankly, some track announcers, including several of the greats on this list, might improve their approach to this important facet of their work.

12. *John Dooley*

Regular announcer at Arlington Park and the Fair Grounds in New Orleans has improved noticeably during recent years to become one of the better announcers in America, with more room to grow ahead. Has improved his cadence and accuracy and is moderately dramatic without going overboard. His strength is in capturing the final furlong as well as anyone on this list. His weakness is the occassional high pitch of his voice.

13. *Bobby Neuman*

Took over for retired Phil Saltzman in 2005 and after a shaky start, has established himself as a solid race caller, with improvements noted in 2006. Increasingly accurate calls, with more detail than many on this list, and tries to provide pace issues and positioning from a horseplayer's perspective. Any further improvement would put him in the Top 10.

14. *Dave Johnson*

Once the heir apparent to Capossela, Johnson called races at the NYRA tracks from 1972 through 1977, when he moved across the Hudson River to become the regular track announcer at the Meadowlands. Known for his oft-imitated, frequently entertaining, highly distinctive "And down the stretch they come," Johnson called Triple Crown races and other major stakes for the ABC television network during the late 1970s and 80s, when he was frequently excellent.

After lightening his schedule and becoming a popular voice for commercial enterprises in the early 1990s, Johnson continued to call some races for ESPN and various radio networks, but only occasionally performed up to his prior high standards.

15. *Phil Georgeff*

An acquired taste, who nevertheless was beloved by Chicago-area racing fans for his pet phrases "Here they come spinning out of the turn," and "He's moving like a shot!" Called thousands of races and claimed he never made a serious mistake. Not sure about that, but after spending a few weeks at Arlington Park, I began to appreciate his calls more every day. He retired after the 2002 Breeders' Cup at Arlington.

16. *Larry Collmus*

Suffolk Downs regular caller also is the prime track announcer during the summer at Monmouth Park. Very good, generally informative, middle-of-the-road announcer whose improving form may eventually lead him to New York after Durkin chooses to retire. Only noticeable flaw is his occasional drift into a higher pitch than needed.

17. *Luke Kruytbosch*

Regular track announcer at Churchill Downs during the spring and fall also is the regular race caller at Turf Paradise in Arizona during the winter and Ellis Park in Kentucky during the summer. A rapid-fire style, very accurate with minimum dramatic overtones. Overall, quite good, and some love his work above all but a few. But frankly, his whispy, raspy voice occasionally sounds hollow to many ears.

18. *Paul Allen*

Canterbury Park's regular track announcer in the 21st century also is the radio voice of the Minnesota Vikings and a talk-show host on one of the Twin Cities' major radio stations. Overall, Allen has considerable talent, and provides good race calls with a flair for the local angle and the dramatic. The question I have is whether he will improve sufficiently to become a national race caller, or will his other gigs mute his progress?

19. *David Rodman*

Generally good but overly dramatic race caller in Maryland probably owns one of the all-time greatest race calls—the 1997 Preakness, with Silver Charm edging out Free House and Captain Bodgit with an adventurous trip by fourth-place finisher Touch Gold. The race was as accurately described as if he had studied under the wing of Trevor Denman and Tom Durkin and is worth repetitious play by budding track announcers and fans of the race-calling art. Rodman may be forced to deal with many mundane races on the Maryland and Virginia circuits, but he calls every horse race with an eye for the pace and the positioning of well-bet horses as if he understands that he is providing race details for horseplayers. His chief flaws are the speed at which he provides these details and his tendency to go over the top.

20. *Dan Loiselle*

The longtime, steady track announcer for Woodbine racecourse, Loiselle has a distinctive, low-toned, appealing voice and is at his best calling races on Woodbine's turf course, over which many of the track's most important races are run. The Woodbine course is 1 ½ miles in circumference and features a stretch run of 1,440 feet, the longest of any track or racing surface in North America. Just as a jockey has to make timing adjustments on this course, so too does Loiselle have to deal with the unusually late developments in Woodbine turf races.

21. *Marshall Cassidy*

Former NYRA announcer from 1979 through 1990, was accurate, but dry to a fault, leaving some fans cold and others in vociferous support for his singular approach to his craft. Personally, I sided often with those who did not appreciate his rat-a-tat style, but I also recognized that he was dedicated to providing pristine race calls that kept the dramatics to a minimum.

22. *Vic Stauffer*

Regular race caller at Hollywood Park and Gulfstream Park has a good, resonant voice, understands the dynamics of racing from a horseplayer's standpoint, and tries to model himself after Tom Durkin, which is not a bad thing. But Stauffer also can be overly dramatic and tends to insert a few too many catchphrases to put his personal stamp on the race. Always had promise, and there is room for improvement.

23. *Terry Wallace*

Oaklawn Park's long-term track announcer and publicity director has moments of greatness and can be among the most entertaining race callers in the booth when he picks up on a catchphrase, or exaggerates his emphasis on a syllable or portion of an unusually named horse. But Wallace also is prone to pauses and/or lost concentration during a race, a sign that he is unsure of which horse is making a move between horses or is partially screened from view.

24. *Tony Bentley*

Was the regular announcer for more than a decade at the Fair Grounds in New Orleans and at Canterbury Park. Bentley, an opera singer, expert chef, and tennis buff, was great on occasion, calling many races with pristine accuracy, plus perfect diction and cadence. But his calls also were marred by pauses and errors while he was seemingly distracted by his other pursuits. Had great potential and probably still is better than many in the game, but has only called the Breeders' Cup Steeplechase and other hurdle events in recent years.

25. *Mike Battaglia*

Started out his career with great promise as the regular track announcer for Churchill Downs and has been an institution in Kentucky through his prerace simulcast and in-house television shows as well as managing an extensive workload as analyst-handicapper on network telecasts of major races and doing his daily gigs on local and cable TV. Surprising to me, but Battaglia only occasionally gives flashes of his old brilliance, calling too many races with the identical pattern, as if the horses on the track are fulfilling a preplanned script. Battaglia is the regular race caller at Turfway Park, where he has been on the mike for more than a quarter century.

10 IDEAS AND ISSUES

THE BEST DEVELOPMENTS AND INNOVATIONS IN RACING HISTORY

There is no need to restrict the items listed here by their occurrence since the early 1950s. Nor is it reasonable to rank them in a pseudo order of importance. All instantly changed and simultaneously improved the game's appeal. Some, however, have also been accompanied by lingering negative issues.

The Invention of the Starting Gate

Since the beginning of horse racing in ancient Greece through the formal organization of the sport in England during the Middle Ages and on to much of the 1930s, horse races usually were run from a standing start, or from behind a tape. The invention of the enclosed, electric starting gate by Clay Puett in 1939 changed everything.

The typical starting gate weighs a few dozen tons, and contains metal stalls just wide enough for a Thoroughbred to walk through when opened on both ends. To begin the loading process, the front gates are closed manually by the assistant starters. The gates are kept closed via an electromagnetic circuit that can only be disengaged by the official starter when he is satisfied that all the horses are in their proper starting stalls, facing forward.

Once the rear doors are closed and the horses seem ready for the break, the starter presses the remote-control button to break the electromagnetic circuit, sending the horses on their way. Of course, things do not always go that smoothly. When a horse gets extremely nervous and overanticipates the start, he may nudge on the front doors to no effect, or generate the needed 300 pounds of thrust from his rear legs to his forehead to break the circuit, as Barbaro did in the 2006 Preakness.

On the negative side, the dangers of being in such a cramped space waiting for a start, especially one that is being delayed by nervous horses in adjacent stalls, has contributed to serious injuries, even death. Jockeys, trainers, and racing officials will tell you that the starting-gate routine requires extremely well-coordinated handling to minimize the potential dangers.

In recent years, however, serious incidents at the gate have become a rarity due to improved training of starting-gate crews, more familiarity with the idiosyncrasies of horses on the grounds, more swapping of information between starting-gate crews at different tracks, better padding in the stalls, and more clearance to the beam on the top of the gate. All things considered, there remain some risks, but the starting gate has helped facilitate millions of fairly run races through the years.

Parimutuel Betting

Some might argue that the old method of playing horses with a bookmaker on the track apron was much better for top-notch players who could shop around for the best price offered by competing bookmakers. Often, an informed player would spot weaknesses in the odds line before the bookmakers could adjust. I certainly would have loved to have had a chance to play the game that way. But, the bookmaker system of horserace wagering—which still can be found at many European tracks—lent itself to betting coups and unethical money moves, to the detriment of casual players and legal bookmakers. An example: The legendary

Pittsburgh Phil, one of the great horseplayers of the late 19th century, was so respected that bookmakers regularly lowered their odds on any horse he bet. To take advantage, Phil sometimes bet a few hundred on a horse he didn't like, while waiting until it was nearly post time before dispatching a handful of associates to bet a few thousand on his preferred selection at inflated odds.

All this changed when Pierre Oller, a Parisian perfume shopkeeper, came up with the idea in 1885 to pool all wagers made before the race and to pay out winnings based on the total in the pool, less a 5 percent commission. *Voila*—Oller had just invented *parimutuel wagering*, or "betting among ourselves," a wagering system that became the legalized form of betting in France by 1887 and was imported to America a few years into the 20th century. It eventually became the dominant form of legalized wagering in every racing country in the world.

Actually, there was one more inventive step that made this form of betting truly functional: the use of electronic devices which accurately calculated odds in split seconds. These devices replaced error-prone hand-operated parimutuel machines that the legal bookmakers of the day could not trust. The improvement was made in America by Henry Strauss, a college-trained engineer and Maryland horse bettor who felt cheated when a horse was listed at 12–1 moments before the race and yet paid only 4–1.

With a little investigation, Strauss realized that the public was being ripped off frequently by corrupt mutuel managers at racetracks throughout the country, so he joined with fellow engineers to invent an electric calculating machine that accurately computed the odds to ensure honest payouts. That led to the formation of the American Totalisator Company and the creation of the electronic odds board, which was installed for the first time at Pimlico Racecourse in 1930.

Today, all racetracks in America, and most throughout the world, have computer-driven, fiber-optic linked wagering systems that can bring in bets from hundreds of locations to a host track and compute dozens of minute changes in all wagering pools. It is nevertheless ironic that the reason for this system was to prevent tampering, or disparate payoffs compared to the odds listed on the board before the race. Yet, the biggest complaint made by modern bettors is the plunge in odds that occurs too often to their taste while a race is in progress. This, we are told, is the function of the 30- to 90-second delay needed to electronically process large volumes of wagers from distant locations to the host track.

While Totalisator companies have acknowledged this problem and have promised improvements, perhaps the industry needs another Pierre Oller or Henry Strauss to apply his genius to the task. Moreover, it is not lost on the public that the biggest wagering scandal in racing history was committed, as recounted earlier (see Chapter 1, "Stunners"), by a savvy computer geek who worked on the inside of Autotote, the totalisator company that handled Breeders' Cup bets in 2002. The ability to slip inside the computer system shook fans' confidence in the game and almost led to a multimillion-dollar fleecing of the betting public.

Daily Racing Form *Past Performances*

Daily Racing Form first was published in Chicago in 1894 as a four-page horse-racing newspaper by Frank Brunell. Although Brunell's initial past performances, first published in 1905, were rudimentary by today's standards, they revolutionized playing the horses in America. For the first time anywhere, bettors could compare the records of horses entered against one another with some degree of accuracy.

Daily Racing Form would go through several changes of ownership and many improvements to its past performances through the years to reach levels of sophistication unmatched by any other publication devoted to the coverage of any single sport. The biggest changes occurred in response to the innovations that appeared in the short-lived upstart *The Racing Times* in 1991 and '92, many of which then became regular features in the *Form*.

From its inception, the *Daily Racing Form* was properly labeled America's Turf Authority, and as it grew and became an indispensable source of handicapping information, it has been known informally as the Horseplayer's Bible.

Electrically Timed Racing and Photo-Finish Cameras

For much of the 20th century, races were timed by stopwatch, which led to assorted controversies over race times and fractional splits at every track in the country. The same was true for close finishes, which were decided by track officials who acted as if they were umpires judging safe or out calls at first base.

In 1938, the American Teletimer Company developed and installed the first electronic teletimer for racing purposes at Pimlico in Maryland. This was less than a year after the "circular-flow camera" was installed to provide photographic evidence of close finishes at Del Mar for its inaugural 1937 race meet.

Invented by Lorenzo del Riccio, an engineer who headed Paramount Pictures' technical laboratories during the 1930s, the circular-flow camera had no shutter. It functioned by moving a strip of film horizontally across a vertical slit to record the horses as they passed the finish line. As soon as the first horse started to pass through the line, the camera recorded the horse from its nose back along the length of its body on the rotating film strip. This produced a "strip photograph" of all the horses as they respectively passed the finish line.

While every track in America still uses similar but more sophisticated photographic methods, some small tracks do not utilize electronic timing gear. More absurd is the fact that some larger tracks have not yet installed electronic devices to record accurate fractional splits on their turf courses.

The technology is far ahead of the game's willingness to fully embrace accurate fractional splits at every pole, electronically timed morning workouts, and the precise margins between horses at every point of call.

As far back as 1978, in fact, I personally was invited by an aerospace company in Saratoga to provide an evaluation of a timing system that utilized miniature identification patches (similar to supermarket pricing strips) that could be sewn into saddle cloths. These patches were designed to register their exact location on sensitive computers linked to every furlong and sixteenth pole on the track. Needless to say, I thought the invention would become standard equipment at every track in America. But, when this company made presentations to various racetracks, they were repeatedly told that the technology "wasn't really necessary," or it would "cost too much to implement."

Despite these negative reactions, it was no surprise to learn some years later that a similar technology had been installed at tracks in Hong Kong and Japan to ensure accurate information at their modern racecourses. The only American track in the early 21st century using a photoelectric-based technology for precise margins at every point of call is the Meadowlands—for harness racing—although in 2006 Keeneland adopted the new Trakus video race technology, which tracks horses digitally via sensor chips in the saddlecloths.

Introduction of Turf Racing in America

American racing woke up to the benefits of racing on grass in the 1950s. Grass racing provided a large population of horses with opportunities to thrive, and it fostered competition with European-based runners who race almost exclusively on grass. Moreover, its popularity with horsemen and fans led to larger fields and exciting races to bet. All these things continue into the 21st century, with more turf courses being built, more international competition, and more to come. Indeed, the mere popularity of turf racing has become its biggest problem.

Courses that see heavy use in warm, dry weather tend to wear out in a month of constant pounding, while in multi-weather climes, a series of heavy rain storms can force an inordinate number of scratches (and very small fields) when turf races are switched necessarily to the main track.

Exotic Wagering

Win, place, show, and the daily double might have been enough to excite horseplayers through the 1950s, but the game changed radically in the early 1960s with the introduction of the quinella and perfecta. Both of these "exotic" bets were borrowed from the Basque game of jai alai, a parimutuel form of racquet-handball.

The object of the quinella was to select the first two official finishers in any order; the object of the perfecta—also known as the exacta—was, of course, to pick the first two in *exact* order. Fans responded enthusiastically to these bets because they paid much more than straight win, place, and show wagers, so it was natural to see a wave of multihorse and multirace exotic bets added to the betting menus of adventurous tracks. Among them were the twin double, trifecta, superfecta, pick three, pick four, and pick six, all of which were introduced at different times of inspiration during the 1960s and 70s. Each spiced up the game with opportunities to catch big payoffs—sometimes life-changing payoffs—and they appealed equally to high rollers and small bettors.

Without these exotic bets, the game would have died a fast death against the emerging competition from heavily advertised state and regional lotteries as well as the expansion of gambling casinos in Nevada, New Jersey, and on Native American reservations in more than three dozen states. With the prospect of higher payoffs, skilled horseplayers knew they had a fighting chance to apply their expertise toward a meaningful score.

Yet, experienced players have been disappointed to see the industry fail to spend advertising dollars pointing out the benefits of the skill-based racing game versus the luck-based lottery and casino games. The lack of promotional effort geared to show that horse playing skill can lead to success at the track is beyond rational explanation. So is the avoidance of television to deal with the nuances of the handicapping-betting side of the major races it covers.

Ironically, the industry with the Kentucky Derby, the Triple Crown, and the Breeders' Cup, the game with huge payoffs in the pick six, pick four, and superfecta, now is embracing the need for slot machines to improve the sport's financial picture. While this already has occurred at some tracks, with some benefit to purses and the bottom line, it is my personal view that slots will only help racing in the long run if track officials use the added revenue to reduce the takeout for horse wagers, while gaining new players from the armies of slot players coming out to the track.

Multidenominational, Multifunctional Betting Windows

While the old parimutuel tickets used to be colorful, sturdy, and useful keepsakes for special occasions, the modern parimutuel ticket is just an antiseptic $2 \frac{1}{2}$-inch square of white computer paper with the crucial numbers printed on it. It's nothing glamorous, nothing worth preserving except for the rarest of victories or defeats.

But with the end of the old parimutuel ticket also came the end of a very annoying parimutuel practice—the $2 win window, as distinguished from the $2 cashier's window, and the $2 place window, and the window to bet $2 to show, $5 to win, $5 to place, etc., etc.—a parimutuel window for every purpose. What a nightmare of logistical planning and design, so typical of racetrack management in the 1950s and 60s, when racing was the only game in town and crowds flocked to their gates.

Can you imagine the waste of time standing behind 40 people waiting to bet $15 to place after you had already put a $10 win bet down? While today's lines on busy days can be equally frustrating, can you imagine what it was like to bet different denominations for you and your friends?

The new computerized parimutuel systems introduced in the early 1980s consolidated all those functions and made tellers learn how to take and cash any bet in one continuous transaction. During that decade, self-automated machines, or SAMs, also were introduced, which permitted you to make your own bets using cash vouchers purchased at teller windows and/or directly at the SAM.

Recent advances, including smaller versions of the SAMs placed at dining tables and well-positioned kiosks where you can spread out your *Racing Form* and play the game at your seat, provide even more convenience. Convenience is the operating concept and there is nothing negative about that.

Off-Track Betting, Simulcasting, Phone Betting, the Internet

In the 1950s and 60s horseplayers could only wager at the track, or via an illegal bookmaker. While it was always good to see 40,000 fans at Aqueduct on most Saturday afternoons, it often was difficult to postpone real life to get there. In the 1970s, Off Track Betting parlors were introduced in New York, followed by a handful of adventurous tracks that entered into simulcast agreements to permit wagering on each other's races.

Soon, a few other OTB networks came into existence, followed by phone-betting accounts in Pennsylvania that were emulated in several other states, despite resistance from state legislatures that continue well into the 21st century.

In the modern world, we have numerous connection devices and computer-linked web sites that provide amazing access to information never before available. Just as important, the world is coming closer together for more wagering networks through the Internet, more international races attracting worldwide play, and much more of that to come.

The globalization of the racing game and its convenience to players in America and around the world is one of the most positive developments in decades.

For people who think racing is dying, here are just a few amazing facts that speak volumes to the contrary. In Hong Kong, more than $100 million is wagered on several different Saturday racing cards each year, with an average daily handle in excess of $70 million—on just one racetrack! Virtually the same passion for parimutuel play is exhibited in Japan, a nation that boosted the quality of its racing dramatically after importing Americas 1989 Horse of the Year, Sunday Silence, to become a foundation stallion for its burgeoning horse industry.

While attendance at American tracks may be down (except for Saratoga and a few premium race meets), more information is available, more races are seen on television, and more people are betting more money on high-quality races here and abroad than ever before. The modern technological advances that permit this are a big plus, but it could become a major minus if American racetrack executives remain reticent to deal with over-saturated racing schedules in neighboring markets, conflicting dates for major races, and the untapped potential of worldwide markets.

The Kentucky Derby and the Triple Crown

The memory, the emotions, the smells and the visual cues of my first Kentucky Derby still remain locked in my brain for instant recall whenever something from out of the blue triggers the memory. Secretariat's Derby was the finest of all time; I was lucky enough to be there. It is that feeling—being witness to something important, something rare—that invites so many people to the Kentucky Derby every year; but it did not happen overnight.

There were all the other great horses and memorable confrontations on and off the track that helped feed the popularity of this American classic. And before any of us was born, there was Matt Winn. Two decades after Colonel Matt Winn took over Churchill Downs in 1902, he commemorated the 50th Kentucky Derby in 1924 with a trophy that has been given to every winner since. Winn, a man of imagination with a touch of P. T. Barnum, realized the Derby was a special race that would make a success of his track and the breeding industry in his state.

He came up with the blanket of roses for the winner's-circle ceremony, arranged for the first radio broadcast of the Derby in 1925, and raised the purse steadily from a flat $6,000 when he took over to $10,000-added in 1914, with the added money coming from nominating fees paid by owners of Derby horses. In 1917, Winn raised the purse to $15,000-added ($20,375, gross total). During the First World War years he raised it again to $20,000, then $50,000, just as he would raise it to $75,000-added in 1940 through the World War II years. Except for the brand-new Santa Anita Handicap for older horses on the distant West Coast—a region ignored by most Eastern track owners—Winn insisted that the Derby should be the richest race in the country.

In 1945, even though the federal government had banned horse racing in January, Winn made sure the Derby was run—on June 9—a month and a day after the ban was lifted when victory in Europe was declared. The purse was $75,000-added, the last year the Derby purse would not be at least $100,000, and Winn also made sure that the attendance figures would be listed as 100,000 or more, no matter how many people actually were on hand. (By comparison, the Preakness and Belmont Stakes were $40,000 to $60,000 races during the corresponding period, and the Travers was worth $20,000 to $25,000.)

Matt Winn passed away at the age of 88 in 1949, but did see his 75th consecutive Derby, having witnessed Aristides's inaugural victory in 1875, when he was 13 years old. In his final major policy decision as president of Churchill Downs, Winn authorized the first television broadcast of the Derby by local Louisville TV and looked to the future when the race would be seen by millions throughout the country.

In the later half of the 20th century and in the early years of the 21st, the Kentucky Derby grew steadily in popularity, stature, and importance from a racing and financial standpoint. Among other indications, more than 100,000 people really did begin attending the event in the late 1960s. Also, breeders began to fall all over themselves trying to lock up the Derby winner with multimillion-dollar syndication offers. The purse itself went up, from $100,000, to $125,000, to $150, 000, but it took a long time to reach $1 million in 1996 and $2 million in 2005.

If Matt Winn were still alive, many observers believe the Derby purse would be $5 million or $6 million, given the enormous profit the race generates via the on-site attendance, reserved seats at high-end prices, the growth of the Kentucky Oaks, which also plays to crowds of 100,000 or more the day before the Derby, plus the multimillion-dollar fees paid by national television networks to broadcast the race. Moreover, through simulcasting, the Derby Day handle has exceeded $125 million and sets records every year.

The run for Matt Winn's blanket of roses has enormous appeal as a stand-alone event. It captures the public imagination more than any other race in America. It is the race that every semi-serious horseplayer tries to win just as much as every breeder, owner, trainer, or jockey. Beyond its singular importance, the Derby also has benefited enormously from a phrase written by a *Daily Racing Form* racing writer after Gallant Fox won the 1930 Belmont Stakes to complete what Charles Hatton labeled a sweep of the "Triple Crown."

The Triple Crown had a ring to it and was not easy to win. Sir Barton in 1919 was the first horse to win all three races, but it is not widely known that he won the Preakness in Baltimore *only four days after he took the Derby* in Louisville. Sir Barton also won the Withers in New York, 10 days after the Preakness, and the Belmont at $1\frac{3}{8}$ miles, not $1\frac{1}{2}$ miles, 17 days after the Withers. In essence, Sir Barton completed a four-race sweep of important stakes for 3-year-old horses in a month, at a time when there were no cargo airplane carriers to make transportation a piece of cake.

When Gallant Fox won the second Triple Crown, the one that moved Charles Hatton to immortal hyperbole, the Preakness was the first of the three races, the Derby was eight days later, and the Belmont three weeks after that. This flies in the face of the misconception that the Kentucky Derby always was run on the first Saturday in May and that the Triple Crown has not undergone major changes in its scheduling.

Not until 1932 did the Kentucky Derby become permanently established as the first race in the series, one year after the Belmont settled on the $1\frac{1}{2}$-mile distance. In the 1930s there were two more Triple Crown winners, Omaha in 1935 and War Admiral in '37. In the 40s, there were four: Whirlaway (1941), Count Fleet (1943), Assault (1946), and Citation (1948). Then followed the 25-year drought that Secretariat quenched in 1973. Seattle Slew followed suit in '77 and Affirmed did the same in '78.

The quarter-century gap between Citation and Secretariat only fueled the appetite for another Triple Crown winner, and that anticipation has been intensified logarithmically by the absence of one since 1978.

In the modern era, the clamor for a Triple Crown winner occurs every year and the hype begins immediately after the Derby winner crosses the finish line. Thus, in most years, the Preakness has one very important thing that the Derby does not: the Derby winner. Likewise, when a single horse wins both the Derby and Preakness, the Belmont gets the big bonanza: another chance to see a horse attempt to add his name to the elite list of 11 others who accomplished the sweep in the 20th century.

In the 21st century, casual fans and horse lovers tune in to see the Derby and tune back to see a possible Triple Crown sweep. Serious fans get to see dozens of Derby prep races on the ESPN, NBC, and ABC television networks, as well as dozens more on TVG and HRTV, the two satellite/cable networks exclusively dedicated to racing. Newspaper stories about potential Triple Crown prospects begin appearing the day after the Breeders' Cup Juvenile for 2-year-olds is run each fall. *Daily Racing Form* dedicates hundreds of pages each year to Triple Crown coverage and there are countless web sites providing opinion forums and relevant statistics for any related purpose.

The Kentucky Derby is a very big deal, certainly the game's biggest single race; but the Triple Crown is even bigger than the sum of its individual parts. Horseplayers and casual racing fans tell time by it, and the game is better for its existence as a complete entity, as compared to having three high-class races in the spring for 3-year-olds, or only one.

Should the Triple Crown be redesigned to reflect the tendency of shorter racing careers and longer breaks between starts? Some argue for a three-week gap between the Derby and Preakness, to match the three-week break between the Preakness and Belmont. While that would not completely ruin the integrity of the three-race series, it certainly would tamper with the degree of difficulty to complete a historic sweep. My personal vote is to leave it intact, the toughest three-race series in the world and one of the most satisfying accomplishments horse and man can aspire to achieve.

Handicapping Contests

The first handicapping contest I ever played in, the Penn National World Series of Handicapping, was the most prestigious, the richest, and the best-run tournament in America for 25 years.

In the 1970s, 80s, and 90s, there were very few handicapping tournaments worth taking seriously. After much promotion, some had to be canceled due to lack of entries; some were manipulated unfairly to permit sharpies to control the outcome; and some had poorly conceived rules. Yet, the Penn National World Series of Handicapping survived, prospered, and helped bring into play several other contests, only to be knocked out of business by the emergence of richer, more accessible competitions that have cornered the marketplace.

In the 21st century, there are hundreds of handicapping tournaments at racetracks, on the Internet, in Nevada race books, and at simulcast sites and OTB parlors. Cumulative prize money has climbed into the multimillions, and more contests are added to the schedule every year, giving good handicappers the opportunity to construct their own handicapping-contest circuit, one that informally resembles the pro bowling or golf tours.

This is a tremendous development in the history of horse racing, as more fans, more players are being drawn into the game through these competitions. Meanwhile, experienced players can pursue big payoffs for a modest investment, or no cost at all.

Winners can earn as much as $250,000 in these tournaments and there are trips to the Kentucky Derby, the Breeders' Cup, and other lucrative prizes up for grabs, including tickets to the most prestigious handicapping tournaments in Las Vegas. In the early 21st century, the two richest are the Horseplayer's World Series at the Orleans Hotel and the Daily Racing Form/National Thoroughbred Racing Association's annual National Handicapping Championship.

Seats at the HWS at the Orleans can be purchased outright, or won in a satellite; but the only way to get to the prestigious DRF/NTRA contest is to win a seat in one of the many qualifying tournaments at tracks and other outlets throughout the year. The winner of the seventh DRF/NTRA tournament in 2005 earned $200,000, plus a spot on the Eclipse Award stage to receive acknowledgment as Handicapper of the Year—no small honor. The total prize money for the 2006 final, to be held in January 2007, is projected at $550,000 and rising.

The Breeders' Cup

When Kentucky breeder John Gaines gave a speech during Derby Week in 1982, most of the people who heard him talk of a single racing card of championship races with $10 million to $15 million in total purses snickered under their collective breath. Who could believe such a thing would actually happen? Who could take seriously the idea that a breeder, or any group of breeders, could convince farm owners throughout North America to contribute many thousands of dollars to this new concept?

Surprise, surprise; with unprecedented cooperation from various segments of the racing industry, with plenty of inside steering by John Nerud, the retired Hall of Fame trainer who was managing Tartan Farms, and with the executive genius of D. G. Van Clief and help from many others, the Breeders' Cup was funded. The first Breeders' Cup racing card was set for Hollywood Park in 1984 with seven Cup races worth $1 million to $3 million.

The day went too fast for anyone to really stop long enough to appreciate its finer details, but it felt as if we were watching and handicapping and writing and thinking about seven Kentucky Derbies on the same day, each a half hour apart.

There was the disqualification that took place in the Juvenile Fillies; the dramatic and roughly run $3 million Breeders' Cup Classic and a DQ that that cost Gate Dancer's connections the difference between $675,000 for second and $324,000 for third. That disqualification also provided some of the best racing coverage of the modern era, with the cameras right inside the stewards' room as they reviewed the infraction from several different angles. A new era had been born. The game was changed forever. Suddenly we had an Olympics of Thoroughbred racing that would attract our best horses, jockeys, and trainers along with many of the best from abroad.

The payoffs were good too. The large fields of high-class contenders invariably created satisfying mutuel returns for any well-placed wager. The Breeders' Cup was an enormous success.

More than two decades later, the Breeders' Cup has been hosted by 10 different tracks, counting Monmouth Park, where it is scheduled for 2007. It is indisputably the best day of racing anywhere in the world; an amazing program of eight championship-style races worth $2 million to $5 million apiece, plus a Breeders' Cup steeplechase event held separately at various locations. In 2006, purses for the eight Cup races were set at $20 million, amid hints of more BC races in the future.

Just as important, the Breeders' Cup has become a perfect annual complement to the spring classics—a date all horseplayers, owners, breeders, trainers, and jockeys circle on their calendar just as they do for the Kentucky Derby, Preakness, and Belmont Stakes. Six months after the Triple Crown, we can see the best horses in every division, including those who survived, or were the stars of, that series of classics.

There were and are flaws in the program, including the extremely high late-nominating fees that made it nearly impossible for several great horses to participate. But in 2006, many of the weaknesses in the nominating structure finally were rectified. Fewer horses that were not nominated by their breeders at birth will have to miss future Breeders' Cup Days, because the rules finally were amended to permit lower fees to be paid during the racing season.

John Gaines's brainstorm has had a spectacular run, and the future looks exceedingly bright.

Multi-Stakes Racing Cards

As a direct offshoot of the Breeders' Cup program, which demonstrated to racetrack officials that there was value in carding more than one high-profile stakes on a single card, multi-stakes racing programs were put into play at several tracks, several times a year.

There are Breeders' Cup-style days for New York-breds, for Maryland-breds, and for Illinois-, Louisiana-, and California-breds, among others. There are multi-stakes racing cards in the late summer and early fall that prepare horses for various Breeders' Cup races. There are red-letter days, such as the Travers at Saratoga and the Santa Anita Handicap and the Arlington Million, that are supported by two, three, or more rich stakes of high quality. All of these multi-stakes racing cards provide the betting fan with the best-quality sport their home track can offer. In most, but not all, instances, this means more interesting races to handicap, more television exposure on the networks, more newspaper stories about racing, and more opportunities to gain new fans.

The only negative residue of this trend is the increased competition for high-profile horses that sometimes occurs. In their attempts to secure "name" horses, some tracks have positioned comparable stakes races on the same day as, or within a week of, another track's rich stakes.

Too often this produces two five-horse fields with 3–5 betting favorites in each race, instead of one field of nine or 10, with the two top horses in the same race. In most other countries, where there is national supervision of racing dates, this could not happen. In America, where every individual racing state and some tracks within the same state decide what they want to do on their own terms, there will never be a solution without an industry-wide effort to create a national scheduling board. We can only hope.

Saratoga and Del Mar

When Saratoga was built near the end of the Civil War in a rural town 30 miles north of Albany, 30 miles south of Lake George, no one could have imagined that much of the wood used in that original grandstand still would be a functional part of America's oldest racetrack.

Saratoga has been reinforced with more wood and plenty of concrete and steel. The old grandstand has been expanded to stretch from the sixteenth pole all the way to the top of the stretch and around the bend past the quarter pole. An open area behind the grandstand still uses aging trees to mark the place for each horse to be saddled for the next race.

It is hard not to be enchanted by Saratoga, a track that probably has made more fans of the sport upon first visit than any other in America. Not only is the racing the best daily fare every year during its six-week summer session, but the natural-wood ambiance provides priceless inspiration to city dwellers who discover it, or tell time by their annual visits.

Grass is the preferred surface for the parking lot. Home-cooked chicken, barbecued ribs, and carved sandwiches coexist alongside the usual concession fare. Several interconnected picnic areas with hundreds of tables are scattered all around the place, first-come first-possessed. A shoeshine stand is well-placed opposite the entrance to the jockeys' room, and the jockeys pass through the crowd on their way to and from the track for each race.

If you get up early in the morning and watch horses train, you can have a great trackside breakfast and you just might feel the presence of Man o' War, Secretariat, and other great ghosts of racing's past thundering down the stretch. History was made here many times over. Should you wish to learn more about that, just walk across the street to the National Museum of Racing and Hall of Fame. Give yourself a few hours.

Say hello to your neighbor playing the game in the next seat or sitting on a bench near the spring-water fountain. That's exactly how I met Andy Beyer and several other lifelong friends. Feel free to say hello to me; share a handicapping idea or opinion; Saratoga makes horseplayers realize that we are all in this incredible game together.

Del Mar is not the West Coast version of Saratoga. Del Mar is unique unto itself, a racetrack along the Pacific Ocean that is the most pleasant place to play the game in America. Located 20 miles north of San Diego, the weather is spectacular—something that cannot always be said for Saratoga, which suffers through several rainstorms a season. The restaurants and night life in Del Mar and nearby La Jolla and along the Southern California coastline are superb. The beaches are free and accessible, complete with all the beautiful bodies—male and female— anyone would hope to see, or need to invoke a creative idea while handicapping the usually lucrative pick six.

The quality of racing may be excellent several days a season, especially most weekends, but California's problem in attracting large fields and new stables to ship out west does not end when the racing shifts from Hollywood Park to Del Mar in late July.

Some days are very disappointing for such a wonderful track. Some days the racing office struggles to attract fields of six or more horses and some days the Del Mar program may have two good races, while the rest of the card resembles a level of quality just a cut above the county-fair tracks in Northern California. Yet, despite that serious demerit, I love Del Mar, almost as much as Saratoga, and I try to split my August by spending half the month in Saratoga, half at Del Mar, or some variation of that.

Just as Saratoga is a mecca for 2-year-old racing, plenty of good 2-year-olds make their debuts at Del Mar. Seeing these youngsters firsthand provides an early line on horses that may develop into next year's Derby prospects.

Built by Bing Crosby and other Hollywood pals in 1936, Del Mar was beautifully refurbished and expanded in the 1990s, which has helped it maintain its appeal to friendly crowds of experienced players as well as newcomers who are more likely to return after watching fast horses in such a colorful, pleasant environment.

Despite the erratic quality of the racing, there are good wagering opportunities at Del Mar, especially in the pick-six pools that tend to produce $125,000 or higher carryovers in a single day.

If you are a West Coast-based racing fan who has experienced Del Mar, I strongly urge a cross-country visit to Saratoga. If you are an East Coast fan who knows all about Saratoga, I strongly urge a cross-country visit to Del Mar. They are both compelling, and the game is much better with both in operation, even though they occupy virtually the same racing schedule each summer. Of course, through the benefits of simulcasting and telephone-betting accounts, modern players can play both tracks. What a country! What a game!

THE BEST HANDICAPPING CONTRIBUTIONS AND/OR WINNING ANGLES

10. *Consistent Horses Usually Beat Inconsistent Ones*

Robert Sanders Dowst, a handicapper in the 1940s and 50s, wrote many articles on this subject for *Turf and Sport Digest* magazine during its heyday. Most of the principles Dowst explained still apply, but the consistent horse tends to attract much more play at the windows than in his era. Moreover, the modern era accents fewer starts per horse per season, so there is less chance to take advantage of this straightforward handicapping principle.

9. *The Drop-Down from Maiden Special Weight to Maiden Claiming*

There is no more potent handicapping angle in the game than to prefer horses that have run against nonclaiming maidens in races where all the horses are entered for a selling price. This angle alone has dominated maiden-claiming races from coast to coast for several decades and surprisingly, it still can produce its share of overlooked longshot winners.

8. *The Turn-Back Angle*

Speed at one mile or 1 $\frac{1}{16}$ miles turning back to 6 $\frac{1}{2}$ or seven furlongs . . . this "turn-back" angle accents the powerful combination of inherent speed matched with the added stamina gained from the longer race. In the shorter sprint, this type of horse usually rallies from a midpack or stalking position, or perhaps even from back in the pack.

7. *Pace Makes the Race*

In some quarters this means pace numbers. In the best handicapping approaches, however, it simply refers to the need to determine which horse or horses will be involved in an uncontested or hotly contested pace and which ones will therefore benefit from the pace configuration. Obviously, a hotly contested pace usually will favor horses who make their best bid after the pacesetters are tired from their efforts. Conversely, an uncontested, relatively modest pace tends to favor horses on or near the lead who reach the final furlongs with energy in reserve.

6. *Track Bias*

The term refers to the way a racetrack may be naturally bent or manicured to favor front-runners, or closers, or horses breaking from favorable or unfavorable post positions.

When such a "bias" exists, it is possible to upgrade or downgrade contenders based on their running styles, or post positions. Likewise, when a track bias has been detected, it is possible to appreciate or discount performances of horses according to whether they ran with or against such a bias.

Basically, track bias is a tool to identify horses that might benefit from the prevailing tendency of the racing surface to influence performance. I coined the term in the mid-1960s while learning the game at different tracks in the East, studying handicapping in between classes at Rutgers.

5. *Workout Interpretation*

Workout clockings that are recorded each day are useful to detect soundness and overall preparedness, but they are not nearly as useful as workouts that have been professionally observed and annotated for a wide variety of characteristics. These may include whether the work was in company with another horse—perhaps with an older horse or a recent winner—with or without serious urging, or from the starting gate.

Also, raw workout clockings are only as accurate as the supervision provided by official clockers on the scene, something that must be judged by each handicapper in each jurisdiction. It would help if all racing commissioners and stewards in every racing state insisted upon accurate clocking and identification procedures with strict penalties for trainers who violated the protocol.

Because some enterprising horseplayers with clocking skills recognized the value of interpreting the way workouts are accomplished, several professional services were introduced in the 1990s to fill the void.

Bruno DeJulio's workout report in *Today's Racing Digest,* which covers Southern California racing, is one of the best. Another is "Handicapper's Report," which commissions clockers in different regions to provide similar reports. Still another is sponsored by a touting service, "National Turf," which also focuses on Southern California racing. All three are subscription services that distribute their analysis via web sites. In the age of simulcasting, the door is surprisingly wide open for similar services to be created elsewhere, especially New York, Florida, and Kentucky

4. *Trip Handicapping*

Essentially, this is the practice of using video replays to review races already run to glean important tidbits about how the horses performed. In the modern game, almost all good handicappers utilize trip notes published in *Daily Racing Form* result charts and past-performance lines, or add their own annotated notes for more subtle clues. Studying the pace pattern, traffic issues, the prevailing bias, if any, as well as the way jockeys did or did not maneuver inside or outside, with the pace or away from it, is a dynamic, almost mandatory aspect of professional class handicapping.

A good DVD recorder helps quite a bit in this regard, as did the VCR for its run of popularity during the 1980s and 90s.

3. *Trainer Patterns*

In my earliest handicapping research, charting the winning "tells" of trainers was one of the most potent handicapping approaches in the game. It remains a consistent price-getting angle, one of the best ways to anticipate an improved performance, or a winning effort by a first-time starter or an absentee, a recently claimed runner and/or a horse making his debut in a grass race. Beyond statistical summaries, which can be helpful, winning trainers repeat winning patterns—it is that simple.

2. *Beyer Speed Figures*

Perfecting a method developed by Andy's college roommate, Sheldon Kovitz, the approach was to compare all the clockings in a single day and factor out the relative speed or lack of speed in the racetrack that day. Doing that made it possible to compare clockings of 1:10 ^{2}/$_5$ or 1:12 for six furlongs on one day to other six-furlong clockings on other days. It also permitted comparisons between different distances and different racetracks. Taking this one step further, Beyer developed a numerical scale that made it possible to refer to any adjusted clocking as a Beyer Speed Figure.

Beyer Speed Figures first became available in print when they were published in *The Racing Times*'s enhanced past performances in 1991; they became a staple in *Daily Racing Form* past performances in 1992.

In addition, this approach to comparing the relative ability of horses has spawned many variations, including private speed-figure methods and the publicly sold Ragozin "Sheets" and similar performance figures published as "Thorograph" by Ragozin's estranged disciple, Jerry Brown. All of these approaches have made positive contributions to the art/science of handicapping.

1. *Internet-Based Information for Handicappers*

The *Daily Racing Form*, TrackMaster, Bloodstock Research Information Services, Equibase, The Jockey Club, and dozens of private information web sites have large volumes of statistical material that can be used by discriminating handicappers to refine insights on trainers, horses, breeding lines, and a host of other handicapping issues. This was not possible before the computer and the Internet linked up for business in the early 1990s. Moreover, the technology is improving logarithmically every year.

For example, DRF's Formulator program, available on its web site, provides lifetime past performances on demand and several years of a specific trainer's horses and their respective patterns with the click of a computer button. In the modern era, it is almost impossible to handicap effectively without using some of these ready-made tools and resources. It also is foolish to ignore them.

TWO GREAT RACING IDEAS
THAT WERE BOTCHED OR FORGOTTEN

The following two racing concepts rank among the best innovative ideas of the modern era. They were badly handled, or botched into oblivion by unfortunate circumstances and other flaws that never were corrected.

The Matchmaker Stakes

The Matchmaker Stakes was an ingenious racing idea developed by Atlantic City Racecourse during the late 1960s. It was extremely popular with owners and trainers of top-quality fillies and mares.

The idea was to bolster the actual purse with free mating seasons to highly prized stallions. While the concept was unique and exciting, it took yeoman legwork and considerable negotiating to get owners of top stallions to provide the requested breeding rights. But once set in motion, the Matchmaker became one of the premier, most sought-after racing events for female Thoroughbreds.

Consider the four national champions who won this race during its glory years from 1968 through 1975: Gallant Bloom, Numbered Account, Desert Vixen, and Susan's Girl, plus two more national champions who finished second or third: Gamely (second in 1969) and Office Queen (third in 1970).

Here are the three or four stallions who were available to the top finishers in the Matchmaker during its greatest years. The order of finish in the race determined the order of choice.

Year	Winning Filly	Stallions		
1967	Politely	Hail to Reason	Jaipur	Round Table
1968	Politely	Hail to Reason	Intentionally	Ribot
1969	Gallant Bloom	Dr. Fager	Nearctic	Sea-Bird
1970	Dedicated to Sue	Buckpasser	Northern Dancer	Jaipur
1971	Deceit	Arts and Letters	Tom Rolfe	Cornish Prince
1972	Numbered Account	Raise a Native	Ack Ack	Delta Judge
1973	Alma North	Northern Dancer	Hoist the Flag	Silent Screen & Cougar II
1974	Desert Vixen	Graustark	Maribeau	Nijinsky II & What a Pleasure
1975	Susan's Girl	Secretariat	Mr. Prospector	Shecky Greene

The stallion roster is a virtual Hall of Fame of historically potent sires. Among them were many acclaimed champions whose get would win hundreds of graded stakes: Northern Dancer, Mr. Prospector, Sea-Bird, Raise a Native, Secretariat, Nijinsky II, Buckpasser, Dr. Fager, Intentionally, Round Table, and Hoist the Flag. These were expensive sires, difficult to book for the impending breeding season and in some cases completely unavailable to the majority of horse owners.

Although the Matchmaker was to remain an important race though 1984 and has been continuously run through the early 21st century, the quality of its participants and stallions bears no resemblance to the race that was once a major target for the best fillies and mares in America.

The decline paralleled Atlantic City Racecourse's financial difficulties, which led to a vastly reduced racing schedule and the need to switch the race over to Monmouth Park. The latter track accepted the race, but did not invest in the event with the same promotional fervor as its New Jersey neighbor. Once the Breeders' Cup Distaff was inaugurated in 1984, the Matchmaker steadily declined into a borderline Grade 3 stakes. In my judgment, this was an unfortunate loss to a sport that needs periodic innovation in its racing concepts. But it was not the only such loss of an important, highly innovative racing concept. Another new concept went down the tubes barely three years after it began with great fanfare: The American Championship Racing Series.

The ACRS (1991–1993)

For only three years, there was a linked schedule of high-class stakes designed to focus on 4-year-olds and up, horses no longer in the spotlight of Triple Crown racing.

Created by horse owner Barry Weisbord, the American Championship Racing Series was one of the best, most innovative ideas during my lifetime. Among other positives, it provided the handicap division with a national stage it has lacked since Kelso, Carry Back, and other top older horses of the 1960s regularly drew large crowds to any of the leading handicap stakes on the national racing calendar. But, as good as the ACRS was, it had at least two major flaws that corrupted its designed intentions.

While a point system was created to reward the top finishers in each designated ACRS race and a television network provided adequate coverage throughout the series, the ACRS did not make it past its third year because it did not include the needed link to the two premier dates on the American racing calendar.

Seeking to operate as a completely independent entity, the ACRS was drowned out by the Triple Crown during the spring and completely lost in the shuffle of the Breeders' Cup in the fall. The organizers were so intent upon creating a totally independent racing entity that they ignored an interaction with the two thriving institutions already in place.

This was a definite loss to every segment of the racing industry, which could have used something to provide continuity from the Triple Crown races to the Breeders' Cup, instead of a disjointed, unorganized middle that has no direct relationship to any seasonal championship.

THE TWO WORST THINGS IN THE GAME

Volponi's surprise victory at 43–1 in the 2002 Breeders' Cup Classic opened up a Pandora's box of problems for the racing industry. Yet, in a way, it was the best thing to happen that day, considering how the unusual pick-six betting payoffs triggered by his long odds helped investigators unravel the biggest criminal betting coup in racing history.

That often is the nature of the worst things that occur in all forms of life; a tragic personal loss may lead to a more closely knit family, or the accidental breaking of a right arm can lead to a stronger left. I can attest personally to this yin-yang of cause and effect, having missed out on a baseball career when I injured my pitching arm in a motor-boat accident at the ripe old age of 18. The following spring, while unable to recover my fastball, I had time to accidentally discover horse racing—really discover horse racing—and moved on.

In contemporary baseball, the BALCO drug case opened people's eyes to the way Barry Bonds, Mark McGwire, Sammy Sosa, and others were probably pumping themselves up with steroids and human growth hormones. But that negative exposure led to a congressional hearing and intense pressure on the lords of baseball to step up efforts to improve testing and penalize abusers of performance-enhancing drugs. That is a *big* positive from a *big* negative with plenty left to do.

In horse racing, where blood and urine testing have been going on for many years, the majority of racing officials have been unable to assure astute horseplayers that there isn't a drug scandal lurking in the shadows.

I subscribe to the lament that nature alone can't possibly account for a long list of trainers who are winning at 25 percent and higher when such percentages were rare in previous decades. In 1963, only eight trainers out of the top 30 (in races won) were able to win at a 20 percent or higher rate. In 1993, 17 of the top 30 were 20 percent winners. In 2005, 22 of the top 30 were 20 percent winners.

Among those who cracked 24 percent was Cole Norman, who had a 28 percent win rate in 2005 and was banned from running a horse in California without special stewards' permission after a positive drug test. Another was Dick Dutrow Jr., who won at a 26 percent rate and had a positive drug test in New York that resulted in a 30-day suspension. Steve Asmussen, the leading trainer in 2005 with 474 victories from 2,227 starters, had two positive drug tests in 2006 that resulted in a pair of six-month suspensions.

Having seen dozens of similar findings and having watched thousands of racehorses train and race, it is not hard to come to this inescapable conclusion: There is more than hay, oats, and water at work here. Too many horses look "brand new" a few weeks or a month after changing hands from a competent trainer to one of these "supertrainers." Too many of the horses under their care suddenly show staying power that they did not previously posses. Beyond the speculation among horseplayers and racing writers, the sudden impact of these supertrainers has negatively thrown out of balance the logic inherent to the handicapping equation.

To pick winners, a good horseplayer used to blend in speed, class, pace, distance, and recent form. Now, when a supertrainer brings a newly acquired horse into a race, you have to expect that horse to outrun anything it has done before. That's not handicapping, and it leads to suspicions that some of these trainers are taking an unfair edge.

Drugs and the suspicions they arouse are threatening racing's credibility, just as they threaten baseball's most sanctified historical records. The simple fact is that the majority of racing commissions do not have the political clout, or the budget, or the insight to investigate what has been going on, or seem unwilling to press for answers.

I have my own concrete reasons for suspicions about drug use in the sport that go beyond inference. I have in fact seen a number of things up close and personal that should raise some red flags.

One such experience involves an Oklahoma-born trainer named Bill W. Cunningham, who hired me as a special consultant in 1977 for a summer of racing at Atlantic City racetrack, where Cunningham was going to have a small stable of less than 20 horses in training. Cunningham hired me to make private speed figures and wanted my counsel on where to run his horses and which ones to claim. I helped him lead the Atlantic City trainers' standings for six weeks before I left after personally witnessing the following events.

While I was sitting in Cunningham's private box during an Atlantic City racing card, he summoned Philadelphia-based trainer Joe Graci to join us. Following simple chitchat, Cunningham asked Graci what he was using to deal with his "problem horses" and Graci said simply, "Bute and some easy gallops rather than hard workouts." Cunningham said point-blank, "I have something much better than Bute. In fact what I got they have no test for."

When Graci awkwardly asked Cunningham to name his preferred preparation, Cunningham said, "Sublimaze."

The answer made Graci flinch before he excused himself and walked away. Sublimaze is a powerful drug that surely can do more for pain than Bute, but it was and remains a banned substance for racing purposes.

The second disturbing thing I witnessed that summer occurred a day later, when I went into the stall of a Cunningham-trained filly to touch her back ever so lightly. The filly was Old Music, a 4-year-old by Olden Times, who had flashed brief early speed before finishing last in her prior two outings at the meet. The filly flinched noticeably when I lightly touched her back right behind where the saddle usually sits. Cunningham saw me, saw the filly's reaction, and angrily ordered me out of the stall, warning me never to do that again. That same evening, this filly won a $5,000 claiming route at 55–1, something I believe she never could have done without a dose of a Sublimaze or another equally powerful painkilling drug.

Before the race I asked Cunningham how this filly possibly could be fit to run, given the condition of her back, and he said simply, "I took care of it."

After the race, the winning jockey, Francisco Calderon, dismounted before completing the gallop back to the winner's circle. She appeared to be in such pain she could not bear the jockey's weight.

The next day I left Cunningham's employment, never to return.

The other story that I have to share about drugs in racing involves Oscar Barrera, a dominant winner of more than 25 percent of his attempts in New York during the 1980s and early 90s.

Oscar Barrera was the brother of Laz Barrera. Both had migrated to America from Cuba; both had made significant marks on the sport—in decidedly different ways.

Laz applied genuine touches of genius while getting the most out of well-bred, fast stock, winning many stakes on the highest level of competition the sport has to offer. For his part, Oscar was responsible for more form reversals of newly acquired horses than any man in his era.

Operating in the manner of some of the modern supertrainers, Oscar bought an assortment of cheap horses via claiming races and promptly won a high percentage of higher-priced races, many within a week. As a result, Oscar often was suspected of using illegal drugs to "move his horses up,'" but, aside from a few minor violations, he never had a serious positive drug test.

My friendship with Laz traced back to numerous conversations during the 1976 Triple Crown and became even closer during Affirmed's 1978 Triple Crown sweep. So, I asked Laz if he would help me set up an interview with his brother. At the time, Oscar Barrera was giving no interviews and trying to maintain a low profile while working apparent miracles with almost every horse he acquired.

I asked Laz to pass on to Oscar that I only wanted to give him a fair opportunity to tell "his side of the story." I asked him as a matter of trust to let me sit down with his brother at a place of Oscar's choosing for one interview.

A week later, Laz called me in New Hope, Pennsylvania, and told me that Oscar was willing to meet me for an hour at a diner in the Bronx, far away from Aqueduct or Belmont Park.

I decided that my best approach would not be to ask direct questions about drugs, but instead to give Oscar a chance to explain how he had improved the form of so many horses so dramatically within such a short span of time. Most horseplayers found it difficult to believe that simple horsemanship could be responsible for so many form reversals and so much dramatic improvement.

Oscar Barrera was already at the diner on Grand Concourse Boulevard, not far from Yankee Stadium. He spoke only broken English, but shook my hand and gave a faint smile. A friend of his was outside, waiting in the car.

I thanked Oscar for coming, ordered a cup of coffee, and pulled out of my briefcase 15 pieces of paper that had the past performances of the 15 most recent horses Barrera had claimed and moved up sharply to win races in their next outings. I placed the past-performance sheets on the table and pointed to them one by one, asking Oscar to explain what he did to make these horses run so much better.

The notorious Oscar Barrera responded in a way that answered no questions and all questions at the same time. He looked at me, looked at the past performances in silence for less than a minute, and angrily pushed them over to my side of the table. He left without speaking a word.

"Drugs in racing" is not the worst thing in the game, however—it is the second-worst thing. The worst is the way the media, politicians, trainers, owners, jockeys, and racetrack veterinarians disregard their responsibilities in dealing with it.

The public at large has no idea how much of a stake it has in what is going on in horse racing. Media coverage is so weak it should be an embarrassment to every serious editor or student of journalism. When newspapers add space to cover racing beyond the basic elements of handicapping, race results, and the Triple Crown events, they tend to focus strictly on the latest hot jockey, or the sentimental story of the week. What is missing is the journalistically important watchdog function that other sports and other megabusinesses get every day.

Racing deserves and needs scrutiny from an attentive press because the sport annually attracts millions of fans to dozens of racetracks and produces billions of dollars in tax revenue, many billions more in employment dollars, and gazillions of dollars in related agribusinesses. All of this is fueled by people like me who make thousands of bets each year on the supposition that the game is played on the level.

Thankfully, race-fixing in contemporary racing is rare because the vast majority of jockeys and trainers are honorable men and women. A fixed race also would invariably involve a conspiracy that could unravel at a moment's notice. But, on all the accumulated anecdotal evidence, reasonable people and practicing veterinarians already know there are sophisticated ways to affect the relative performances of racehorses, positively and negatively.

While it may be unfair to be suspicious of all trainers winning at a 25 percent clip, it is all too common to see dozens of horses each season improve 20 to 30 Beyer Speed Figure points when moved to one of the trainers doing miracles with their stock.

Only a fool would believe that performance-altering drugs are not being used on the racetrack just as they have been on the baseball diamond. The only difference is that Congress and the general media care about baseball, while racing is left to its own devices to investigate itself or be condemned to live on the fringes of sport through its own silence. As I said, that, not the actual use of drugs, is the worst thing in the game.

POSITIVE AND NEGATIVE TRENDS

Along with the many memorable moments and great performances by horses, jockeys, and trainers, it is impossible to do a book such as this without looking forward to some of the most positive trends in the sport, as well as the most pressing issues needing attention. First, the positives:

5. *The Emergence of New Riding Stars*

From 2002 to 2005, the racing game lost six of the top jockeys in history when Hall of Famers Laffit Pincay Jr., Eddie Delahoussaye, Chris McCarron, Pat Day, Gary Stevens, and Jerry Bailey all retired, leaving only Russell Baze, Mike Smith, Earlie Fires, and Kent Desormeaux as active Hall of Fame riders.

To fill the void, trainers with high-class stakes horses continued to seek out potential Hall of Famers John R. Velazquez, Edgar Prado, Alex Solis, Victor Espinoza, Pat Valenzuela, and Garrett Gomez, while solid journeymen Ramon Dominguez, Javier Castellano, and Cornelio Velasquez also came into demand for important engagements. But the most promising development regarding jockeys was the sudden rise of three young riders who have the talent to develop into Hall of Fame candidates: Rafael Bejarano, Fernando Jara, and Julien Leparoux.

Emerging from near obscurity, Rafael Bejarano took over from Pat Day with lightning speed to become the dominant jockey in Kentucky during 2004 and 2005. Bejarano was on his way to repeating the feat in 2006 until the French-born apprentice Julien Leparoux burst on the scene to narrowly edge past Bejarano to win the spring meet title at Churchill Downs. Under the guidance of trainer Patrick Biancone, Leparoux became one of the leaders at several successive meets including Saratoga, which usually humbles the best apprentice jockeys in the land.

In 2006, Jara emerged from his apprenticeship with a confidence rarely seen since Steve Cauthen won the Triple Crown as an 18-year-old riding prodigy in 1978. Much like Cauthen, Jara demonstrated nerves of steel under extreme pressure to win the 2006 Belmont Stakes with a flawless ride aboard Jazil, and went on to win several other graded stakes during the late spring and summer, most notably the Whitney Handicap and the Breeders' Cup Classic aboard Invasor.

With these three superb young riders making such a positive impact on the national stage, it is encouraging to know that a new generation of top jockeys has stepped up to take up some of the slack caused by the retirement of the six great jockeys who left the game in such a relatively short span of time.

4. *The Thriving Breeders' Cup*

The Breeders' Cup continues to grow, prosper, and become more accessible to more horse owners and breeders. In 2006, for example, purses were increased for the eight Breeders' Cup races from $14 million in 2005 to $20 million in 2006, making it the largest payday in racing history.

In early 2006, the Breeders' Cup Racing and Nominations Committee also took a major step forward by adjusting its previous rigid policy pertaining to exorbitant late-nomination fees. Prior to the adjustment, owners of worthy Breeders' Cup contenders who were not originally made eligible for the series at birth, or by the owner of the horse's sire, were forced into untenable financial decisions regarding late-nominating fees that ranged as high as $800,000 for the Breeders' Cup Classic when it was a $4 million race, and would have reached $1 million for the $5 million Classic of 2006.

While late-nominating fees still rank among the highest for any race in America, they have been reduced sensibly to make it feasible for owners to nominate top horses that may not have been nominated as weanlings, or even before birth.

These changes ensure the continued success of the Breeders' Cup from a competitive standpoint, which in turn will help maintain the status of the Breeders' Cup as the racing industry's biggest day, bigger than the extremely popular Kentucky Derby. Without a thriving Breeders' Cup, racing would be a winter-spring sport with little pull on media attention.

3. *Increased Television and Electronic-Media Exposure*

As racing moves into the 21st century, actual attendance at most American racetracks has continued to slip a few percentage points each year, but that trend is misleading if not contradicted by these facts: Far more people are playing the game at home; there are much larger wagering handles for the highest-profile races; attendance and handle is booming in other countries, especially Japan and Hong Kong; and the gradual increase in telephone wagering and other high-tech wagering outlets have fueled growth in other countries. All of these developments may have been underreported in the general media, but they have been providing ambitious racing investors with opportunities for growth, marked by noticeable increases in media exposure for the sport.

This trend is directly attributable to the creation of two dedicated cable and satellite-television channels—Television Games Network and Horse

Racing TV—as well as the omnipresent ESPN, which signed a contract in 2006 to promote and broadcast a long series of races leading up to and including the Breeders' Cup. But, the positive increase in media exposure also extends to a boom in radio broadcasts devoted to racing and handicapping in virtually every region of the country.

To top off the trend, the expansion of the Internet and the use racing is making of it are extremely encouraging facets of this increased exposure.

Where useful handicapping information once was obscure, now the Internet provides dozens of web sites that feature substantial statistical material, streaming live video of races in progress, archives of races already run, discussion groups, and simulcast broadcasts of radio shows and interviews of key racing personalities on a near-daily basis. While all this already was having a positive impact heading into the 21st century, no one should underestimate the potential of the rapidly expanding Internet to become a vehicle to reach both casual and serious-minded horseplayers, potential investors, advertisers, horse buyers, and officials at every level of every racing-related group.

As powerful as the Internet has been for racing during its relatively short lifespan, it is my view, shared by several racing executives, that we have only seen the tip of the proverbial iceberg.

2. *Cooperation Between Competing Racetrack Owners*

The willingness of competing racetrack ownership groups, such as Churchill Downs and Magna Entertainment, to join forces on selected projects is a trend that finally may address inconveniences imposed on their overlapping fan bases.

While operating numerous racetracks, each organization fought tooth and nail to develop separate Internet and phone-line wagering outlets and separate international satellite-television networks. This forced fans to subscribe to both wagering outlets and both networks at considerable expense and/or inconvenience. In early 2006, Churchill and Magna realized they could help each other save money and efficiently provide their various tracks' signals to British-based horseplayers via one mutual agreement. This foray into uncharted territory was followed in the summer of 2006 by an agreement to work together while seeking or assisting a possible third party to bid for the New York Racing Association franchise, up for renewal at the close of 2007.

The foundation for these and other racing organizations to work for the common good has been laid. Hopefully there is much more to come.

1. *Practical Awareness of Negative Issues, Such as Drugs*

In the early years of the 21st century, a scismic shift in thinking by several racing officials targeted some of the most pressing issues in the sport. While this shift in thinking received little fanfare in the press, it is one of the most hopeful developments of the modern era. Indeed, it has the potential to produce an equal seismic shift in direction for the sport.

In one such example, and for the first time in many years, questions were raised in prominent circles about the reasons for the increasing number of breakdowns occurring at tracks from coast to coast. Some officials pointed to possible problems with racing surfaces, others pointed to year-round racing schedules and the extreme length of various race meets where racing surfaces, especially turf courses, get worn out. Still others courageously cited the possible negative impact of drugs, legal and illegal, that have permeated racing in the modern era.

While such views hardly were shared by the majority of racing officials—especially in public—the change of thinking on the executive level began to surface at round-table forums and other symposiums with increasing intensity. Worried about the breakdown factor, a handful of important tracks even scheduled installation of presumably safer artificial surfaces to replace the standard dirt tracks that have been a staple of American racing for more than a century.

In California, the California Horse Racing Board issued an edict commanding all of the major tracks in the state to install such surfaces by the end of 2007. Not willing to wait, Hollywood Park went right ahead and replaced its dirt track with an artificial surface for the fall 2006 race meet. Woodbine, in Canada, and Keeneland, in Kentucky, also installed artificial tracks for their fall 2006 race meets. This followed the lead of Turfway Park in Florence, Kentucky, which put Polytrack in place for its 2005–06 fall and winter meets.

In addition to this response to the breakdown problem, which might not prove to be the ultimate answer, a few racing officials openly stated the case for a simultaneous attack on the sport's drug problem.

For example, in Kentucky—which has allowed decades of the most lax drug rules of any major racing state—a special panel convened by the Kentucky State Racing Commission recommended stiffer drug rules, penalties, and supervisory procedures that would bring the state in line with other more progressive jurisdictions. Indeed, should the recommendations overcome some stiff opposition within partisan circles, including the state legislature, new standards would be established on several fronts. The signs were encouraging.

While it may be naïve to believe that the ancient sport of horse racing actually can become a progressive institution in the 21st century, the mere fact that serious questions are being raised about the game's lingering problems is an encouraging trend that has the potential to set in motion a much-needed era of positive reform.

Now for the negative trends:

3. *Attendance Is Down and the Solutions Are Temporary*

Attendance is flagging at most tracks, and not enough effort is being put into educating the general public about the overall fairness of the racetrack gamble and the beautiful aspects of the sport's history and contemporary stars.

In today's racing world, most tracks are seeking slot machines to bolster their purse funds. Several, in fact, have received legislative permission to add slots and have boosted their purses accordingly. But, there is no guarantee that any state gaining large sums of tax revenue from legalized "one-armed bandits" will not decide someday to turn the track into a casino at the expense of racing. Moreover, many of the tracks that have installed slots are being permitted to set the "take" from those slots at exorbitant levels that make the parimutuel takeout seem like a bargain.

Whether tracks are willing to commit more creative energy and more resources toward genuine fan education and well-thought-out promotions is not certain. Whether or not tracks are willing to organize legislative efforts to lower the parimutuel takeout rates and drastically reduce the withholding of taxes against significant winnings are two more crucial issues that need action to boost interest in the game. As we move forward into the 21st century, the industry's failure to address any and all of these initiatives suggests that slots will be merely a temporary solution, a solution that may raise revenues of track owners and horsemen in the short term, while doing nothing to provide the racing game with a positive future.

2. *Oversaturation of Racing*

As previously stated, we are in an era when horses race less frequently for a variety of reasons. Yet tracks in neighboring states continue to put pressure on the horse population while cannibalizing their overlapping fan base by running long race meets in competition with each other. The fact that these two trends are mixed together in an era when simulcasting allows for wagering across state lines raises the question of why there continues to be an inexplicable lack of interest in working out compatible racing schedules, with fewer live racing dates.

Some say it is because horsemen need to have racing opportunities to make their financials work. Others point to the number of jobs that would be lost for a few months a year at tracks presently running year-long schedules. While there is no doubt that a reduction in racing dates would bring a corresponding reduction in the number of purses awarded and the available days of racetrack work, it is also likely that fewer racing dates could result in higher purses from larger wagering handles, due to the premium value of better-quality races with larger fields. Likewise, the added revenue from larger handles for fewer dates might increase the daily worker's paycheck. Meanwhile, an increase in wagering through simulcasting during a one- or two-month break from live racing could keep more employees on the job than the rank and file are willing to believe.

The excess of racing dates on many racing circuits is contributing to the dilution of the sport's appeal and is affecting the pocketbook of everyone who fears or believes in a more sensible yearly schedule.

1. *The Fragility of the Modern Thoroughbred*

Thoroughbred racehorses are 850- to 1,100-pound animals that run fast in a rhythmic, beautiful stride that is supported on very thin ankles. But to blame the overall fragility and relatively short racing careers of the modern Thoroughbred on this genetic fact is to deny a simple truth: The majority of racehorses in the decades preceding the 1990s ran many more times per year and were solid performers through their 5- and 6-year-old racing seasons.

The truth is that shortened careers and the overall decline in durability are at least coincidental, or cause-related to this fact: Modern breeders often choose to accent precocious speed over stamina in their planned matings to produce a racehorse capable of winning the huge amounts of money targeted for 2-year-old races. To force-feed this emphasis on speed and quick production, some breeders bulk up their flashiest prospects with growth hormones and steroids to attract inflated prices at the elite yearling sales.

While ultrafast track conditions have been a contributing factor to debilitating injury, the same is true of the manner in which early speed is accented in the training techniques employed to win high-value purses of early-season 2-year-old races, when horses are just growing into their immature bodies. But, again, the emphasis on 2-year-old racing is not a recent phenomenon. Nor are racing surfaces that are tuned up to promote possible track records on high-profile racing days.

By all indications, drugs—legal and illegal—have become the real problem, and so it will remain until all elements of the racing industry appreciate the need to rid them from the game. Drug use for racing purposes always has existed, but it has been a growing presence in the modern era, to a troubling degree that parallels the use of steroids in baseball, professional cycling, and other performance-related sports. I am talking about the worst thing ever to happen to the Thoroughbred sport.

Consider the testimony given to New York State legislators in October 1999, by Dr. George Maylin, director of the New York State Racing and Wagering Board's Drug Testing and Research Program at Cornell's College of Veterinary Medicine.

"In the 1970s, there were only several dozen major drugs of concern [to the racing industry], but that number has spiraled to hundreds, if not thousands of drugs," Maylin said. "New York, like all other racing jurisdictions, has a growing drug problem that must be addressed if the integrity of the sport is to remain intact. It will not go away by itself. It must be addressed now."

Maylin explained that illegal drugs include those used "to mask tissue damage to pass prerace veterinary inspections," as well as "performance-influencing drugs." Maylin specifically indicted the racing industry as a whole for its lack of "uniformity in equine drug policy across the country" adding that the "rapid development of designer and synthetic drugs, undermines New York's attempt to administer an efficient testing program."

While there have been well-intentioned efforts by some veterinary organizations and racing officials to unify and standardize drug testing throughout the country, such attempts continue to face insidious resistance in the 21st century from influential vets and others with a vested interest in keeping the status quo. For example, in 2003, a committee formed by the National Thoroughbred Racing Association in conjunction with The Jockey Club specifically proposed a series of sensible drug reforms that would establish specific tests and penalties across the country. Unfortunately, action on their suggested reforms was blocked by track vets in several states.

In the 21st century, "Bute" (phenylbutazone) continues to be widely used legally for racing purposes to reduce pain and inflammation in troubled joints. But any vet will tell you that it also serves to reduce the running horse's sensitivity to his natural warning system—pain, which may be signaling a small bone chip or crack.

The diuretic Lasix (furosemide), which helps curb capillary bleeding in the pulmonary system under racing stress, generally is given to approximately 85 percent of all horses about four hours prior to a given race, whether they have a bleeding problem or not. Despite this, there never has been a long-term veterinary study to say what effect the repetitious use of this powerful flushing agent has been having on the breed. Anecdotally, it is strangely coincidental that the decline in the ruggedness of Thoroughbred racehorses can be traced to the introduction of these two drugs in the late 1970s and the expansion of their use to virtually every racing state in the late 1980s and early 1990s.

Maylin, a most respected veterinarian during his tenure with the NYRA, was not merely talking about Bute and Lasix. In private interviews, he clearly stated his disgust over the rampant use of many performance-enhancing drugs that are not detectable—including anabolic steroids and growth hormones—drugs that have plagued all performance-related sports in the 1990s and beyond.

The good vets at many tracks who work with horses know this is true, and so do many of the trainers who are forced to compete against the cheaters.

On this score, it is worthwhile to consider the official testimony taken from the Congressional Record and supplied by the late congressman Robert McClory of Illinois to members of a House subcommittee investigating a racing-related bill as far back as 1986:

"The United States is the only country that permits the practice of drugging and numbing of racehorses. Although various racing states have legalized what is termed controlled medication, it is anything but that. Horse racing is becoming drug-dependent. Many of the drugs used are illegal and untested. All are inadequately controlled at the state level. While they push for increased revenues from racing, prolonged seasons and lenient drug policies, state legislatures are ignoring the horse as a living creature. The artificial means to enhance a horse's moneymaking capacity defeats integrity."

Frankly, Congress has huffed and puffed with indignation at racing's drug problem for decades while showing no interest in putting state racing officials to the fire, officials who rarely allocate sufficient funds to develop sophisticated testing techniques. This despite billions of tax dollars generated by racing-related enterprises in America.

Surely, protecting the public interest and the interest of Thoroughbreds who can't speak for themselves should command some attention from national agencies when state governments and track owners and other racing organizations have been struggling to find the courage to cope with the problem in a public, open manner.

At the bottom line, the modern-day drug problem in the sport leaves rational horseplayers and honest, hard-working racing folk with plenty of doubts about the legitimacy of playing the game fair and square. To put it even more bluntly, the continuation of permissive policies about drugs in racing remains a national disgrace.

11

The Very Best of All Time of Any Age or Sex

ON ANY GIVEN day any of these 20 might have beaten each other. If my life depended upon betting the winner of a race involving some or all of these horses, the deciding factor would be distance and the next most important factor would be the projected pace. On the other hand, the rankings below, as subjective as any rankings can possibly be across different generations, come from considerable research into their respective best performances and the quality of the competition each horse had to beat.

My conclusion: I can hardly imagine any horse taking the measure of the top horse on this list on his best day.

20. Miesque:
European filly was best turf miler to race in this country.

19. Manila:
Best American turf horse; beat Europe's best.

18. *Personal Ensign:*

Unbeaten filly champion, with sensational final win.

17. *John Henry:*

A Horse of the Year at 6 and 9 years old, strong on dirt and turf.

16. *Ta Wee:*

America's greatest sprinter, beat males with 140 pounds.

15. *Seabiscuit:*

Late-blooming, very popular, hard-hitting campaigner.

14. *Forego:*

Game, persistent, three-time Horse of the Year carried weight.

13. *Ruffian:*

The best filly of all time, unbeaten until tragic match race.

12. *Swaps:*

Kentucky Derby winner at 3, was an even better 4-year-old.

11. *Affirmed:*

Great Triple Crown sweep over stubborn rival, solid at 4.

10. *Seattle Slew:*

Underappreciated Triple Crown winner, was superb at 4.

9. *Damascus:*

One of the great 3-year-olds of all time, slipped a little at 4.

8. *Buckpasser:*

Set world record for the mile, won 15 straight.

7. *Dr. Fager:*

Set world records; carried heavy weight assignments.

6. *Spectacular Bid:*
Ran very fast very often, unbeaten as a 4-year-old.

5. *Citation:*
Superior 3-year-old campaign included 15 straight wins.

4. *Kelso:*
Five-time Horse of the Year, many great performances.

3. *Count Fleet:*
Awesome Triple Crown sweep in 1943.

2. *Man o' War:*
Lost only one race and was frequent dominating winner.

1. *Secretariat:*
Incredible performer on dirt and turf at classic distances.

About the Author

STEVE DAVIDOWITZ has been a professional handicapper, reporter, editor, consultant, and columnist for more than three decades. He is the author of the influential and best-selling handicapping book *Betting Thoroughbreds*, which he updated a few years ago to cover modern handicapping situations and a variety of advanced exotic-wagering strategies.

A highly touted baseball star at Rutgers University who lost a potential pitching career due to a freak boating mishap, Davidowitz has a wide-ranging background that includes solo travel to Cuba as a teenager; scuba diving in the Caribbean; playing folk guitar in the clubs of New Orleans; and photographic magazine covers and exhibitions of his work. As a single parent, Steve also raised his son, Brad, now a corporate program analyst in Minneapolis, married with two children.

Davidowitz says he "began to major in horse-racing studies at Rutgers University, Garden State Park Division," when a New Brunswick, New Jersey, bookmaker gave him a copy of the 1959 *American Racing Manual*. Some 40 years later, Davidowitz would help *Daily Racing Form* bring that prestigious annual back to print as the ARM's editor from 2000-03.

An active horseplayer who manages a pick-six syndicate, Steve has contributed articles to *The New York Times* and been a featured columnist and/or racing editor for *Turf and Sport Digest* magazine, the Minneapolis *Star Tribune*, *The Oakland Tribune*, *The Philadelphia Journal*, *The Racing Times*, the *St. Petersburg Times*, and the *Houston Post*, among other publications.

Today, Davidowitz writes handicapping columns for *DRF Simulcast Weekly*, trackmaster.com, and other outlets on the Internet. In addition to his horse-race writings and commentaries, Davidowitz is the co-author of *They Can't Hide Us Anymore* with singer/songwriter Richie Havens. He now lives in Las Vegas, Nevada.